The Good
Country House
Guide

C000179424

The Good Country House Guide

The Essential Critical Guide to the Best Country Houses Open to the Public

Lydia Greeves

PAVILION

First published in Great Britain in 1994 by
PAVILION BOOKS LIMITED
26 Upper Ground, London SE1 9PD

Text copyright © Lydia Greeves 1994
Illustrations copyright © Nick Farnell 1994

Designed by Roy Cole

Maps by Martin Collins

The moral right of the author has been asserted

All rights reserved. No part of this publication
may be reproduced, stored in a retrieval
system, or transmitted, in any form or by any
means, electronic, mechanical, photocopying,
recording or otherwise, without the prior
permission of the copyright holder

A CIP catalogue record for this book is
available from the British Library

ISBN 1 85145 834 4

Printed and bound in Great Britain by WBC Ltd

2 4 6 8 10 9 7 5 3 1

Contents

Introduction 7

Introduction

Visiting over 500 houses throughout the length and breadth of Great Britain was an exhilarating experience. Seeing these places day after day, week after week, you soon realise what a rich source of pleasure they are, but also how many rarely-considered factors, including such intangibles as the friendliness of the room stewards or guides, affect the enjoyment of a visit. Too often, guidebooks concentrate on facts without in any way conveying what it is like to be at the place described. By contrast, I have set out to convey the flavour of a house, bringing in everything that impinges on a visit, and have tried to evaluate the total experience. The essential background on architecture and builder is all here of course, and there are descriptions of furniture and paintings, with pointers to the most exceptional rooms and contents. But I have mixed such details with comments on setting and atmosphere, and with an indication of how much of the house is shown, drawing attention to places where you need to pace yourself carefully.

The spread of houses included is very wide, ranging from medieval manors and Scottish tower houses to neat Georgian boxes and Victorian extravaganzas, and also includes a sprinkling of cottages. Some are still privately owned, some are now in the hands of the National Trust or National Trust for Scotland, or some other official body. All are of the country rather than the town, even if some are now attached to what have become substantial villages or have seen their estates swallowed up by the spread of a city, in particular London and the industrial conurbations of the Midlands and north. This means that some of the places included here, among them Osterley, Saltram, and the heart-rending Aston Hall, are like beached whales, with housing estates and motorways beyond the park rather than green fields and woods. Most of the places included are also furnished, if not by any means always lived in, but I have also included some atmospheric and rewarding ruins. And all have set opening days each year, even though some can be visited only infrequently.

The grading system, in which houses are awarded from one to four stars, takes into account all factors which relate to the enjoyment of a visit. The half dozen or so places which have been given four stars are all houses of considerable historic and aesthetic importance, with period interiors filled with fine paintings and furniture. These are houses that anyone interested in Britain's cultural heritage should make a point of visiting. But the grading system should not be used blindly. All houses awarded a star have something of merit about them, and some of the most delightful are the quiet, little-visited places with little or nothing in the way of contents but strongly atmospheric buildings, such as Cadhay, or a superb setting, such as Muncaster Castle. Then, too, it is useful to be clear what you want to get out of a visit to a country house. In many of the grander places, the visitor tour concentrates on the lavishly appointed state rooms. From the first, these were intended for special occasions, and for receiving honoured guests, not for everyday use. The finest furniture and paintings are usually here, but such apartments never feel remotely lived in, even if, as in the case of the saloon at Blenheim, the family has Christmas lunch in them once a year. If your preference is for places which you can relate to, and where you might find the family dog curled up on an armchair, then it is better to go for a house where the rooms shown are still part of everyday life, or somewhere which strongly reflects a particular personality, such as Winston Churchill's Chartwell, or Bernard Shaw's ugly red-brick villa at Ayot St Lawrence.

Where the condition of houses in private ownership varies enormously, all properties of the National Trust and the National Trust of Scotland are looked after to a very high standard, and you can be sure the accompanying tea-rooms etc will also meet with approval. There is, though, a blandness to some of these places, and a feeling that something essential has been sacrificed along with the cobwebs, dingy paintwork and unkempt grounds. In country house visiting, quirkiness and eccentricity are the icing on the cake. Certainly, ghosts seem to prefer private houses, although legends and traditions abound everywhere. Every manor from Somerset to Cornwall seems to have been slept in by Charles I when he visited the West Country in 1645, and both this misguided king and the equally impolitic Mary Queen of Scots seem to have gone to the gallows wearing layer upon layer of lacy shifts and, in Mary's case, clutching a fine collection of rosaries, crucifixes and illuminated missals.

Finally, I must record a very big debt of thanks to the many friends and relations who allowed me to use their houses as hotels, producing wonderful meals every evening when I came in after a hard day's research. Without this hospitality, I would not have been able to undertake the book. All the following, therefore, have had a part in this work: Elizabeth and Nigel Ashby, Bridget Barkham, John and Suzy Barkham, Tony and Betty Brightman, Patrick Greeves, Joanna Hayes, Brian and Dill Hughes, Jane and Stephen Jarvis, James and Melissa Mahon, Jenifer Mahon, Daffodil and Charles Marriage, Ben and Christine Mayo, Elizabeth and Paul Rutledge, Fred and Polly Strickland Constable, Stella and Peter Vaines, Arnrid and Charles Wood.

Opening times

The opening times given relate only to the house, not to the garden or any surrounding park, which will often be open for longer. Several National Trust houses now limit visitors by issuing timed tickets, which allow a set number of people into the house every quarter of an hour or so. Usually, it is possible to book these tickets in advance. Otherwise, anyone interested in seeing a place where this system operates should arrive as early in the day, or afternoon, as they can, and certainly before 3 pm, unless it is a slack time of year. Most houses, too, have a last admission time that is 30 to 45 minutes before the official closing. The opening times are as correct as I have been able to make them, but it is always wise to check beforehand, particularly if you are driving any distance.

Abbreviations

Cadw Welsh Historic Monuments
EH   English Heritage
HS   Historic Scotland
NT   The National Trust
NTS   The National Trust for Scotland

Houses awarded four stars

Boughton House, Northamptonshire
Chatsworth, Derbyshire
Hardwick Hall, Derbyshire
Knole, Kent
Wilton House, Wiltshire

South-west England

Avon, Cornwall, Devon, Dorset, Somerset

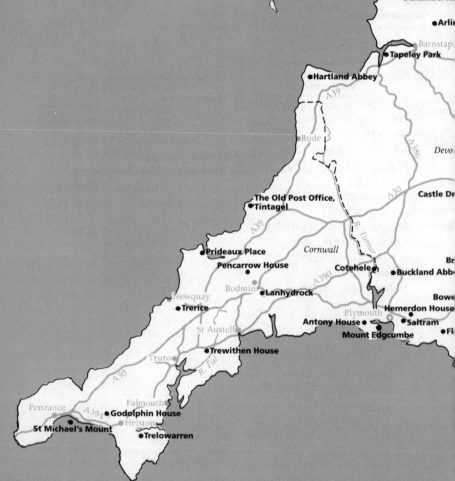

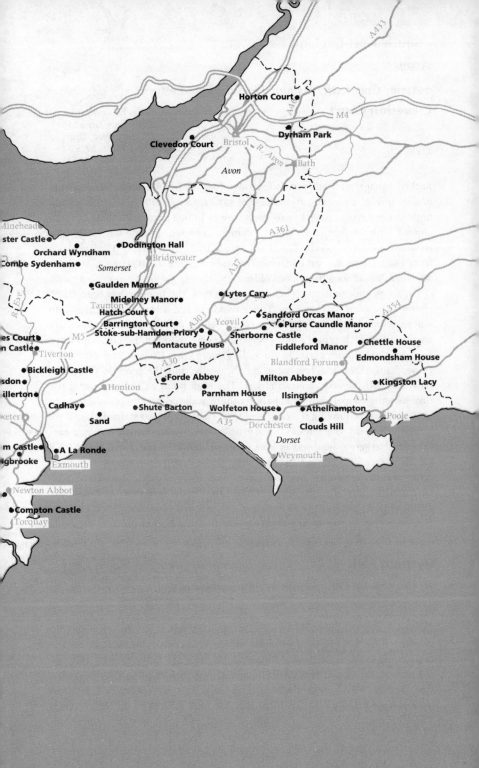

Clevedon Court

1½ m E Clevedon, on B3130, signed from M5, exit 20; NT; refreshments; terraced garden; *open:* Apr–end Sept, Wed, Thurs, Sun and BH Mon, 2.30–5.30; tel: 0275 872257

Backed up against a steep wooded ridge just off the M5 is this unexpected medieval relic, a pleasing assemblage of gables, stone-mullioned windows and high pitched roofs, with a four-storey tower in one corner. Nothing is quite aligned with anything else, and the manor is entered through a heavily buttressed two-storey porch. The main house, built to a chunky H-plan, dates from 1320, but at the east end, clustered askew round a little triangular court, are fragments of something even older.

Although the medieval ground plan survives, the interior has been much altered. The great hall has huge Tudor windows and a 14th-century arch into a deep window bay, but the lofty, coved ceiling and the classical screen are among many 18th-century and later changes by the Elton family, who came here in 1709. Elton portraits, including works by Hudson and Nathaniel Hone, hang three and four deep on the walls, and the room is positively crowded with carved Carolean chairs. The high point of a short tour is the tiny hanging chapel above the hall, its south wall, pointing the dedication to St Peter, a net of flowing tracery filled with richly coloured stained glass.

Those hunting the Eltons' literary links are rewarded with Boehm's cartoon of Thackeray, who was in love with a daughter of the house, and with a profile sketch of Arthur Hallam, friend of the family, for whom Tennyson composed his emotional *In Memoriam*. And there are displays of the self-taught Sir Edmund's distinctive Eltonware, made between 1880 and the 1920s, with its metallic glazes and deep colours, and of walking sticks, rolling pins and other fripperies in pastel twists of the local Nailsea glass.

Dyrham Park ☆☆

8 m N Bath, off A46; NT; tearoom; garden and park with views across Severn Valley; *open:* Apr–end Oct, daily, except Thurs and Fri, 12–5.30; tel: 0272 372501

Tucked under the Cotswold escarpment, in a narrow valley between steeply swelling hills, is a splendid example of late 17th-century taste. Built by the high-flying William Blathwayt following his marriage to the estate's 36-year-old heiress, Dyrham is really two houses placed back to back. On the garden side, looking west across the Severn, is the attractive two-storey façade set back behind a raised courtyard that was designed in 1692 by the little-known Samuel Hauduroy, with a balustraded, urn-topped roofline and a central balcony carried on scrolled brackets. In the same year Blathwayt began acting as

William III's Secretary of State and by the time he started on the east front, in 1698, he was in a position to secure the services of William Talman, Wren's second in command. Where Hauduroy's work has a French accent, Talman's baroque three-storey façade crowned by the eagle of the Blathwayt crest looks more like an Italian palace, with tall windows lighting the *piano nobile* on the first floor and a rusticated ground storey.

Inside, the baroque plan survives, with suites of modest, high-ceilinged rooms on both fronts arranged either side of the lofty portrait-hung hall that is the only remnant of the old Tudor building. The furnishings reflect the Dutch taste of Blathwayt's time. Richly glowing panelling, some of it walnut and cedar, some of it painted deal, sets off blue and white Delftware, gleaming brass locks and hinges engraved with tulips, daffodils, and roses, and much original furniture, including the baroque state bed with faded crimson and yellow hangings now shown in a darkened room, some William III walnut and marquetry pieces and book presses of the kind designed by Pepys. One room is still hung with the gilded, embossed leather that Blathwayt bought in The Hague on one of his extended trips to Holland, and almost every wall shows off one or more of his collection of Dutch paintings. Here are several of Hondecoeter's huge bird compositions, quiet corners of Amsterdam by Storck and Hendrik Mommers, an evening view of Antwerp across the glassy River Scheldt by Hendrik van Minderhout, and two of Samuel van Hoogstraeten's perspective paintings, one of them – of a peaceful domestic interior – hung at the end of an enfilade so that the open doors in Hoogstraeten's work seem just a continuation of those in the house.

Horton Court

¹/₄ m N Horton, 3 m NE Chipping Sodbury, off A46; NT; rose garden; *open:* Apr–end Oct, Wed, Sat 2–6, or dusk if earlier; tel: none

Two architectural curiosities are on show at this peaceful, stone-built Cotswold manor. The buttressed north wing, only feet away from the little village church, is a rare, late-Norman, one-storey hall of c. 1140, with a couple of original splayed windows and round-headed doorways carved with dogtooth decoration. A six-arched Renaissance loggia in the garden, its interior ornamented with caricature-like medallion heads, was the work of Henry VIII's chaplain William Knight, who enjoyed Horton as one of his many livings. Perhaps this worldly cleric was inspired by what he had seen in Italy when he travelled to Rome in a vain attempt to secure the Pope's blessing on the King's divorce from Catherine of Aragon.

Cornwall

Antony House ☆☆

> 5 m W Plymouth, off A374, via Torpoint car ferry; NT; guided tours; garden; woodland and estuary walks; *open:* Apr–end Oct, Tues, Wed, Thurs, BH Mon, also Sun in June, July, Aug 1.30–5.30; tel: 0752 812191

A serene, early-18th-century house of silver-grey stone, Antony sits on a gentle slope above the tidal reaches of the lower Lynher, with vistas to the river through the woodland fringing the water. Shallow pediments dignify the two main façades, dormers poke from the hipped roof, and low arcaded wings of warm red brick frame the grassy entrance court. The Carew family for whom it was built, by an unknown architect, have been at Antony since the 15th century, and they live here still.

Despite the double hall filling about a third of the ground floor, this is not a grand place. Modest oak-panelled rooms are comfortably and sympathetically furnished, with several pieces that have always been here, and hung with sporting paintings and portraits, among them pictures by Jan Wyck, John Wootton and Jan Weenix, works by Reynolds, Dahl and Hudson, and Mary Beale's rather dull likeness of Rachel Carew, the girl who inspired Daphne du Maurier's *My Cousin Rachel*.

Earlier paintings, such as Edward Bower's haunting portrait of Charles I at his trial, recall the Carew's prominence in county and national affairs. A small exhibition room displays such treasures as an Edwardian visitor's book, with the cramped signature of Lawrence of Arabia among the entries, a recipe book of 1713, and a copy of Richard Carew's great *Survey of Cornwall*, published in 1602 and one of the first such works ever produced.

Cotehele ☆☆☆

> 8 m SW Tavistock, 6 m W Calstock, signed from A390 at St Anne's Chapel; NT; barn restaurant; formal and woodland garden; wood and river walks; mill and quay complex; *open:* Apr–end Oct, daily, except Fri, 12–5.30 (5 in Oct); tel: 0579 50434

This isolated, atmospheric Tudor house, reached only through a web of twisting lanes, sits at the head of a steep, wooded valley running down to the Tamar. A buttressed medieval barn flanks the approach to the gatehouse tower, where a cobbled passage, just wide enough for a packhorse, leads through to a grassy courtyard, the largest of three, surrounded by low ranges of rubbly slatestone and rough-hewn granite. Inside, Cotehele is a rambling sequence of small, tapestry hung, chilly rooms, with heavy wooden doors, granite arches, steep stairs and bare, undulating floors much in evidence. The house has no electricity and is always dark.

Built between 1485 and 1539 by Sir Richard Edgcumbe and his son Sir Piers, who transformed an existing medieval building, Cotehele has miraculously survived largely unaltered. Shortly after it was finished Piers' son built a new house at *Mount Edgcumbe*, overlooking Plymouth Sound, and this became the family's principal seat. There were some improvements in the 17th century, when the main staircase and a castellated tower were added, and in the 1860s one wing was remodelled for a dowager countess, but the essentially Tudor character of the place is unchanged.

One side of the main courtyard is filled by a traditional great hall, still with its original, rough limeash floor and with a decorative, arch-braced timber roof high overhead. Built by the Edgcumbes as an armoury as well as an eating place, the walls are authentically covered with ancient matchlocks, swords, halberds and gauntlets, and a moulded granite fireplace warms the high-table end.

Beyond is a two-storey solar block, with a squint into the hall from what would have been the family's private room on the first floor. The furnishings here and in the adjoining tower include four-posters in the bedrooms, crewelwork hangings, an enchanting stumpwork mirror, beautifully worked upholstery on chairs and settees (much of it, unfortunately, hidden beneath protective covers), and a couple of virtuoso cabinets, one carved in high relief with little naked figures. Everything looks just right, but in fact most pieces date from the 17th and 18th centuries and were probably introduced by the antiquarian 1st Earl of Mount Edgcumbe to enhance Cotehele's romantic appeal.

Most striking, and most unusual, is the wealth of faded Flemish and English 17th-century tapestry which lines almost every room, with panels looped back over doors and ruthlessly cut and patched to fit. Some show bloody scenes from Roman history, some classical myths, others bucolic scenes, but they are so mixed up and intermingled that pieces from any one set are found all over the house.

The one interior that still has many of its Tudor fittings is the tiny, late-15th century, barrel-vaulted chapel, its exterior marked by the fine traceried window looking on to the main court. Inside are medieval floor tiles, the original oak screen and a 16th-century Flemish triptych, with portraits of the donor and his wife flanking an Adoration of the Magi on the central panel, while a cupboard at the back of the room holds the pre-pendulum clock installed here between 1485 and 1489, its hand-wrought machinery connected to an hour-bell in an ornate granite bellcote on the roof.

From the sheltered valley garden below the east range, a path leads half a mile downstream to a cluster of granite buildings around Cotehele quay, among them an offshoot of the National Maritime Museum, the gaping arches of former lime kilns, and a berth for *Shamrock*, the last of the traditional barges which once plied up and down the river. And in a wooded side valley is Cotehele's 18th-century water mill, now restored to working order, and a picturesque group of estate workshops.

Godolphin House ☆

5 m NW Helston, between villages of Godolphin Cross and Townsend; tea room; *open:* May, June, Thurs 2–5, July, Aug, Sept, Tues, Thurs 2–5 (Aug Thurs from 10), also BH Mons; tel: 0736 762409

This old granite house is one of the most atmospheric in the West Country. Once with over a hundred rooms set round two courtyards, it was largely pulled down in 1805 and what remained left to crumble away. Although now rescued by the present owners, Godolphin still has a romantic melancholy about it: ferns and ivy blur steps and walls, the stone is weathered and lichen-spotted, and moss encrusts a cobbled forecourt and the Cornish slates of the roof.

The first sight is of the long, low, 17th-century north front, with the upper floor carried on a granite-columned loggia, a crenellated roofline parapet, and drain pipes moulded with the leaping dolphin and double-headed eagle of the Godolphin crest and arms. An Elizabethan arch closed with massive oak doors leads through into the grassy square at the centre of the house, with the ruinous Great Hall range on the south side, stone-mullioned Tudor façades to east and west. Inside, all is small-scale and homely, with a sequence of modest, lived-in rooms leading up to a spacious, sparsely furnished chamber with a high coved ceiling at the end of the west wing. Downstairs, in a tiny panelled dining-room in the oldest part of the house, is Godolphin's prize possession, a painting by John Wootton of the bay known as the Godolphin Arab. Owned by Sir Frances, the 2nd Earl, in the mid-18th century, this high-spirited stallion sired one of the three lines from which all British racing stock is descended.

Lanhydrock ☆☆

2¹/₂ m SE Bodmin, off B3268, signed from A38; NT; restaurant; hillside garden and park walks; *open:* Apr–end Oct, daily, except Mon (but open BH Mon), 11–5.30 (5 in Oct); tel: 0208 73320

In a hollow beneath steeply rising slopes, looking east over the wooded valley of the Fowey, is a sprawling house of local granite and slate built round three sides of a courtyard, and with a little church set back into the hill behind. Although dating from 1640, with stone-mullioned windows and a battlemented roofline, most of what you see was rebuilt after a fire in 1881. Only the projecting two-storey porch and the north range are genuinely 17th century, and so too is the exquisite gatehouse, its roof crowned with a forest of stumpy obelisks.

This is a huge house, with a tour that takes in 36 rooms on three floors. The main interest of the place is its complete evocation of Edwardian country-house life, with extensive servants' quarters contrasting with the comfortable, spacious rooms used by the Robartes family, who lived at Lanhydrock from 1620 until 1969.

In one part are thickly carpeted corridors, William Morris wallpapers, heavy silk lampshades and potted plants, with several echoes of social conventions at the turn of the century. There are French menu cards in the stiff and formal dining-room, and comfortable leather armchairs protected by anti-macassars in the masculine billiard room and smoking room, where the walls are hung with an array of college photographs, Eton boaters and prefects' canes, neatly tied with white ribbon. The latest conveniences include a post box and stamp machine on the table in the hall, a luggage lift to carry boxes, trunks and cat-baskets to the third floor, and light fittings on pulleys.

In the much barer servants' domain, there are glimpses into the housemaids' closet, with its array of bedpans, earthenware hot water bottles, and pottery slop pails; into tiny, plainly furnished bedrooms, atmospherically supplied with a basket of knitting here, a battered suitcase there; and into the room lined with wardrobes of dresses for the ladies of the house, with a table for mending and pressing. And there is an astonishing array of kitchens, larders and sculleries. Apart from the lofty kitchen itself, with its rows of copper pans and moulds, there are fish and meat larders, a bakehouse, and two dairy rooms, one with a long trough to hold pans of fresh milk, the other with a marble slab for jellies, blancmanges and other cold delights, with water from a spring on the hill above channelled round the edge to keep the confections cool.

Two of Lanhydrock's most attractive interiors come almost at the end of the tour. A panelled drawing-room shows off some fine 18th-century furniture brought here from *Wimpole Hall*, and portraits by Romney and Devis, while the 116 ft gallery running off it down the length of the north wing is the only part of the Jacobean house to have survived the fire. Lit by windows on three sides, this is a glorious room. A high barrel ceiling is a riot of 17th-century plasterwork, with a menagerie of strange beasts, from hairy porcupines to leaping dogs, surrounding unsophisticated illustrations of Old Testament stories. On display is the Lanhydrock *Atlas* of 1693–4. showing every meadow, wood and copse on the estate.

Mount Edgcumbe

On Rame peninsula overlooking Plymouth Sound; long road approach from Plymouth via Torpoint ferry, A374 and B3247, or direct Cremyll ferry, pedestrians only, from Admirals Hard, Stonehouse; café; gardens, park and coastal walks; *open:* Apr–end Oct, Wed–Sun and BH Mon, 11–5.30; tel: 0752 822236

The seat of the Edgcumbe family, which had stood looking over Plymouth Sound since 1553, was gutted by incendiary bombs in 1941, its contents, including several portraits by Joshua Reynolds, largely destroyed. The present house is a post-war reconstruction, carried out for the 6th Earl of Mount Edgcumbe by Adrian Gilbert Scott.

Visitors toiling up the long grassy ride from the Cremyll ferry see a rectangular battlemented building with startlingly ruddy limestone and granite walls, and stumpy octagonal corner towers. The interior, planned round a top-lit hall rising through the centre of the house, as on the 16th-century plan, is currently being restored and refurnished by the two local authorities that now own the estate. The spacious main rooms feel unreal and unlived-in, with newly finished decorative schemes in 18th-century style and period furniture largely assembled from elsewhere. Only a few bits and pieces, such as the seascapes by Van de Velde the Younger, the hassocks and prayer books in the first floor chapel, the mostly 19th- and 20th-century portraits, or the 4th Earl's diary for 1880, with its notes of work to be done on the estate, evoke echoes of the family who lived here for almost 500 years.

Ironically, *Cotehele*, the Edgcumbes' medieval manor 10 miles up the River Tamar, which they largely abandoned for Mount Edgcumbe, has survived with its contents intact. Mount Edgcumbe's 18th-century landscape park, though, is as spectacular as it ever was, with wooded slopes falling to the water's edge and sweeping views over Plymouth Sound.

The Old Post Office, Tintagel ☆

In centre of Tintagel, opposite large public car park; NT; *open:* Apr–end Oct, daily, 11–5.30 (5 in Oct); tel: 0840 770024

Despite its name, this pixy-sized building of Cornish slate is a medieval manor house, dating from the 14th century. Low to the ground, as if shrinking from the unsightly tide of tea shops, car parks and gift emporia that has engulfed Tintagel, it is a place of tiny casements, sturdy chimney stacks, slate window seats and ladder-like stairs, with a pint-sized hall open to the rafters and a wildly undulating roof tufted with grass and moss. The rooms are simply furnished with traditional, sturdy oak pieces, and the former Post Room, in use from 1844 to 1892, has been fitted out as a Victorian post office.

Pencarrow House ☆☆

On A389 at Washaway, 4 m NW Bodmin; guided tours, *c*. 40 mins; tea room; gardens and woodland walks; *open:* Easter–mid Oct, Sun–Thurs, 1.30–5 (from 11 BH Mon and Jun–early Sept); tel: 020 884 369

After the long wooded drive lined with banks of rhododendrons, camellias and hydrangeas, Pencarrow itself may seem an anti-climax, its rather austere, Palladian entrance front not improved by the dirty yellow rendering. Inside, though, the charm returns, with a series of modest, mostly mid-Georgian rooms filled with the Molesworth family's portraits and furniture.

Curiously, the entrance leads straight into a cosy, pine-panelled library, with portraits hanging above the cases of leather-bound books. A music room next door is grander, with a Grecian nude filling the pedimented niche intended for an organ, while through a concealed jib door from the library is the sugary drawing-room, with gilded furniture, curtains of deepest pink and a fanciful Collard and Collard grand, a reminder that Sir Arthur Sullivan composed much of the music for *Iolanthe* while staying at Pencarrow.

Begun in 1765 by Sir John Molesworth, 4th Baronet, who employed an obscure Yorkshire architect, the house was altered a century or so later by the 8th Baronet, who arranged the present entrance, installed pine panelling (painted to resemble maplewood), and laid out the extensive gardens. Molesworths and their relatives stare down from almost every wall, among them works by Raeburn, Beechey and Northcote, and 11 portraits by Reynolds – three of them devoted to Sir Joshua's patron, the 5th Baronet – grouped together in the dining-room. There is a Devis of the St Aubyn sisters of *St Michael's Mount*, some Samuel Scott views of 18th-century London, and two Richard Wilson landscapes, one showing the Thames at *Marble Hill*. A tiny George II rosewood table, its corners doubling over like the folds of an envelope, stands out from the period furniture, and a collection of Chinese porcelain is headed by a large 18th-century bowl, its interior painted with a foxless hunting scene featuring inscrutable orientals on horseback.

Prideaux Place ☆☆

On edge of Padstow, 7 m from Wadebridge; use public car park on A389 ring road, from which house is signed; guided tours (*c*.1 hr); tea room; garden and park walk; *open:* 2 weeks from Easter Sat, then Spring BH–end Sept, Sun–Thurs, 1.30–5 (from 11 Spring and Aug BH Mon); tel: 0841 532411

Set high above one of Cornwall's most popular fishing ports, Prideaux Place stands apart from the crowded streets down the hill. A low, creeper-covered, two-storey house of local grey stone and Cornish slate, it looks out across an ancient deer park to the sandy estuary of the Camel. Although the 16th-century gables have gone, the long entrance front still has the three bays, granite porch and stone-mullioned windows of the E-shaped Elizabethan plan, but round the corner is a sash-windowed Georgian frontage, with a gothick traceried window partly filled with stained glass.

Inside, there are similar contrasts. The sombre dining-room formed out of the Elizabethan Great Hall, with its inlaid panelling of Spanish oak, is a world away from the salmon-pink morning-room and its panel of art-deco light switches, from the churchlike library, with its vaulted plaster ceiling, or from the drawing-room, with its huge rococo mirror, gothick frieze and murals by Alec Cobbe, the artist who is now ensconced in *Hatchlands*. There is a gothick staircase hall, with busts set in pinnacled, canopied niches and a traceried window, and the Elizabethan Great Chamber on the first floor has a barrel vault with plaster panels telling the story of Susannah and the Elders.

The Prideaux family still lives here, as their ancestors have done for 400 years, and the place is full of accumulated treasures. There are paintings by David Teniers the Younger, inset panels by Antonio Verrio, whose florid cherubs came attached to some Restoration panelling from a house near Bude, and portraits by Zoffany, Lely and Opie, who left his own likeness here as a tip for the housekeeper. A chest rescued from the treacherous Doom Bar at the mouth of the Camel is encrusted with fishscale slivers of mother-of-pearl, cabinets are stuffed with a collection of Spode and Royal Worcester and a blue-and-white Nanking dinner service, and Sèvres and Meissen vases and other *objets* clutter mantelpieces and rub shoulders with a display of family photographs.

St Michael's Mount ☆☆

At Marazion, off A394, 3 m E Penzance, on island in Mount's Bay; access by causeway or boat (summer only), allow 45 mins from car park to castle entrance; NT; island cafe; *open:* Apr–end Oct, Mon–Fri 10.30–5.30, Nov–March, Mon, Wed, Fri, as tide, weather and circumstances permit; also open many summer weekends for charity; tel: 0736 710507

Spectacularly sited on the crest of a sea-girt rocky crag, the Mount has one of the most dramatic settings of any house in England. From a distance it looks superb, with massive walls rising directly from bare rock, and battlements, thrusting chimneys and a tall central tower silhouetted against the sky. Just getting there is something of an adventure. At low tide, an ant-like thread of visitors approaches cautiously across the causeway linking the Mount to the mainland; at high tide there are long queues for the little boats which appear as if by magic the moment the water is too deep for paddling. On the other side, beyond the lobster-claw harbour ringed with whitewashed cottages, there is a stiff climb up a rough and slippery path.

St Michael's Mount is a curious hybrid: part-fortress, part-religious retreat, part-elegant country house, its romantic skyline owing much to extensive 19th-century remodelling. At the highest point of the island is a little 14th-century granite church, the most obvious survival of the Benedictine priory established here as a daughter house of the much grander Mont St Michel on the other side of the Channel. The Mount had been a place of pilgrimage ever since St Michael appeared to some local fishermen in the 5th century, and when the saint's shrine was enhanced with a jawbone of St Appolonia, who had the power to relieve toothache, the faithful came in their thousands.

At the Dissolution, the Mount was transformed into a fortress and it was the last military governor, the parliamentarian Colonel John St Aubyn, who began to convert it into a private house shortly after the Civil War. Both priory and castle are still very much in evidence. A dungeon-like garrison room is embedded deep in the rock, gun batteries point out to sea, and an old sentry box watches visitors struggling up the path. The coolly elegant blue drawing rooms, decorated with gothick plasterwork and hung with portraits by Opie, Gainsborough and Hudson, were created out of the ruined lady chapel, and the monastic refectory was turned into what is now the lofty Chevy Chase Room, its open timber roof incorporating medieval timbers, some 15th-century Flemish glass in the windows and an engaging hunting frieze, all eager dogs and unsuspecting rabbits, running round the walls.

Going round the Mount is a curious experience. Only a small part of the extensive house is shown, several of the rooms are given over to displays of historical and family relics, and visitors are channelled along a one-way system which sometimes funnels them through narrow stone passages, sometimes leads out on to great terraces, before plunging back inside once again. From the south terrace – the roof of the large Victorian wing grafted on in 1875–7 – you can look down on the St Aubyn family's private garden far below; from the north terrace there are panoramic views along the coast and inland to the moors of Cornwall.

Trelowarren

6 m SE Helston, off B3293 to St Keverne; guided tours; teas; gardens and 4 m woodland walk; *open:* mid Apr–early Oct, Wed and BH Mon, 2.30–5; tel: 032 622 366

This secluded manor, home of the Vyvyan family since 1426, looks more exciting than it is. Three low ranges are set round a grassy courtyard, one still with Tudor mullions and gables, one clearly a chapel, and the third, the main block of the house, marked by stepped buttresses and a battlemented roofline. With one exception, though, the interiors shown are all heavily Victorian. More than this, Trelowarren is now occupied by an ecumenical Christian fellowship and, although there are still Vyvyan family portraits here, the furnishings are institutional and drab. The one joy is the chapel. A frothy exercise in Strawberry Hill gothick, this tunnel-vaulted room is lined by elaborately canopied stalls and another canopy sits crown-like over the double doors at the west end. Recently restored, all is freshly cream and white, with slate-blue highlights.

Trerice ☆

3 m SE Newquay, off A3058; NT; lawn mower museum; barn restaurant; garden; *open:* Apr–end Oct, daily, except Tues, 11–5.30 (5 in Oct); tel: 0637 875404

Reached through narrow, high-sided lanes, Trerice is a seductive, unspoilt Elizabethan manor house, built for Sir John Arundell, one of the great men of Cornwall, in 1570–2. A small turfed entrance court sets off an E-shaped

façade of honey-grey limestone, topped off by five curvaceous Dutch gables and with a huge, stone-mullioned window lighting the Great Hall to the left of the porch. Inside, there is rich Elizabethan plasterwork on the barrel ceiling of the sunny Great Chamber, and a caryatid-flanked overmantel is endearingly dated 'MCCCCCLXX3', as if the plasterer simply ran out of space.

The original contents have been dispersed, but the half-dozen modest rooms on show have been sympathetically furnished by the Trust, with some Cornish pieces and two clocks by Thomas Tompion among a collection of 17th- and 18th-century oak and walnut furniture. The paintings also have an appropriately Cornish flavour, with several works, including a rather severe self-portrait, by John Opie, who was born 15 miles away. Royal portraits recall the Arundells' loyalty to the Stuart cause, and there are also some panels of Jacobean stumpwork, one of them showing Charles I and Henrietta Maria in a charmingly rural setting, watched by a long-eared rabbit.

Trewithen House ☆☆

On A390 between Probus and Grampound; guided tours (c. 45 mins); tearoom; outstanding garden; *open:* Apr–July, Mon, Tues, and Aug BH Mon 2–4.30; tel: 0726 883794

Spring displays in Trewithen's woodland gardens tend to deflect attention from the charming early Georgian house, its neat, sash-windowed façades touched with a pink blush of lichen. The north front, with a prospect over park and lake and with two cupola-topped stable blocks framing the grassy entrance court, was begun in c.1730, soon after Philip Hawkins, son of a wealthy Cornish attorney, bought the estate. The south front on to the gardens, faced in silvery grey Pentewan stone, is later, dating from Sir Robert Taylor's work on the house in 1763–4.

The tour takes visitors over the ground floor of what is very much a family house, lived in by Hawkins' descendants and filled with a rich accumulation of furniture and paintings. The one grand interior is the spacious, mid-18th-century dining-room occupying the centre of the south front, with rococo plasterwork white on pale green walls, and screens of Ionic columns either end, one shading a round-headed niche full of blue and rust Imari ware. Possibly intended by Taylor to be the entrance hall, this impressive room is hung with some of the best of the family paintings, including Reynolds' portrait of Dr Zacchariah Mudge imitating his friend Dr Johnson, two works by Vanderbank, and three Allan Ramsays in ornate gilded frames.

Four paintings by Northcote, including a warts-and-all self-portrait, are gathered in the parlour, the only room to retain its early 18th-century oak panelling, and there is some fine furniture, including pieces by Chippendale, in the yellow-walled drawing-room. Family connections account for the desk inlaid with amboyna wood that once belonged to the colourful Sir Stamford Raffles, founder of Singapore, and for the longcase clock by the Plymouth-born Thomas Mudge, Zacchariah's son, who was apprenticed to Thomas Tompion.

A la Ronde ☆

2 m N Exmouth on A376; NT; tea-room;
open: Apr–end Oct, daily, except Fri and
Sat, 11–5.30; tel: 0395 265514

This bizarre, 16-sided villa looking west over the Exe estuary is like a giant African hut built of stone and tile, with a steep, conical roof above rough limestone walls. Green-shuttered sashes and diamond-shaped casements in rust-red frames add to the whimsical effect, as do the tall brick chimneys and prominent catwalk sprouting from the roof.

Built in 1796 for the intrepid Jane and Mary Parminter, newly returned from a Continental tour, A la Ronde originally stood in country outside Exmouth, but is now within the spread of the resort. The interest of the place lies not in fine furnishings or the beauty of its setting, but in the ingenious layout and the survival of the Misses Parminter's intricate handiwork. The main floor is designed like a wheel, with seven strangely shaped rooms radiating out from a central octagon. Every inch is used: little lobbies have been created in awkward corners, seats fold down across the doorways of the hall, bookshelves have been dovetailed back into triangular recesses.

Jane and Mary were as inventive in what they created. A frieze of feathers still adorns the drawing-room, skirting and doorframes are carefully marbled, shells have been sculpted into flower arrangements and used as a mosaic round a fireplace, and there are pictures made of sand and seaweed, or of cut paper, with tiny trees waving feathery branches. The detail is ethereal. A little box is covered with minute scrolls of paper used like marquetry, knitted bootees are only millimetres across, and the tiny scissors used for paperwork are almost too small to handle. Most astonishing is the gallery high above the octagon, where every inch is encrusted with shell decoration and bird pictures made out of feathers, moss and twigs. Sadly, the gallery is considered too fragile to show, and visitors must admire it on video or by looking up from below.

Few of A la Ronde's treasures are as obvious as the gallery. Several rooms strike drab and unpromising, or are painted in virulent colours, and only those who take time to stand and stare will find what is here.

Arlington Court ☆

7 m NE Barnstaple, on A39; NT; tearoom,
garden; carriage collection and rides; park
walks; *open:* Apr–end Oct, Sun–Fri and BH
Sats 11–5.30; tel: 0271 850296

At the centre of a glorious 3,500-acre estate embracing the deep-cut, wooded valleys of the River Yeo is a stuccoed Regency villa by the local architect Thomas Lee, with a plain stone 19th-century wing built on to the north. Seat of the Chichester family since the 16th century, Arlington as it is now bears the stamp of the high-living Sir Bruce Chichester, who presided over a Victorian heyday, and of his only child, Rosalie, who lived on here until 1949. A compulsive hoarder, with a child's delight in little things, Miss Chichester filled room after room with model ships, stuffed birds, *objets*, tea caddies, pewter plates and mugs, and exotic souvenirs acquired on round-the-world trips.

A modest entrance leads into a huge staircase hall taking up a good third of the house, added in the 1860s by the extravagant Sir Bruce. Cannon from the *Erminia*, in which he cruised the Mediterranean, guard the imperial staircase, and paintings of the topsail schooner hang round the walls. Off here are a boudoir and the three most important rooms in the house, forming a sunny 70 ft gallery down the south front, and upstairs visitors can see Rosalie's modest bedroom, with the silver dressing-table set which she was given by her Austrian godmother.

Alas, the whole place is now a watered-down, tidied-up version of how it was in Rosalie's day, when a huge cage bursting with budgerigars filled the central bay of the gallery, when Polly the parrot flew free, and when every cupboard and surface was crammed with pieces from her collections. Choice items – a sinuous rock crystal cat, a red amber elephant, snuff boxes, ornaments of ivory, enamel and silver – are carefully displayed in the gallery, elsewhere are cupboards of orderly pewter and intricate arrangements of shells, and a robin and a blue tit modelled in bread and a couple of stuffed mice preside over the room fitted out as a nursery. But only a couple of unobtrusive watercolours in the hall, painted by Miss Peters, Rosalie's diminutive companion, really convey how Arlington was.

Bickleigh Castle ☆

Off A3072, across the River Exe from Bickleigh, 4 m S Tiverton; tearoom; garden; guided tour (c.50 mins) except at peak times; *open:* Easter week, then Wed, Sun and BH Mon to end May, then daily, except Sat, to early Oct, 2–5.30; tel: 0884 855 363

Idyllically set between the Exe and steeply rising wooded slopes is a picturesque group of cottages clustered round a red sandstone gatehouse. Castle in name only, Bickleigh is a remnant of a medieval fortified manor slighted in the Civil War, with a 17th-century farmhouse of cob and thatch added on behind. All is prettily set off by the water garden created in the former moat and by a pair of rococo Italianate gates screening the house.

The tour takes in the gatehouse and some low-ceilinged, lived-in rooms in the farmhouse. There is an intriguing, re-assembled, Jacobean stone overmantel, an assortment of arms and armour in one of the former guardrooms flanking the stone-vaulted archway, and some 17th- and 18th-century furniture, but the 50 ft great hall stretching across the gatehouse arch is a creation of the 1920s, when the whole place was much restored. A mixed bag of exhibits in the outbuildings includes World War II spy equipment invented by Charles Fraser-Smith, the original of Ian Fleming's 'Q', who dreamed up a compass disguised as a button, maps on handkerchiefs and shoe laces which doubled as saws.

Bickleigh's best feature lies across the road. Here, in a cob-walled enclosure on the edge of the river, is a tiny Norman chapel, its rough walls smothered in roses, its roof thatched, and its plain interior spanned by a 15th-century wagon roof.

Bowden House

1 m S Totnes, signed from A381 to Kingsbridge; guided tours (c. 50 mins); teas; photographic museum; open: Easter–end Sept, Tues, Wed, Thurs and BH Sun and Mon, 2–4 (last tour); tel: 0803 863664

Over a steep rise from tourist-thronged Totnes and the Dart estuary is this secluded house, tucked under the shoulder of the hill amongst fields and woods. Charming early Georgian façades of pinkish-grey stone, with plain pilasters cutting through rows of narrow sash windows, mark the principal fronts. Behind, focused on two small cobbled courts, is a much older house, dating back to early Tudor times, with a surviving stone-mullioned window and some original panelling and plasterwork. The guided tour takes in rooms of both periods, including the lofty Tudor great hall, with its Elizabethan ribbed ceiling and plaster frieze; a sitting-room lined with re-used 16th-century panelling and with a carved overmantel of 1585; and an elegant first-floor drawing-room, with three long windows looking down-valley, its 18th-century panelling painted in deepest pink and white. Most impressive is the stone-flagged baroque hall picked out in pink, white and blue which ends the tour, with the figure of Mercury and a scrawny version of Pegasus boldly depicted among the plasterwork on the ceiling, broken pediments over the doors, and round-headed niches in the walls, two of them painted with the figures of Bowden's past owners. Alas, most rooms are spoilt by obtrusive modern furnishings, and the great hall, seen by a flickering light with curtains drawn, has been given a gothick cast, with fake cobwebs smothering the pikes and muskets hung on the walls, a scattering of bats, spiders and mice, and chairs reserved for ghosts.

Bradley Manor ☆

Drive leads N off A381 Totnes road, just outside Newton Abbot; signed only inside gates; NT; garden; river and woodland walks; open: Apr–end Sept, Wed 2–5, and some Thurs in Apr and Sept; tel: none

This homely, 15th-century manor of local limestone and Dartmoor granite lies deep in a secluded valley on the edge of Newton Abbot, surrounded by unbroken woodland. A path leads across the river to the long, low-slung entrance front, with tiny oriels in each of the gables, heavily buttressed, whitewashed walls, and a round-headed arch opening into the screens passage which runs across the house. A barrel-roofed chapel juts out to the north, with a traceried gothic window in the east end.

Inside, visitors see a succession of low-ceilinged, rough-walled, lived-in lit-tle rooms. One is the old kitchen, with a massive granite fireplace at one end, while upstairs, in what was part of the 13th-century house, is some early Tudor painted decoration: a repeated pattern of black fleur de lys, and a gory IHS monogram, surrounded by the instruments of the passion. The one spa-cious interior is the Great Hall, its roof open to the rafters, a gaudy Tudor coat of arms prominent on a gable end, and a 16th-century carved oak screen filling the arch leading to the chapel.

Buckland Abbey ☆

6 m S Tavistock, off A386 near Yelverton; NT and Plymouth CC; restaurant; garden and waymarked walks; open: Apr–end Oct, daily, except Thurs, 10.30–5.30, Nov–end March, Sat, Sun, Sun 2–5; tel: 0822 853607

This secluded place, hidden in a side valley of the River Tavy, was home to two of the best-known of Elizabethan adventurers: Sir Richard Grenville and Sir Francis Drake. Grenville's father had bought the former Cistercian monastery at the Dissolution – for the princely sum of £233 3s 4d – but it was his son who converted it into a house, only to sell it on to Sir Francis Drake, for £3,400, just a few years later.

Despite these associations, visitors should not expect too much. Badly dam-aged by a fire in 1938, and sold by Drake's descendants a few years later, Buckland Abbey is now more museum than home, with only a couple of fully furnished rooms. Then, too, its originally Elizabethan character was pro-foundly altered by 18th-century improvements.

The path leading down to the house takes visitors past attractive farm buildings, including sheds for the ox teams that worked the estate until 1881, and the heavily-buttressed, 160 ft, medieval monastic barn, its vast bare inte-rior, like the nave of some primitive cathedral, rising to a 15th-century arch-braced timber roof.

The house, not as long as the barn, was created out of the shell of the monastic church, with floors built into the nave and chancel and the squat crossing tower left rising at the east end. The arch of the blocked south transept and the gable of the demolished roof are etched on the south front, while inside there are carved corbels that once supported the vault beneath the tower and a traceried arch.

Climbing the elegant staircase put in in the 1770s, still with its original dog gates, visitors then work their way down through the house, starting with the long, top-floor gallery detailing the history of the estate from medieval times. Historically, the most interesting room is the darkened gallery devoted to Drake, the exhibits here including a list of expenses incurred in fighting the Armada, annotated in Lord Chancellor Burghley's spidery hand; lead shot, pewter and other finds from Spanish ships wrecked off the Irish coast; the commission from Elizabeth I to 'singe the king of Spain's beard' at Cadiz in 1587; and the legendary side drum painted with Drake's coat of arms. A Georgian dining-room, hung with portraits by Northcote and Opie, is more gloomy than elegant, but on the ground floor, directly beneath the crossing tower, is Grenville's great hall, panelled in inlaid oak, floored in colourful pink and white tiles, and with a decorative plasterwork ceiling and frieze.

Cadhay ☆

1 m NW Ottery St Mary on B3176; guided tours only; garden; open: July, Aug, Tues–Thurs, 2–6, also late May and Aug BH Sun and Mon; tel: 0404 81 2432

Set in water meadows by the River Otter, with a chain of medieval fish ponds incorporated in the garden, is a picturesque Tudor courtyard house. The gabled east façade, with walls of warm brownish sandstone, stone-mullioned windows, and a projecting octagonal stair turret, is as built by the prosperous lawyer John Haydon, legal adviser to the city of Exeter, who constructed a three-armed manor here. A long gallery wing and the enchanting courtyard façades, faced in a chequer of flint and sandstone and with Renaissance-style niches carrying endearingly unsophisticated statues of Henry VIII and his three children, were early Jacobean embellishments by John's great-nephew Robert, and an 18th-century owner was responsible for the Georgian north front, with its sash windows, pedimented doorway and facing of grey Beer stone.

The interior, although sensitively restored in the early years of this century, has been much altered. An informal tour focusing on architectural history takes in the former long gallery, the mutilated remains of a medieval hammerbeam roof, now spanning a draughty attic, a huge Tudor fireplace in the lower half of what was the great hall, and a spiral stair. The modest rooms, some with Georgian panelling and fireplaces, have been furnished with good 17th- and 18th-century pieces by the present owner.

Castle Drogo ☆☆

Drewsteignton, via A30 Exeter–Okehampton road, or A382 Moretonhampstead–Whiddon Down road (signposted); NT; tearoom; garden; moor and river walks; open: Apr–end Oct, Sat–Thurs 11–5.30; tel: 0647 433306

Castle Drogo, a long finger of Dartmoor granite set high on a moorland spur, is in a class of its own. Built by Sir Edwin Lutyens between 1911 and 1930, it was commissioned by the 33-year-old Julius Drewe, who had made a fortune from his Home and Colonial Stores. Determined to join the Victorian establishment, Drewe wanted a house that would set him up as a landed gentleman and an ancestry to match. Castle Drogo gave him both. A helpful genealogist traced descent from the Norman baron who had given his name to the nearby village of Drewsteignton, while no-one could fail to be impressed by the building that rose slowly above the deep cleft of the River Teign, its site almost 1,000 ft above sea level.

From the outside, Castle Drogo is angular and severe, with great expanses

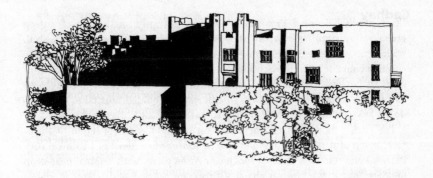

of wall rising to a parapeted and battlemented skyline, and a fortified entrance tower with arrow slits and a real portcullis. Only the generous mullioned windows with views south over the valley suggest this carapace has a softer centre. Inside, the place is a strange, unsettling mix of castle-like austerity and comfortable Edwardian interiors. There are bare granite walls, vaulted corridors and constant changes of level, as if to remind people of the difficulties of the site, while the poor servants were condemned to work in a dungeon-like kitchen, lit from a lantern in the roof. There is even exposed granite in the rather chilly bathroom, and a crypt of a chapel feels as if it has been dug out of the rock.

Quite different is the spacious, airy drawing-room, lit by windows on three sides, the panelled walls painted a restful green, comfortable chintzy sofas round the fire, a grand piano tucked away in a corner, and Venetian chandeliers cascading from the ceiling. There are the ghosts of a hundred house parties here, with guests assembling before dinner and then processing down the majestic staircase to the portrait-hung dining-room directly underneath, its long table lit by electric candlesticks attached to a circuit beneath the cloth. Such gimmicks and period furnishings rub shoulders with tapestries, exotic, leather-covered chairs and other Spanish antiques acquired by Julian Drewe in 1899, when he bought the home of the banker Adrian de Murietta. Most impressive is the sheer quality of the workmanship that has gone into the castle, with every smooth surface, rounded corner, and thin, tapering slab of granite modelled with hammer and chisel alone.

Sadly, Julian Drewe died shortly after the castle was finally completed, his declining years shadowed by the loss of his eldest son in World War I. His social ambitions, though, were fully realised. Drewe was listed in Burke's *Landed Gentry*, an honour which his rivals Lipton and Sainsbury never had.

Chambercombe ☆

On E edge of Ilfracombe, off A399 and B3230; guided tour (c. 60 mins); tearoom; garden; open: Easter–Sept, Mon–Fri 10–4.30, Sun 2–4.30; tel: 0271 862624

Ilfracombe's balconied Victorian villas stop abruptly on the rim of a deep green valley running down to Hele Bay. Tucked into the slope of the hill, with low, whitewashed buildings of cob and stone clustered round a tiny cobbled court, is what is essentially an old farmhouse, dating back to the 15th century but much altered and restored. Starting in the beamed, one-storey hall with a sloping limeash floor, an entertaining guided tour takes in half-a-dozen low-ceilinged, interconnecting rooms with rough, plastered walls.

For such a modest place, there is a surprisingly good collection of furniture, much of it 17th century, but also including such items as a 13th-century Peter's Pence chest, a lovely yew Queen Anne piece, with original pear-drop handles, and a Mackintosh chair. Visitors are regaled with stores of smuggling and of the well-attested discovery of a woman's skeleton in a walled-up chamber, possibly a lady rescued from a wrecked ship and murdered here for her jewels. The tour ends in Chambercombe's tiny private chapel licensed in 1404, no more than 10 ft long, and still entered through a medieval door.

Sadly, the manor's immediate surroundings are raw and depressing and Ilfracombe presses too close.

Compton Castle ☆

At Compton, 3 m W Torquay, off Torbay ringroad, 1 mile N Marldon; NT; garden; open: Apr–end Oct, Mon, Wed, Thurs, 10–12.15, 2–5; tel: 0803 872112

Only a mile or two from the rash of modern development fringing Tor Bay is this magical fortified manor cocooned in a narrow, steep-sided valley. The winding lane from the village suddenly reveals a cliff-like expanse of roughly built, battlemented and buttressed wall, with tall, gabled towers at the corners and portcullis-protected gateways. A thatched, 18th-century barn frames one side of the grassy approach and the impressive entrance façade links into a curtain wall ringing the whole complex. Started in the early 1300s by Geoffrey Gilbert, direct ancestor of the family that still lives here, the castle was gradually enlarged over the next 200 years, with the final defences, as if the place were expecting to withstand a siege, added in the 1520s. Little has been altered since, but extensive restoration in this century involved rebuilding the Great Hall.

Although only a couple of rooms are shown, and there are no original contents to admire, Compton Castle is wonderfully atmospheric. There are Tudor traceried windows in the chapel and a detached medieval kitchen has a massive hearth filling one wall and a stone barrel vault for a ceiling. Then, too, the castle links in to one of the greatest periods in English history. It was two 16th-century Gilberts, John and Humphrey, who, with their half-brother

Walter Raleigh, their cousin Richard Grenville and Sir Francis Drake, formed that band of Devon sea-captains who played such a prominent role in the defeat of the Armada and in Elizabethan expeditions to the New World.

Flete

11 m E Plymouth, entrance on A379 opposite junction with B3210; guided tours; garden; *open:* May–Sept, Wed, Thurs, 2–5; tel: none

An austere, fortress-like edifice in pinkish limestone and Dartmoor granite with a five-storey tower dominating the entrance front and a battlemented roofline, Flete may well have inspired Sir Edwin Lutyens in his design of *Castle Drogo* on the other side of Dartmoor. Unlike Drogo, though, Flete was a remodelling of an earlier house, carried out for the Mildmay family in 1878 by Richard Norman Shaw. At the back, a fragment of a gabled Tudor wing extending into the gardens is a taste of what was destroyed.

The house is now divided into apartments, and visitors are shown just the few public rooms. There is much heavy oak panelling, some Jacobethan plasterwork and massive chimney-pieces carved out of granite and marble.

Fursdon

6 m SW Tiverton, just outside Thorverton village, approach via A3072 or A396; guided tours (*c.* 45 mins); tearoom; garden; *open:* Apr–end Sept, Thurs and BH Mon, 2–4.30; tel: 0392 860860

Narrow, twisting Devon lanes lead to this modest, cement-rendered house of 1732 tucked into a hillside high on the edge of the Exe valley. An informal tour of a few ground-floor rooms takes in lived-in Georgian interiors, the comfortless Regency library-cum-dancing room built on in 1815, and museum rooms created out of what were once cobbled larders and cellars. Fursdons have lived on this spot since the 13th century and there are still some traces of their earlier house, such as the Jacobean oak panelling in the dining-room, but the furniture and paintings on show, including an undistinguished set of family portraits, are mostly of the mid-18th century or later. The museum is principally a costume collection, its most important exhibit a blue and silver court dress of 1753.

Hartland Abbey ☆

15 m W Bideford in NW corner of Devon, ¼ mile from Hartland, on road to Hartland Quay, signposted from A39; tearoom; coast walks; *open:* May–Sept, Wed, BH Sun, Mon 2–5.30, also Sun in July and Aug, and 1st two in Sept; tel: 02374 41264

Hartland Abbey is buried in a deep gash of a valley, just one field wide, running down to a stretch of wild and beautiful coast. Tree-covered slopes climb above the house on either side and the sea is only a mile away. The house is wedged across the valley, its walls of rough grey stone like a dam against unseen waters. It was built on the remains of an Augustinian abbey, dissolved in 1539, and the seaward side still has cusped openings that were once part of the monks' cloister. Most of the exterior, though, is the result of rebuilding in the 18th century, when the principal façade was given its playful gothick windows and the whole ensemble was finished off with a battlemented roofline.

The tour of the house concentrates on the three large reception rooms facing up-valley. Redecorated in the mid-19th century, like much else at Hartland, these are a display of heavy linenfold panelling, Jacobethan overmantels and painted ceilings, with oak drawing-room furniture to match and some gaudy murals illustrating romanticized scenes from the Middle Ages. A similarly colourful, vaulted and stencilled corridor is by Sir George Gilbert Scott, who was commissioned in 1862 to design a new entrance and front hall, and whose handwritten request for £100 can be seen among the display of documents.

Hartland has passed through marriage from one family to another and, as a result, the paintings here are an intriguingly mixed bag. Among them are portraits of the family of the Elizabethan adventurer Sir Richard Grenville, a clutch of admirals by Reynolds, Northcote and Beechey, works by the Bideford-born Thomas Hudson, and a likeness of the Georgian antiquary William Stukeley, one of the first to realize the importance of Avebury and Stonehenge.

Hemerdon House

2 m from Plympton, just E Hemerdon village, off road to Sparkwell and Cornwood; open : 30 days in May and Aug, 2–5.30; tel: 0752 223816 (office hours), 337350 (weekends)

Looking south over a peaceful valley is this square, rendered house, with unobtrusive pediments on the two show façades. Begun in the late-18th century, it was built over some time, as the differences in the windows levels suggest, and has a library fitted out about a hundred years later. A homely, lived-in place, it is full of Woollcombe family treasures and paintings, among them portraits by Reynolds and Northcote and the latter's *Worthies of Devon*, with a little boy kneeling before such legendary figures as Walter Raleigh and Francis Drake.

Killerton

7 m NE Exeter, on W side of B3181, entrance off B3185; NT; tearoom; hillside garden with rare trees and shrubs; park walks; *open:* Apr–end Oct, daily, except Tues, 11–5.30; tel: 0392 881345

Most people come here to enjoy the woodland garden laid out on the slopes of the volcanic hump rising behind the house rather than to see the low, apricot-washed building that burrows back into the hill. Former home of the Aclands, one of Devon's oldest and most prominent families, and still the centre of a major agricultural estate, Killerton is a low-key and undistinguished house. In 1778, Sir Thomas, 7th Baronet, asked the provincial architect John Johnson to put up a stop-gap residence to replace the Elizabethan mansion he had inherited, while a palace by James Wyatt was constructed on the hill above, but in the event he made do with the modest building Johnson produced, and later generations simply extended it as required.

Major alterations by the 12th Baronet gave the house its Edwardian character, with a suite of reception rooms – all scagliola pillars, reproduction 18th-century plasterwork and marble fireplaces – designed for lavish house parties. Sadly, the original contents were largely destroyed while in store during World War II, and the house lacks character. The inner hall, where gentlemen gathered before dinner to watch the ladies sweep down the massive oak staircase, still has the 1807 chamber organ on which Lydia Acland, wife of the 10th Baronet, had lessons from Samuel Wesley, then organist of Exeter Cathedral, and the dining-room, where sleeveless evening dresses were the rule even in the depths of winter, has a table laid with 18th-century Acland silver and is hung with family portraits. But on the whole, apart from some fine carpets and the drawings of members of the political Grillion's club, among them likenesses of Gladstone and Lord Shaftesbury, there is not a great deal of interest here, although some visitors may enjoy trying out the organ. The upstairs rooms are devoted to changing tableaux displaying 18th- and 19th-century costumes from the extensive Paulise de Bush collection.

Knightshayes Court ☆☆

2 m N Tiverton, off A396; NT; teas; formal and woodland garden; *open:* Apr–end Oct, daily, except Fri (but open Good Fri), 1.30–5.30; tel: 0884 254665

High above Tiverton sits this sinister, red-sandstone mansion, with thrusting gables and dormers, huge, vaguely Elizabethan windows and menacing gargoyles. Designed by William Burges, one of the most fanatical of the gothic revivalists, it was built in the early 1870s for Sir John Heathcoat-Amory, fox-hunting squire and local MP, whose grandfather had made a fortune out of the lace factory that still dominates the town in the valley below.

Burges planned the interior as a richly coloured medieval dream, lavishly decorated with sculpture, mosaics, metalwork and stained glass, but his more conservative client, returning from a fishing holiday in Norway, took fright at the 57 pages of meticulous watercolours from the opium-fuelled imagination of his architect, and sent Burges packing. The house was completed by the safer J. D. Crace, but even his more restrained painted decoration was considered over the top and much was covered up or removed in later years.

Visitors see several rooms on the two main floors, where family paintings and furnishings are now combined with the Trust's re-creations of the 19th-century decorative schemes and with period pictures and features brought from elsewhere. A medieval-style great hall is the only room which is almost as Burges envisaged it, with massive beams in an open timber roof, four stout columns of polished black marble supporting a balustraded gallery for addressing the assembled tenantry, and delicious carved corbels, some devised as medieval rustics, others as a frog, a fox and other animals.

Upstairs, there is a panoramic view of Tiverton from a sunny, bay-windowed bedroom, stencilled decoration by Crace, and paintings of local scenes by the Devon artist F. J. Widgery, and the tour ends with the principal rooms forming an enfilade down the south front. The dining room has a beamed and painted ceiling and a gilded frieze made up of quotations from Robert Burns; gothic niches in the octagonal morning-room are filled with 17th-century majolica; and the richly coloured ceiling in the egg-yellow library is punctuated with Burges' favourite 'jelly-mould' cavities, looking for all the world like huge gold daisies.

Most splendid is the scarlet-walled drawing-room, with a monumental carved marble chimneypiece that Burges designed for an Oxford college and the original, compartmental ceiling, the brilliantly coloured decoration again involving lavish gilding. Apart from the contemporary table by Anthony Salvin, the room is rather bare, but the lack of furnishing is more than compensated for by what is on the walls. Here and in the library are displayed the cabinet paintings collected by the late John Heathcoat-Amory, among them a 15th-century Flemish annunciation, with Mary looking over her shoulder at the angel as if to greet a casual visitor, a dreamy Claude, Holbein's *Lady in a White Cap*, a tiny Rembrandt self-portrait, two flower paintings by Constable, an impressionistic Turner seascape and a charming nativity by Lucas Cranach the Elder, with an ass gently snuffling at the baby and Joseph bringing in more straw. Even if some of the attributions are in doubt, they look splendid.

Overbecks

1½ m SW Salcombe, signposted from Malborough and Salcombe; NT; tearoom; exotic garden; *open:* Apr–end Oct, daily, except Sat, 11–5.30 ; tel: 054 884 2893

Those who brave the steep and narrow lanes leading to this individual property generally come to enjoy the steeply terraced, almost Mediterranean garden and the stunning views over Salcombe bay rather than to visit the undistinguished, double-fronted Edwardian villa sitting at the top of the slope. The house is now a museum, with displays on local natural history, a children's corner, and a room devoted to ships and the sea, recalling Salcombe's heyday as a port. Part of the collection came from Mr Overbeck, the eccentric scientist who gave the house to the Trust. Visitors can see his electronic rejuvenator and a clipping from the *Daily Sketch* for 21 January 1911 heralding his non-alcoholic beer.

Powderham Castle ☆☆

8 m SE Exeter, off A379 to Dawlish; guided tours (c. 50 mins); tearoom; small garden; *open:* Easter–end Sept, daily, except Sat, 10–5.30; tel: 0626 890243

Seat of the Courtenay family, Earls of Devon, Powderham is an imposing, many-towered building looking east over a wooded deer park to the wide estuary of the Exe. At its heart are the remains of the medieval fortress built by Sir Philip Courtenay between 1390 and 1420 to guard the approaches of the river, but most of the castle-like exterior was the creation of the Devon-born architect Charles Fowler, better known for his Covent Garden market, who added battlements, gothic windows, the fortified gatehouse and other medieval touches in the 1840s. The interior, on the other hand, is largely Georgian, the result of remodelling in the mid-18th century and by James Wyatt in the 1790s.

Inside, visitors see some dozen rooms on two floors. Fowler's oppressive panelled dining hall leads into the elegant mid-Georgian wing, with delicate plaster ceilings and marble fireplaces and a glorious double library, bare-floored and sparsely furnished, as if cleared for dancing. James Wyatt's flamboyant music room – more barn than boudoir – juts out beyond, a concoction of urn-filled niches and gilded Regency furniture, with a chamber organ in pastel blues and pinks at one end. Similarly unrestrained is the staircase hall of 1755 rising through the building, with cascades of plasterwork fruit and flowers on brilliantly blue walls. This riot of rococo decoration by a talented local craftsman includes realistic birds, a tambourine and pipes, a hunting horn, an artist's palette and other motifs celebrating war, peace and love.

The staircase was created out of the original Great Hall, one of the oldest parts of the castle, and the marble-floored room next door still retains a carved overmantel dated 1533 and the stone arches of 1390 which led to the medieval kitchens and buttery. Also medieval, although originally used as a granary, is the little chapel reached across the rose terrace at the back of the house, its open roof made of 15th-century timbers and ancient carvings on the pews ends.

There is some delicate embroidery on a couple of Georgian *chaises-longues* and a long run of family portraits, the earliest dating from Tudor times, the most distinguished a number of works by Kneller and Hudson, and the most romantic the local artist Richard Cosway's studies of some of the numerous daughters of the 2nd Viscount. The girls all appear in a group portrait of the 2nd Viscount and his family, his only son surrounded by 11 young ladies.

Saltram ☆☆☆

2 m W Plympton, 3½ m E Plymouth city centre, between A38 and A379; NT; restaurant; chapel art gallery; garden and park; *open:* Apr–end Oct, Sun–Thurs 12.30–5.30; tel: 0752 336546

Allow plenty of time to visit Saltram. Although Plymouth now presses close

against the park, with views of housing estates where once there were vistas of fields and woods, and the house itself is an austere Georgian box with plain, stuccoed façades, the interior is a treat.

Saltram was largely created by two John Parkers, father and son, who straddle the 18th century. John the Elder was responsible for enlarging an originally Tudor and Stuart house, and for the rich rococo plasterwork, carved marble fireplaces and other period details in the stone-floored hall, the rich, red-walled velvet drawing-room, and the morning room between them, while John Parker II, 1st Lord Boringdon, engaged Robert Adam to create the vast and elegant Saloon which is one of the least altered examples of the Scotsman's work. Everything here has been designed by Adam, from the Venetian window and the delicate plasterwork on the high coved ceiling to the huge wall-mirrors and the lacy gold filigree surrounding the door handles. Gilded chairs and settees were produced to Adam's designs and the richly coloured carpet echoes the swirls of his ceiling.

The great architect also sketched in the picture plan, but the 1st Lord decided what would hang here. An avid collector and friend of Sir Joshua Reynolds, who was born in the nearby village of Plympton, John II acquired most of Saltram's paintings. Those in the Saloon are difficult to see, as visitors can no longer walk the length of the room, but there is much to enjoy elsewhere: several Reynolds' portraits of the family, including a full-length of the rotund Lord Boringdon, leaning against a gate; views of Naples by Gabrielle Ricciardelli; an improbable Stubbs of *The Fall of Phaeton*, with four terrified horses harnessed to a gilded chariot; an early Rubens of the Duke of Mantua, curly-haired and fish-eyed in black armour; Angelica Kauffmann's likeness of Sir Joshua and her own self-portrait; bucolic Dutch and Flemish pictures, such as Pieter de Hoogh's tavern scene; and the charming local views which were commissioned from the Devon artist William Tomkins. Walls are covered two and three deep in the 18th-century manner, with landscapes, portraits and classical and religious paintings all mixed up together.

Upstairs are rooms hung with 18th-century Chinese wallpaper and a cluttered

Victorian boudoir, and then comes the atmospheric, tobacco-coloured library, more 19th-century than Georgian in spirit, with portraits above the bookshelves and a thick accumulation of sofas, easy chairs and desks. Some of the finer books are shown in a separate display and there is an exhibition on the engaging Lord Boringdon's racing stables, built up, no doubt, with some of the £32,000 he found hidden in bags all over the house when he inherited.

Sand ☆

¼ m NE Sidbury, off A375; guided tours (*c.* 60 mins); teas; garden; *open:* 8 days, Suns and Mons, over season, 2–5.30; tel: 03957 230

The grandest feature of Sand is the shady lime avenue in which visitors leave their cars. From here, a path through the garden leads past a stone-built Jacobean summer house to the gabled, Elizabethan manor tucked into the slope of the hill. Home of the Huyshe family since the 16th century, it is an unpretentious, rustic place, built of rough brown and grey-pink local chert, and with extensive renovations of 1908–9 merging almost imperceptibly with the Tudor work. Inside, large stone-mullioned and transomed windows, one of them glowing with armorial glass, light what was the great hall, and there are original stone fireplaces and woodwork, notably the panelled partitions flanking the screens passage running across the house. Nearby is the thatched remnant of a medieval hall house, with an arch-braced timber roof at the east end. The buildings are explained in an excellent and wide-ranging guided tour, about half of which takes place outside.

Shute Barton ☆

3 m SW Axminster, on B3161 to Colyton; NT; guided tours; *open:* Apr–end Oct, Wed, Sat 2–5.30; tel: 0297 34692

The gargoyle-studded Elizabethan gatehouse on a corner of the road would stop anyone in their tracks. Beyond, hidden in the trees, are the remains of a medieval and early Tudor manor, more tower than house, with two rough-built, three-storey wings standing high over a tiny cobbled court, a crenellated roofline, mullioned and transomed windows, some of them with cusped medieval heads, and buttressed walls.

A gothic door leads into the stone-floored, 14th-century kitchen, with a massive fireplace filling one wall and a medieval timber screen dividing off the next room. A middle floor was a later insertion, but in the spacious chamber at the top of the house, reached by way of a 15th-century spiral stair in the angle of the court, is an arch-braced chestnut roof of *c.*1400 and a garderobe fitted with smoke outlets for the fire. A level lawn at the back of the house was once a tiltyard, and to the north, across the drive, is the tiny, much-restored, medieval church.

The brief tour is of largely architectural interest, but this is an unusual, atmospheric place, with lovely views across the valley of the Axe.

Tapeley Park

Instow, on B3233, signposted off A39
Barnstaple–Bideford road; tearoom; garden;
jousting on BHs and Suns; *open:* Easter–Oct,
Sun–Fri, guided tours at 12 or 12.30 and
2.30 or 3 (15 minimum); tel: 0271 860528

Views of the sea and Italianate terraced gardens bring a touch of the Mediterranean to this solid, red-brick house set high above the estuary of the Torridge. The classical pediment and stone pilasters on the south-facing entrance front and the long verandah-cum-colonnade down the side of the house were added by John Belcher between 1898 and 1916, but the building behind dates from *c.* 1700; fortunately, wisteria and other climbers do much to soften the harsh Victorian shell of red brick with which most of it has been encased.

Belcher was working for Augustus and Lady Rosamond Christie, and the latter was largely responsible for the hotch-potch of furnishings on show, the result of limited funds and an eye for a bargain. The whistle-stop tour, on which enthusiasm and humour more than make up for an almost total lack of knowledge, is conducted at great speed, so nothing can be examined very closely. You will be left with a vague memory of panelled rooms, marble fireplaces and some 18th-century decorative ceilings, of over-romantic paintings and a sculpture by Lord Leighton, of Sir William Richmond's rose-winged vision of Icarus, of Minton vases and inlaid cabinets, and of a grand piano with a silver-gilt and gesso case by William Morris, who was a friend of the family.

Tiverton Castle

N side of Tiverton, next to St Peter's
church, on A396 through town; tearoom;
open: Good Fri–last Sun in Sept,
Sun–Thurs, 2.30–5.30; tel: 0884 253200

Visitors drive in through the splendid crenellated gatehouse on the A396. Together with a round corner turret, and some evocative ruins on the south side of the inner courtyard, this tower of dusky red sandstone is almost all that remains of the Courtenay stronghold built on a cliff above the River Exe in the 13th century. Substantially remodelled in Elizabethan times, the castle was attacked by a Parliamentary army during the Civil War, and largely destroyed. The present L-shaped building is an amalgam of periods and styles, with a substantial William and Mary wing running west from the battlemented medieval and Elizabethan gatehouse range.

The rooms on show, largely lit by stone-mullioned windows, are all in the older part of the building. Now used to display the present owner's collection of Jacobean armour, 17th-and 18th-century furniture and clocks, the castle feels more like a museum than a home, and, apart from a garderobe shaft in the round tower, there are few original internal features. There are views to Exmoor from the roof of the gatehouse, and a glimpse of the entrance to one of the castle's many secret passages from the parapet wall above the river.

Ugbrooke ☆

Just outside Chudleigh, off A38, signposted from centre of town; teas; garden and lakeside walks; *open:* late May BH Sat, Sun, Mon, late July–end Aug, Sun, Tues, Wed, Thurs, guided tours at 2, 3.45; tel: 0626 852179

The young Robert Adam's first attempt at a mock castle, Ugbrooke is built round three sides of a square, with angular corner towers topped by pink plaster battlements and long two-storey façades faced in muddy stucco. The first-floor windows are conventional enough, but the ground-floor sashes are enclosed in clumsy, round-headed frames of reddish cement – not, it must be said, by Adam, but a later addition of 1874.

Built between 1763 and 1771 for the 4th Lord Clifford, Ugbrooke has remained in the family ever since. Sadly, though, the original interiors did not survive being used as a grain store in the middle of this century, and the present decoration, with some uncompromisingly strong colour schemes, is largely as restored in recent years. Most attractive is the elegantly furnished drawing-room looking west down the valley of the little Ug brook to a chain of lakes created by Capability Brown. Here, deep yellow walls set off a collection of Stuart portraits and Lely's painting of the 1st Lord Clifford, Lord Treasurer to Charles II, who acquired many of the most notable contents. Here, too, are three pieces of fresh 16th-century needlework, with scenes from the life of Jesus set in a peaceful Elizabethan countryside. Elsewhere you can see 17th-century tapestries, a mixed bag of furniture, including an early 18th-century blanket chest of mottled burr yew, family porcelain, and the ornate silver ewer and enormous dish, over 3 ft across, which Charles II gave his godson Charles Clifford as a christening present.

After the informal guided tour, visitors can wander into the top-lit, originally 17th-century chapel in a remnant of a much earlier house, its Italian Renaissance interior, with walls lined with a rich selection of coloured marbles, reflecting 19th-century attention. The family have been Roman Catholic since the first lord was converted in 1673, and the Victorian 7th Lord even found himself with a cardinal for a father-in-law. This illustrious relative, who entered the Church late in life, was the source of the pink vestments trimmed with Honiton lace which are draped over one of the bedrooms.

Yarde

N Salcombe, on N side of A381 just E of Malborough; *open:* Easter–end Sept, Sun, Wed, Fri, 2–5; tel: 054884 2367

A steep, potholed drive leads down to this sadly dilapidated farmhouse, with a dignified Queen Anne frontage of mellow, lichen-stained stone backing on to the remains of an Elizabethan building. More atmospheric than the house itself is the tiny, cobbled courtyard enclosed by Tudor outbuildings, among them the original bakehouse with a 14 ft fireplace and a built-in pigeon loft, while beyond is a grassy farmyard, one side framed by a cob-walled stable, another with the ancient barn, its roof supported on rough pillars of local stone. Entrance charges here go towards much-needed restoration.

Dorset

Athelhampton ☆☆

5½ m NE Dorchester, 1 m E Puddletown, on A35; teas; formal gardens; *open:* Easter–end Oct, Wed, Thurs, Sun, and BH Mon 12–5, also Tues May–Sept, and Mon and Fri in Aug; tel: 0305 848363

Almost moated by the River Piddle, and set off by a flint and stone dovecote and a strongly architectural walled and hedged garden, is the picturesque Tudor house begun by Sir William Martyn, Lord Mayor of London, in the 1480s. The earliest part, facing visitors as they approach, is a low battlemented range with an assertive two-storey porch and a projecting bay lighting the great hall. Sticking out to form a wide-angled L is a taller, more self-important gabled wing of *c*.1530, with large stone-mullioned windows, and pinnacled angle buttresses crowned by the monkey of the family crest. Moss and lichen encrust every ledge and hood mould, and a general spikiness is picked up by the stone obelisks and yew pyramids of the gardens.

Sold by the Martyns in 1848, Athelhampton passed through various hands before being bought by the present owner's father-in-law in 1957. Massively restored in the 19th century, when further ranges were added on behind, and again in the 1950s, the interior is partly original, partly reconstructed, with some period fittings brought from elsewhere. Visitors see a series of mellow, lived-in, beautifully furnished rooms in the medieval and Tudor wing, most of them panelled, but with some walls covered with gothic papers derived from 19th-century designs. The lofty great hall, partly lined with linenfold panelling, still has its decorative 15th-century timber roof, and there is some Tudor heraldic glass in the vaulted bay lighting the high table end.

There are very few paintings here, but a fine collection of antique furniture includes 17th-century oak pieces in the hall, a show of William and Mary walnut and an inlaid Kirckman harpsichord in the former great chamber, and rococo gilded mirrors and 18th-century mahogany in the dining-room. Following a major fire in 1992, several rooms have been closed for restoration, but all is scheduled to reopen by the spring of 1994.

Chettle House

6½ m NE Blandford Forum off A354; teas usually available; garden; *open:* Apr–early Oct, daily, except Tues and Sat, 11–5; tel: 0258 89 209

A baroque, Queen Anne house of rich red brick with dressings of Chilmark and Ham stone sits on a grassy platform above a vineyard stretching away to the south, with a little flint and stone church like a gothic eyecatcher at the end of the garden. Begun by Thomas Archer in 1710, it shows the architect's fondness for imposing frontages, rounded corners and tapering pilasters, but it is not nearly as grand as it looks, and the interior is disappointing. Apart from the brick-vaulted basement, now used as a picture gallery, visitors see only a white-and-gold drawing-room decorated in the French style in the mid-19th century and two halls, in one of which Archer's double staircase rises to a galleried landing.

Clouds Hill ☆

9 m E Dorchester, 1 m N Bovington Camp, signposted from B3390; NT; *open:* Apr–end Oct, Wed, Thur, Fri, Sun, BH Mon 2–5, or dusk if earlier; tel: none

This primitive, four-roomed cottage is where the solitary, restless T. E. Lawrence – Lawrence of Arabia – came to live after his discharge from the Air Force in 1935. He had rented it some twelve years earlier, as somewhere to work on revising *The Seven Pillars of Wisdom*; he bought it in 1925 and fitted it out as he wanted it. More hut than house, and largely without modern conveniences, Clouds Hill directly reflects Lawrence's austere, unconventional lifestyle.

Upstairs, open to the roof, is the attic music room, the huge wind-up gramophone on which Lawrence played Beethoven and Mozart filling one corner and a row of candle-holders fixed to a dividing beam. His bedroom is a kind of cabin, with a porthole for a window, a bunk bed wedged across the end, and the deep purple Arab robe which he used as a dressing-gown on the wall. There is no kitchen, or anywhere to store food, just three glass domes to cover such essentials as bread, butter and cheese, and an extendable toasting fork attached to the fender in the cluttered room downstairs. This den is where Lawrence entertained his all-male gatherings, fuelling fireside discussions with tea, and picnics of olives, salted almonds and baked beans. His huge leather divan, more bed than sofa, still fills the room, but the shelves lining the walls are now used to display a mass of drawings and photographs rather than Lawrence's books. Sadly, he never lived to enjoy his retirement, dying in a motorcycle accident only weeks later.

Edmondsham House

In the middle of Edmondsham, off B3081 between Cranborne and Verwood, no signs to house; guided tours; teas; garden; *open:* Easter Sun, BH Mons, Wed in Apr and Oct, 2–5; tel: 072 57 207

Edmondsham's tall, gabled entrance front still proclaims the outlines of the Elizabethan manor completed here in 1589, but the original red brick has been covered over with an unlovely grey render and the Tudor frontage is sandwiched between two Georgian extensions, their rounded, gabled ends topped with urns to match the earlier finials. Inside, a Jacobean staircase survives, but the rest of the relatively modest interior has been extensively altered. Four lived-in, ground-floor rooms display a mixed bag of family treasures and furniture, and there is a sweet, octagonal Victorian dairy in the yard at the back.

Fiddleford Manor

1 m E Sturminster Newton, off A357; EH; *open:* key from keeper; tel: 0305 860853

This unfurnished, rough-walled building on the banks of the Stour is the much-restored remnant of a medieval manor. Laid out to a traditional plan, it has a galleried hall and first-floor solar, both of them with decorative 14th-century timber roofs, but little atmosphere.

Forde Abbey ☆☆

4 m SE Chard, off B3167, signposted from Chard–Broadwindsor road; tearoom; lush and extensive garden; *open:* Apr–mid Oct, Sun, Wed, BH Mon, 1–4.30; tel: 0460 20231

Monasticism went out in a blaze of glory at Forde. So magnificent were the improvements of the wordly Thomas Chard, the last abbot, that his work was adopted as the centrepiece of the mansion created by Edmund Prideaux, one of Cromwell's right-hand men, who bought the estate in 1649. Forde is still largely as Prideaux left it, half-monastic, half Cromwellian, with some elaborate 17th-century plaster ceilings, contemporary panelling and just a gloss of later changes.

A long, low, L-shaped building, of lichen-spotted, Ham Hill stone, the abbey lies in a hollow, its showy main front looking south over sweeping lawns and a romantic water garden based on a chain of fishponds.

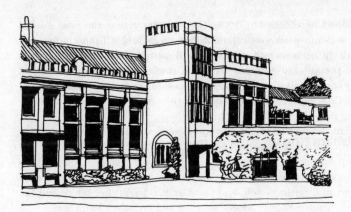

Dominating the façade is Chard's flamboyant, three-storey entrance tower, with two oriel windows projecting over a vaulted porch and lacy friezes of carved decoration. The windows of the abbot's great hall fill the wall to the left, while to the right, beyond a castellated tower, is the delicate tracery of the surviving arm of Chard's cloisters, now a plant-filled conservatory, and the sturdy bulk of the Norman chapter house, converted into a chapel. From the north and east the abbey is more austere, with 13th-century lancets lighting the long wing over a vaulted undercroft that was once the monks' dormitory.

Now lived in by the Roper family, who have been here since the mid-19th century, almost all the original contents were sold when the last of Prideaux's descendants died in 1846. As a result, it is the building and its decoration, rather than paintings and furnishings, which are the main interest. Beyond the Great Hall, still with the curiously bare-headed columns that were left unfinished at the Dissolution, Prideaux's richly decorated Jacobean staircase forms a grand approach to the principal rooms. Sir Edmund's Saloon is hung with biblical Mortlake tapestries woven from Raphael cartoons painted for the Sistine Chapel. Ordered by Sir Edmund, these richly red and blue hangings were kept back, like the graceful 16th-century brass chandelier in the hall, from the 1846 sale. Three bedrooms show a mix of Jacobean, 18th-century and modern features, and then comes the atmospheric library created out of the abbey refectory, spanned by a 15th-century, arch-braced roof, with a traceried niche where improving books would be read to the monks as they ate, and with a splendid screen made up of carved Breton bedsteads.

Ilsington

At Puddletown, 4 m from Dorchester on A35, entrance behind Puddletown church; guided tour (c. 45 mins); garden; open: early May–end Sept, Wed, Thurs, Sun and BH Mon 2–6; tel: 0305 848454

This dignified William and Mary house has not been improved by later alterations, such as the grey render now covering the façades and the plate glass in the windows on the garden front. The main interest of the brief guided tour is the present owner's collection of modern art and sculpture. There are several startling canvases by the Australian Robert Lebkowitz, among them a leonine self-portrait and a hippie version of the legend of the golden apple, while a crowded display on the oak-panelled stairs includes a black and red portrait by Cecil Beaton, drawings of blowsy women by Toulouse-Lautrec, and a rolling horse by Elisabeth Frink.

Visitors are also regaled with a rumoured royal scandal. From 1780 to 1830 the house was leased to General Thomas Garth, Equerry to George III, and Puddletown became a staging post on the royal family's journeys to Weymouth each summer. The story goes that 22-year-old Princess Sophia gave birth to an illegitimate son, and that Garth, 33 years her senior and the putative father, subsequently adopted the lad and brought him up here.

Kingston Lacy ☆☆

1½ m W Wimborne Minster, off B3082; NT; audio guide; restaurant; garden; *open:* Apr–end Oct, Sat–Wed, 12–5.30; tel: 0202 883402

A lush, tree-dotted park grazed by shaggy cattle sweeps right up to this compact, strongly vertical house, with prominent, French-style dormers in the hipped roof, a central lantern and tall chimneys at each corner, as if it were a creature flipped on to its back. Preserved within the stone carapace is the shape of an originally Restoration house, built 1663–5 by Roger Pratt, but Kingston Lacy as it is today was largely created by Sir Charles Barry between 1835 and 1841, with some earlier 1780s decorative schemes by R. F. Brettingham. Barry's client, William Bankes, was the most original of the family who lived here for over 300 years. Friend of Byron and bohemian wanderer, whose remodelling of the house came to an abrupt end when an indiscretion with a guardsman prompted a quick flight abroad, William was responsible for acquiring the Continental paintings which, added to some first-rate family portraits, are the main interest.

Barry's Italianate marble staircase, with an illusion of an open loggia on to the garden, leads to the state rooms shown to visitors. Back to back across the centre of the house, with views to the Egyptian obelisk which William planted in the garden, are the high-ceilinged drawing-room and Saloon, the one a rose-pink, Edwardian clutter, with photographs out on every surface and a cloth-covered grand piano, the other stiffly formal beneath a delicately painted barrel ceiling, but both hung with paintings two and three deep. In the drawing-room are Romney's full-length portrait of William's mother, languid in a white dress, two Van Dyck's, works by Reynolds and Lawrence and a frieze of 55 enamelled miniatures by Henry Bone, although few can easily be seen. Freer access in the Saloon allows a good view of Rubens' portraits of the Grimaldi sisters, stiff as dolls in their huge ruffs and all-enveloping dresses, their porcelain complexions contrasting with the blotched face of the Italian nobleman painted by Titian that hangs between them.

Next door is William's *tour de force*, a jewelled box of a room with an ornate ceiling brought from a Venetian palace, walls hung with red and gold leather, and a show of Spanish paintings acquired in the aftermath of the Peninsular War. The general effect is more striking than the individual works, several of which were purchased in a flush of uncritical enthusiasm, but in among them is Velazquez's painting of the Papal Nuncio to Spain, Cardinal Massimi, thick-lipped and fleshy-faced, his peacock blue robe painted in costly ultramarine pigments. William's love of woodwork emerges in the panelled dining-room with its carved boxwood doors and also here is Sebastiano del Piombo's unfinished *Judgement of Solomon*, all eyes and the executioner's uplifted arm focused on a baby which has yet to be painted in. A library packed with the family's leather-bound books has an exceptional collection of Lely portraits and Batoni's painting of William's father, but, again, many works are difficult to see.

Milton Abbey

Milton Abbas, 7 m SW Blandford Forum, just N of A354; cafe; *open:* over Easter and July and Aug during school holidays, daily, 10–6.30; tel: 0258 880484

What is now a public school started life in the 10th century as a Benedictine abbey. In a grassy amphitheatre framed by steep wooded slopes stands the 14th-century monastic church, blank arches at both ends showing where it was never completed. Only yards away is the Georgian courtyard house which William Chambers created from 1771 for the future 1st Earl of Dorchester, its principal façades designed in an uneasy, constipated gothic, with a pinnacled, fretted roofline and rows of neatly pointed windows only partly disguising what is really a classical composition.

Chambers built so near to the church in order to incorporate the abbey's Tudor great hall, completed only a few years before the Dissolution, in the south range of the house. This huge, stone-floored space, rising to a hammer-beam roof of 1498 and with a carved Tudor screen at one end, is now the boys' dining-hall and is what visitors see first. Beyond, institutional passages lead to the classically decorated state rooms on the west front, the best of them, notably the bare, barrel-vaulted saloon with Adamesque plasterwork picked out in pastel shades of mauve, green and blue, by James Wyatt rather than Chambers.

Alas, the lawns are now cricket and rugger pitches, modern accretions mar the view, and the whole place feels like the school it is.

Parnham House ☆

On A3066, 1 m S Beaminster, signposted from town; restaurant; furniture workshop; garden; *open:* Apr–end Oct, Wed, Sun and BHs 10–5; tel: 0308 862204

Set among wooded hills, and with Elizabethan-style gardens falling away in giant steps to the lake south of the house, is a satisfying, many-gabled building of honey-coloured stone, with a battlemented and pinnacled roofline and an array of stone-mullioned windows. If it were not for a certain heavy-handedness about the garden front, this could almost be another *Montacute*. In fact, although the core of the house *is* Tudor and Elizabethan, Parnham was remodelled and enlarged in 1807–11 by John Nash, who was largely responsible for the present skyline.

Parnham is now the home of John Makepeace's furniture workshops and craft school, and pieces from the collection are on show throughout the building, some displayed in lived-in rooms used by the family, others in the main show rooms, with discreet labels and price lists attached. No decoration original to the house remains. Some period fittings, such as the screen in the hall, or the splendid linenfold panelling and Renaissance frieze in the room used as a restaurant, were brought to Parnham from elsewhere, while a painted staircase, with *trompe l'oeil* strapwork, caryatids and masks, is a 20th-century pastiche. The visitor is assaulted with modern lighting systems and some startlingly bold colour schemes, while Makepeace's uncompromisingly individual furniture shouts for attention, some of the pieces made of wood so contorted that they look as if they are writhing with pain.

Purse Caundle Manor

In Purse Caundle village, S of A30 4 m E of Sherborne; guided tour (30 mins); garden; *open:* Easter Mon, May–Sept, Thurs, Sun, BH Mon 2–5; tel: 0963 250400

In a quiet, stone-built Dorset village, with a stream bubbling through, is this gabled 15th-and 16th-century manor, with stone-mullioned windows and licheny roofs. Although altered over the years and substantially restored in the 1920s, Purse Caundle still has many ancient features. At its heart is a pint-sized great hall, open to a 15th-century timber roof with a carved gothic frieze, and with two stone arches that once led into the buttery and kitchen. A cosy winter parlour is lined with Jacobean panelling and upstairs, with a delicious 15th-century oriel overhanging the road, is an enchanting barrel-roofed drawing-room, once the great chamber, its walls hung with a leafy William Morris paper in blue green and dusky pink. Visitors to this comfortable family house are treated to a friendly informal tour that concentrates on architectural history.

Sandford Orcas Manor

In Sandford Orcas village, 3 m N Sherborne, off B3148; guided tour (*c*. 30 mins); garden; *open:* Easter Mon 10–6, May–Sept, Sun 2–6, Mon 10–6; tel: 0963 220206

High above the twisting lane from Marston Magna, at the north end of the village, is this almost unaltered small Tudor manor of licheny Ham Hill stone, cheek by jowl with the tiny church. A gabled frontage with stone-mullioned

windows and a two-storey porch looks east, away from the traffic on the road, and the house is approached through a charming gatehouse curiously attached to the north wall. The present owner shows the one-storey hall, with its spikily crested Jacobean screen and two huge window bays, the upper lights hung with armorial glass, and four other lived-in rooms, taking visitors up one Tudor spiral staircase and down another, and through original plank doors.

Sherborne Castle ☆

On E side of Sherborne, off A352 and A30; tearoom; lakeside walks; *open:* Easter Sat–end Sept, Thurs, Sat, Sun, BH Mon 2–5.30; tel: 0935 813182

In a letter to Martha Blount of *Mapledurham House*, Alexander Pope wrote enthusiastically about Sherborne. Perhaps it was its strangeness that the poet relished. Perched on a grassy hilltop, with views across a deep, lake-filled valley to the ruins of Sherborne's Norman fortress, the castle is an ungainly H-shaped building, like a four-armed spider, with flat-topped hexagonal turrets at the corners of a gabled central block and at the ends of the low projecting wings. The skyline is crowded with chimneys and heraldic beasts, large stone-mullioned windows light every floor and the walls are covered in an ugly, dirty-yellow render. The central block was created by Sir Walter Raleigh from 1592 out of a Tudor hunting lodge; the wings were added by Sir John Digby in about 1625, seven years after Raleigh's execution for treason.

Visitors see a succession of mostly formal rooms on three floors, all of them clearly for show only and arranged to no very obvious plan. Much altered in Georgian times and again in the mid-19th century, when elegant classical schemes were overlain by Philip Hardwick's restoration in a loud Jacobean style, the castle has only traces of 17th-century and earlier work, among them a gilded stone fireplace displaying the Digby arms, a ceiling featuring the heraldic Digby ostrich and a couple of carved interior porches. There is an elegant library in restrained Strawberry Hill gothick, with a copy of Raleigh's unfinished *History of the World*, written while he was imprisoned in the Tower of London, among its leather-bound books, but most rooms are curiously unconvincing.

The furniture, though, is superb. Some sturdy Stuart pieces stand out among a feast of Georgian mirrors and pier tables, commodes, sofas and pole screens, with several pieces by Hepplewhite, and displays of rich veneer and marquetry. One room is devoted to cases of blue and white Chinese porcelain; another is lined with ornate cabinets. Digby family portraits hang on almost every wall, among them works by Gainsborough, Lely, Kneller, Reynolds and Angelica Kauffmann, and there are miniatures by Isaac Oliver, Nicholas Hilliard and Samuel Cooper. Among such riches, only Robert Peake's stylized canvas of Elizabeth I, shown carried shoulder-high by a group of courtiers, reminds visitors of the uncompromising adventurer who first created a house here.

Wolfeton House ☆

1 ½ m N Dorchester, off B3143 Charminster road, signposted from roundabout junction with A37 bypass; garden; *open:* May–Sept, Tues, Thurs, BH Mon, 2–6; tel: 0305 263500

A rough drive with a gate that visitors must open for themselves sets the tone for this atmospheric remnant of weathered, lichen-stained grey stone set in meadows north of Dorchester. The entrance is through a drum-towered gatehouse, with arrow slits overlooking the road and dovecotes in the towers. Beyond is just one range of the double-courtyard, 15th-and 16th-century house built by a family of wealthy sheep farmers, its south front, on to the garden, filled with six stone-mullioned windows in a piece of typically Elizabethan display. The interior, through a porch added on in 1864, is just as intriguing, with a grand stone staircase of 1570, built as for a family of giants, leading to the rough-walled, bare-floored Great Chamber on the first floor;

exuberantly carved door surrounds and overmantels; ornamental plaster ceilings; and fine linenfold panelling. Some of this decoration, such as the pedimented Renaissance stone doorway to the Great Chamber, is refined Elizabethan work. Other details are Jacobean, and a perfect carving of a little monkey with two bowls of fruit dates from 1530. The few rooms shown are furnished with carved 17th-century oak pieces, and there is a tiny chapel on the north side of the Tudor gatehouse.

Somerset

Barrington Court ☆

In Barrington village, 5 m NE Ilminster off A303 and B3168; NT; guided tours only (c. 35 mins); teas; enchanting, compartmental garden; *open:* Apr–end Sept, Wed 1.30–5; tel: 0985 847777

From the present approach, to the north, Barrington looks rather severe. To see this Elizabethan manor as it should be seen, go round to the south side, where a sweep of grass sets off a symmetrical E-shaped façade of lichen-spotted Ham Hill stone, with gabled and buttressed bays stepping inwards to the prominent central porch. Above, erupting from the roofline like a growth of vigorous spring shoots, is a flamboyant array of spiral chimneys and finials, while just to one side, as if providing a foil for the house, sits a four-square red-brick stable block of 1674.

By the early years of this century, Barrington was little more than a gutted shell. The interiors that visitors see, with some fine linenfold panelling and a couple of Jacobean overmantels, are as restored from 1920 by Col. A. A. Lyle, who fitted the house out with a collection of oak panelling, beams, floorboards and other period fittings culled from derelict 16th- and 17th-century houses. The colonel's furniture has all gone and in its place is an odd assortment of period pieces dangling prominent price tags; Barrington is now sublet to Stuart Interiors who use the house as their showroom. In some ways this adds spice to a tour which necessarily concentrates on architectural features, among them a Tudor kitchen with original charcoal braziers, a plaster overmantel of the Judgment of Solomon, and the colonel's rebuilt staircase, spanned by huge ships' timbers.

Combe Sydenham

5 m N Wiveliscombe, on B3188; tearoom; garden; country park; *open:* end Mar–Oct, Mon–Fri, 11–3.30; tel: 0984 56284

This moated Elizabethan and Restoration house, with one gabled tower rising above buttressed sandstone façades lime-washed a soft, earthy pink, and a ruinous gatehouse, looks splendid from a distance, when it is seen silhouetted against steeply wooded slopes. Close to, it is soon clear that the current owner's restoration programme still has many years to run. Only a couple of rooms in the west wing are shown, one with a restored barrel ceiling and painted walls, the other two much in need of attention. This was the childhood home of Francis Drake's second wife, Elizabeth Sydenham, but visitors would do best to spend their time in the country park.

Dodington Hall

1 m E of Nether Stowey, N of A39, follow signs to Dodington; garden; *open:* late May–late July, Sun, 2–5; tel: 0278 74 400

Dodington Hall is a small, Elizabethan manor of local red sandstone built into the side of a hill, with a fine, two-storey porch, stone-mullioned windows and a bell turret. The main feature is the tiny hall rising to the roof, still with its original oak screen, minstrel's gallery and carved fireplace of 1581, but marred by Victorian floor tiles. A path leads from the house to a pocket-sized church.

Dunster Castle

In Dunster village, 3 m SE Minehead, off A39, NT: hillside garden; *open:* Apr–end Oct, Sat–Wed, 11–5 (4 in Oct); tel: 0643 821314

From the coast road to Minehead, Dunster is a tawny mass of towers, turrets and battlements rising from a steep, wooded tor. A stiff ten-minute climb from the car park takes visitors past the 17th-century stables to the 15th-century gatehouse, and to a medieval gateway beyond, but these outer defences are among the few genuine remains of the former fortress. The house itself, built of rough local sandstone and set on the southern side of what was once the castle's lower ward, is primarily a picturesque fantasy by Anthony Salvin, who remodelled an existing Jacobean mansion between 1868 and 1872. There are remnants of the medieval curtain walls, but the site of the former keep on the top of the tor is a grassy plateau.

After the build-up of the approach, the interior is something of a disappointment. Visitors see about a dozen rooms on two floors, but the house has no central focus or climax and the contents are not as rich as might be expected in a place that has been the home of the Luttrell family for 400 years. Jacobethan decoration and heavy Victorian schemes by Salvin, as in the hall, billiard room and library, contrast with some surviving 17th-century work, in particular the elaborate plaster ceiling in the dining-room and the staircase of oak and elm built within a medieval D-shaped tower. Newel posts carry carved vases piled high with fruit and the sculptural pierced balustrade is nicely dated by a clutch of Charles II shillings in one of the panels. No great chamber opens from the upper landing, but a bedroom with a crude Jacobean overmantel is said to be the one where the future Charles II slept when he visited the West Country in 1645, and an adjoining gallery is hung with glowing, richly coloured wall hangings of painted, silver-embossed leather telling the story of Antony and Cleopatra, the chubby childlike figures and their toy mounts obviously created by a 17th-century Beryl Cook.

There are several family portraits, including Hans Eworth's confused allegorical painting of Sir John Luttrell, dated 1550, and some delightful 18th-century views of the castle. Much of the charm of this place derives from the setting shown in these paintings; the sea only half a mile away, a picturesque village (sadly thronged with tourists in summer) huddled at the foot of the tor, and views inland over a deeply rural, hilly countryside.

Gaulden Manor ☆

9 m NW Taunton, 1 m E Tolland, signposted from B3188 and A358; guided tours; tearoom; valley garden; *open:* Easter Sun and Mon, early May–early Sept, Sun, Thurs, BH Mons 2–5.30; tel: 09847 213

Tucked away in a secluded valley and approached only down narrow lanes is this modest, lived-in farmhouse of rough local sandstone, dating largely from the 16th century. Once the home of the Turberville family – Thomas Hardy's D'Urbervilles – it is distinguished by some intriguing early plasterwork which just might date from the time of James Turberville, Bishop of Exeter, who was imprisoned in the Tower in 1559 for refusing to take the Oath of Supremacy.

The most striking decoration is in the cosy, comfortable great hall, partly walled with a panelled Jacobean screen, where a pendanted ceiling carries biblical vignettes: an angel trumpeter raising the dead, here represented by a lively skeleton; Adam and Eve in the Garden; King David playing his harp. The tour takes in some four rooms in all, their Tudor fireplaces, old plank doors, low ceilings and period furniture all contributing to a sense of age; opinions about the bold colour schemes are likely to be more divided.

Hatch Court ☆

In village of Hatch Beauchamp, 6 m SE Taunton, off A358; guided tours; teas; garden; *open:* mid July–mid Sept, Thurs and Aug BH Mon, 2.30–5.30; tel: 0823 480120

This dignified house looking south over unspoilt wooded countryside appears much grander than it is. Built in 1755 for a local wool merchant by the gentleman architect Thomas Prowse, it is a square, two-storey Palladian block of lichen-spotted Bath stone, with a turret at each corner, a roofline balustrade, and an unusual five-arched Italianate loggia stretching across the entrance front. Inside, a stone-floored hall running right through the house to a cantilevered staircase is similarly imposing, but the rooms to either side, the best of them a sunny, bay-windowed drawing-room with a rococo plasterwork ceiling, are relatively modest.

The court passed through many hands before ancestors of the present owners came here in the 1890s. The few lived-in rooms on view are nicely furnished with an eclectic mix that includes three horse paintings and a study of a dog by Alfred Munnings and a couple of Lely-like portraits by Mary Beale. Nothing is very remarkable, but the presentation is friendly and unhurried and spiced with gobbets of family history. The tour ends in what was the housekeeper's sitting-room, across a yard at the back, where visitors are shown a fine display of china, including some deep green Wedgwood and an olive Minton dessert service of c.1750, and relics of the Canadian regiment raised with lightning speed by Andrew Hamilton Gault, the present owner's great uncle, at the outbreak of World War I.

Lytes Cary ☆

1 m N A303 Ilchester bypass, via Bridgwater road (A372); NT: garden; *open:* Apr–end Oct, Mon, Wed, Sat 2–6 or dusk; tel: 0985 847777 (NT regional office)

Home of the Lyte family for 500 years, this unassuming, gabled manor of rough local stone is a hotch-potch of many periods. The Great Hall open to the roof, its rafters decorated with carved angels, was built in 1453; a tiny chapel reached by an outside door dates back to 1343; and the long south wing and most of the finer features were additions of the 1530s by John Lyte. The old manor was once a more substantial courtyard house, but one range was destroyed in order to build the Georgian farmhouse that now rises above the older buildings. A 20th-century extension was added by Walter Jenner, who bought the house in 1906 and set about restoring it, acquiring the largely 17th-century furnishings seen today.

Visitors are shown the medieval and Tudor house, a place of small, panelled rooms, interior porches, stone floors and arches, heavy old doors, and with a worn stone stair to the upper floor. Muted colours are lifted, in the hall, by Thomas Lyte's rich armorial glass featuring the Lyte swan, and by two splendid blue and white Delft tulip vases. The Great Chamber, with the arms of Henry VIII emblazoned at one end, has a gently arched plaster ceiling, with thin ribs tracing an intricate web of star- and kite-shaped panels, and more Lyte swans.

Where John Lyte was the builder of the family, his son Henry was a gardener and plantsman. The house is set off by an Elizabethan-style garden and a copy of the 1578 herbal which Henry translated from the Flemish, annotated with his observations, is on show in the hall.

Midelney Manor ☆

Drayton, signposted off A378 Curry Rivel–Langport road; guided tours (c. 40 mins); garden; *open:* May–late Sept, Thurs, BH Mon, 2.30–5.30; tel: 0458 251229

Originally an island manor attached to Muchelney abbey, this lonely, greystone, Tudor house, home of the Trevilian family since the Dissolution, was once reached largely by boat. The single track approach road, which goes no further, feels like the causeway it was, particularly when the water meadows on either side are flooded. The manor is a long, low, U-shaped house with stone-mullioned casements and lichen-spotted walls. Strangely, because of a family feud, it was built like a modern semi-detached, with a thick partition wall and two main entrances either side of the forecourt. Although now a single dwelling, it still looks divided, with gabled dormers on one side only and a change in roof height half way down.

Inside, visitors are shown the stone-floored, low-ceilinged hall and cosy, lived-in rooms with 18th-century panelling. There are family portraits, some interesting porcelain, and in the garden is a delightful sequence of forecourts and gateways of Ham Hill stone, once part of a grand 18th-century approach.

Montacute House ☆☆

In Montacute village, 4 m W Yeovil, on A3088; NT; restaurant; garden; park walks; *open:* : Apr–end Oct, daily, except Tues and Gd Fri 12–5.30; tel: 0935 823289

A tall, many windowed E-shaped mansion of Ham Hill stone, Montacute is a prodigy Elizabethan house, more conventional than *Hardwick*, but none the less splendid for that. The original entrance front, looking east down a grassy lime avenue, is ornamented with curvaceous Flemish gables and engaging classical details: chimneys disguised as columns and endearingly clumsy statues in Roman dress set high on the façade. Obelisks and finials crowd the roofline, their sharp profiles picked up in the spiky balustrade enclosing the forecourt and in the ogee roofs of the little pavilions to either side. All around is smoothly mown grass and clipped yew, with wide views over the park and the Somerset countryside beyond.

This enchanting place was built for the Elizabethan lawyer Sir Edward Phelips at the end of the 16th century, probably by the local stonemason William Arnold. Phelips's continued to live here for another 300 years, and it was a later Sir Edward who created Montacute's more fantastic west front, embellished with heraldic beasts on barley-sugar columns and other stonework brought here in 1786 from another Tudor house. In the late 19th and early 20th century, though, the family fell on hard times: for some years the house was let, most notably to Lord Curzon, who lived here with the colourful Elinor Glyn, and the original contents were dispersed.

While the exterior is magical, the extensive tour of the interior is a mixed experience. Sympathetic furnishings acquired by the Trust are allied to Phelips' family portraits and to original Elizabethan plasterwork and chimney-pieces, but some rooms appear bare and stark, and the long gallery stretching 172 ft across the third floor is used to display some 100 Tudor and Jacobean portraits from the National Portrait Gallery. The paintings are of considerable interest, but what should be the most glorious room in the house now lacks atmosphere. Most satisfactory is the sunny library created out of the former Great Chamber, lit by windows on three sides, entered through a richly carved internal porch and containing the only Phelips furniture in the house, some cane-backed, walnut chairs. The plaster ceiling is 19th-century, but the deep frieze is original, as is the armorial glass in the windows and the double-tier, columned chimney-piece, sadly now without the female nudes which once stood in niches to either side and which proved too much for Victorian sensibilities. By contrast, Montacute's low-ceilinged great hall is curiously low-key, despite some Elizabethan glass, the rustic 16th-century plaster cartoon, showing the fate of husbands who drink while minding the baby, and the virtuoso stone screen, with a strapwork crest and prominent rams'-head capitals.

Several superb hangings and a collection of 17th- to 20th-century samplers are dominated by a 15th-century French tapestry of an armoured knight riding through a sea of spring flowers, while the portraits on the top floor show a nice contrast between stylized, icon-like earlier works and more naturalistic 17th-century paintings by such as Marcus Gheeraerts the Younger, Cornelius Johnson, William Dobson and Paul van Somer. The last's sympathetic group portrait of the Earl of Monmouth and his family is particularly striking.

Orchard Wyndham ☆☆

Williton, off A39 to Minehead; follow signs to Orchard Mill and parish church; guided tours (c. 60 mins), advance booking advisable; *open:* 8 days in Aug, 2–4.30; tel: 0984 32309

An attractive jumble of roofs, suggesting a hamlet tucked away in a hollow of the hills, is in fact a rambling medieval and Tudor house built round two courtyards. Except for the mid-16th-century north front, with its large mullioned and transomed windows, Orchard Wyndham looks picturesque rather than particularly old, with an obviously 18th-century addition adjoining the north front, and a show of cottagey Victorian dormers and carved bargeboards. But 19th-century embellishments are just a veneer on ranges that go back to the 13th century. Owned by the Wyndhams since 1528, the house has been both enriched and preserved by being connected with a family who have had grander properties elsewhere, notably *Petworth*.

Visitors see the atmospheric Tudor great hall range at the north end of the house and a couple of 18th-century extensions off this wing, one of them a Georgian staircase built over a former courtyard. The lofty hall is still open to an arch-braced timber roof, and there is an original beamed and coffered ceiling in the little library at the western end, but the rooms have been altered over the centuries and are comfortable and lived in rather than period pieces. Carolean pine panelling in the hall is hung with a Madonna and Child by Zurbarán, a distant view of the house painted in c.1750 by Robert Griffier, a portrait by van Mierevelt, and a huge turtleshell brought back from the Pacific by Sir Francis Drake; a little sitting-room displays one of the irascible Evelyn Waugh's ear trumpets as well as busts by Westmacott, landscapes by Poussin and Pieter Brueghel the Younger and a painting of card players by David Teniers; and a lovely 17th-century writing table in the library sits easily with purposeful filing cabinets. The tour ends in the Georgian drawing-room facing west over the garden, with dove-grey panelling hung with portraits by Hudson, Gainsborough and Reynolds – one a version of his middle-aged self-portrait – and Queen Anne settees and marquetry chairs grouped round the fire.

Stoke-sub-Hamdon Priory

In village of Stoke-sub-Hamdon, on road to Martock N from High Street; NT, but not signed; use village car park; *open:* all year, daily, 10–6 (or dusk); tel: none

An arch in a high, curving wall on North Street leads into the quiet grassy courtyard at the centre of this somnolent clutch of medieval buildings, originally built for a community of priests. On one side is a buttressed and gabled house dating from the 15th century, where visitors can see the rough-floored, unfurnished, bare-walled great hall with a large stone-mullioned window looking on to the yard. A thatched medieval barn, ancient stables and other ruined outbuildings complete the ensemble, all of it in glowing Ham Hill stone.

Southern England

Hampshire, Isle of Wight, Kent, Surrey, East Sussex, West Sussex, Wiltshire

Charlton Park
Lydiard Park
Swindon

Sheldon Manor
Chippenham
Corsham Court
Bowood House
Littlecote
M4
Lacock Abbey
Marlborough
A4
A30
Great Chalfield Manor
Tottenham House
Westwood Manor
Highclere Castle
Stratfield Saye
Trowbridge
The Vyne
Farnboro
Wilts
Basingstoke
Clandon P
Andover
Guildford
Warminster
M3
Farnham
Loseley House
A303
Hampshire
Longleat
A3
Wilton House
Jane Austen's House
A31
Stourhead
Avington Park
The Wakes
Salisbury
Winchester
Rotherfield Park
W. Sus
Pythouse
A36
Mottisfont Abbey
Hinton Ampner
A30
Petworth
Newhouse
Hamptworth Lodge
Breamore House
Parhan
A338
Broadlands
Stansted Park
Southampton
St
M27
Goodwood
Ringwood
A3(M)
Chichester
Arundel
Beaulieu Palace House
Portsmouth
Bournemouth
Cowes
Osborne House
Ryde
Newport
Nunwell House
Isle of Wight
Shanklin
Appuldurcombe House

Avington Park

4 m NE Winchester, off B3047, S from Itchen Abbas; guided tours; teas; garden; *open:* May–Sept, Sun, BH Mon 2.30–5.30; tel: 0962 779260

This sprawling, red-brick house is a shadow of what it must once have been – when the 3rd Duke of Chandos, who inherited in 1751, planted his lime avenue, or when a later owner entertained George IV and Mrs Fitzherbert here. Now divided into flats, it is a sad, soulless place. The entrance front of 1710, probably by the John James who designed *Appuldurcombe*, is imposing enough, with substantial two-storey blocks framing a vast recessed portico topped by giant lead statues. Round the side, though, the grandeur collapses, with two curvaceous Victorian conservatories bulging out of what turns out to be nothing more than a screen wall.

Inside, visitors are taken on a tour of the state rooms. Apart from the gilded, mid 18th-century staircase, with a mahogany rail inlaid with holly, the principal interest is the painted decoration. Most is of *c.*1760, but some paintings of the Four Seasons in the gilded saloon, the most splendid and also the most desolate of the interiors, may just be late 17th-century work by Verrio.

Whatever you think of the house, spare a minute to visit the brick Georgian church across the grass, complete with box pews, three-decker pulpit and wig pegs.

Beaulieu Palace House

In Beaulieu, 6 m NE Lymington, signed from M27; restaurant; national motor museum; monorail; garden; *open:* all year, daily, summer 10–6, winter, except Christmas Day, 10–5; tel: 0590 612345

Beaulieu's commercialism is disconcertingly upfront, with crowd-pulling attractions clustered round the entrance. The house is furthest from the gates, looking south over the broad Beaulieu river to a red-roofed village. Despite its name, this is no palace. One end was the gatehouse of a great Cistercian abbey founded in 1204, but the place was much enlarged and remodelled by Sir Arthur Blomfield between 1871 and 1874 for Henry Scott, lst Lord Montagu, whose ancestor, the Earl of Southampton, bought the estate at the Dissolution. Many chimneyed, with staring stone-mullioned windows and stiff gables, Beaulieu is principally a Victorian mansion in Elizabethan style, complete with baronial fireplaces and stained glass.

Visitors see some seven rooms on two floors, most of them as impersonal as a hotel, but showing off portraits by Wissing, Hudson, Dahl and Kneller and some family treasures, such as the lst Lord's paint box and sketching stool, and the premature obituary of the 2nd Lord, written when his ship was torpedoed. A dining-hall and adjoining drawing-room in the original gatehouse

have what is said to be 14th-century fan vaulting, and upstairs traceried windows and a little trefoil-headed piscina mark the chapels that once stood side by side here. More atmospheric are the ruins of the abbey cloister north-east of the house, ringed with skeletal arcades and with a weedy and crumbling night stair. The former monk's refectory, like some primitive Italian *chiesa*, is now the village church.

Breamore House ☆

In village of Breamore, off A338, 8 m S Salisbury; guided tours; teas; carriage and countryside museums; maze; jousting in high summer; *open:* Apr, Tues, Wed, Sun; May–Sept, Tues, Wed, Thurs, Sat, Sun, BHs (daily in Aug), 2–5.30; tel: 0725 22468

Close by a flint church dating back to Saxon times is a many-gabled, E-shaped Elizabethan mansion of soft red brick, with huge mullioned and transomed windows and thrusting chimney stacks. Still owned by the Hulse family who bought the estate in 1748, the house is rich in 17th- and 18th-century furniture and paintings. With the exception of some rather splendid carved stone fireplaces, though, the decorative schemes, including a couple of 'Elizabethan' plaster ceilings, are the result of sensitive Victorian restoration following a fire which virtually gutted the interior in 1856.

Visitors are whisked round in large parties. The formal blue drawing-room, filled with ornate Dutch marquetry pieces and with a gilded rococo mirror over the fireplace, has a predominantly 18th-century feel. The dining-room, with its original fireplace, Charles II mahogany chairs and Dutch still-lifes, seems older, and this is even more true of the great hall, an 84 ft gallery of a room looking south over the Avon valley. Re-created panelling and plaster-work set off two fine stone fireplaces, a couple of Brussels tapestries and some of the most interesting paintings, among them Teniers the Younger's bucolic *The Coming of the Storm* and two full-length Jacobean portraits.

Elsewhere you can see an apple-green, early English pile carpet with the date it was made, 1614, woven into one end, royal portraits by Beach and Kneller, a sensitive, unfinished sketch of the Duke of Wellington, said to be the great man's favourite likeness, pastels of the 1st Baronet's family by Francis Cotes, whose teacher, the better known Thomas Hudson, is also represented in the house, and one of the earliest records of a cricketer, painted in *c.* 1760.

Broadlands ☆☆

Romsey, 8 m N Southampton, entrance from A31 Romsey bypass; guided tours; restaurant; Mountbatten exhibition; grounds; *open:* Easter–end Sept, daily, except Fri, 12–5.30, open Gd Fri and Fri in Aug; tel: 0794 516878

Looking out to the River Test over sweeping lawns is the square Georgian house of yellowish brick and stone which Capability Brown created for Henry Temple, 2nd Viscount Palmerston, between 1767 and 1780. The show front, with steps leading down from a central portico, pedimented windows and dormers in the gently hipped roof, is towards the river; the entrance is on the other side, through the recessed loggia with which Brown's son-in-law Henry Holland filled in an open courtyard in 1788.

Broadlands, home of Lord and Lady Romsey, is where both the Queen and her eldest son spent the first days of their honeymoon, was the much-loved house of Lord Louis Mountbatten, and was where, in the 19th century, the 3rd Viscount Palmerston, foreign secretary and prime minister, escaped from London whenever he could. Not surprisingly, the friendly guided tour tends to focus on recent history and connections, and those who like to linger may find they are moved on before they are ready.

Henry Holland's classical hall shows off the 2nd Viscount's collection of antique and 18th-century sculpture, among them an animated wall relief of a boar hunt, vases by Piranesi, and Joseph Nollekens' erotic *Boy on a Dolphin*.

Beyond are elegant, if sometimes chilly, Georgian reception rooms, the best of them with fluid, Adamesque plasterwork by Joseph Rose the Elder. The white and gold saloon, the grandest room in the house, is filled with gilded, 18th-century chairs and settees, boasts a grand piano on which Sir Malcolm Sargent often entertained the family, and has two alcoves lined with Sèvres and Meissen porcelain.

Portraits are everywhere, among them three full-length works by Van Dyck, and paintings by Reynolds, Romney, Raeburn, Hoppner and Lawrence. But there are also startlingly strident carpets by the interior designer David Hicks, who married Lady Pamela, Lord Romsey's aunt, and some other curiously inappropriate modern furnishings. Upstairs, a succession of chintzy bedrooms leaves little impression, but among them is the coolly beautiful green room, with mirrored shutters to enhance the view of the river, and a de Laszlo portrait of Lady Mountbatten, subject of Noel Coward's: 'I could really not be keener, on a weekend with Edwina'.

The old Tudor manor which was swallowed by the 1st Viscount's new house emerges only in a curving Jacobean staircase and in the oak-panelled room, now the family cinema, that is curiously used to display a painting of a dramatically lit forge by Wright of Derby.

Highclere Castle ☆☆

4¹/₂ m S Newbury, off A34; tearoom; garden; *open:* Jul, Aug, Sept, Wed–Sun 2–6, and Easter, May and Aug BH Sun and Mon; tel: 0635 253210

The vast, four-square Victorian palace designed by Charles Barry for Henry Herbert, 3rd Earl of Carnarvon, rises from a sea of grass, relieved only by a few majestic cedars. Faced in golden Bath stone, and with a sturdy tower erupting from the middle of the house, Highclere is a domestic version of Barry's Houses of Parliament, with Elizabethan details, such as the strapwork parapet, sculpted stonework and pinnacled corner turrets, decorating classically symmetrical façades with rows of identical windows. Buried somewhere in this pile is the Georgian brick house which the self-important 3rd Earl asked Barry to transform.

Both Barry and his noble client were dead before much work on the interior had been done, and the house was largely completed, after 1861, by the much less talented Thomas Allom. Stylistically, it is a mess, the only unifying thread a feeling of Victorian opulence. Plushest of all is the long, T-shaped library running down the east side of the house, with a screen of gilded, fluted columns dividing off one end, a heavy, coffered ceiling, ornate bookcases, lamps made out of elegant oriental vases, and mahogany furniture. From here, interconnecting reception rooms lead one into another down the castle's south front, the most appealing of them the cosy smoking-room with leather-covered chairs round the fire and a nice, if undistinguished, collection of 17th-century Dutch canvases and Canaletto-style Venetian views on the apricot walls. Elsewhere is some rather heavy-handed late Victorian plasterwork and a run of family portraits from Stuart times, among them works by Kneller, Hudson and Gainsborough, several paintings by Sir William Beechey, whom the Carnarvons particularly admired, and what must be Sir Joshua Reynold's most embarrassing work, of the baby 2nd Earl as Bacchus, with two sleepy lions.

Repetitive bedroom suites ring the first floor, and the tour ends in the splendid Moorish hall rising through the centre of the house, ringed with gothic arcades, encrusted with carved stonework and hung with gilded Spanish leather. Among the portraits here is a raffish likeness of the moustachioed 5th Earl, whose passion for ancient Egypt led to his association with the similarly obsessed Howard Carter and the discovery of the tomb of Tutankhamen in the Valley of the Kings in November 1922. An exhibition devoted to the 5th Earl displays those finds the Egyptian authorities allowed him to keep, among them bracelets, mummy wrappings, beads and a painted coffin, and some more personal items, such as a much-thumbed Baedecker on Egypt, letters from Howard Carter, a pencilled expedition shopping list, the stores to be purchased including tins of jam and sardines, and the Earl's photograph albums. An array of pigeon-holes hidden in the thickness of a wall are where some Egyptian artefacts were concealed until discovered by the butler in 1987.

Hinton Ampner ☆

8 m E Winchester, entrance gates on A272; NT; tearoom; garden; *open:* April–end Sept, Tues, Wed, and Aug weekends, 1.30–5.30; tel: 0962 771305

Hinton Ampner is a 20th-century creation in the spirit of the 18th century. Ralph Dutton, the 8th and last Lord Sherborne, who died in 1985, lived here like a Georgian country gentleman, remodelling house and park and laying out the enchanting garden, with its terraced walks, unexpected vistas, and secretive dell. Architecturally, the house is nothing special. Created out of a Victorian monstrosity, and largely rebuilt after a disastrous fire in 1960, it is a quiet, red-brick, neo-Georgian affair with long, low façades smothered in climbers. The five rooms on show are strongly Georgian and Regency in character, fitted out with chimneypieces, doorcases and even ceilings acquired from other houses, including an Adam fireplace from Adelphi Terrace. Fussily furnished to a strongly masculine taste, they are filled with formal and ornate period pieces and *objets d'art* reflecting Ralph Dutton's passion for precious materials and fine workmanship, and hung with mythological and religious works by 17th- and 18th-century Italian artists, including a dramatic landscape by Locatelli and two works by Pellegrini.

There are gilded, Adam-style side-tables and mirrors; Savonnerie carpets and a white marble fireplace that may have been made for Marie Antoinette; tops inlaid with *pietra dura*, onyx and blue-john; and cluttered surfaces carrying ornate French clocks, little statuettes, Sèvres vases, gilded candelabra and urns of blue-john, pink marble, or porphyry. Most attractive is the long cool drawing-room, hung with yellow-and-white striped silk and with a big bay to the garden. Most comfortable is a little red-walled sitting-room, the paintings here including two monochromatic, nightmarish Fuselis, and a landscape by Gaspard Poussin.

Jane Austen's House

In Chawton village, 1 m SW Alton off A31 and B3006; garden; *open:* Apr–Oct, daily, Nov, Dec, March, Wed–Sun, Jan, Feb, Sat, Sun 11–4.30; tel: 0420 83262

A small, red-brick house set sideways on to the main street through the village is where Jane Austen, her sister Cassandra and their widowed mother came to live on 19 July 1809, when the novelist was 33. A quiet, ordered existence, with dinner at an unfashionably early hour and long evenings spent sewing and reading, was shattered by Jane's death, from Addison's disease, eight years later; Mrs Austen survived her younger daughter by a decade, and Cassandra then lived on here alone until 1845.

The house is now primarily a museum, its low-ceilinged, bare-floored, cottagey rooms devoted to memorabilia of the novelist and her family, among them a song book written out in the author's neat, slanting hand, her lacquered needlework basket, a turquoise bracelet, and the cup and bell with which she used to amuse her nieces and nephews. Apart from the round tripod table at which Jane wrote, working and reworking her closely observed novels, most of the few pieces of furniture, although in period, were not here in her time, and there are too many glass cases for comfort. It takes imagination to see Jane boiling water for the family breakfast at the original cast-iron hob in the dining parlour, locking away the tea and coffee in the built-in cupboard beside it, or hiding what she was writing when the creaking door at the bottom of the stairs warned her of approaching visitors.

On the first floor is the tiny bedroom looking on to the stableyard which she shared with Cassandra and Jane's donkey cart, in which she explored the lanes round about, sits in the brick-floored bakehouse out the back, where a woman from the village came in to do the washing.

Mottisfont Abbey ☆

4¹/₂ m NW Romsey, ¹/₄ m W A3057; NT; garden; *open:* Apr–end Oct, Tues, Wed, Sun 1–5; tel: 0794 341220/340757

Mottisfont stands end-on to the River Test, a backdrop to sweeping lawns shaded by mature trees. The house itself, a mix of medieval, Tudor and Georgian work, is firmly rooted in the Augustinian priory which stood here for some 350 years, with one wall of the church now forming the long, heavily buttressed north façade. Visitors are ushered first into a cool, dimly lit monastic undercroft, with a vaulted roof carried on massive, half-buried pillars. Beyond, tile-floored passages follow the north and west walks of the priory cloister, with bare rooms off showing fragments of medieval and Tudor

Hampshire

work. The initial transformation was carried out by William lst Lord Sandys, Henry VIII's Lord Chamberlain, who bought the priory at the Dissolution; much of his double courtyard house disappeared when Mottisfont was remodelled in the 1740s and given its brick south front, but there is still a Tudor fireplace to be seen, and stone-mullioned windows sit below Georgian sashes on the north front.

A steep stair leads up to the inhabited part of the house and the high point of the short tour: the drawing-room painted by Rex Whistler in 1938–9. Slender *trompe-l'oeil* columns, trophy panels and lacy tracery in pink and white transform the room into a gothic icecream palace, the theatrical, fairy-tale effect enhanced by heavy, ermine-trimmed, blue velvet curtains drawn across the windows. Nothing is quite what it seems. The drapery pelmets are painted wood, the ermine itself is a fur fabric speckled with black flecks, while the paint pot Whistler has left balanced high on a cornice and a smoking urn are both illusions.

Rotherfield Park

4¹/₂ m S Alton, on A32; teas; large garden; *open:* first 7 days of June, July and Aug, also BH Sun and Mon 2–5; tel: 042 058 204

Set on a rise looking east towards Selborne, with the tower of East Tisted church rising out of a clump of trees in the valley below, is the Scott family's sprawling 19th-century house, with huge mullioned windows, Tudor-style chimneys and an aggressive roofline balustrade. Built in the early 1820s to the design of Joseph Parkinson, Rotherfield Park was romanticized in the 1880s, when a slender corner turret and various towers were added, one a Camelot-like confection straight out of a medieval manuscript. Visitors see the impressive staircase hall with its stencilled decoration, and a few comfortable lived-in ground floor rooms. There are period mirrors, chandeliers and wall-paper, vaguely Jacobean strapwork ceilings touched with gold, and much mahogany and rosewood 19th-century furniture, but also portraits attributed to Zoffany and Northcote, some 17th-century Dutch paintings, and a show of porcelain that includes some huge oriental vases.

Stratfield Saye ☆☆

6¹/₂ m NE Basingstoke, 1 m W A33, well signposted; restaurant; garden; *open:* May–last Sun in Sept, daily, except Fri, 11.30–4; tel: 0256 882882

This long low house with shaped gables on the stubby wings is the Duke of Wellington's answer to *Blenheim*. Offered £600,000 by a grateful nation after Waterloo with which to acquire a country house, Wellington purchased this relatively modest mansion on the banks of the River Loddon. At first, he had plans to replace it with a colonnaded classical palace, designs for which were submitted by Benjamin Dean Wyatt, Cockerell and others, but these came to nothing; the Duke's resources would not stretch so far, and, it seems, he began to love the old place.

At heart, Stratfield Saye is a Jacobean house of *c.*1630 built by Sir William Pitt, some time Controller of the Household to James I, but 18th-century improvements radically altered the interior and account for the long rows of sash windows and the stuccoed walls. Inside, Georgian classicism is overlain by the strong personality of the Duke, whose character and achievements pervade almost all the rooms on show, who introduced some of his own decorative schemes, and who acquired many of the furnishings and paintings. But be prepared for a slightly gloomy atmosphere and for a feeling that everything here is gently fading, as if the house were being slowly overlain by a sepia wash.

The stone-floored, classical hall is hung with tattered, faded banners embroidered with imperial bees and self-important Ns; gilded leather-bound books that once belonged to Napoleon fill the shelves of the library; there are several portraits and other mementoes of Copenhagen, the chestnut charger who carried Wellington at Waterloo, and a collection of small Dutch cabinet paintings by Teniers the Younger, Jan Griffier, Cuyp and others are just some of many pictures from the Spanish royal collection captured from the fleeing Joseph Bonaparte in the Peninsular War. Interestingly, too, the Iron Duke had a taste for French furniture, ornate pieces he acquired in Paris in 1817, and a row of gilded busts, now lining the 18th-century long gallery looking over lawns to the river. This room, as several others in the house, is decorated with prints stuck on to the walls in the 18th-century fashion, the original Georgian scheme here much enhanced by the softly glowing gold leaf added as a background in Victorian times.

The circuit of the ground floor ends in a corridor displaying the Duke's spy glass, compasses, locks of hair (in 1813 a rich auburn, by 1852 a straw-coloured wisp), and hearing aid, essential for a man who had been continually deafened by cannon. And in the rustic, ochre-washed outbuildings lining the drive is a more stagey exhibition, its highpoint the sinister funeral carriage which carried the Duke's coffin through the streets of London. While his master faces eternity in the crypt of St Paul's Cathedral, Copenhagen was buried with military honours at Stratfield Saye, his grave marked by a dignified headstone.

The Vyne ☆☆

4 m N Basingstoke, off A340, signposted from A33; NT; tearoom; garden; *open:* Apr–end Oct, daily, except Mon and Fri (but open Good Fri, BH Mon, closed Tues following), 1.30–5.30 (4 in late Oct); tel: 0256 881337

This long, red-brick house crouched in a shallow valley disguises its origins well. Orderly sash windows and a pedimented portico on the garden front seem entirely 18th-century in spirit. Inside, modest, low-ceilinged rooms decorated with rococo plasterwork and lined with faded crimson and white damask show off elegant Queen Anne furniture. The showiest interior is a classical staircase hall forming a narrow cleft through the house, with busts of scowling Roman emperors on the newel posts, Corinthian columns screening the upper landing, and relentlessly geometrical plasterwork picked out in white and blue.

Beneath this gloss is a very much older place. The Vyne's E-shaped plan, with two long wings framing the entrance court, gives the shape of the Tudor mansion built by William, lst Lord Sandys, Lord Chamberlain to Henry VIII. And two fine early 16th-century interiors have survived later alterations. On the ground floor, forming the climax to the long sequence of rooms down the north front, is a candlelit chapel, with a carved canopy arching over two tiers of stalls, a fringe of decorative Tudor floor-tiles in grass-green, blue and ochre, and three windows filled with richly coloured glass depicting the king and his first wife, Catherine of Aragon. The tour ends in Sandys' sparsely furnished long gallery filling the first floor of the west wing. A classical fireplace and busts on fluted pedestals are later introductions, but the linenfold panelling is original and carved with allusions to Sandys and the prevailing regime, among them the pomegranates of Queen Catherine, and Thomas Wolsey's cardinal's hat.

For its date, Sandys's house was ahead of its time, with one of the earliest long galleries in England. Chaloner Chute, the lawyer and Speaker of the House of Commons who bought The Vyne in 1653, was similarly innovatory, and it was he who commissioned John Webb, Inigo Jones's disciple, to add the grandiose portico, the first of its kind in the country. Other classical features, such as the staircase, were the work of John Chute in the mid-18th century, and this friend of Horace Walpole was also responsible for some less successful embellishments in Strawberry Hill gothick, such as the flimsy, skin-deep decoration of the Ante-Chapel. More convincing is the grandiose monument to Chaloner Chute that John added on to the chapel in *c.* 1770. An effigy of the great man reclines atop a kind of classical temple, his head propped up on his arm.

The Wakes

In centre of Selborne, on B3006, 4 m SE Alton; garden; *open:* mid March–end Oct, Tues–Sun and BH Mon 11–5.30, also Sat, Sun in Nov, Dec; tel: 042 050 275

The ghost of Gilbert White, the 18th-century clergyman and naturalist who lived at Selborne for 64 years, hovers only fitfully over his much-altered former home, which has largely disappeared under Victorian and Edwardian remodelling. In addition, many visitors may be surprised to find galleries commemorating the 19th-century African explorer Francis Oates, and his nephew Capt Lawrence Oates, who went with Scott to the South Pole in 1912 and so bravely sacrificed himself on the return journey.

The downstairs rooms have little to recommend them. Most atmospheric is the rough-walled, low-ceilinged bedroom in the 17th-century wing, furnished with White's footstool and a desk carved with his initials, with hangings embroidered by his aunts on the four-poster, and with casement windows looking on to the garden he loved and beyond it to the steep, beech-covered hanger immortalized in his *The Natural History and Antiquities of Selborne.*

Isle of Wight

Appuldurcombe House ☆

$\frac{1}{2}$ m W Wroxall, off B3327; EH; access on foot along a rough, uphill track; open: summer, daily, 10–6, winter, Tues–Sun 10–4; tel: 0983 852484

Appuldurcombe is the only house of its kind on the Isle of Wight. Although now an empty, ruined shell, its lichen-stained stonework attractively decayed, it still looks like the magnificent baroque mansion it once was, with pedimented pavilions projecting from each corner, giant Corinthian pilasters between the windows, and swags of drapery and a bloated satyr's mask above the main entrance. Largely built between 1701 and 1713, to plans by the London architect John James, Appuldurcombe was not finished until the 1770s, and has been unoccupied since 1909. Set in a natural hollow, with the downs swelling up behind the house, the ruin is at its most romantic when the sea mist rolls in, veiling the rash of Wroxall on the opposite hillside.

Nunwell House ☆

$\frac{1}{2}$ m from Brading, signed from the A3055 Ryde to Sandown road; guided tours; garden; *open:* July–late Sept, Sun–Thurs 10–5; tel: 0983 407240

This attractive, lived-in house, bought by the present owners in 1982, offers a succession of comfortable, well-furnished rooms. Architecturally it is a mongrel, with one wing of an H-shaped, stone built Jacobean house attached to a much grander front of 1765, an elegant, three-storey façade of lilac-tinged brick looking over park and farmland to the sea. Between the two, like the filling in a sandwich, is a tile-hung early-Georgian improvement, with a rusticated classical doorway. There is some 18th-century panelling and a delicate Adamesque plaster ceiling in the library, but Jacobean woodwork in the room said to have been slept in by Charles I was sadly removed, by John Nash, in 1810. A family collection of militaria, largely devoted to World Wars I and II, fills a couple of rooms and a former wine cellar is devoted to the Home Guard who operated from here in 1940–4.

Osborne House ☆☆

1 m SE East Cowes on A3021; EH; restaurant; grounds; ¹/₂ m walk or Victorian carriage rides to Swiss Cottage, toy fort and Victoria's bathing machine; *open:* Apr–end Oct, daily, 10–6 (5 in Oct); tel: 0983 200022

Built between 1845 and 1850 as a country retreat for Queen Victoria and her family, and designed by Prince Albert, with a little help from Thomas Cubitt, Osborne is an ungainly, barracks-like, Italianate villa in a magnificent position on the north coast of the Isle of Wight, with terraced gardens falling away to the Solent. A rather confused sprawl of buildings round two main courtyards makes most sense from the garden side, where the three-floored pavilion for the family's use, with a striped awning over a first-floor balcony, juts seaward from the main mass of the house. A campanile-like clock tower at one end of the façade is balanced by a flag tower on the pavilion.

Visitors have an extensive tour of the royal family's private apartments, and also see a couple of more impersonal rooms that were used for council meetings, audiences and state receptions, one of them, the Indian-style Durbar Room added on in 1890–91, now filled with presents given to mark Victoria's jubilee. The fascination of the place is that it has been preserved as it was when the Prince Consort died in 1861. Victoria continued to visit Osborne until her own death, 40 years later, but she gave orders that nothing should be changed and Edward VII, whose childhood memories were rather less than rosy, gave the estate to the nation as soon as he decently could.

Like the exterior, the principal rooms are conceived in Italian Renaissance style, with elaborate painted ceilings by the German Ludwig Gruner, screens of marbled columns, and a surfeit of heavy gilded mirrors and mock candelabra. Saccharine portraits by Winterhalter, Landseer and others, the best of them a rather touching painting of Victoria in her widowhood, are complemented by idealized sculptures of the children by Mary Thornycroft, including a cloying study of one-year-old Princess Beatrice in a nautilus-shell cradle.

The private apartments above these public rooms suggest something of Victoria's obsessional, all-controlling personality. In the queen's sitting-room, with a big bay towards the Solent, two identical desks sit side by side in the middle of the room, that used by the Prince Consort, who acted as his wife's private secretary, distinguished only by the higher chair. For a little relaxation Victoria and Albert could play together on the ornate, ivory and rosewood piano against one of the walls, where two stools await the royal performers. Every surface is crammed with photographs and *objets*, and with glass domes covering withered fragments of funeral wreaths and casts of the royal infants' hands. On the floor above is the royal nursery, with miniature, Charles II-style chairs marked with the children's initials and a fully equipped night-nursery, with a narrow single bed for the nurse watching over a row of high-sided cots and a canopied cradle.

There is much else to enjoy, including a hideous collection of antler furniture, and the sculpture commissioned by the royal couple. Here is Sir Joseph Boehm's life-size image of Victoria's collie, every hair of the animal's fur faithfully reproduced, and Emil Wolff's statue of the Prince Consort as a bare-legged Roman soldier, Albert's neat moustache looking quite out of place above the period dress.

Kent

Belmont ☆

4 m SW Faversham, follow signs from Badlesmere on A251; guided tours, *c.* 60 mins; teas (from June); *open:* Easter Sun–end Sept, Sat, Sun BH Mon, 2–5; tel: 0795 890202

Built between 1789 and 1793 for the future 1st Lord Harris, whose military career in India had left him a wealthy man, Belmont is an exercise in restrained neo-classicism by Samuel Wyatt, elder brother of the more famous James. Gentle domed bows bulge out of the east front, with its glorious views over the park, while to south and north the house is fronted by colonnaded, verandah-like porticos. Wyatt's individuality and use of up-to-the-minute techniques comes through in the glazed, lighthouse-like look-outs in the domes, in the facing of fashionable yellow tiles, in the underfloor heating, and in the Coade stone plaques decorating the exterior, one showing the muse of architecture with Belmont in the background. An earlier red-brick Georgian house was relegated to one side of the sunny stable yard.

The guided tour focuses on the three east-facing reception rooms. An apse-ended drawing-room is fitted out in French style, with white and gold 'Louis XV' seat furniture and ornate French clocks against a silver and white striped paper; the Regency dining-room is all solid mahogany, with a family group by Arthur Devis on the end wall; and the more relaxed, tobacco-tinged library, with prominent globes in Wyatt's plaster frieze, has original recessed bookshelves grained to resemble walnut. A portrait-hung, top-lit staircase hall rises through the house, with gallery-like landings off the cantilevered staircase. There are reminders of India, such as the snarling lion and tiger caged by the entrance, and there is the 5th Lord Harris's catholic collection of clocks, ranging from instruments by Thomas Tompion and Joseph Knibb to Victorian extravaganzas in the shape of a candlestick, or a tiered church steeple.

Boughton Monchelsea Place ☆

Off M20, 5 m S Maidstone on B2163, signed from A229; guided tour (*c.* 1 hour); teas; garden and grounds; *open:* Good Fri–early Oct, Sun and BHs, and Wed in Jul and Aug, 2.15–6; tel: 0622 743120

A long, rough drive through coppice woodland suddenly emerges on the crest of a ridge, with breathtaking views south over an unspoilt, wooded expanse of the Weald. Poised on the shoulder of the hill is this low, L-shaped house of creamy-grey ragstone, its originally Elizabethan frontage, with stone dormers and a projecting two-storey porch, embellished with Georgian gothick windows and battlements. Stone mullions from an earlier house survive on the south side, and, at the back, a grassy courtyard is enclosed by early 19th-century brick buildings which replaced the original north and west ranges.

Boughton Monchelsea is a modest, retiring place, and the rooms visitors see, as varied as the exterior, are comfortable and domestic rather than grand. The only attempt at show is the gently-vaulted, gothick hall, with white cluster columns set against khaki-coloured walls. A wine-red dining-room, with a gothick screen at one end, has a Regency feel, but the cluttered drawing-room on the south-east corner of the house is an eclectic mix, with a gilded rococo mirror over the fireplace, marquetry and lacquer cabinets, white oriental porcelain arranged on a grand piano, and comfortable sofas by the fire. These rooms and a broad William and Mary staircase with twisted, barley-sugar balusters contrast with a remnant of the tight Elizabethan stairs, with treads of solid oak, with the 16th-century herb closet, still fitted out with the original oak shelves and cupboards, and with a little panelled bedroom furnished with a bulbous four-poster, one of a few early pieces that have always been in the house.

Chartwell ☆☆

2 m S Westerham, off B2026; NT; entry by timed ticket; tearoom; extensive garden; *open:* March and Nov, Sat, Sun, Wed 11–4.30; Apr–end Oct, Tues–Thurs, 12–5.30, Sat, Sun, BH Mon 11–5.30; tel: 0732 866368

This red-brick, family house set high on the shoulder of a peaceful Kentish valley is a shrine to Sir Winston Churchill, who bought the place in 1922 and lived here, whenever he could, for the rest of his life. Virtually rebuilt for the Churchills by Philip Tilden, the house itself is on the ugly side of unexceptional, with strongly vertical, crow-stepped gables towering over the garden that falls away into the combe.

The interior, now largely returned to the way it looked in the years before World War II, is much more attractive. Here is the family sitting-room, with comfortable chairs and sofas round the fire, a card table set for bezique, which Churchill loved, an array of newspapers, and fresh flowers on the mantelpiece. On the floor below is the low-ceilinged, white and green dining-room, from which the family could step straight into the garden, while upstairs are Lady Churchill's cool and airy barrel-vaulted bedroom and the great man's study, both with views over the valley and the Weald beyond.

Displays of documents, uniforms, and other Churchilliana include political cartoons and copies of historic dispatches, among them the terse directive sent to Field Marshal Alexander on 10 August 1942, ordering him to drive the Germans and Italians from north Africa. Churchill the sensualist comes through in the piles of cigar boxes, the velvet siren suits, which he wore with all the panache of an 18th-century dandy, and in his brash impressionistic paintings, his bold use of colour as uncompromising as the man himself. His landscapes, still lifes and portraits hang all over the house and fill the surprisingly large garden studio, where a whisky and soda set ready by his chair and the half-empty decanter reflect another of his essential pleasures. Also on show is a painting of his prize-winning colt, Colonist II, a reminder of the racing stable and stud farm which he kept for many years and of his prowess as a polo player. There are many family mementoes too, among them a charcoal drawing of his beautiful mother by John Sargent and photographs of his little daughter Marigold, who died in infancy, and of his beloved Nanny Everest.

Chiddingstone Castle

In village of Chiddingstone, off the B2027 Edenbridge to Tonbridge road; tearoom; garden; *open:* Apr, May, Oct, Wed, Sun, BHs, June–Sept, Tues–Sun, all BHs 2–5.30 (from 11.30 Sun and BHs); tel: 0892 870347

People come to this toy castle in the Kentish Weald to see the collections of the eccentric Denys Eyre Bower (1905–77), who managed to acquire a remarkable range of treasures on the salary of a bank clerk and bought Chiddingstone in 1955 as somewhere to display them. Always, his obsession took precedence, his last great purchase, a 17th-century Flemish tapestry, being bought with funds for repairing the roof.

Apart from a couple of rooms, such as the galleried great hall, Chiddingstone is more museum than home, with objects displayed in glass cases. Then, too, Mr Bower's tastes inclined towards Ancient Egypt and the Far East, and much of what is here, such as the army of Egyptian funerary statuettes, the Samurai armour and masks, or the important collection of ornate Japanese lacquered boxes, is of primarily specialist interest. Some Jacobite drinking glasses and other relics, such as a rather grubby handkerchief that Charles I is said to have carried to the block, Bonnie Prince Charlie's wooden porringer, a miniature of Charles II by Samuel Cooper, and Lely's portrait of a fleshy nude who may or may not be Nell Gwynn, have more general appeal. Most precious are an Egyptian head of red porphyry dating from the lst century BC and a Japanese jewel casket of *c*.1636–9, but these are inadequately labelled, as is much else here.

The castle itself dates from *c*.1805, when a red-brick Carolean house was transformed into a towered and battlemented mock castle by James Wyatt's pupil William Atkinson. Funds ran out before all the work was done, though, so the place is something of an architectural mongrel.

Cobham Hall ☆

4 m W Rochester, just off A2(M2) on B2009; guided tour (*c*. 60 mins); teas; grounds; *open:* 24 days in Apr, July and Aug, 2–5; tel: 0474 823371

Set in sweeping wooded grounds is one of the most arresting houses in Kent. A grassy court is framed by two long Elizabethan wings of diapered red brick, with stone-mullioned windows, tall Tudor chimneys and ogee-capped octagonal turrets, and with a Renaissance stone frontispiece marking what was the entrance to the chapel. Joining them, on the site of an originally medieval block, is a Charles II range in the style of Inigo Jones, with fluted Corinthian pilasters and a baroque central doorway.

Later alterations, such as an attic storey by William Chambers, have only blurred the original work, but the interior was extensively remodelled between 1785 and 1810 by James Wyatt, who gave the house its gothick entrance hall and a number of classical interiors. Cobham is now a girls' school, and the informal tour sweeping through all three ranges takes in a series of once grand rooms filled with functional furniture. The only place where the 20th century is left behind is the bare and lofty, grey and gold hall rising through the 1660s block, with gilded plasterwork on the ceiling, sculpted figures playing the pipe and tambourine framing the marble fireplace, and with Wyatt's crimson seat furniture against the walls.

Finchcocks ☆

1½ m W Goudhurst, 10 m E Tunbridge Wells, off A262; teas; garden; *open:* Easter–late Sept, Sun, BH Mon and Wed–Sun in Aug, 2–6; tel: 0580 211702

Only music lovers should visit this early Georgian brick house, where the steep admission fee covers an afternoon of wittily introduced recitals on period instruments. Architecturally, Finchcocks is interesting enough, its imposing baroque entrance façade, built of a pleasing mix of red and blue bricks, and with a battered, armless statue of Queen Anne in a round-headed niche below the floating central pediment, actually fronting a comparatively small house, only 40 ft deep. Low wings curve out from the four-storey central block, its apparent height exaggerated by a heavy parapet and massive chimney stacks. Built for the London barrister Edward Bathurst in 1725, Finchcocks seems to have been the work of a local man, although possibly based on a design by Thomas Archer.

Since the 1970s, the bare-floored panelled rooms have been filled with the present owner's collection of 18th- and 19th-century pianos, harpsichords, virginals, spinets and clavichords. Visitors can wander among these beautifully crafted objects, but the main draw is the almost continuous music going on in the hall, for which some of the audience is seated on the 18th-century staircase.

Godinton Park ☆☆☆

1½ m W Ashford, signed off A20; guided tours (c. 60 mins); garden; *open:* Easter Sat, Sun, Mon, June–Sept, Sun and BH Mon 2–5; tel: 0233 620773

Despite the outskirts of Ashford faintly visible across the park, this Jacobean courtyard house sheltering behind a wall of yew is one of the most pleasing and unpressured houses in the south-east of England. Home of the Toke family for some 400 years, from 1440 to 1895, the present building owes most to the colourful, five times married Royalist, Captain Nicholas Toke, who extensively reconstructed an originally 14th-century house in 1627–30, and to a 19th-century Toke with antiquarian tastes, who acquired much of the carved woodwork that is such a feature of the place. Godinton's mellow brick ranges with their wood-mullioned windows and curving Flemish gables are now set off by a topiary garden designed by Sir Reginald Blomfield in 1902, part of a scheme of Edwardian alterations. Sadly, apart from some portraits and a few other things, most of the original contents have gone, but the rooms have been refurnished with a fine collection of 17th- and 18th-century pieces.

One of the best guided tours, assuming both intelligence and real interest, takes visitors into some half-dozen widely-varied rooms. Surprisingly, there is still a great hall at the heart of the house, its 14th-century hammerbeam roof hidden behind Sir Nicholas's arching ribbed ceiling, the walls richly panelled with a frieze of Flemish medallion heads, and Renaissance arcades screening a corridor and the gallery at the far end. This piece of 19th-century romanticism is enhanced by a set of royal portraits, including works by Lely and Kneller, and by Jacobean furniture standing on a softly coloured oriental silk carpet.

As memorable is the long, well-lit great chamber of 1635 on the first floor of the east front, its Georgian panelling crested with gay, lacey finials, and carved with a frieze of animated figures engaged in musketry and pike drill. A chimneypiece of the local Bethersden marble is carved with a strange assortment of creatures, and portraits by Mytens, Raeburn and Reynolds complement some fine walnut and marquetry furniture from the turn of the 17th century and a collection of Worcester, Chelsea and Dresden porcelain.

Also on show are two of Blomfield's Edwardian interiors, the one fitted out like a French boudoir, with gilded, tapestry-covered chairs and apple-green Sèvres, the other a white-panelled sitting-room hung with pastels and water-colours. The dining-room is a cavernous 18th-century interior, and a chinoiserie garden hall is furnished with a Chinese Chippendale table and chairs.

Great Maytham Hall

$^1/_2$ m E Rolvenden village, on road to Rolvenden Layne; guided tours; open: May–Sept, Wed, Thurs 2–5; tel: none

Looking south over the Weald, with the valley of the Rother falling away steeply below the garden, is an enormous mansion of red and grey brick in a vaguely Georgian style, with dormers in a steeply pitched roof and prominent chimneys. Built in 1909–10 by Sir Edwin Lutyens, who was faced with incorporating an existing Georgian and Victorian house, Great Maytham Hall is not the great architect's happiest creation. It is now divided into flats and visitors see just the main reception rooms and the brick-vaulted Georgian cellars. The now-immaculate walled garden on the slope below the house is said to have inspired Frances Hodgson Burnett, who rented Great Maytham at the turn of the century, to write *The Secret Garden*.

Hever Castle ☆

3 m SE Edenbridge off B2026, signposted from M25; restaurant; garden; open: mid March–early Nov, daily, 12–6; tel: 0732 865224

This double-moated, medieval manor still looks much as it did when the Boleyn family lived here in the early sixteenth century and the dark-haired Anne was courted by Henry VIII. Although called a castle, the only defences are the drawbridge over the moat and the three-storey battlemented gatehouse with its original portcullises. Beyond the entrance arch is a domestic cobbled courtyard, framed by half-timbered, gabled ranges.

Inside, another world takes over. By the end of the 19th century, Hever was in a decayed, dilapidated state and was only saved, at the eleventh hour, by the American millionaire William Waldorf Astor, who bought the ruin in

1903 and poured his fortune into its restoration. With the help of the architect F. L. Pearson (son of J. L.), the millionaire created a lavish, rose-tinted evocation of the age of Anne Boleyn. Edwardian craftsmen produced the inlaid and linenfold panelling, carved screens, stone fireplaces, moulded plaster ceilings (which Astor insisted were produced by eye alone), and heraldic glass which now adorn the principal rooms.

Astor's agents combed Europe for antique furnishings, acquiring Brussels and Aubusson tapestries, Persian carpets, and an eclectic mix of Italian, French, Scandinavian, Spanish and English pieces. Where he could not find the real thing, Astor had copies made, reproducing 16th-century silver chandeliers at Hampton Court for the long gallery. And the improbably perfect huddle of Tudor half-timbered cottages to the north of the moat was built to house guests and servants.

Amidst all this confident luxury, the spirit of the 16th century largely disappears. The bare room where Anne Boleyn is supposed to have slept contains the illuminated Book of Hours that she is said to have carried with her to the scaffold, and a display of Tudor and Stuart needlework in a gallery-like corridor includes a headpiece and coif with embroidery by Anne, as well as the layette which Elizabeth I is said to have produced during her half-sister Mary's phantom pregnancy. After Anne's death, Henry appropriated the Boleyn family home for himself and, with characteristic insensitivity, granted it to his divorced fourth wife, Anne of Cleves, but there is nothing of her here.

Rooms devoted to the Astors celebrate more recent history. Here is the ledger of works of art purchased for Hever, written in a neat, confident hand, and a display of curiously trite letters. Apart from Winston Churchill's advice to John Astor, 2nd son of William Waldorf, about his painting – 'use brighter colours' – these are mostly smoothly worded bread-and-butter missives, or rejections of invitations to lunch at *The Times*, of which John Astor was chairman. Only the 92-year-old Bernard Shaw is witty, pointing out he would be a Banquo's ghost at such a gathering.

Sadly, Hever is now in the hands of a leisure company and a spirit of commercialism threatens to destroy the castle's atmosphere. Visit, if you can, out of season, when you are less likely to be disturbed by the cars parked in full view of the house or by Morris dancers cavorting outside.

Ightham Mote ☆☆

6 m E Sevenoaks, 2½ m S Ightham, off A227; NT; tearoom; garden; *open:* Apr–end Oct, daily, except Tues and Sat, 12–5.30 (from 11 Sun and BH Mon); tel: 0732 810378

One of the most beautiful and tranquil of houses lies hidden away in a narrow wooded valley in the Kentish Weald. Built of rough Kentish ragstone and local oak, with walls rising sheer from the surrounding moat and half-timbered upper storeys jettied out over the water, Ightham Mote grew piecemeal from the mid-14th century, gradually developing into the picturesque agglomeration that now surrounds a spacious, shady courtyard. Despite substantial restoration in the 19th century, and the loss of the contents in a sale in 1951, the essential character of the house is unspoilt, and it has been sympathetically refurnished.

The oldest part, facing the Tudor gatehouse across the courtyard, is the great hall, with sculpted corbels, an open roof borne on ribs of wood and stone, a massive fireplace, and a handsome five-light window glowing with richly coloured armorial glass – portraying the scarlet Tudor rose, the golden pomegranate of Aragon, and the portcullis of Henry VIII – inserted by the high-flying courtier Sir Richard Clement, who bought the house in 1521.

A Jacobean staircase leads to a trio of interconnecting rooms on the first floor and to what was Sir Richard's long gallery running down the north wing. Long converted into a chapel, this atmospheric chamber is a clever mélange of 16th-century linenfold panelling, Continental glass, and late medieval stalls and screen, with the faded paintwork of the Tudor wagon roof displaying another batch of royal symbols: the *fleur-de-lis* of France, the castle of Castile, and the rose of England. Through a medieval oak door, its lock many times renewed, is the one gracious interior, a long, uncluttered, faintly exotic drawing-room, lit by an 18th-century Venetian window, speckled with potted plants and blue and white oriental porcelain, and with an uninhibited Jacobean fireplace carved with saracens' heads.

The current extensive restoration, expected to last for at least 15 years, means that visitors are unlikely to see everything described in the guidebook, but the Trust is making a feature of the work, with opportunities to see conservation in progress. Sadly, as a result of the renewal of wood and stone, Ightham has lost its air of picturesque decay, and the mature beeches which once formed a green wall on the shoulder of the valley have been devastated by recent storms.

Knole ☆☆☆☆

S end of Sevenoaks, off A225; NT: guided tours in Oct; tearoom; garden (rarely open) and park; *open:* Apr–end Oct, Wed–Sun and BH Mon 11–5 (Thurs 2–5); tel: 0732 450608

Once through the unobtrusive entrance on the A225, Sevenoaks is shaken off in a switchback drive across the deer park that cocoons this magical place, home of the Sackville family since 1603. Set on a rise, with rabbit-cropped turf right up to the walls, Knole's cluster of turrets, towers and chimneys, of pinnacles, finials, gables and battlements, seems more like a town or some vast monastery than a house. Outside, the place is four-square and sharply defined; inside, it is a sprawling warren of interconnecting courtyards and lodgings. The main ranges are of rough Kentish flagstone with warm red-tiled roofs, but the inquisitive will catch glimpses of half-timbered, overhung façades hidden away behind, as if the walls also embrace a village.

First built by Thomas Bourchier, Archbishop of Canterbury, in the late 15th century, Knole was seized from Archbishop Cranmer by Henry VIII,

who greatly enlarged his prize. The ground plan is still largely as it was when the avaricious Henry died in 1545, but the rooms shown are Jacobean rather than Tudor, with rippling plasterwork, ribbed ceilings and bravura fireplaces dating from Thomas Sackville, 1st Earl of Dorset's alterations in the first years of the 17th century. The contents are later arrivals still. The original furnishings were mostly lost in the Civil War, when Knole was plundered by the Parliamentarians, but this loss is more than remedied by the quantity of early 17th-century pieces still upholstered in original velvets, silks and brocades. Acquired by the 6th Earl from royal palaces, these were perquisites of his position as Lord Chamberlain to William III.

Avoid, if you can, that brief period when there are compulsory guided tours. This is a house that needs to be lingered in. Beyond the bare great hall, with a musicians' gallery for the Sackvilles' private orchestra at one end, visitors are plunged into a succession of panelled, tapestry-hung galleries and intimate bed-chambers, all shielded from the sun in a curtained twilight. And there are two painted staircases, one with a life-size plaster nude of Giannetta Baccelli, mistress of the 3rd Duke of Dorset, reclining on a rumpled couch at its foot. Some 300 paintings include a set of identikit portraits in the brown gallery; Netherlandish cabinet pictures; and a splendid collection of works by Reynolds, among them likenesses of the 3rd Duke's Chinese page and a haunting vision of the near-blind Samuel Johnson, his hands clenched as if in pain. Mytens, Van Dyck, Dobson, Gainsborough and Hoppner are all represented, and there is a charming portrait by Madame Vigée-Lebrun, of a curly-headed girl in a red hat.

Four-posters are hung with precious hangings, the most sumptuous, on a richly carved and gilded bed, made of blue-green Italian velvet, and once-royal chairs are covered in silk shot through with silver thread. Among such riches, particular treasures, such as the Louis XIV table inlaid with pewter and brass to resemble silver and gold, are easily lost. The tour ends in the darkened and theatrically lit King's room, with glittering, silver-plated furniture surrounding a bed hung with cloth of gold. But even the most mundane details are beautifully crafted, each of the rainwater heads in Stone Court, for example, being fashioned as a little castle, and each different.

Leeds Castle ☆

4 m E Maidstone, on B2163 (junction 8, M20); restaurant; garden with maze and aviary; park; transport from car park for elderly and disabled; dog collar museum; *open:* mid Mar–end Oct, daily, 11–6, Nov–mid Mar, Sat, Sun and daily in Christmas week 11–5, but closed sometimes for functions and high-level conferences; tel: 0622 765400

Like an ageing beauty, Leeds Castle is best seen from a distance, and in the soft, misty light of a winter afternoon rather than the full glare of summer. From afar, as when first seen on the 20-minute walk from the car park, it is a fairytale place, with rolling wooded parkland setting off a vision of battle-mented walls and turrets rising out of a glassy lake. Close too, though, it has the slightly brassy, tired air of any much-visited, commercial attraction, and only part is genuinely ancient.

What is old dates back to Norman times, and to the 300 years, from 1278 to 1552, when Leeds was in royal hands. Jutting furthest into the lake, com-pletely enveloping the little island on which it is built, is the original strong-hold, a 13th-century keep with huge bay windows inserted by Henry VIII softening the massive walls rising sheer from the water. A cobbled bridge leads to the weathered gatehouse range of c.1280 that guards the approach to the larger island. One side of the grassy court here is framed by a Tudor range, the remains of a medieval wall circles the edge, but the main house, set self-confidently across the inner end, dates only from 1822–4, when a Jacobean mansion was replaced by a late-Georgian gothic fantasy designed by the little-known William Baskett of Camberwell.

Inside, the castle is a cross between a luxury hotel and a film set, with stone-mullioned windows, deep-set alcoves, gothic arches, a 16th-century oak staircase and old stone fireplaces curiously mixed with unsubtle, theatrical recreations of medieval interiors and with the discreet, carpeted corridors and a cocoon-like seminar room used for the high-level conferences that are now held here. Almost all the present furnishings, beautiful as many of them are, date only from 1926, when the Anglo-American Lady Baillie bought the place in a dilapidated state and spent decades restoring and refurnishing, importing Jacobean panelling and other period bits and pieces and enlisting the help of the French designers Rateau and Stéphane Boudin.

Most atmospheric is the 75 ft gallery known as Henry VIII's banqueting hall, with a deep Tudor window bay, a floor of polished ebony, tapestry-hung walls and a mix of 15th-century furniture round the French Renaissance chimneypiece. A quite different era pervades the two sumptuous drawing-rooms in the 19th-century block, where the deep sofas and pleated lampshades for the use of conference delegates are surrounded, in one case, by 17th-century panelling and richly coloured Chinese porcelain birds, in the other by walls of yellow silk damask setting off flower paintings by Monnoyer and a Tiepolo. A museum room displaying miniatures and other treasures, such as a late 17th-century collect book embroidered with silver thread, or a watch that was used at the Battle of Naseby in 1645, recalls some of the many high-born figures who have been associated with the castle. But only the most unquestioning will thrill to the recreation of the apartment used by Catherine de Valois, Henry V's queen, in about 1430, the garish hangings enveloping both walls and bed so obviously not made of rich old fabrics.

Lullingstone Castle ☆

½ m SW Eynsford, off A225 Sevenoaks road; teas; garden and river walk; *open:* Apr–Oct, Sat, Sun, BHs 2–6; tel: 0322 862114

A turreted Tudor gatehouse in warm red brick leads in to a spacious grassy court, big as a cricket pitch. On the far side is the house, with rows of orderly sashes in a Queen Anne façade; to the left is a flint-faced 14th-century church, to the right a long, tree-fringed lake formed out of the River Darent. All is serene and very English.

Lullingstone is still owned by descendants of Sir John Peche, companion of the young Henry VIII, who built a manor here at the end of the 15th century and embellished the church, adding the family chapel and the splendid canopied screen. Although Sir John's house seems to have disappeared, the 18th-century elegance disguises an older building. From the river path to the east, there is a view of stone-mullioned windows and tall Tudor chimneys, while on the north the deep cornice of the entrance front turns into a brick parapet and octagonal brick turrets flank a Tudor doorcase.

The interior shown is largely Queen Anne, with well-proportioned, panelled rooms leading off the two-storey hall in the centre of the house. The queen frequently visited Lullingstone and the story goes that the wide wooden staircase was given specially shallow treads so as to make it easier for her to heave her vast bulk upwards. Forming an anteroom to the queen's first-floor apartment is the sparsely furnished Elizabethan Great Chamber, the finest room in the house, with caricatures of Roman emperors, all sly eyes and hideous noses, among the decorative plasterwork covering the barrel-vaulted ceiling.

Family portraits hang throughout the house, among them a triptych of 1575 showing Sir John Peche's nephew, Sir Percival Hart, with his two adult sons. Apart from the paintings, some of which are difficult to see, the contents are generally of less interest than the building.

Owletts

S end of Cobham village, opposite turning to Sole Street; no advance signs; NT; garden; *open:* Apr–end Sept, Wed, Thurs 2–5; tel: none

A modest yeoman's house built in the last years of Charles II's reign, Owletts is a pleasing red-brick building with closely spaced sash windows, tall chimneys rising from a steep hipped roof, and narrow bays coming forward either side of the entrance front. Inside, visitors see the Carolean staircase with its bold plaster ceiling, and two lived-in downstairs rooms. Here, the presiding spirit is the architect Sir Herbert Baker (1862–1946), whose house this was. Sir Herbert installed the cedar panelling in the little dining-room, and designed the chairs and sideboards, with their motifs based on his family and his distinguished career in South Africa and India, where he worked in New Delhi with Sir Edwin Lutyens. Some of his watercolours, including a painting of *Port Lympne*, hang in the cream-walled sitting-room opposite; the empire clock he designed, telling the time round the world, is above the fire; and in the garden beyond is his classical bird bath, composed of Corinthian capitals saved from his remodelling of Sir John Soane's Bank of England.

Penshurst Place ☆☆

In Penshurst village on B2176, 3 m SW Tonbridge; restaurant; toy and farm museums; outstanding formal garden; *open:* late Mar–end Sept, daily, 1–5.30; tel: 0892 870307

Penshurst, home of the Sidney family for centuries and with an untouched medieval core, both excites and frustrates. One of those houses that grew gradually over the years, it is a huge rambling place, shaped like an untidy H, with a wing heading off from one of its legs like a final flourish of the pen. Visitors are admitted to only one side of the H – including the final flourish – and must work out the rest of the building as best they can (for the determined, the north and west fronts can best be glimpsed from the B2176). Then, the rooms seen, impressive as they are, are very obviously set pieces, some of them arranged with museum-like unreality.

It is best to drift through, letting the house take over. The approach through the gardens is magic. Past luxuriant borders backed by yew hedges and ancient walls, an isolated gatehouse, part of the 14th-century defences, leads to the irregular, many-turreted south front, built of warm, weathered sandstone and lit by stone-mullioned windows of every shape and size. Towards one end is the spacious hall built by Sir John de Pulteney in c.1340, rising 60 ft to a chestnut roof and still with its original central hearth and 15th-century, elm-topped trestle tables. Edward IV dined here, and perhaps Henry V too, as he had brothers living at Penshurst.

Up the stone staircase beyond, a succession of formal, rather dark state rooms, not improved by 19th-century alterations, do little to warm the heart, but there is a splendid collection of 16th- and 17th-century Sidney portraits, among them Marcus Gheeraerts the Elder's charming picture of an Elizabethan Lady Sidney with six of her children. There are also fine William and Mary furnishings, such as a day bed with a huge shell curving over one end, and various other treasures, including a Dutch cabinet with each drawer painted by a different artist.

The one place to linger is the long gallery. Added on in the early years of the 17th century, and lit by windows on three sides, this is a sunny, oak-panelled room some 80 ft long, hung with portraits by Lely and Kneller and furnished with gilded and ebonised late 17th- and early-18th-century pieces. In the armour- and weapon-hung stone-floored lower gallery at the end of the tour is the porcupine-crested helm carried in the funeral procession for Sir Philip Sidney, who was born at Penshurst in 1554, wrote much of his poetry here and died, aged only 31, fighting in the Netherlands against Spain.

Port Lympne

3 m W Hythe, off A20 and B2067; guided tours in high season; restaurant; garden and zoo park; *open:* all year, daily, except Christmas Day, 10–5 (dusk in winter); tel: 0303 264646

At the centre of John Aspinall's 300-acre zoo park is a sprawling, red-brick, Lutyens-style mansion with curving Dutch gables, tall chimneys, and steeply pitched roofs. It sits high on a cliff-like bluff, with panoramic views along the coast and terraced gardens falling steeply away to the green expanses of Romney Marsh. Started in 1911 and completed after World War I, Port Lympne was built for the millionaire MP Sir Philip Sassoon, some time Private Secretary to Lloyd George, and designed by Sir Herbert Baker and Ernest Willmott, with later additions by Philip Tilden.

Sadly, there is only a faint echo of Port Lympne's heyday, when the great and the famous flocked to Sir Philip's legendary house parties, and when international peace conferences were held in Tilden's intimate octagonal library. You can still see the marble-floored hall, the stone staircase, and Tilden's shady Moorish patio, with arcades of delicate marble columns and a green marble pavement, but the handful of rooms on show are largely devoted to animal art and to displays related to the zoo, the panelled library is now a shop, and the place as a whole has a tawdry, commercial air. The one feature which makes a visit worthwhile is the room painted as a *trompe l'oeil* tent by Rex Whistler in 1933, with the green-and-white candy stripes of the canopy open on one side to reveal a vista over an elegant 18th-century town.

Quebec House

At E end of Westerham village, on N side of A25, facing junction with B2026; NT; no car park; garden; *open:* Apr–end Oct, daily, except Thurs and Sat, 2–6; tel: 0959 562206

This gabled, early-17th century brick house on a bend on the busy A25 is a shrine to General James Wolfe, whose victory over the French at Quebec in 1759 has passed from history into legend. In fact, Wolfe only lived here as a child, up to the age of 11, and most of the furniture in the modest, panelled rooms, although appropriate to the house, has nothing to do with either him or his family. The connection is made through paintings and engravings, and through such personal relics as his fruitwood snuff box, his high-collared, white-linen dressing-gown, and his travelling canteen, complete with glass decanters. Also here is a rough pencil portrait drawn by Wolfe's ADC. An unflattering image of a slight young man with a pointed nose and a receding chin, it is one of only a couple of likenesses made from the life.

Smallhythe Place ☆

S end of Smallhythe village, on E side B2082; NT; garden; parking in layby beyond house; *open:* Apr–end Oct, Sat–Wed and Gd Fri 2–6 (or dusk); tel: 058 06 2334

This crooked, timber-framed 16th-century house with a sweeping red-tiled roof is where the actress Dame Ellen Terry lived for nearly 30 years, dying here at the age of 81 in 1928. The intimate, low-ceilinged rooms, lit by small-paned casements, and with a steep rope-railed stair to the upper floor, are now primarily a theatrical museum, devoted to relics of Terry's eventful career.

The brick-floored kitchen, with a settle drawn up by the fire, is given over to the wider theatrical scene and mementoes of Terry's contemporaries, among them a cast of Eleonora Duse's hand, Sir Arthur Sullivan's monocle, and a gushing scrawl from Sarah Bernhardt. The other five rooms on show concentrate more closely on the great actress. There are cases of extravagant costumes, including the dress decorated with beetle wings which she wore as Lady Macbeth, a fan-letter from Oscar Wilde, a spartan make-up box, containing little more than a mirror, a sponge and a swatch of grey hair, and reminders of her long professional partnership with Sir Henry Irving. Something of Terry herself comes through in the simply furnished, almost austere bedroom, with her Globe Shakespeare and a crucifix by the bed and plump pottery pigs on the dressing-table. Also here are pastels of her two children, offspring of a six-year relationship with the architect Edwin Godwin, not of her three short-lived marriages.

Squerryes Court ☆☆☆

Western outskirts of Westerham, off A25 and B269; tearoom (weekends only); garden; *open:* Mar, Sun 2–6, Apr–end Sept, Wed, Sat, Sun, BH Mon 2–6; tel: 0959 562345

This desirable, red-brick, William and Mary house sits above a reed-fringed lake looking out over an unspoilt stretch of wooded Kentish countryside. Inside, a few well-proportioned, lived-in rooms are the setting for the Warde family collection of paintings, porcelain and furniture, mostly acquired in the decades after John Warde I bought the place in 1731.

The dining-room, with long shuttered windows on to the garden, is hung with 17th-century Dutch paintings, among them atmospheric landscapes and river scenes by Van Ruisdael and Van Goyen, domestic interiors, and a Van der Helst of a burgher family out for a walk, a red-tiled, step-gabled town in the distance behind them. Family portraits are gathered in the hall and the comfortable drawing-room, where two languid young men by Devis, a Romney and a couple of slightly saccharine Opies accompany John Wootton's delightful painting of the first Warde owner and his family, all on horseback, and William Barraud's picture of a corpulent, fox-hunting Regency Warde.

Much grander canvases line the broad landing upstairs, among them a version of Rubens's portrait of Philip II on horseback, two overblown, mythological Giordanos, and a vast still-life by Pieter de Ring, with a gold ring as a play on his name hidden among a mouth-watering array of grapes, peaches and pomegranates. These paintings are complemented by fine 18th-century furniture, including two delicate rococo music stands, by a blue and orange K'ang-hsi dinner service bearing the Warde crest, and by the three Soho tapestries of 1720 set into the panelling of an upstairs room, the exuberant floral arabesques and exotic birds of the design still as fresh as when they were woven. And there is a corner devoted to James Wolfe, who lived as a boy in *Quebec House* nearby and was a friend of the young George Warde, John I's son. Relics of the great general include the sword he wore during the

Quebec campaign, and a portrait done at the time of his first commission, when he was 14, the only likeness for which Wolfe ever sat.

Stoneacre ☆

3 m SE Maidstone, at N end of Otham village, via narrow lane S from A20; NT; guided tours; garden; *open:* Apr–end Oct, Wed, Sat, 2–6; tel: 0622 862871

A steep uphill walk from the car park brings visitors to this substantial, half-timbered house overlooking a secluded valley, one wing heavily buttressed to stop it sliding downhill. Like *Great Dixter*, Stoneacre is a piece of creative restoration, only a 15th-century hall to the left of the porch and the solar block beyond being original to the site. Ranges to either side, and a spiral staircase in an octagonal brick turret, were added on by the antiquarian Aymer Vallance, who bought the property in 1920 and augmented it with pieces of other Tudor houses. Windows were moved about, fireplaces and panelling introduced, and suitable furniture and paintings zealously collected.

Visitors are shown the hall, parlour and solar of the original house. Most impressive are the two open timber roofs, with cluster-column crown posts supporting the rafters, but some of the introduced details are just as intriguing, in particular the stone fireplace carved with curly-tailed dragons that Vallance rescued from The George, a former medieval inn in Sittingbourne.

Surrey

Albury Park

Just east of Albury, 4 m SE Guildford, on A248; grounds; *open:* May–end Sept, Wed, Thurs 2–5; tel: none

In a magical setting, looking over a secluded valley dotted with mature specimen trees, is a house of little distinction. Gabled and battlemented Tudoresque façades of black ironstone and moulded red brick with a profusion of tall ornamental chimneys were slapped onto an older but already much altered building in the mid-19th century by the failing Augustus Welby Pugin, soon to lose his mind, and his son Edward. The house is now divided into flats and visitors see only the public rooms, a mix of styles and periods that includes an elegant staircase and high-ceilinged drawing-room designed by John Soane and two 17th-century overmantels. A tiny Saxon and medieval church in the grounds has a chapel richly decorated in blue, red and gold by the elder Pugin, and across the valley can be seen the long grassy terraces of the formal garden designed by the 17th-century diarist John Evelyn.

Clandon Park ☆

At West Clandon, 3 m E Guildford on A247;
NT; tearoom; museum of Queen's Royal
Surrey Regiment; garden; *open:* Apr–end
Oct, Sat–Wed, Gd Fri l.30–5.30, BH Mon
11–5.30; tel: 0483 222482

This austere, red-brick block, with a pedimented, stone-faced bay standing out strongly white on the entrance front, was built in *c*.1730 for Thomas, 2nd Baron Onslow, member of a distinguished political family which produced three speakers of the House of Commons. Designed by Giacomo Leoni, Clandon is one of a very few English buildings by this Venetian architect. It is also one of those places that have been rescued and refurnished by the National Trust. Although owned by the 2nd Baron's descendants until 1956, Clandon's contents were largely sold off over the years, and most of the delicate inlaid furniture and porcelain now in the house was bequeathed by Mrs David Gubbay, who built up an outstanding collection in the interwar years. Be prepared for some museum-like interiors and a generally unlived-in atmosphere.

Visitors step straight into Leoni's grand marble hall, the high point of a tour which takes in some dozen rooms on two floors and a basement kitchen. Floored in marble, and with carved chimney-pieces by Michael Rysbrack to either side, this cool and lofty space rises to a fluid, unrestrained plaster ceiling by the stuccoists Artari and Bagutti. This Italian duo were at their most adventurous and daring at Clandon, producing a *tour-de-force* of foreshortening and perspective. Life-size figures balance on the cornice, their bare legs dangling free, the weight of the ceiling apparently on their shoulders.

No other interior – even the marble-floored saloon on the garden front – matches up to the hall, but Mrs Gubbay's collection of 17th- and 18th-century porcelain birds gives Clandon a distinctive character. Brightly plumaged in rich reds, ochres, greens and blues, these ducks, pheasants, parrots and cranes perch on mantelpieces and on the gilded rococo brackets that were bought specially for them. Also on show are capacious 18th-century walnut chairs, inlaid French and English pieces, such as a satinwood secretaire bookcase of *c*. 1775 decorated with marquetry baskets of flowers, and faded needlework carpets. Paintings by Zoffany, Dahl, Kneller, de Laszlo and others include some Onslow family portraits and Knyff's early 18th-century view of the old red-brick house, surrounded by formal gardens and a wooded park.

Hatchlands Park ☆

On N side of A246 Guildford–Leatherhead
road, just E of East Clandon; NT; teas;
gardens; *open:* Apr–end Oct, Tues, Wed,
Thurs, Sun and BH Mon, and Sats in Aug
2–5.30; tel: 0483 222482

Set in a peaceful 420-acre park, this mid-18th-century brick box seems much further from London than stockbroker Surrey. Designed by the obscure Stiff

Leadbetter, an Eton builder, for Admiral Edward Boscawen, who distinguished himself in campaigns against the French, Hatchlands is remarkable for its different floor levels, signalled on the outside by the way a two-storey façade on the west turns into three floors on the south. The visitor, though, sees only the ground floor, where some powerful sculptural chimneypieces and decorative plasterwork by the young Robert Adam, with much use of dolphins, mermaids, sea horses and other suitably nautical motifs, are allied to pictures and period furnishings introduced by Mr Alec Cobbe, the picture-restorer, painter and musician who now lives in the house. The high-ceilinged, panelled drawing-room and the adjoining red-walled saloon are hung with paintings two and three deep in the 18th-century fashion, among them works by Gainsborough and Rubens, self-portraits by John Opie and Angelica Kauffmann, a collection of religious Italian art, and a landscape or two, such as a red-roofed village in the wooded Arno valley by the Italophile François-Xavier Fabre.

More unusually, almost every room displays one or more of Alec Cobbe's early keyboard instruments, among them a square piano that is said to have been made for Marie Antoinette. Lucky visitors will hear Mr Cobbe demonstrating, and usually there is someone playing the concert grand in the domed music room added on by Sir Reginald Blomfield in 1903. Where the sound of music adds greatly to the atmosphere of the house, visitors may be less sure about Mr Cobbe's contributions to the decorations, in particular his vivid arabesques on a lime-green ground painted on the dining-room walls.

Loseley House ☆

2¹/₂ m SW Guildford, off B3000 or A3100; guided tours (c. 60 mins); teas; moatside garden and farm tours; open: end May–early Oct, Wed, Thurs, Fri, Sat and Aug BH Mon 2–5; tel: 0483 304440

This three-storey Elizabethan house, its gabled bays alternately advancing and retreating and chalk-mullioned windows standing out white against rough grey walls, looks north over parkland to a low downland ridge. Loseley was built between 1562 and 1568 by Sir William More, one of Elizabeth I's most trusted advisers. A long gallery wing has gone, and a brick and stone range on the back is a Victorian addition, but essentially the house is unchanged, and it is still lived in by Sir William's descendants. It is a popular venue for coach parties, and has a restaurant area to match, but the house has kept its integrity.

Visitors see some half-dozen rooms on two floors, all well preserved. The heart of the place, in every sense, is the portrait-hung great hall rising through two storeys, with a richly carved and galleried screen – perhaps made up of pieces from the demolished wing – at the east end, and *trompe l'oeil* panelling, said to have come from Henry VIII's Nonsuch palace, giving the illusion of arcades at the other. Colourful canvas panels hanging above the gallery, as gay and insubstantial as theatrical props, are also thought to have been painted for the King. A panelled library has Victorian overtones, but the drawing-room has a ribbed and pendanted ceiling that was gilded for a visit by James I and a superb chalk chimneypiece carved with complaining caryatids.

Fine 17th- and 18th-century furniture includes a collection of English and Continental cabinets, one inlaid with seaweed marquetry, another lacquered, a third with a rich assortment of woods making up an architectural fantasy. There is a show of Jacobean needlework in a trio of tapestry-hung bedrooms, and among the family portraits are an eerily lit shipwreck by Van de Velde the Younger, paintings of James I and his queen attributed to John de Critz, and an anonymous likeness of the boy king Edward VI. Modern religious works associated with the Loseley Christian Trust strike a discordant note, their banality pointed up by a 16th-century Flemish triptych from the demolished chapel.

Polesden Lacey ☆☆

5 m NW Dorking, off A246
Leatherhead–Guildford road; NT;
restaurant; garden; woodland walks; *open:*
Mar, Nov, Sat, Sun, 1.30–4.30, Apr–end
Oct, Wed–Sun 1.30–5.30, also open BH Mon
and preceding Sun 11–5.30; tel: 0372
458203

Polesden Lacey has to be imagined in its Edwardian heyday, filled with a glittering house party. Gatherings of royalty, statesmen, literary lions and the simply well-feathered were hosted by Mrs Ronald Greville, one of the most determined social climbers of her day, who used her father's brewery fortune to transform a modest Regency villa into the large country house that she needed as a base for her ambitions, filling it with fine paintings and furniture. Her creation is a low, architecturally undistinguished building set round a courtyard, with green shutters framing the windows and roughcast, yellow walls. It sits high on a ridge, with views over a pastoral valley to the woods of Ranmore Common on the opposite slope, the whole estate now a remarkable island of tranquillity along the suburbanized ribbon of the A246.

Inside, there is something of the atmosphere of a luxury hotel, perhaps because Mrs Greville called on Mewes and Davis, the architects of the Ritz, to remodel the house, but also because so much of the furniture seems ornamental rather than practical. Visitors see the formal, elegant rooms ranged along the south front, the most splendid of them the golden drawing-room, with long wall mirrors reflecting a glistening chandelier, carved and gilded panelling, and elegant 18th-century French furniture, such as a delicate heart-shaped dressing-table, and a little Louis XV writing desk. Cabinets of oriental, English and Continental porcelain include a Chinese version of a European, with bulging eyes, elongated ears and handkerchief at the ready.

The best of the paintings hang in less showy settings. Portraits by Lawrence, Raeburn, Reynolds and Jonathan Richardson are ranged round the dining-room, while Dutch cabinet paintings and early Italian works, among them an oval Perugino and an icon-like 14th-century triptych, line the cool, shuttered corridor giving on to the central courtyard. There are river and coastal scenes by Jan van Goyen and Salomon van Ruysdael, interiors by David Teniers the Younger, Pieter de Hoogh and Gerard Terborch, and some tiny early portraits, among them an old woman in a whimple and a fur-lined coat by the Master of St Severin.

The one comfortable interior is the L-shaped billiards room, with leather armchairs grouped round the fire. A display case here shows the Polesden Lacey visitors' book, some of Mrs Greville's French menus, and the record of a round of bridge, in which Edward VII partnered his mistress Mrs Keppel. Monogrammed fripperies that the king gave his hostess are on show in the drawing-room, among some Fabergé trinkets.

East Sussex

Alfriston Clergy House

By St Andrew's Church in Alfriston, 4 m NE Seaford; NT; use village car park; *open:* Apr–end Oct, daily, 11–6 (or sunset); tel: 0323 870001

The timber-framed, thatched cottage sandwiched between the River Cuckmere and the village green was built in 1350 for the parish priests and their resident housekeeper. Part was rebuilt in the 17th century, but the sparsely furnished rooms on show include the original Great Hall, its roof open to the rafters and the rough, uneven floor made of lumps of chalk sealed with sour milk.

Bateman's ☆☆

¹/₂ m S Burwash, signposted from A265 through village; NT; tearoom; garden; working mill; open: Apr–end Oct, Sat–Wed and Gd Fri 11–5.30; tel: 0435 882302

This attractive Jacobean house of yellowish sandstone is where the writer Rudyard Kipling lived from 1902 until his death in 1936, and where he produced some of his best work. It is an unpretentious place, with stone-mullioned windows, brick chimneys arranged in a massive central stack, creeper and wisteria covering the garden front, and with two oast houses for company.

The rooms are comfortably furnished, as the Kiplings had them, with some solid 17th-century pieces complementing the house, and rich oriental rugs and statuettes of eastern deities reflecting the writer's passion for India. Upstairs you can see Kipling's low-ceilinged, book-lined study. The long table at which he wrote, with a large Indian waste-paper basket to take his discarded drafts, is now unnaturally tidy, but the view – over the fields and red-tiled farm which Kipling also owned – is the same, and the sealskin-covered day bed where he threw himself down when inspiration left him is still here. Next door, there are displays of first editions, facsimile manuscripts, letters and some personal items, among them the rough necklace of stone, iron, glass and ivory which inspired 'How the alphabet was made' in the *Just So Stories*, the Bateman's visitors' book, and the writer's bookplate, dominated by a magnificently caparisoned elephant. John Collier's portrait on the stairs, painted in 1900, shows a fresh-faced man with a walrus moustache and disconcerting eyes, one blue, the other hazel, and in the modest bedroom is a pastel portrait of Kipling's fair-haired daughter Josephine, who died of pneumonia when only seven.

Bentley House ☆

7 m NE Lewes, off A22 and A26; tearoom; garden and wildfowl reserve; open: Apr–end Oct, daily, 12–5; tel: 0825 840573

Bentley's exaggeratedly long red-brick façade is a 20th-century creation, the result of Raymond Erith's 1960s extension of a cottagey, 16th-century farmhouse for Gerald Askew and his wife. Simply carrying on the original lines without a break, Erith sandwiched the original building between two high-ceilinged Palladian rooms, lighting them with the Venetian windows that stand out like punctuation marks at either end. The only vertical accents are two bands of flint dividing the old work from the new, and four prominent dormers adding a third storey to the central section.

Visitors walk the length of the ground floor. In the middle are the cosy, low-ceilinged rooms of the old farmhouse; at either end, furnished with flair and originality, are the show-pieces that make Bentley special. One is a marble-floored cross between a conservatory and a sitting-room, its egg-yellow walls hung with gouaches of wildfowl by the Sussex artist Philip Rickman, a scatter of giant oriental urns forming brilliant blue splashes, and four life-size cast-iron swans, from a Belgium balcony, supporting a virtuoso central table. The other, lined with leaf-green, 18th-century Chinese wallpaper, is more flamboyant, with a show of rococo mirrors and sconces, gilded and painted tables and chairs and a large chinoiserie birdcage. Where the constant references to birds are a reminder of Mr Askew's collection of wildfowl, horse paintings by Herring, Wootton and others recall the stud he once had here.

Brickwall House

East end of Northiam on B2088, 7 m NW Rye; topiary garden; guided tours (c. 20 mins); *open:* Apr–end Sept, Sat and BH Mon 2–5; tel: 0797 223329

A curving brick wall and lion-crowned gate piers flag this much altered 17th-century house, now a school, with its original frontage hidden behind black-and-white, mock-Tudor half-timbering added in the 19th century. Visitors are shown only the hall, drawing room and staircase. Apart from a few portraits of the Frewen family, whose house this was, and a fine William and Mary cabinet on barley-sugar legs, the main attraction is a couple of bold 17th-century plaster ceilings.

Charleston Farmhouse

Off A27 6 m E Lewes, between Firle and Selmeston, signposted from main road; *open:* Apr–end Oct, Wed, Thurs, Sat (guided tours), Suns, BH Mon (unguided), also Fri late July–end Aug 2–6; tel: 0323 811626

Vanessa Bell, Virginia Woolf's sister, moved into this unassuming 18th-century farmhouse tucked under the South Downs in 1916. It was originally seen only as a wartime let, where the Bells' friends, the painter Duncan Grant and the writer David Garnett, branded as conscientious objectors, could do farm work, but Vanessa, her art-critic husband Clive and Duncan Grant were to use the house for the rest of their lives. Here she and Grant were lovers, here their daughter Angelica was born in the last months of World War I, and here Vanessa died in 1961. Cold, unsympathetic interiors were brightened with richly painted walls and furniture and the guests flooded in, among them the economist Maynard Keynes, who stayed for weeks at a time, Lytton Strachey, who regaled the company with drafts of his *Eminent Victorians*, T. S. Eliot, the critic and painter Roger Fry, and the novelist E. M. Forster. Charleston is now the principal monument to the Bloomsbury group, its rooms still filled with their paintings, ceramics, textiles and furniture.

The rooms all have the same distinctive, almost childlike look, the few pieces of conventional furniture, like a marquetry table and a glass-fronted cabinet that once belonged to Thackeray, standing incongruously among the painted chairs and tables, the stencilled wallpaper and the unsophisticated friezes and murals. Colours are dove grey, dusky pink, apple green, russet or terracotta, a piece of jewel-like stained-glass inset in a bedroom door glowing unexpectedly scarlet. Pottery lampshades by Vanessa's son Quentin look like upturned colanders, Duncan's tile-topped tables are smudges of blue, green and russet, and his painted door and window panels include an india-rubber acrobat and, in what was once Vanessa's bedroom, a strangely elongated cock (to waken her) and a dog (to guard her while she sleeps). Paint disguises lack of comfort: bedrooms are unheated; faded rugs lie on bare boards.

The room where Vanessa died is downstairs, with French windows to the walled garden, a painted screen hiding a bath in the corner, and, over her desk, two portraits of her baby son Julian, from whose death in the Spanish Civil War she never recovered. Next door, in the capacious, cluttered studio built on in 1925, is the last portrait Duncan did of her, leaning forward with intense concentration as she works at her easel, grey hair caught back, a shoe slipping from her foot. They were very versatile, these two, the many examples of their art here including skilled copies of Impressionists and Old Masters. In every room, too, there are paintings by friends and associates, with some blob-like ballerinas by Sickert, a Matisse, and Renoir's plaster head of his seven-year-old son Coco in among them.

Firle Place ☆☆☆

5 m SE Lewes, off A27; guided tour (c. 60 mins) except on first Wed in month; tearoom; garden; *open:* May–end Sept, Wed, Thurs, Sun and BH Mon, also Easter Sun and Mon 2–5; tel: 0273 858335

Beneath the steep wooded slopes of the South Downs and the 700 ft Firle Beacon is this quirky, double-courtyard house of mottled limestone, its apparently Georgian façades just a dressing-up of a much older building. Despite a couple of grand touches, such as the Venetian window over the arch into the main courtyard, no architect seems to have been employed; hence the endearingly amateur touches, with a mass of dummy windows filling one side of the courtyard, and a cobbled join in the south-west corner.

Still lived in by the descendants of Sir John Gage, the Tudor builder, Firle is a family house, but also a show place. The guided tour, which does a complete circuit of the main courtyard, takes in only half a dozen rooms in all, but these are so rich it feels like a feast. The starting point is the stone-floored, tapestry-hung great hall, with the original hammer-beams hidden beneath a Georgian coved ceiling and Van Dyck's arresting portrait of the professional mercenary Count John of Nassau with his family on the end wall. Off the elegant staircase hall, with its sophisticated rococo plasterwork and a tiny Tudor doorway uncovered in one corner, elegant, low-ceilinged drawing-rooms sit one on top of the other along the south front. The lower, a white and gold Palladian room with two screens of fluted Ionic columns, is furnished with rare console tables and Chinese Chippendale chairs and hung with a fine show of 18th-century portraits, among them a dignified Gainsborough, David Martin's studies of General Thomas Gage, commander of the British forces in the American War of Independence, and his indiscreet, black-haired wife, and Reynolds' painting of the son of a Jewish financier, an academic gown trimmed with gold braid over his plum velvet suit. The upper is more artificial, marrying delicate French marquetry pieces and porcelain-filled Chippendale cabinets with a collection of largely Italian paintings. Here is Fra Bartolommeo's Holy Family, a florid Rubens head, a Puligo self-portrait, a pair of tiny, postcard-sized Guardis, and Moroni's astonishingly modern portrayal of a red-haired man.

The cherry on the icing is a yellow-walled, parquet-floored long gallery running the length of the east front, broad enough for dancing, and used to display some of the finest furniture: generous, gilded Venetian chairs, Louis XIV and Louis XV serpentine-fronted, marquetry commodes and a commanding Louis XVI rolltop desk. There is a show of apple green, rose pink and blue Sèvres, and a panoramic landscape by de Koninck and a rustic wine harvest by Teniers stand out from another flourish of family portraits, among them works by Reynolds and Lawrence, a charming Devis, and two Zoffanys, one showing the collector 3rd Earl Cowper, source of many of Firle's riches, in Italy, his hat raised as if to greet visitors.

Glynde Place ☆

4 m SE Lewes, off A27; tearoom; garden; *open:* Easter Sun and Mon, June–Sept, Wed, Thurs, 1st and last Sun of month, BHs 2.15–5.30; tel: 0273 858337

At the top of the village straggling up the hill is this unassuming Elizabethan courtyard house, its gabled façades of grey flint and stone warmed with patches of red brick, like darns on an old coat. A carefully orchestrated approach through the cupola-topped archway of the Georgian stable block and past brick gatepiers topped by vigorous wyverns keeps both the house and the panoramic view east hidden until the last moment.

Built in 1579, Glynde was substantially remodelled in the mid-18th century by the handsome Bishop of Durham. Referred to by George II as 'the beauty of holiness', and one of the most colourful of the long line who have inherited the estate since the 12th century, the bishop was responsible for turning the house round, to look east, and for the predominantly 18th-century flavour of the interior.

The tour takes in two floors of the entrance range, starting with the chilly, high-ceilinged, stone-floored hall, with its screens of wooden columns painted to look like marble. The most attractive room, a portrait-hung panelled gallery with a high coved ceiling, lies directly above. Despite some 18th-century alterations, and the capacious Georgian chairs, the flavour here is Jacobean, with two Lelys on an end wall, portraits by Cornelius Johnson in elaborately carved frames either side of the bishop's classical fireplace, and a Grinling Gibbons-style overmantel above. The little dining-room next door, with its Tudor floor of split pine, boasts Zoffany's portrait of the bishop's nephew, the 2nd Viscount Hampden, and an unusually attractive still-life by Snyders, a pile of luscious grapes and apricots, figs, raspberries and asparagus, with not a slaughtered deer to be seen.

On the way up, visitors use the grand, late 17th-century staircase added to the north side of the house, warmed by a fireplace on the half-landing and with copies of well-known paintings – notably a now-lost Caravaggio of some card players – inset in the panelling. The way down is by a warped Tudor stair. From several windows there are glimpses of the grassy central courtyard, with a projecting porch marking the original entrance, and there are a few family treasures, among them a contemporary illustrated account of the Armada, and a fragment of John of Gaunt's household accounts for 1381, written in a mix of Latin and French and with individuals grouped by status. Dress warmly to come here – this is one of the coldest houses in England.

Great Dixter ☆

'/₂ m N Northiam, off A28, signed from centre of village; guided tours (c. 35 mins); teas; garden; *open:* Apr–early Oct, Tues–Sun and BH Mon 2–5, also two weekends in Oct; tel: 0797 253160

Great Dixter is a piece of creative restoration. Surrounded by a beautiful garden, with oast houses and a barn used as backdrops to the planting, the house sits just below a shoulder of the Weald, with views south over wooded ridges. The west end, to one side of a drunken, two-storey porch, is a half-timbered, late medieval manor, with a great hall open to the roof and a two-storeyed cross range beyond. Left of the porch is a totally successful addition of 1910–14 by Sir Edwin Lutyens, a long, gabled, tile-hung façade with case-ment windows, massive brick chimney stacks, and a sweeping red-tiled roof that matches the pitch of the medieval structure. A re-erected timber-framed 16th-century yeoman's house brought from 8 miles away forms another wing on the south side.

This atmospheric hybrid was the work of Nathaniel Lloyd, who bought the derelict property in 1910. Inside, visitors are shown three rooms of the medieval wing. The cluttered hall, which is partly used as a shop, has imper-sonal displays of antique furniture and the Lloyd family's needlework, but the low-ceilinged parlour, smelling of a wood fire even in summer and with a clutter of hastily tidied books, and the solar above, lit by oriel windows at both ends, are much more evocative. A beam has been carved with the name of one John Harrison, who rented the house in Elizabethan times, and the solar, which is now a comfortable sitting-room, still has its original, 16th-cen-tury fireplace. Nathaniel's son Christopher, the gardening writer, now lives here.

Hammerwood Park ☆

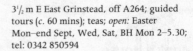

3½ m E East Grinstead, off A264; guided tours (c. 60 mins); teas; open: Easter Mon–end Sept, Wed, Sat, BH Mon 2–5.30; tel: 0342 850594

At the end of a rough and narrow lane, looking out to a green valley over the wreck of a terraced garden, is this sculptural Greek revival house, designed to be seen from a distant hilltop. One of only two surviving English works by Benjamin Latrobe, who emigrated to the infant USA, Hammerwood was built in the 1790s, with a severe, pilastered central block and low wings enfolding what look like tiny, porticoed Greek temples. Rabbit-heaved turf and cracked and crumbling stonework advertise the heroic task facing the present owner, who bought the house in 1982 and is single-handedly bringing it back from a ruinous state.

Visitors are swept along in the most informal and enthusiastic of guided tours, into one high-ceilinged cavernous room after another. Some have re-created plasterwork, a frieze reproducing the Elgin marbles rings the old squash court, now the tearoom, and the hall is frescoed with pleasing *trompe l'oeil* architectural murals, full of references to the house and its history. Ad hoc furnishings have been picked up in job lots, and there is a general air of make do and mend, but nowhere else will you find such ebullient dedication.

Michelham Priory ☆

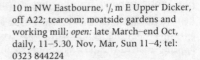

10 m NW Eastbourne, ½ m E Upper Dicker, off A22; tearoom; moatside gardens and working mill; open: late March–end Oct, daily, 11–5.30, Nov, Mar, Sun 11–4; tel: 0323 844224

A 14th-century gatehouse tower guards the only approach to the moated island that was once the site of an Augustinian priory. The medieval church is now only outlines in the grass, but ranges on the south and west sides of the cloister were absorbed in the picturesque house, with its walls of rough brown stone, tall chimneys and steep tiled roofs.

Sadly, except for those fascinated by architectural detective work, the interior is not up to the promise of the outside. The originally Elizabethan house, partly gutted by fire in 1927, has been massively restored, and the priory is no longer lived in. Now in the hands of the local archaeological society, it has the feel of a museum, with all exhibits conspicuously numbered, collections of musical instruments and samplers which have nothing to do with the house, and other interiors invaded by ghostly plain-chant and robed and tonsured dummies.

The priory comes through most strongly in a stone-vaulted undercroft, with a central pillar supporting an umbrella of stone, and elsewhere there are glimpses of trefoil-headed, medieval lights, delicate arches with sculpted capitals, and truncated tracery. Strangely, the Elizabethan house is more elusive, but two panelled and tapestry-hung rooms with original Tudor fireplaces show off sturdy 17th-century furniture, pewter and ironwork, and some lovely Turkish carpets.

Monk's House ☆

In Rodmell, on S side of lane leading to church; NT; garden; *open:* Apr–end Oct, Wed, Sat 2–5.30; tel: 0892 890651

This weatherboarded, cottagey house is where, from 1919, the novelist Virginia Woolf and her husband Leonard came to escape London, often walking over the fields to visit Virginia's sister Vanessa at *Charleston Farmhouse* just a few miles away.

And it is Charleston, not Virginia or Leonard, that dominates the small, low-ceilinged rooms, with their bare, tiled floors, painted furniture, and homespun pottery and fabrics. Virginia enlisted her sister's help in choosing furnishings, and bought tables, chairs and other pieces decorated by Vanessa and Duncan Grant, among them the tile-topped table and cane-backed chairs in the sitting-room, and the painted music cabinet. Vanessa's pictures are everywhere, and even the apple-green walls echo a colour used at the farmhouse.

Sadly, the books that once filled every corner, and which must have added so much atmosphere, were sold on Leonard's death, and the few here now have been bought by the National Trust. Still here, though, are the old-fashioned gramophone which the Woolfs listened to as they sat by the fire; the blue pottery bowl for the dogs' drinking water; and the tank in which Leonard nursed ailing fish from the garden ponds. And in the garden there is Virginia's writing hut, with its rough wooden desk and a big picture window looking east to the downs above Seaford. It was across these fields that she walked to drown herself in the River Ouse, weighing down her pockets with stones.

Arundel Castle ☆☆

In Arundel, 9 m W Worthing; tea garden; *open:* Apr–late Oct, Sun–Fri 11–5; tel: 0903 883136

Arundel Castle is best seen from a distance. For those who hurry past on the A27, it is a Camelot-like vision rising above the red-roofed town at its feet, a romantic assemblage of massive walls, rounded towers and square turrets, its battlemented roofline enhanced by a forest of chimneys. Close to, much of the charm disappears. All is too elephantine, too ham-fisted, too out of scale with the straggle of visitors who toil up from the entrance gate. And it is not what it seems. Despite the drawbridge, the remains of a medieval gateway, and the shell of a round Norman keep set high on a mound, this is no castle. Almost everything that you see was part of a grandiose and lengthy reconstruction in the 19th century, most of it to designs by the heavy-handed C. A. Buckler.

The main house frames three sides of a grassy quadrangle, once the bailey of the Norman castle. An extensive tour takes visitors through a sequence of high-ceilinged, vast and largely unwelcoming reception rooms in two of the ranges, a procession of bare stone walls, gothic arches, and huge baronial fire-places. There is an outstanding picture collection here, with portraits by Mytens, Van Dyck, Lely, Reynolds, Gainsborough, Lawrence, Millais and de Laszlo, and fine 18th-century furniture, but some paintings are difficult to see, particularly those in the vast, cathedral-like Great Hall, and the carefully controlled route means visitors cannot stroll down the portrait-hung long gallery but are forced to take a zig-zag course, darting in and out from the rooms on either side.

Arundel is the seat of the Fitzalan-Howards, Dukes of Norfolk and Earls of Arundel, whose ancestors have held the castle since Norman times. This great Roman Catholic family, headed by the country's premier duke, has always lived dangerously, paying with their lives for courtly intrigues and their staunchly held faith. Something of this history can be sensed at the castle. Here is Mytens' portrait of the ambitious and self-seeking 3rd Duke, who introduced his two most attractive nieces, Anne Boleyn and Catherine Howard, to Henry VIII's court, callously deserting the girls when their marriages to the king turned sour. Here, too, is a posthumous painting of the 3rd Duke's eldest son, the poet earl, executed on a trumped-up charge of treason at the end of Henry's reign. And a rosary of gold and enamel which Mary, Queen of Scots reputedly carried with her to the block recalls the impolitic 4th Duke, whose bid to marry the queen, seen as an attempt on the English throne, cost him his life.

These treasures often seem overwhelmed by their surroundings. The ele-gantly furnished dining-room, for example, has been created out of a former chapel, with a high ribbed vault and three slender gothic windows soaring over wine coolers by Paul de Lamerie, a boulle clock, and a set of mid-18th-century chairs covered in contemporary needlework, brought here, with much else, after the sale of the family's London house in 1938. The most successful and atmospheric interior is Buckler's private chapel, with slender columns of dark Purbeck marble against pale stone, graceful gothic arches, and a striped stone vault.

Danny

6 m N Brighton, via New Way Lane off B2116 between Hassocks and Hurstpierpoint, no advance signs; garden; *open:* May–Sept, Wed, Thurs 2–5; tel: none

At the foot of the whale-like hump of Wolstonbury Hill, looking out over a serene park, is this attractive house of warm red brick. The gabled, E-shaped entrance front is Elizabethan, with two huge stone-mullioned windows lighting what was the great hall, but round the corner is a handsome, sash-windowed façade of 1728, ornamented with brick and stone pilasters and with a parapet hiding dormers in the roof. Danny is now divided into flats and visitors see only a few public rooms, most of them substantially altered in Victorian times. There is some 16th-century panelling and an elegant, twisting Georgian staircase, while an oak refectory table in the former great hall is where Lloyd George conferred with his war cabinet when the house was rented for his use during the summer and autumn of 1918.

Goodwood ☆☆

3¹/₂ m NE Chichester, approached via A285, A286 or A27; teas when no evening function; country park; *open:* Easter Sun and Mon, then early May–late Sept, Sun, Mon 2–5, and Tues, Wed, Thurs in Aug (but closed event days); tel: 0243 774107

This strange, elongated house, like a section from an angular wheel, is the seat of the Dukes of Richmond, descendants of Charles II and the captivating French spy Louise de Kéroualle. Like *Euston Hall,* home of another bastard Stuart line, Goodwood is primarily a splendid picture gallery, with a sequence of elegant, restrained interiors that are mostly bare-floored and sparsely furnished.

Centre of a 12,000-acre estate on the Sussex Downs, and approached through well-wooded parkland, the house is the result of a dream that failed. The 3rd Duke commissioned James Wyatt in 1790 to build a two-storeyed, hollow octagon, with domed turrets at each corner, but the money ran out when only three segments were finished. The walls, of rough flint and stone, are curiously homely for such a grand project, and a wing of the original Jacobean house, remodelled by Sir William Chambers, projects behind like a broken spoke. A circular lily pond in the triangular garden courtyard marks what would have been the centre of this enormous mansion.

The 3rd Duke was Ambassador to Louis XV, and seems to have spent his time in Paris acquiring furnishings. Many pieces were destroyed in a fire in 1946, but the finest of what survives, an array of Louis XV chairs, boulle mantel clocks and marquetry commodes, is gathered in the Yellow Drawing-Room. An apse-like alcove here and the walls of the adjoining turret are lined with cases of 18th-century Sèvres, some of it the familiar apple green, some the very rare rose pompadour, and some midnight blue picked out in gold.

The paintings are everywhere. As at Euston Hall, there is a Lely of Charles II, but here he hangs next to a Kneller of Louise. The young 1st Duke stares out of a canvas by Wissing, and several Van Dycks are headed by a relaxed portrait of Charles I with Henrietta and their two eldest children. Goodwood also boasts Sir Thomas Lawrence's favourite painting, of the 5th Duchess, works by Reynolds and Romney, and a Lely of La Belle Stewart, Duchess of Richmond, the revealing costume in which she appears said to have been copied for the figure of Britannia on the coinage.

The 2nd Duke's Canalettos are tucked away behind a screen of pillars in the main hall. Two are Venetian scenes, the others panoramic views over London painted from the windows of the duke's town house that were specially commissioned for Goodwood. The sporting pictures, too, are linked to the estate. Wootton's hunters were painted at Goodwood in the 1740s, and the three works by Stubbs were executed for the 3rd Duke, who started the horse-racing for which the house is now best known.

Newtimber Place ☆

7 m N Brighton off A281 between Poynings and Pyecombe, no advance signs; garden; guided tours; open: May–Aug, Thurs, 2–5; tel: 0273 833104

Under the hump of the South Downs, hidden away at the end of a narrow lane, is this enchanting moated manor dating from the 16th and 17th centuries. The flint and brick frontage with a central porch and dormers in the hipped roof is work of 1681 and there is some Tudor panelling and a carved Elizabethan fireplace to be seen, but the few beautifully furnished, lived-in interiors shown to visitors largely reflect later alterations. Most striking is the hall, where walls and doors are covered with 18th-century murals in sepia, black and white imitating the decoration on Greek and Etruscan vases. Possibly by Biagio Rebecca, or J. F. Rigaud, these sombre reliefs contrast with much softer painted panels of the same period in the dining-room. Visitors also see a south-facing drawing-room, with a Charles II cabinet of tortoiseshell and silver, and the sunny library, with a big bay jettied out over the moat.

Parham ☆☆

4 m SE Pulborough, off A283 (signposted off A24 and A29); audio tours; tearoom; garden; open: Easter–first Sun in Oct, Sun, Wed, Thurs, BH Mon, 2–6; tel: 0903 742021

Set in an extensive deer park beneath the grassy hump of the South Downs is this tall, atmospheric Elizabethan house of rough local stone, built to a typical E plan. The show front, with two gabled wings coming forward either side of a central porch and huge, stone-mullioned windows, looks towards the Downs, over the little church which marks the site of old Parham village. The first view, though, is of the gaunt east front, from where a long wall running north embraces both the 18th-century service court and the walled garden beyond, giving the impression Parham is much larger than it is. A circular 18th-century dovecote stands just outside the walls, and the remains of a water tower seem to guard the whole complex.

Inside, much remains from the 16th century, but much, too, has been altered. A sale in 1922 largely disposed of the original contents, and the house was extensively restored, with recreations of Jacobean plasterwork, and sympathetically refurnished in the 1930s by Clive Pearson. There is an outstanding collection of 16th- and 17th-century portraits, much early furniture, oriental carpets, and an abundance of fine needlework, from Elizabethan bed hangings and Jacobean pictorial panels to an exquisite quilted cot coverlet of 1705.

Visitors see about a dozen rooms on three floors, working their way slowly upward through the house. The heart of the place is still the lofty great hall, lit by a wall of glass on the south front. The great fireplace, the silvery oak panelling and the Renaissance screen with mullioned windows opening on to a former steward's room above are all original; the furniture, including a bulbous-legged central table, is in period; while the array of portraits includes works by Antonio Mor and Mytens and Robert Peake's intriguing painting of Prince Henry, James I's ill-fated elder son, with opportunity, symbolized by a naked old man, at his back. Similarly striking is the light and airy, 160 ft long gallery running the length of the third floor, with splayed window bays on

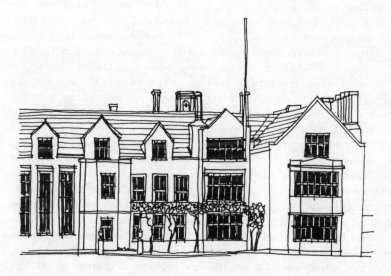

both sides as well as each end, silvery panelling, and leafy foliage painted by Oliver Messel in the 1930s on the barrel ceiling. In between, some rooms are Elizabethan recreations, others have no period feel, while the white and gold saloon is pure 18th-century, its furnishings including several Sheraton pieces and a couple of ornate French clocks.

Throughout the house, paintings and furniture are skilfully grouped. In one room is an array of hard-faced ladies by Lely, Kneller and Dahl; in another are softer portraits by Reynolds and Romney; and on the stairs is a splendid Gainsborough, of a scarlet-suited major, and a tiny Devis, his sitter reduced to mannekin proportions. In among the portraits are one of Claude's Italianate landscapes, views of 18th-century London by William James, a Samuel Scott seascape and Stubbs's enchanting painting of a kangaroo, based on a skin brought back by Captain Cook and the first likeness of the animal seen in Europe.

Petworth House ☆☆☆

In centre of Petworth (A272/A283), 5½ m E Midhurst; NT; tearoom; pleasure grounds and park; *open:* April–end Oct, Tues–Thurs, Sat, Sun (but open Good Fri, BH Mon, closed Tues following) 1–5.30; extra rooms shown Tues–Thurs; tel: 0798 42207

There is nothing homely or domestic about Petworth. More art gallery than house, it offers an important collection of paintings and sculpture arranged in a sequence of high-ceilinged, sparsely furnished rooms.

The house itself is something of an oddity. For a start, it is crammed close against Petworth town, right on the edge of the huge landscape park which rolls away westwards. Then, despite its size and the status of its owners, only one front has anything showy about it. The east side, by which visitors enter, is a roughly built hotchpotch supported by huge buttresses. The principal frontage, an assured, 320 ft William and Mary façade, is towards the park. This piece of proud display was the work of the arrogant Charles Seymour, 6th Duke of Somerset, who between 1688 and 1693 remodelled the ancient manor of the Percy family inherited by his wife. Of what visitors see, only the chapel, lined with 13th-century window arcades, dates from this earlier house, and the 6th Duke's decorative schemes have largely disappeared under late 18th- and early-19th-century alterations for his descendants, Charles and George Wyndham, the 2nd and 3rd Earls of Egremont. Just two important interiors of the Proud Duke's time survive: the baroque Marble Hall, with the bull and unicorn of the Seymour crest crouched over the fireplaces at either end, and the painted staircase, decorated with cloud-borne cherubs and half-clothed deities by Louis Laguerre. The Duke also commissioned the fluid limewood carvings by Grinling Gibbons and the talented local craftsman John Selden which encrust one of the rooms on the west front, but these virtuoso pieces, with naturalistic crabs, lobsters, flowers and musical instruments erupting from darker panelling behind, were all re-arranged by the 3rd Earl.

Apart from these schemes, and an exceptional assemblage of rococo wall mirrors, Petworth is primarily notable for the wide-ranging collection of paintings and sculpture acquired by the 2nd and 3rd Earls and by their Jacobean forbears, the 9th and 10th Earls of Northumberland. When the family was here, pictures were arranged as the fancy took them, but the National Trust, initially with advice from Sir Anthony Blunt, have grouped like with like, giving each room a coherent theme. 16th- and 17th-century Dutch canvases are concentrated in the Somerset Room, among them a sinister Van Ruisdael landscape, jewel-like religious paintings on copper by Adam Elsheimer, and works by David Teniers the Younger, Aelbert Cuyp and Hobbema. There are several Van Dycks, among them paintings of the colourful Sir Robert Shirley, dressed as an eastern potentate, and his exotic Circassian wife, and a whole room devoted to Kneller's and Michael Dahl's likenesses of the disdainful ladies of the court of Queen Anne, several of them apparently wearing the same dress. A memorable Titian, of a fair-haired, sharp-nosed character in a black hat, is put in among them, as if to show up the later pictures for what they are.

This inappropriately named Beauty Room is part of the long enfilade down the west front, with the climax of the tour coming at the north end. Through a long gallery, where Gibbons' and Selden's limewood swags frame portraits by Joshua Reynolds, Lely and others, is a bare-floored room entirely devoted to the works which Turner painted for the 3rd Earl, his patron for some thirty years. A constant visitor to Petworth in the 1830s, when an old library with a strong north-east light was fitted up as his studio, Turner recorded the park, with deer drinking from the lake, in some of his most luminous, elegiac works. Beyond is the 3rd Earl's sculpture gallery, where antique marbles collected by his father are displayed with pieces by 19th-century English sculptors, the most striking of them John Flaxman's powerful St Michael and Satan. Roman portrait busts of the 1st and 2nd centuries AD are lined up along the walls, with works by contemporary English artists acquired by the 3rd Earl hung two and three deep above them. This gallery is one of very few such collections to have survived intact.

St Mary's House ☆

In village of Bramber, 10 m NW Brighton, off A283; teas; small garden; guided tours (c. 50 mins); *open:* Easter Sun–late Sept, Sun, Thurs, BH Mon, and Mon in July, Aug, Sept 2–6; tel: 0903 816205

End on to the village street, with one corner sticking out into the traffic, is a picturesque, black and white, half-timbered house, with the upper floor jettied over the lower and crooked small-paned casements. The surviving wing of a medieval courtyard building, St Mary's once housed the warden of the old bridge across the River Adur, now just a trickle down the road but then a broad tidal inlet and major gateway to southern England. A lively tour by the present owner takes in a series of intimate, panelled rooms, one of them painted with early 17th-century *trompe l'oeil* arcading framing tiny land-scapes, another with a marquetry overmantel that was probably taken off a four-poster. There are connections with Elizabeth I and Charles II, and the tour ends in the barn-like music room added on in the 19th century, where the fireplaces are canopied Venetian tombs.

Standen ☆

2 m S East Grinstead, signposted from B2110; NT; teas; garden and woodland walk; *open:* Apr–end Oct, Wed–Sun and BH Mon 1.30–5.30; tel: 0342 323029

Although built in 1892–4, Standen is the antithesis of a stuffy Victorian house. A country retreat designed by Philip Webb, friend and associate of William Morris, for the family of a prosperous London solicitor, it is an unpretentious, picturesque blend of local brick and stone, with tall chimneys rising from steeply pitched, red-tiled roofs, a gabled and tile-hung frontage on to the garden, and a mix of sashes and leaded casements. Inside, light, airy rooms with glorious views over the Medway valley, some lined with painted deal panelling, others hung with Morris wallpapers and fabrics in restful greens and blues, are filled with Webb's practical furniture. Richly coloured carpets came from Morris's company, there is wine-red William de Morgan pottery, and metalwork made for the house includes a copper log box, brass finger plates and delicate light fittings, those in the L-shaped drawing-room decorated with a sunflower motif that reappears on the wallpaper and the cheeks of the fireplace.

A sunny, plant-filled conservatory is a kind of garden sitting-room, and upstairs are a series of chaste bedrooms, with white counterpanes on brass beds and a suite of furniture with silver handles. William Nicholson's por-traits of the Beales, for whom Standen was built, are not original, and neither is much else that is here, but the house is a period piece.

Stansted Park

Rowlands Castle, 8 m S Petersfield, follow signs to house from E end of village (4 m by road, 2 on foot); tearoom; walled garden and grounds; *open:* Easter Sun, Mon, May–end Sept, Sun, Mon, Tues 2–5.30; tel: 0705 412265

Alas, the late 17th-century house which once looked west down the magnifi-cent 2-mile beech avenue leading to the village was burnt to the ground in 1900; the undistinguished red-brick replacement in a stolid William and Mary style was built by A. C. Blomfield in 1903, with later alterations by H. S. Goodhart-Rendel. The few ground-floor rooms shown are pleasant enough but unremarkable, with a mix of furnishings and paintings. Most welcoming is the golden-walled music room, with its capacious Queen Anne walnut chairs and modern family portraits, and the finest object in the house, a Louis XV desk of inlaid kingwood, is in the cluttered blue drawing-room next door.

There are portraits by Lawrence, Angelica Kauffmann and Hoppner, and several pieces of Irish Chippendale recall the Kilkenny origins of the Earl of Bessborough, whose house this now is. Better than the house is the little chapel by the walled garden, with a Tudor brick porch and a richly decorated sanctuary, part of Goodhart-Rendel's work of the 1920s. Walk from the village if you can: the unmade-up drive is rough indeed.

Wiltshire

Bowood House ☆

2¹/₂ m W Calne, off A4 Chippenham road, 8 m S M4, Junction 17; restaurant; park and rhododendron walks, *open:* Apr–end Oct, daily, inc BHs, 11–6; tel: 0249 812102

A ten-minute walk through extensive landscaped grounds leads to a long conservatory looking south over Italianate terraces to a lake-filled valley. This giant greenhouse, designed by Robert Adam in the 1760s but remodelled since, is the principal room on show, the orange and lemon trees which once stood here now replaced by pedestalled busts and paintings. Elsewhere, apart from a box of a chapel designed by Cockerell in 1821 and the classically inspired library decorated in tones of acid green and brown, the visitor is treated to a series of purpose-made exhibition rooms created out of what were stables and grooms' quarters. These museum-like settings display what remains of the collections acquired by the 1st and 3rd Marquesses of Lansdowne, father and son. At the death of the 1st Marquess, in 1805, almost everything had to be sold to pay his debts, and further sales this century have again depleted what is here. There is still plenty to engage anyone interested in art and sculpture, but it is vital to arm yourself with the most recent picture list, as many works are not labelled or not where they once were.

Sculpture is concentrated in Adam's orangery and the adjoining, tapestry-hung gallery, where the family once kept a private zoo (the 18th-century philosopher Jeremy Bentham records stroking a leopard here). Antique pieces include a bull-necked bust of the debauched 1st-century Emperor Vitellius, favourite of Caligula, and a poised discus-thrower, made in *c.* AD 50 as a copy of a much older original, but most pieces are 19th-century, with examples of the work of Sir Richard Westmacott, William Theed and Thorwaldsen. The paintings are a mixed bag. The 3rd Marquess's patronage of contemporary artists led to the romanticized, highly finished Italianate scenes by Clarkson Stanfield and Eastlake and Callcott's view of the pool of London which dominate the conservatory, overshadowing a group of 16th- and 17th-century Italian works, such as a portrait of Baldassare Castiglione. The same policy resulted in an extensive collection of English watercolours, enlarged by the present Earl, which includes work by Turner, Lear, Cox, Nash, Varley, Roberts and Buckler, and drawings and sketches by Richard Parkes Bonington.

These subtle works are curiously grouped with a showy display of glittering early-19th-century jewellery acquired by the 4th Marchioness's grandfather during the Napoleonic wars, and with cases of ornate silver and inlaid ivory furniture dating from the 5th Lord's stint as Viceroy of India in 1888–94. You can also see the Albanian peasant costume once sported by Lord Byron and the little room where Dr Joseph Priestley, engaged as a tutor, discovered oxygen in 1774.

The great house was demolished in 1955–6. Only the two service courtyards built by Henry Keene in the mid-18th century remain, one end now converted into a substantial residence for the present Lord Lansdowne.

Charlton Park

1½ m NE Malmesbury, via signed entrance on A429 only; *open:* May–end Oct, Mon, Thurs 2–4; tel: none

The west front of the Earl of Suffolk's prodigy Jacobean house beckons visitors onwards in a show of stone-mullioned windows, finialled gables and ogee-capped angle turrets, the whole topped off with an exuberant strapwork parapet that positively shouts across the park. Substantially remodelled in the 1770s by Matthew Brettingham the Younger, who roofed in a central courtyard to form a huge top-lit hall, the house is now divided into flats, and the hall and the east-facing saloon are all that visitors see. The saloon, with delicate plasterwork on walls and ceiling, is pretty enough, but the hall, freshly painted in peppermint green and white, is breathtaking – a vast marble-floored space rising to an oval dome, with galleried landings carried on fluted classical columns, apsidal ends, and a restrained embellishment of plasterwork medallions and trophies.

Corsham Court ☆☆

In Corsham, signposted from A4 Bath–Chippenham road; garden; *open:* Jan–end Nov, daily, except Mon and Fri, 2–4.30 (6 Easter–Sept, when also open Fri and BH Mon); tel: 0249 712214

In contrast to the lovely, stone-built village in which it sits, Corsham Court, home of the 6th Lord Methuen, is not a beautiful building. But the rather bleak and forbidding exterior conceals rich state rooms and an outstanding collection of art and furniture. The house dates from 1582, but has been so much altered that only the E-shaped entrance front, with its gables, projecting wings and two-storey porch, has a 16th-century flavour. Mostly, Corsham reflects remodelling in the 1840s by the inferior Thomas Bellamy, who gave the place its pinnacled 'Jacobean' north front, its grandiose hall and staircase, and long, arcaded corridors. Only 40 years earlier, John Nash had created one of his most flamboyant exercises in Strawberry Hill gothick here, but his work was so unsound it had to be destroyed and only some castellations and a few other details remain.

The visitor tour is largely concentrated on the four rooms making up the 18th-century state apartments, created by Capability Brown for the clothier Mr Paul Methuen shortly after he bought the house in 1745. Here, the outstanding art collection Mr Methuen inherited from his cousin, the diplomat Sir Paul Methuen, is blended with fine paintings and other pieces brought to Corsham by marriage in 1844. The accent is on Italian and Flemish works, and on specially commissioned furniture by Robert Adam, Chippendale, and the similarly outstanding John Cobb. From Bellamy's gloomy, stone-floored corridors, you walk straight into a lush, crimson-walled, 72 ft gallery, with plasterwork by Thomas Stocking of Bristol on the high coved ceiling. This is the grandest of the interiors, with extravagantly crested Adam mirrors between the windows, gilded rococo girandoles, Chippendale settees and armchairs upholstered in crimson silk damask set round the walls, and a sculptural marble fireplace by Scheemakers. Paintings hang two and three deep, with altarpieces by Tintoretto and Veronese, landscapes by Salvator Rosa, a William Dobson portrait and other works arranged around a few huge canvases dominating the room, notably Van Dyck's restless *The Betrayal of Christ*.

The apartments that follow are smaller, but similarly full of treasures. In one are three Italian *pietra-dura* cabinets, an inlaid commode and matching torchères by John Cobb, and two contrasting annunciations, the first, richly coloured and set against a Tuscan landscape, by Filippo Lippi, the second, sparser, more focused, and half a century or so later, by Francesco Granacci. The octagon room is devoted to small cabinet paintings, among them a still-life by Brueghel the elder, a tiny Claude landscape, Francken's *Death and the Miser*, with a jaunty skeleton playing the violin to a frightened old man, and a portrait of a weary, aged, Elizabeth I, while Bellamy's bleak dining-room down the corridor is the setting for some family portraits by Romney and Reynolds and for a gothick fireplace and sideboard by Nash.

Great Chalfield Manor

2¹/₂ m NE Bradford on Avon, S of road from Broughton Gifford to Atworth, N of B3107; NT; garden; *open:* Apr–end Oct, Tues–Thurs, guided tours (*c.* 35 mins) at 12.15, 2.15, 3, 3.45 and 4.30; tel: 0985 847777 (regional office)

Across a rush-fringed moat at the end of a long approach is an enchanting ensemble of honey-coloured walls and licheny, stone-tiled roofs set round a gravelled court. Facing the road is the north front of Thomas Tropnell's manor of 1465–80, with a buttressed great hall range sandwiched between gabled bays. Two delicious oriel windows – one semicircular, the other octagonal – light first-floor rooms, engaging griffons and other heraldic figures perch on the gables, and a two-storey porch opens into the screens passage leading across the house. A tiny church topped with Tropnell's crocketed spire and belfry faces across the court to a long Tudor west range, smothered in climbers, and with an ancient gatehouse at the north end.

Left half-ruined at the end of the 19th century, Great Chalfield was fully restored for Robert Fuller, including some rebuilding in period style, in 1905–12. The manor is still the Fuller family home, and the few interiors shown are well-furnished and lived-in. The lofty, tapestry-hung hall, filled with a mix of old oak pieces and comfortable sofas, has a copy of the 15th-century oak screen, and an original but much mutilated timber roof. Staircases at either end lead to the two oriel rooms, one a bedroom with a Tudor arch-baced roof and some ancient stained glass, the other a sitting-room, with chambers off where hidden onlookers could watch proceedings in the hall through three intriguing carved stone masks.

Hamptworth Lodge

10 m SE Salisbury, on road from Redlynch to Landford between A36 and A338; garden; *open:* Mar–late April, daily, except Suns, guided tours at 2.30 and 3.45; tel: 0794 390215

The owner's disembodied, tape-recorded voice guides visitors round this bizarre reproduction of a Jacobean manor, built in 1910–12 for his grandfather, Henry Charles Moffatt, by Sir Guy Dawber. Picturesque façades are a mix of brick and half-timbering, with jutting gables, carved bargeboards, moulded brick chimneys, and leaded casements. Inside, rooms panelled with oak from the estate and decorated with Jacobean-style plasterwork ceilings, one a barrel arch, are filled with intricately inlaid and beautifully carved furniture. Some of the pieces are Tudor and Jacobean, but many have been made by Henry Charles Moffatt himself, in oak, cherry, chestnut and other hardwoods, and almost every surface shows off one or more tiny chairs, chests, and other apprentice pieces. In the great hall, open to a timber roof in the traditional way but unconventionally placed on a corner of the house, is a 'Jacobean' stone fireplace carved with strapwork and obelisks, and one end is filled with Moffatt's decorative case for a massive organ.

Lacock Abbey ☆☆☆

In Lacock village, 3 m S Chippenham, just E A350; NT; museum of photography; garden; *open:* Apr–end Oct, daily, except Tues and Gd Fri, 1–5.30; tel: 0249 730227

Attached to one of the most carefully preserved villages in England, with not a single television aerial to mar the stone-tiled roofs, Lacock Abbey has a similarly serene, other-worldly atmosphere. Set in water meadows by the River Avon, with placidly chewing cows beyond the ha-ha, this sprawling, double-courtyard house was created, from 1539, out of the Augustinian nunnery that had flourished here for 300 years. There is nothing very special about the furnishings and paintings, but the building itself, developed by the high-flying Tudor courtier Sir William Sharington, whose political intriguing and dabbling in debased coinage nearly cost him his life, is unique. Sharington adapted rather than building anew, creating his living quarters out of the former nuns' dormitory, refectory and other ranges above the cloister walks. Only the church was totally destroyed, although its north wall now forms the south façade of the house.

Visitors make two tours here: the first takes them round the house; the second, which should really be done first, involves a rather colder circuit of the cloister garth. Opening off this grassy square are the vaulted chapter house and warming room, and three sides of the court are framed by the original cloister walks, with carved bosses pinning the slender ribs of the vaulting.

Some medieval features – corbels that once supported the refectory roof and a section of monastic floor – survive inside the house too, but here other influences predominate. A circuit of all four ranges takes in three corridor-like galleries, and a floor of the tall octagonal tower on the south-west corner of the house that is Sharington's most individual addition to the abbey. Here, a skewed passage leads to a high-ceilinged, vaulted chamber designed as a strong room, its width – only 9 ft across – almost bridged by a carved stone table. Supported on four grinning satyrs and with the scorpions of the Sharington crest crawling round the base, this virtuoso piece was commissioned from the exceptional John Chapman, who also supplied the refined Renaissance fireplace in one of the galleries. Georgian alterations account for the sash-windowed blue parlour and the barn-like, pea-green dining-room, and in 1754–5 the gentleman-architect Sanderson Miller was commissioned by Sir William's descendant, John Ivory Talbot, to remodel the hall into a gothick fantasy, with baroque terracotta statues striking improbable attitudes from ornate canopied niches in every wall, like a cast of ham actors practising their parts.

Littlecote ☆

2 m NW Hungerford, off B4192, signed from M4 Junction 14; restaurant; garden and grounds, with remains of Roman villa; many other attractions; *open:* Apr–end Sept, daily, 10.30–5; tel: 0488 684000

There is nothing little about Littlecote. Sheltered in the pastoral valley of the Kennet is an immense, many-gabled house, with a long and largely flint-built medieval and Tudor frontage set back to back with a symmetrical, E-shaped Elizabethan range in rosy brick. The stone-mullioned windows are pleasingly varied, tall Tudor chimneys rise from the stone-tiled roof, and at the back walled and hedged gardens slope down to the river. Brasher, redder brickwork betrays an early 19th-century addition in period style.

Once, this must have been a magical place. In the hands of the present owner, though, the house is just one facet of a highly commercial venture, its tone set by the gibbet beside the drive. Some of the original contents are still here, but little is explained in the woefully inadequate guidebook, and dummies in Jacobean costume and inappropriate fitted carpets do little for the atmosphere.

Visitors are shown rooms of all periods in a tour that starts in the Elizabethan hall, takes in a 19th-century drawing-room hung with hand-painted Chinese wallpaper and the tobacco-tinged Regency library, and ends in the medieval wing. The lofty, oak-panelled hall still has its long refectory table and 17th-century court cupboards and is still hung with the private armoury – yellow-leather buff-coats, glistening breastplates and helmets and an array of muskets – with which the Littlecote contingent was fitted out during the Civil War. At the back of the house, with five great windows looking onto the gardens, is a 110 ft long gallery, now unfurnished but still portrait-hung and with a deep plaster frieze, and the warren of low-ceilinged rooms in the oldest part of the house includes a fine brick-floored, panelled parlour, a haunted bedroom, and a little painted room.

Best of all, and miraculously well preserved, is the Cromwellian chapel created out of the buttressed medieval hall. Open to the roof and lit by windows on both sides, this austere room has all its original fittings, with a tall, canopied pulpit in the place of the altar, balustraded galleries carried on slender columns above the narrow, candlelit pews, and a skeletal screen of slender turned posts. And it is worth wandering along the river to the excavated Roman villa, with its restored 4th-century mosaic floor.

Longleat ☆☆

4 m SW Warminster, off A362; guided tours in winter months and early in day (*c.* 90 mins); restaurant; garden and park; many other attractions; *open:* all year, daily (except Christmas Day), 10–6 (4 in winter); tel: 0985 844400

Although Longleat and its safari park are now a major money-making business, the commercial attractions have not been allowed to mar the first view of this Elizabethan prodigy house. Suddenly, the woodland hemming in the drive opens out and the ground falls steeply away to reveal a square stone palace in the valley below, its symmetrical, three-storey façades stained white and yellow with lichen. All around stretches Capability Brown's serene landscape park, with mature beech trees planted like a wall on the crest of the hill and a stream widening to a lake below the house. One of the earliest Renaissance buildings in England, Longleat is an individual blend of classical and gothic, with a rhythmical parade of enormous mullioned windows combined with chimneys disguised as columns, pilasters and medallion heads of Roman emperors. And on the roof, most clearly seen from the shoulder of the valley, are seven pepperpot turrets, little pavilions where the Elizabethan company would wander up after dinner to savour the sunset over another glass of wine.

Built and rebuilt by Sir John Thynne, with the aid of Robert Smythson, architect of *Hardwick*, and the Frenchman Allan Maynard, Longleat was finally completed in 1580, the year of its perfectionist creator's death. The façades are still essentially 16th century, but the interior is another story. Apart from the great hall, with its Tudor hammerbeam roof and sculpted stone fireplace, all that you see is 19th century, the result of remodelling by Sir Jeffry Wyatville between 1806 and 1820 and of J. D. Crace's redecoration from 1874 for Sir John's descendant, the 4th Marquess of Bath. No expense was spared in the creation of showy Italianate interiors, with richly painted and gilded ceilings copied from those Crace had seen in Genoa, Venice and Parma and extravagant hangings – 17th-century crimson velvet from a Genoese church, or tooled Spanish leather from Cordoba – adding a suitably exotic touch. There are doorcases of marble and alabaster, inlaid shutters, carved marble fireplaces and much ornate, formal furniture, including 17th-century Japanese cabinets embossed with silver, Boulle pieces inlaid with tortoiseshell and brass, a desk that once belonged to Talleyrand, and Flemish cabinets of carved ebony. Among the few English pieces is an uncompromisingly loud table made by John Makepeace, of *Parnham House*.

Visitors see a succession of these formal, lush interiors, among them the portrait-hung, brown and black state dining-room, with 16th-century Venetian paintings incorporated in the ceiling; the tapestry-hung, 90 ft saloon, made out of the Elizabethan long gallery; and the state drawing-room, designed to show the 4th Marquess's collection of religious Italian art, including works by Titian and Tintoretto. The paintings here and elsewhere, though, are not well displayed and only a very few are referred to in the skeletal guidebook. Wootton's hunting scenes are a feature of the Great Hall, and family portraits stretching back to Tudor times include a lovely G. F. Watts of the 4th Marchioness, a Sargent charcoal drawing of the 5th Marchioness, and a discordant Graham Sutherland of the 6th Marquess. One wall is thickly hung with Dutch cabinet paintings, placed here, so we are told, to give the unconventional 7th Marquess more room for the murals with which he is decorating his wing of the house, and which are on show.

Lydiard Park

5 m W Swindon, just off M4, junction 16; refreshments in park; *open:* all year, weekdays 10–1, 2–5.30, Sun 2–5.30 (closes at 4 Nov–Feb and closed Good Fri, Dec 25, 26); tel: 0793 770401

All that remains of the once extensive estate of the St John family is this chaste 18th-century house faced in Bath stone, with stumpy corner towers like those at *Wilton*, and some 140 acres of landscaped grounds, now a popular country park. Its contents dispersed in sales and its fabric decayed and rotting, Lydiard Park was only saved from almost certain demolition by the local council, who turned much of the mansion into a management training centre, but restored and refurnished the 18th- and 19th-century state rooms looking on to the park. The china and silver on show, including a dessert service painted with wild flowers, are original to the house, as is some of the furniture, and there are many family portraits, but the rooms feel like museum pieces. The greatest treasure, a relic of an earlier house, is an early 17th-century window painted in glowing, translucent colours by the Netherlandish artist Abraham van Linge, whose work also adorns the medieval and Jacobean church next to the house.

Newhouse ☆

Redlynch, 9 m S Salisbury, 2^1/$_2$ m SW Whiteparish, off B3080; teas; *open:* Aug, daily, except Sun, 2–5.30; tel: 0725 20055

Unkempt surroundings and crumbling, cupola-topped stables add to the charm of this architecturally exceptional house. Built some time before 1619 as a hunting lodge, it is a tall, many-gabled hexagon of weathered red brick, with three faces lengthened to form a Y. Low castellated wings added on in 1742 give the impression the house has flung wide its arms in welcome. Inside, are modest, lived-in, panelled rooms, an 18th-century staircase, and one grand, unfurnished, Georgian-style drawing-room. Nelsonian relics reflect the family's descent from the admiral's younger sister.

Pythouse

4^1/$_2$ m NE Shaftesbury, off Semley-Tisbury road; grounds; *open:* May–Sept, Wed, Thurs 2–5; tel: none

Set in a natural amphitheatre in the Wiltshire Downs, with a wooded ridge rising steeply behind and an enviable view across an unspoilt valley, is a stately Palladian house. Built by the then owner in the late 18th century to his own designs, the front, with its dignified portico, is conventional enough, but the sides have unusual recessed loggias rising the height of the building and the whole thing is set off by a delicious, gaily-finialled orangery to one side. The house is now divided into flats and visitors see only a couple of high-ceilinged reception rooms and the intriguing staircase, carried on iron shafts.

Sheldon Manor ☆

1½ m W Chippenham, off A420; teas; garden; *open:* Easter–early Oct, Sun, Thurs, and BHs 2–6; tel: 0249 653120

This stone-built, gabled manor, with mullioned windows and lichen-spotted roofs, sits above a sloping forecourt. A 13th-century porch is flanked, on one side, by a 15th-century wing, on the other by a generously windowed range rebuilt in 1659, its outward lurch held by a heavy buttress. Decorative 18th-century gates guard the entrance to the court, a tiny medieval chapel, more summer house than church, sits by the house, and two stone-tiled barns frame a second grassy square.

Inside, Sheldon is a place of dark, lived-in rooms, seen by a watery, greenery-filtered light. Some features, such as the stone water trough fed by pipes from the roof, the dog gate on the 17th-century stairs, or mint-green William and Mary panelling, are original, others, such as the fine linenfold in the dining-room, were additions of the early 20th century, and the house has been furnished by the Gibbs family, who bought Sheldon in 1917. A rich clutter in the panelled hall includes a gilded Spanish *vargueño* and other decorative chests, a marquetry longcase clock, sofas and chairs covered with Persian saddlebags of the deepest red, and a show of Nailsea glass and William de Morgan pottery set out on Jacobean tables. A little priest's room over the porch has a high, cobwebby wagon roof and a tiny, two-light trefoil-headed

window; an atmospheric library in the 15th-century wing is open to the rafters; and some interesting paintings include one of Tissot's Faust-inspired costume pieces and a child portrait by John Callcott Horsley.

Stourhead ☆

At Stourton, 3 m NW Mere on A303; NT; teas in NT inn; world-famous landscape garden; *open:* Apr–end Oct, Sat–Wed, 12 – 5.30, or dusk if earlier; tel: 0747 840348

Only a few of the thousands who flock to Stourhead's 18th-century landscape garden also visit the Palladian villa out of sight on the slopes above. Created by Colen Campbell between 1718 and 1724 for Henry Hoare I, whose son laid out the valley garden, and reached today by a stiff uphill walk from the car park, the house has been blurred by later additions and alterations and by massive restoration after a fire in 1902. The long entrance front, where the original compact block is framed by low wings added in the 1790s for the antiquary and connoisseur Sir Richard Colt Hoare, is a severely classical composition, with a columned and pedimented portico and balustraded rooflines. Inside, Regency schemes in the wings, where Sir Richard's picture gallery and library both escaped the flames, are married to Edwardian re-creations of the early 18th-century decoration by Doran Webb, whose often clumsily executed work now frames a wide-ranging collection of paintings and original furnishings, many of them made for the house.

The most satisfying interior is the huge, barrel-vaulted library, like an elegant, sparsely furnished engine shed, decorated in shades of green. Colt Hoare's books have gone, but a replica of the original carpet sets off a massive desk, library steps and other pieces made for the room by Chippendale the Younger, and lunettes high in the curve of the ceiling glow with coloured glass. Sir Richard's moss-walled picture gallery at the other end of the house is gloomier, although the paintings, including a double portrait by Carlo Maratta, landscapes by Zuccarelli and Gaspard Poussin and Cigoli's huge *Adoration of the Magi*, are interesting enough.

Smaller rooms in the main body of the house display more Chippendale pieces, including satinwood armchairs inlaid with ebony and accompanying gout stools, a bravura 17th-century cabinet with *pietra-dura* inlay, family portraits by Dahl, Samuel Woodforde, Leighton, Wootton and Ramsay, and small works by such as Orizonte and Teniers the Younger. Many of the pictures are difficult to see, but helpful room stewards and a full list allow visitors to seek out the best of the collection.

Tottenham House

6 m SE Marlborough, on E side of road to Durley and Savernake Forest from the A346, ½ m N Savernake Forest Hotel; *open:* about 24 days a year in school holidays, 10.30–1.30; tel: 0672 870331

A long straight drive leads to the porticoed west front of this vast classical mansion, hidden among the heaths and woods of Savernake Forest. Jaunty-tailed lions stand erect on the colonnaded wings curving out to either side, and a suitably grand stable block stands just north of the house. Begun in the 1820s for the 1st Marquess of Ailesbury by the Cundys, father and son, Tottenham was then extended in the 1870s by the 2nd Marquess, who added the wings and the lions.

Now a boys preparatory school, all former elegance has been largely submerged beneath functional lighting, scuffed paintwork and rows of desks. Visitors see about ten rooms on the ground floor, the most impressive the lofty library, with a coffered plaster ceiling, and the top-lit staircase hall rising through the centre of the house, with gallery-like landings ringing the upper floors.

Westwood Manor ☆

Beside church in Westwood village, 1¹/₂ m SW Bradford on Avon, signed from B3109; NT; small garden; *open:* Apr–end Sept, Sun, Tues, Wed 2–5; tel: 0225 863374

Between the church, with its delicious Elizabethan tower, and a picturesque medieval barn is this secluded, stone-built manor, closing two sides of a grassy court. Westwood's heyday was in the 16th and early 17th century, when an originally medieval building was turned into something with pretensions. Visitors see some half-dozen panelled rooms with fluid and inventive Jacobean plasterwork, a couple of internal porches and stone-mullioned casements, some still filled with the original tinted glass. Period furniture – sturdy oak stools and tables, carved Carolean chairs – was collected by Edgar Lister, who restored Westwood from 1911, and he was also responsible for the richly coloured needlework covering several chairs. The most memorable interior is not the stone-flagged, tapestry-hung hall, but the airy great parlour above, with stumpy plasterwork pendants hanging from a high, gently arched ceiling, a long vista south over green fields from the window looking on to the court, and a spinet by Stephen Keene and an Italian 16th-century virginal among a collection of early musical instruments.

Wilton House ☆☆☆☆

In Wilton, 3 m W Salisbury on A30; restaurant; model soldiers and miniature railway; garden; *open:* Apr–mid Oct, Mon–Sat 11–6, Sun 12 - 6: Tel: 072 274 3115

Built between 1630 and 1655 for the 4th Earl of Pembroke, one of the 'noble and incomparable paire' of brothers to whom Shakespeare dedicated his first folio, Wilton is a four-square, hollow palace, of golden Chilmark stone, with cedar-shaded lawns stretching to a sluggish river. For his innovative, Italianate south façade, with a tall Venetian window as a central focus and low corner towers counteracting the otherwise strongly horizontal lines, the 4th Earl consulted Inigo Jones, although the great man, busy on projects for

Charles I, left the execution to Isaac de Caux. Round the corner, a sturdy, lantern-topped tower with stone-mullioned windows is all that is left of the 16th-century courtyard house that once stood here, but the present building follows the Tudor plan.

Inside are an outstanding collection of paintings, sculpture and furniture and Inigo Jones' state rooms, created after a fire in 1647 and realized by his close associate John Webb. His great set pieces, the Single Cube (30 ft x 30 ft x 30 ft) and Double Cube (60 ft x 30 ft x 30 ft), sit side by side in the middle of the south front, adorned with sculptural marble fireplaces and richly carved and gilded white pine panelling, and now subtly lit to take all eyes upwards to the mythological dramas – the stories of Icarus and Perseus – painted on the high coved ceilings by Giuseppe Cesari and, possibly, Thomas de Critz. The best family portraits are gathered here: Lelys in the Single Cube, Van Dycks in the Double Cube, among them a group portrait of the 4th Earl's family, with the men as gaudy as peacocks. Wide planks of oak are the original Jacobean floorboards and the Double Cube is filled with bravura gilded chairs and sofas designed, 100 years later, by William Kent and Thomas Chippendale the Younger.

Some more intimate interiors follow, and the state rooms are approached through James Wyatt's gothic cloisters of 1801–14, now used to display some of the classical and 17th-century statuary acquired by the 8th Earl, who founded the Wilton carpet factory, and such treasures as a lock of the ageing Elizabeth I's hair, and Napoleon's dispatch case, taken from his carriage during the retreat from Moscow.

The paintings are an eclectic mix of English, Netherlandish and Italian works, of portraits, landscapes and religious pictures. There are canvases by Reynolds, Beechey and Lawrence, a tiny Assumption by Rubens, an equally minute and magical landscape by Claude, works by Andrea del Sarto and Lotto, winter scenes by Pieter Brueghel the Younger and his brother, and views of Wilton by Knyff and Wilson, the former including Stonehenge and the long red-brick façade of the first carpet factory, the latter showing the enchanting Palladian bridge over the river. Star of the show is Rembrandt's portrait of his mother, head poked forward and skin deeply wrinkled, like a venerable tortoise. How ironic that the 4th Earl, whose house reflects, as nowhere else, the splendour of the Stuart court, threw in his lot with the Parliamentarians, thus ensuring the preservation of his collection and the security to rebuild in the 1640s. Today, Wilton stands out not only for what it contains, but also for the friendliness of the staff.

Newport Pagnell

Beds

Chicheley

Houghton House

Chicksands Priory

Banbury

Stowe

A422

Broughton Castle

Milton Keynes

A6

Wrest Park

A505

Buckingham

Woburn Abbey

Chipping Norton

A5

Rousham Park

Bicester

Winslow Hall

A1(M)

Stevenage

A44

Claydon House

Ascott

Mentmore

Luton

Knebworth

Bishop's Stortford

A411

Wotton House

Luton Hoo

Blenheim Palace

Waddesdon Manor

Minster Lovell Hall

Aylesbury

Nether Winchendon

Shaw's Corner

Herts

Witney

Oxon

Welwyn

Oxford

Hemel Hempstead

St Albans

M11

cott

Stanton Harcourt Manor

Gorhambury

Hatfield House

Kingston House

Bucks

Chenies Manor House

M25

A10

t Park

M40

Hughenden Manor

Watford

Milton Manor

High Wycombe

Moor Park Mansion

gton House

West Wycombe Park

ndown House

Stonor Park

Nuffield Place

Fawley Court

Kenwood

Greys Court

Cliveden

Maidenhead

Slough

Osterley Park

London

Basildon Park

Windsor Castle

Chiswick House

R. Thames

Mapledurham House

Dorney Court

Syon House

Marble Hill House

M4

Frogmore

Ham House

Berks

Reading

Staines

Hampton Court

Kingston

A4

Newbury

Swallowfield Park

Croydon

A33

A30

M4

A4

M3

A3

A24

M25

A21

Bedfordshire

Chicksands Priory

In RAF Chicksands off A507, 1¼ m from Shefford; guided tours (c. 45 mins); refreshments; *open:* Apr–Oct, 1st and 3rd Suns of month, 2–5; tel: 02302 4195

Now marooned in the middle of an airforce base, and much in need of restoration, the once-great house of the Osborne family requires imagination and understanding. Formed out of the claustral buildings of one of the few Gilbertine foundations in England, Chicksands was remodelled in the 1740s by Isaac Ware and again, in 1813, by James Wyatt. The exterior is gothick, with rows of pointed windows, pinnacled corner buttresses, and a pseudo-medieval porch. Inside, visitors are taken on an enthusiastic guided tour of empty, decaying interiors, with features of every period on view. One range sits on a vaulted medieval undercroft; James Wyatt was responsible for the gothick entrance hall and for the octagonal King James room, with an umbrella of delicate vaulting pinned by a heavy central pendant; and the intrepid who scale the steep stairs to the attics are rewarded with a close view of Ware's huge brick chimneys and of the late-15th-century oak and chestnut roof. The gobbets of architectural history are enlivened with tales of ghosts and strange happenings.

Houghton House

1 m NE Ampthill, on Bedford road; EH; *open:* any reasonable time; access on foot along a rough track; tel: none

A bleak, windswept scarp of the Chilterns is crowned with this melancholy, brick and stone ruin, the panoramic views over the flat pastureland towards Bedford now spoilt by a clutch of smoking chimneys. Said to have been the inspiration for John Bunyan's House Beautiful in *The Pilgrim's Progress*, Houghton was built in c. 1615 for Philip Sidney's sister, the Countess of Pembroke, with frontispieces added some 20 years later, possibly by Inigo Jones. It is now a roofless shell, with gaping stone-mullioned windows and the remains of grand façades.

Luton Hoo ☆☆

On outskirts of Luton, via A1081 (M1 junction 10); restaurant; garden; *open:* Easter–mid Oct, Fri, Sat, Sun 1.30–5.30, BH Mon 10.30–5.30; tel: 0582 22955

After a depressing approach through the fringe of unlovely Luton comes a long drive through a serene 18th-century landscape, with wide views of the pastoral Lea valley. The house itself is part Palladian villa, part French château, part grand hotel. There are traces of Robert Adam's unfinished work for the 3rd Earl of Bute, but the Scottish architect's classical vision has been blurred by Robert Smirke, who completed the house in the 1820s and added the grandiose entrance portico; by rebuilding after a fire in 1843; and by remodelling early this century by Mewes and Davis, architects of the Ritz, who added the distinctive mansard roof and created the opulent, French-style interiors.

Mewes and Davis were working for the South African diamond magnate Julius Wernher, who bought the property in 1903. His descendants still own the house, but it is no longer lived in. Only occasionally is there a sense of Luton Hoo's Edwardian heyday: in the vast entrance hall, with its mirrored doors; in the dining-room that was designed round a set of Beauvais tapestries, the yellow and green-grey marble lining the walls, the Axminster carpet, and the brownish tinge to the glass in the chandeliers all chosen to complement the strongly red colouring of the hangings; and, above all, in the starkly black and white, oval staircase hall, where marble treads edged by a gleaming brass handrail curve sensuously upwards round Borgonzoli's statue of Cupid and Psyche.

Most rooms are now devoted to museum-like displays of the paintings, porcelain, jewellery and *objets d'art* collected by Sir Julius, his son Harold and daughter-in-law Lady Zia; one shows exquisite medieval ivories and boxwood carvings, another 15th- and 16th-century jewellery from Moorish Spain, a third cabinets of 18th- and 19th-century English porcelain. Early religious paintings, including a rare altar-piece by the 15th-century Spaniard Bartolomé Bermejo, and works by Filippino Lippi and Hans Memling, are hung in a chapel-like setting, with a 15th-century annunciation, in which a scarlet-robed, green-winged angel kneels to the Virgin, above the 'altar'.

Next door is a collection of 17th-century Dutch canvases, among them a curly-headed boy by Frans Hals, and land- and sea-scapes by Hobbema and Van de Velde the Younger. Here, too, are domestic interiors by Pieter de Hoogh and Gerrit Dou, the one showing a woman nursing her baby by an open casement, the other focused on a girl peeling apples, her scarlet bodice a flash of colour across the room, while a corridor is hung with Rubens' *Battle of the Amazons*, all thrashing horses and naked bodies, and with Titian's sombre, hard-faced portrait of Prince Giacomo Doria. Also here is the Russian collection inherited by Lady Zia, daughter of the Grand Duke Michael who took a 21-year lease on *Kenwood* in 1910. She was responsible for the court costumes and for the cases of Fabergé trinkets, among them sprays of jewelled flowers and tiny eggs of jade, turquoise, amethyst and gold, and for mementoes of the imperial family, including a table and chair used by the haemophiliac tsarevitch. A portrait of the last Tsar, Nicholas II, hangs in the recently restored, romanesque chapel created by G. E. Street in 1873, with stained glass by Clayton & Bell and a richly painted ceiling.

Sadly, despite the richness and interest of the collection, it is badly presented, with barely adequate information. An atmosphere of dejection and desolation infects every corner of the house, as if the place were slowly dying, and the feeling is that visitors are tolerated rather than welcomed.

Woburn Abbey ☆☆

8 m NW Dunstable, on A4012, M1 exit 12 or 13; coffee shop; grounds; *open:* Jan–end March, Sat, Sun 11–4.45; end March–end Oct, daily, 11–5.45 (6.15 Suns); tel: 0525 290666

As you drive past on the way to the car park, have a good look at this yellow-stone palace dominating a sweep of deer-grazed turf, as this is the only chance to see Henry Flitcroft's long, Palladian west front of 1747, and the less ostentatious south façade designed by Henry Holland 40 years later. Visitors are ushered into the house through a side door in the north range, and cannot walk round the outside.

Flitcroft and Holland were working for John and Francis Russell, the 4th and 5th Dukes of Bedford, whose family have been here since the mid-16th century, and it was these two, together with the 6th Duke, who largely made Woburn what it is: by remodelling the former Jacobean house, and by acquiring the outstanding collection of paintings, furniture and porcelain, much of it, unfortunately, given scant coverage in the flashy but insubstantial guidebook. The family china and silver, including some delicious Meissen dishes in the shape of the fruit and vegetables they are supposed to contain, and items from a 183-piece, blue and gold, Sèvres dinner service given by Louis XV, are displayed in dramatically lit cases at the end of the tour. If you are fond of such things, pace yourself carefully, because Woburn is a house which could exhaust the most tireless visitor. Some twenty rooms are shown, with some of the most rewarding coming at the end.

State apartments running down the south front, with heavy gilded ceilings by Flitcroft, include the corner room slept in by Queen Victoria, hung with some of her Majesty's careful, uninspired etchings, and a hideous Saloon, its walls now painted with a blue wash of modern murals that sit uneasily with the Rysbrack chimneypieces and high, coffered ceiling. There are splendid paintings here – Italianate landscapes by Claude and Poussin, an elegiac river scene by Cuyp, portraits by Lely and Van Dyck, and works by David Teniers and Jan Steen – but none of these rooms will make you catch your breath.

More rewarding are the family apartments in the south wing (not always open), in particular Henry Holland's sunny classical library, divided by screens of fluted columns and with self-portraits by Tintoretto, Rembrandt, Cuyp and Hogarth, and a painting of a wild-haired bohemian who may, or may not, be Jan Steen, hanging above the bookcases. A white and gold break-fast room displays a group of portraits by Reynolds, among them a painting of Oliver Goldsmith, and a more formal, red-walled dining-room is hung with most of the two-dozen Venetian views which the 4th Duke commissioned from Canaletto. Early family portraits, from the 16th and 17th centuries, are paraded on Flitcroft's staircase and the long room which he created out of the Jacobean gallery, among them a jewel-encrusted image of Elizabeth I by George Gower, a sweet group of children by Marcus Gheeraerts and John de Critz's portrait of Lucy Harrington, Countess of Bedford, wearing a red dress designed for a masque by Inigo Jones. Elsewhere are rooms devoted to the flying Duchess, wife of the 11th Duke, who was lost over the fens in March 1937 when on a solo flight in her de Havilland Gipsy Moth, and to the Russell's long and continuing interest in horse-racing, echoed in paintings by Sartorius and Sawrey Gilpin.

Of the Cistercian monastery that once stood here, there is now no trace, although Woburn's three ranges grouped round a central courtyard preserve the monastic plan; the Jacobean house, on the other hand, underlies much of the later work and the shell-encrusted grotto in the north wing is a 17th-century survival.

Wrest Park

¹/₄ m E Silsoe, off A6; EH: refreshments, garden; *open:* Easter or 1 Apr (whichever earlier)–30 Sept, Sat, Sun, BHs, 10–6; tel: 0525 60718

Wrest Park is an Alice in Wonderland place, where the usual expectations do not apply. Elaborate gateways in the high park wall seem to lead, not to a mansion but to an industrial estate. The house itself is a French château, with a high mansard roof, rows of identical windows and little one-storey pavil-ions either side, while the only building of any architectural distinction, a baroque, domed brick eyecatcher designed by Thomas Archer in 1709–11, sits at the far end of the garden, closing the vista down a long canal. Built in 1834–9 by the 2nd Earl de Grey, the house was based on designs by Mansard, Blondel and other 17th- and 18th-century French architects, with decorations in an exuberant Louis XV style. It is now an agricultural research centre, and the gilded plasterwork and painted ceilings in the state rooms are allied with utilitarian desks and bookcases. Most visitors hurry through to the stunning formal garden which stretches half a mile from the house.

Berkshire

Basildon Park ☆

7 m NW Reading, on W side A329, between Pangbourne and Streatley; NT; tearoom; garden; *open:* Apr–end Oct, Wed–Sat 2–6, Sun and BH Mon 12–6 (closed Wed following BH); tel: 0734 843040

No one would guess that this dignified Palladian house looking out over the wooded Thames valley was left derelict after World War II, stripped of many of its fittings. Built by John Carr of York in 1776–83 for Francis Sykes, one of the richest nabobs to come out of India – but not, the guide comfortably tells us, one of the most corrupt – Basildon as it is today, with period furniture and Italianate paintings complementing delicate 18th-century plasterwork, is almost entirely the work of Lord and Lady Iliffe, who bought the rotting shell in 1952 and took endless trouble to restore it. Another ruinous Carr house was mined for fireplaces and mahogany doors, and appropriate furnishings picked up piece by piece: silk damask curtains from *Blenheim*, a state bed from Ashburnham Place, painted urns from *Fawley Court*, just down the road.

A steep woodland path from the car park brings visitors to the imposing entrance front, with a pedimented central block connected by low screen walls to pavilions either side and a dramatically recessed portico. The front door opens into a surprisingly cosy and intimate interior, more drawing-room than hall, the delicate, gilded plasterwork on walls and ceiling picked out in pink, green, lilac and stone. Like the equally rich dining-room, the hall is best seen on a grey autumnal afternoon, when lamplight brings out the relief in the decoration. A more oppressive spirit rules in the octagonal drawing-room lit by a huge Venetian window. Given a heavy Italianate ceiling by J. B. Papworth in 1840 and furnished with aggressive yellow sofas, this opulent, red-walled room is now the setting for the most unusual pictures from the Iliffe collection of Italian art: Pompeo Batoni's paintings of God the Father and seven of the apostles, among them a weather-beaten St Matthew with his account books and St Thomas with his set-square.

John Carr's splendid top-lit staircase, with round-headed arches circling the first floor, leads to a sequence of bedrooms and an intriguing, decoratively arranged collection of shells, fossils and geological specimens. Lord Iliffe appears in a portrait by Graham Sutherland, his body slipping gently out of the frame as if the effort of sitting were almost too much, and there are some 40 bleak and comfortless Sutherland sketches for the Coventry Cathedral tapestry.

Frogmore House ☆

On B3021, Old Windsor to Datchet road, signposted from A322; refreshments; garden; *open:* early Aug–late Sept; tel: 0753 868286 for details

This Regency villa looking over a serpentine lake and tree-shaded lawns is the least grand of the royal residences open to the public. Buried in the private Home Park attached to *Windsor Castle*, it is also the most secluded. Its connection with the royal family dates back to 1709, when the late 17th-century house that forms the core of the present building was leased to the Duke of Northumberland, Charles II's son by the Duchess of Cleveland. Then, in 1792, Frogmore became a retreat for George III's consort Queen Charlotte. Here she and her daughters pursued self-improving pastimes, and here they all sought relief from the king's increasing insanity. It was Charlotte who employed James Wyatt to create the present stuccoed composition, with low, bowed wings either side of a three-storey main block and a long colonnade on to the lake. After 1861, the house became a residence for Queen Victoria's difficult mother, the Duchess of Kent, and in the 1920s Queen Mary arranged several rooms as a kind of family museum.

Recently restored, Frogmore has been arranged to reflect its principal royal residents, with rooms re-created as they appear in photographs and paintings. The Duchess of Kent's sitting-room, with a big bow on to the gardens, is a restless, discordant clutter, with pale lilac walls and deep yellow curtains struggling with the vivid green, red and orange in the carpet. Potted ferns and palms stand in the windows and a writing desk and a mass of small tables are crammed with ornaments and photographs. Next door is Queen Charlotte's extraordinary Green Pavilion, its windows to the garden and glass doors to the colonnade half-concealed by voluminous swathes of a fringed and tasselled, red-and-green print, like a shawl for a monstrous gipsy. The Queen Mary rooms are filled with painted tea caddies and writing boxes, with lacquered, papier-mâché furniture, and with flowers of silk, wax and shell arranged under glass domes.

Royal talent is displayed in watercolours and drawings by Charlotte's daughters, in works by Queen Victoria, one of them a painting she did at the age of ten, and in accomplished pictures by her more talented daughters Vicky and Louise. Some rather muddy murals by Louis Laguerre recently exposed on the staircase are the only decorative scheme to survive from the era of the Duke of Northumberland.

Swallowfield Park

In village of Swallowfield, 6 m S Reading, off A33; guided tours; garden; *open:* May–Sept, Wed, Thurs, 2–5; tel: none

This dreary, cement-rendered house standing in the ruins of a once-magnificent formal garden does not live up to the promise of its approach – over a five-arched 18th-century bridge and past a pretty, clock-towered service court – or to its history. The stately red-brick mansion built by William Talman for the 2nd Earl of Clarendon at the end of the 17th century has been largely submerged in a remodelling of the 1820s. Only a delicate oval vestibule, adorned with statue niches and with plasterwork white on primrose-yellow walls, and a grand baroque gateway standing forlornly in the garden, survive from Talman's time. The house is now divided into apartments, and visitors are shown only the public rooms.

Windsor Castle ☆☆

Windsor, 21 m W London, off M4; *open:* all year, summer 10.30–5, winter 10.30–4, but state apartments closed when HM the Queen in residence, and advisable to check in advance; tel: 0753 831118

On an outcrop of chalk above the Thames is the largest inhabited castle in the world. Big enough to be a hilltown, Windsor sprawls expansively along the crest of the ridge in a display of battlements, towers and turrets. Originally one of the nine castles with which William the Conqueror defended London, the buildings incorporate work from every century since, but the fairytale skyline, with a great round tower rising high out of the centre of the complex, owes most to Jeffry Wyatville's reconstruction of 1820–40 for George IV, when the place was remodelled in a romantic medieval idiom. Now more palace than fortress, Windsor is still a royal residence, and it was the private part of the castle that was most seriously damaged in the fire of 1992.

Entry is from the south, through the Tudor gateway on Castle Hill that gives access to the town clustered round the walls. The lower ward, shaped by the rock beneath, stretches away uphill, framed on one side by the glorious buttressed and pinnacled south front of St George's chapel, on the other by an endearingly domestic terrace of stone-built medieval and Tudor houses. Beyond the now grassy moat circling the round tower, an originally 14th-century gate gives access to the ranges crowning the escarpment, where the state apartments are on view. Although based on suites created for Charles II and his queen, Catherine of Braganza, in c.1680 by Hugh May, these, like the skyline, were remodelled by Wyatville, and are mostly 19th-century in spirit. Two of the largest reception rooms, still used for banquets and other functions, were gutted in the fire, but the rest escaped the flames, and visitors have the added interest of being able to watch work in progress on the devastated interiors.

A monumental staircase designed by Anthony Salvin in 1866, and dominated by a marble statue of George IV and by a suit of armour made for the corpulent Henry VIII, leads up to a lofty, vaulted chamber by James Wyatt, Jeffry's uncle, who started the gothicizing of the castle in 1796. Used to show off Napoleonic and other military relics, such as the bullet that killed Nelson, and hung with weapons, it is presided over by a stolid marble statue of Queen Victoria. Adjoining is the toplit, grandiose Waterloo Chamber created out of a former courtyard, where some delicate 17th-century carvings by Grinling Gibbons, brought here from elsewhere, frame Sir Thomas Lawrence's triumphalist portraits of those involved in the defeat of Napoleon. In the king's and queen's apartments beyond, most of the rooms, with damask-hung walls and gilded plaster ceilings, are as transformed for George IV and his successor William IV, whose initials appear on some of the decoration, and are unexceptional, differing only in size. Three Stuart interiors survive, although the effect of lofty ceilings painted by Antonio Verrio, more work by Grinling Gibbons surrounding overmantel and overdoor paintings, and panelled walls hung with Gobelins tapestries, is spoilt by some startlingly white Adam fireplaces.

The contents, barely referred to in the guidebook, are another matter. Standing out from the mostly late 18th- and 19th-century furnishings, including a domed bed slept in by Napoleon III and Empress Eugenie, are some exceptional Stuart and William and Mary pieces, among them a seaweed walnut desk and a pier table, mirror and *torchères* made of embossed silver. And the show of paintings from the Royal Collection, although often badly lit, more than makes up for the generally lacklustre atmosphere. Here is Van Dyck's triple portrait of Charles I, from which Bernini carved a bust in Rome without ever seeing the king, and the same artist's picture of Charles's children. There are three portraits by Holbein, a wall of Canalettos, and several works by Rubens, including an assessing self-portrait, with fedora and goatee beard, and a likeness of Van Dyck, who bears a striking resemblance to his mentor. More easily missed are Dürer's portrait of a sharp-nosed man, an interior by Jan Steen, and two Rembrandts, one a painting of his aged mother, the lace at her throat catching the light. A separate gallery has a changing exhibition of drawings from the collection, where it is best to discover what is on show before buying a ticket, and visitors can also see Queen Mary's dolls' house, fitted out as a great house of the 1920s with a mix of antiques and modern conveniences.

Buckinghamshire

Ascott

2 m SW Leighton Buzzard, S side of A418; NT; entry by timed ticket; lovely garden; *open:* mid Apr–mid May and Sept, Tues–Sun and BH Mon (closed Tues following) 2–6; tel: 0296 688242

Of the Rothschild houses that once ringed Aylesbury, turning the Vale into a private fiefdom, Ascott is one of the least pretentious and a pleasing contrast to *Waddesdon*. A ten-minute walk through the garden brings visitors to what looks like a mock-Tudor country hotel, all black-and-white half-timbering, jutting gables, sturdy chimneys and diamond-paned windows. The work of the Victorian architect George Devey, who enlarged a 17th-century building by simply adding on more of the same, Ascott was created for Lionel de Rothschild, grandson of the Frankfurt banker who founded the family fortunes. Like Waddesdon, the house is filled with an outstanding collection of works of art, the focus here being on Dutch and English paintings, on oriental porcelain from the Ming (1368–1644) and K'ang-Hsi (1662–1722) dynasties, and on 18th-century French and English furniture.

Rothschilds still live here, and the five rooms shown have the feel of a beautifully appointed private house. Visitors walk straight into a comfortable sitting-room, hung with portraits by Romney, Gainsborough, Hogarth and Beechey, some subject pictures by Reynolds, and with a study of five mares by Stubbs. In the low-ceilinged dining-room next door, 17th-century Dutch landscapes and bucolic village scenes by Adriaen and Isaac van Ostade, Philips Wouwerman and Jan Steen are overshadowed by Cuyp's luminous view of Dordrecht on a summer evening, a strong vertical line in the middle of the canvas showing where it was once cut up and sold in two halves.

More Dutch paintings – a town square by Jan van der Heyden, Ludolph de Jongh's subtly lit *Lady Receiving a Letter* – hang in the rather dark and sumptuously furnished Common Room, the only Victorian interior to survive later remodelling, but the tone here is more exotic, with a cabinet full of the richly coloured oriental ware – jars decorated with raised chrysanthemums, pyramids of aubergines and pomegranates, peach-shaped wine pots, all in deep purple, aquamarine, and mustard yellow – in which Ascott excels. Oriental ware also fills display cases along the corridors, the more fanciful figurines and vessels leavened by plainer pottery and earthenware of the Han to Sung dynasties (206 BC–AD 1279).

The tour ends in an oak-panelled library lit by windows on two sides. Here is the best of the Georgian furniture, and some prize treasures, among them an elongated Egyptian head of black basalt some 2,600 years old and a beautiful Sung flower bowl of the richest purple. An easel carries Lorenzo Lotto's portrait of a prelate, and facing each other across the room are Turner's dream-like vision of Cicero's villa at Tusculum, with dark poplars and a statue-lined walk floating in front of the house, and Gainsborough's striking painting of the red-headed Duchess of Richmond.

Chenies Manor House

In the village of Chenies, off A404 between Amersham and Rickmansworth (junction 18, M25); guided tours, *c.* 45 mins, late afternoon; teas; garden; *open:* early April–end Oct, Wed, Thurs 2–5, BH Mon 2–6; tel: 0494 762888

This unassuming L-shaped Tudor manor of warm red brick is marked by tall crow-stepped gables and ornamental chimneys. The earlier wing, incorporating a stumpy battlemented tower, is the remnant of a house built about 1460, to which the long south range was added by John Russell, 1st Earl of Bedford, in 1523–6. Here the high-flying Russells entertained Henry VIII and his daughter Elizabeth, and Chenies is one of the places where Henry's fifth queen, the young and foolish Catherine Howard, carried on the dalliance with Thomas Culpepper that was to cost her her life.

The manor's modest, interconnecting rooms seem barely grand enough for royal visitors. Today, too, there is nothing of the Russells here; from 1627 their principal seat was at the much more impressive *Woburn Abbey*, and in the 1950s Chenies was sold to the present owners. The interiors on show are a mix of periods and styles. The lovely stone-floored parlour looking on to the garden, once the open-roofed hall of the 15th-century house, is lined with white Georgian panelling and furnished with a mix of Elizabethan, Jacobean and 18th-century pieces; the upstairs room where Elizabeth I is said to have held court is tapestry-hung and oak-floored; and there are Tudor garderobes, a priest-hole and the brick-floored chamber believed to have once been occupied by Miles Coverdale, chaplain to the Russell family, who is known for his fine translation of the Bible. In contrast, there are also William Morris wallpapers, 19th-century furnishings and several pieces from India.

The earliest part of the manor is a 13th-century vaulted undercroft beneath what is now the shop, while the enchanting garden, a series of beautifully planted 'rooms', embraces the ruin of a Tudor nursery, where the children of the house lived apart, an octagonal brick well-house and the entrance to a brick tunnel, one of several leading into a nearby wood.

Chicheley Hall ☆

2 m E Newport Pagnell, 11 m W Bedford, on A422; guided tours (*c.* 60 mins); teas; garden; *open:* mid Apr–end May and Aug, Sun and BH Mon, 2.30–6; tel: 023 065 252

Chicheley Hall is a treat. Framed by a double avenue of limes is an exuberant brick and stone baroque façade, with a heavy cornice supported on Corinthian pilasters sweeping theatrically upwards to point the projection of the central bay. A bat's wing pediment crowns the entrance and above is a deep stone frieze carved with satyrs' masks and overflowing cornucopia. This playful piece of illusionism was built 1719–23 for Sir John Chester by Francis Smith of Warwick, who designed the other fronts in a kind of rising crescendo, as if visitors were expected to walk round the house before going inside. Flanking pavilions are set so far apart they can only be lined up from across the garden.

Inside, the mood changes. The lofty, stone-floored hall – by Henry Flitcroft – is severely classical, with a confused, inept ceiling painting by William Kent and grey scagliola columns screening the inlaid 18th-century staircase. Mostly panelled rooms with original plasterwork ceilings, including a second-floor library with bookshelves cunningly concealed behind the woodwork, are cosy and lived in rather than grand, and furnished with sofas and easy chairs as well as a show of 18th-century walnut pieces and a couple of splendid gilded mirrors. There are Stuart beer tankards and salt cellars of shimmering mother-of-pearl, portraits by Hudson and de Laszlo, and Sargent's compelling drawing of the distinguished Admiral Beatty, whose son bought the house in 1952 and whose World War I exploits are remembered in a little museum.

Claydon House ☆ ☆

In village of Middle Claydon, 3½ m SW Winslow, signed from A413, A421 and A41; NT; tearoom; garden and park: *open:* Apr–end Oct, Sat–Wed and BH Mon 1–5; tel: 0296 730349/730693

A quiet, stone-faced classical house set on a terrace above the park, Claydon seems the height of restrained 18th-century taste. But this self-contained box, only the west end of what was once a much larger and more ostentatious mansion, has some of the most exuberant and uninhibited rococo decoration in Britain.

In the north hall, woodwork as fanciful as spun-sugar decoration encrusts mirrors, doors and chimney-piece and has even been attached to the ceiling. Writhing foliage supports snake-necked herons and fork-tailed dragons, while the doors are treated like precious pieces of furniture, each panel inlaid with daisies of ivory and ebony. The plasterwork of the adjoining saloon and library is more restrained, but upstairs is the theatrical Chinese room, watched over by a couple of malevolent mandarins, and with one wall filled with a richly carved pagoda hung with a rash of bells. The staircase is a work of art, its walls encrusted with fluid plasterwork, each tread and riser devised as a mosaic of box, mahogany, ebony and ivory, and gilded ears of corn trembling in the ironwork balustrade.

The woodwork was the creation of the eccentric but brilliant Luke Lightfoot, employed by Ralph, 2nd Lord Verney from 1750–1769 to help in the rebuilding of a Jacobean house. Although given his head for some time, this difficult man was eventually ousted by the similarly unsuitable Sir Thomas Robinson, the Yorkshire squire and amateur architect who designed Verney's great rotunda and ballroom, now demolished. The plasterwork is by Joseph Rose, who must often have wondered what he had got himself into.

Verney's descendants still live here, but the furniture has largely gone and some of the rooms seen are noticeably bare. In the 19th century the 2nd baronet, Sir Harry Verney, married Florence Nightingale's sister Parthenope, and the formidable Florence was a frequent visitor. Her bedroom is on show and also some of her letters and objects connected with her exploits in the Crimea, among them the armband she wore while nursing at Scutari, and her travelling Communion set.

Only yards from the house, set on a grassy hillock, is the ancient village church, its chancel almost filled by a grandiose monument to Sir Edmund Verney, killed at Edgehill in 1642.

Cliveden

2 m N Taplow on B476, signposted from A4 (M4, junction 7); NT; entry by timed ticket from kiosk in car park; teas; exceptional garden; *open:* Apr–end Oct, Thurs and Sun 3–6; tel: 0628 605069

Sir Charles Barry's Italianate palace of 1850–1 floating on a terrace high above the Thames is now a luxury hotel, with liveried attendants collecting luggage from cars parked in the forecourt and a pianist to regale guests with Satie and Mozart. In the first half of the century, though, it was known for the brilliant house parties presided over by Nancy, Lady Astor, whose father-in-law, the American millionaire William Waldorf Astor, had bought the house in 1893. As at *Hever Castle*, the lst Lord poured a fortune into restoring the house and garden, acquiring the long Renaissance balustrade that now sits below the main terrace and employing the architect J. L. Pearson to create settings suitable for his collections of furniture and works of art.

Most of the contents have gone, but the taste of the lst Lord lingers on in the three rooms on show. A low-ceilinged, oak-panelled hall, now awash with low sofas and table lamps, still boasts Astor's early 16th-century stone chimney-piece, his Brussels tapestries of 1690, and Sargent's portrait of Nancy Astor. More of a piece is the green and gold breakfast room on a corner of the house, with gilded mirrors reflecting carved and painted rococo panelling, painted overdoors and a marble fireplace, all brought here from a château outside Paris. When discreet figures are laying up the long table, luxury hotel and grand country house seem curiously merged.

Dorney Court ☆

In Dorney village on B3026, 2 m W Eton and Windsor; teas; garden; *open:* Easter weekend, May, Sun, BH Mon, June–Sept, Sun, Mon, Tues 2–5.30; tel: 0628 604638

This pretty Tudor manor house sprawled round a courtyard is an unexpected find in this affluent corner of Buckinghamshire, so close to London. A rough, potholed lane through a dense coppice suddenly reveals a mirage of half-timbering, pink brick, jutting, barge-boarded gables, star-shaped chimneys and undulating red-tiled roofs. It is almost too good to be true, and, indeed, there is more than a touch of romantic 19th-century restoration here. Behind, its Tudor brick tower seeming to rise out of the house, is the tiny parish church.

The manor dates from *c.* 1500 and is filled with the accumulated portraits and furniture of the Palmer family, who have lived here since the mid-16th century. Nothing is outstanding, but the general effect is warm and welcoming: this is a place of uneven floors, deep window bays, richly coloured carpets, gleaming wood and comfortable chairs, many of them covered with intricate needlework done by the family. The lofty Great Hall, lit by a huge window in the south wall, is lined with linenfold panelling from Faversham Abbey and hung with Palmer portraits, among them works by Cornelius

Johnson and Kneller and a Lely of the family's most notorious ancestor, Barbara Villiers, said to be the lewdest and fairest of Charles II's mistresses. There is a parlour with a low, beamed ceiling and a Jacobean overmantel, a barrel-vaulted great chamber, and, by way of contrast, an elegant William and Mary dining-room, with duck-egg blue panelling and a plaster ceiling.

Hughenden Manor ☆

1½ m N High Wycombe, W side of A4128; NT; garden and woodland walks; *open:* March, Sat, Sun 2–6, Apr–end Oct, Wed–Sat 2–6 (but closed Gd Fri), Sun, BH Mon 12–6; tel: 0494 532580

The country estate which Benjamin Disraeli bought in 1847 to bolster his political career sits in a quiet, wooded valley just beyond the reach of High Wycombe. Here he would retreat from Parliamentary business and here he retired in 1880 after his final six-year term as Prime Minister. A Georgian building was transformed by E. B. Lamb into the present forbidding red-brick house, with its curious pinnacled parapet.

Much of the interior is on view, the heavy Victorian gothic of the downstairs rooms, with plaster vaulting and pointed arches, contrasting with the lighter Georgian decoration on the first floor. Sadly, little is as Disraeli had it: after his death Hughenden passed to his nephew Coningsby, who threw out much of the furniture and made his own changes. Some rooms contain only drawings and engravings; others are used to display objects connected with the statesman, among them the withered bunch of primroses which Queen Victoria sent for his funeral; the manuscript of Disraeli's last, unfinished novel; and the robe he wore as Chancellor of the Exchequer, which he refused to pass on to his successor. The sunny, cluttered drawing-room, with its profusion of stools and cloth-covered tables, looks authentic enough, but in Disraeli's time this was the library. Only the little study on the first floor, with its book-lined alcoves, leather armchair, tasselled bell pull and battered trunk for papers, is as he knew it.

Mentmore

In village of Mentmore, 5 m S Leighton
Buzzard, off B488; grounds; *open:* all year,
Sun, guided tour at 2.30 (*c*. 60 mins),
unless house closed for function;
tel: 0296 662183/661881

Crowning a low ridge, with views south-east across a green and wooded valley to Ivinghoe Beacon, is an arresting, ethereal house faced in golden stone.
Huge mullioned and transomed windows fill every wall, towers are angled
out at each corner, and an array of obelisks, heraldic beasts and shaped gables
bristles on the skyline. This Elizabethan parody, inspired by Wollaton Hall
outside Nottingham, was devised 1852–4 by Joseph Paxton, fresh from the
Crystal Palace, for Mayer Amschel Rothschild, grandson of the Frankfurt
banker who founded the family fortunes and the first of the clan to build in
the Vale of Aylesbury.

Its art treasures dispersed in a legendary sale in 1977, with only hooks for
paintings and tapestries and empty plinths to suggest what was once here,
Mentmore is now lived in by disciples of the Maharishi Mahesh Yogi, who
show visitors some half dozen rooms on a tour which mixes past history and
present philosophy. A lobby floored in grey, red and pink Sicilian marble
leads into the astonishing hall, like a roofed over courtyard, that fills the centre of the house. Light and airy, it rises 100 ft to Paxton's glass and iron roof,
and huge doors, with only the thinnest of frames supporting great expanses
of glass, give views out over the vale and onto the grand marble staircase,
with its pink alabaster balusters, and purpose-built niches to take Mayer
Amschel's racing trophies. A vaguely Renaissance arcade rings the first floor,
and the black and white marble fireplace, with bold ram caryatids, one of
many fittings that are older than the building, was brought here from
Rubens's house in Antwerp.

Despite careful refurbishment, the lofty, silk-hung rooms looking onto the
Vale seem dispirited. More impressive is the opulent dining-room, fitted out
with panels of red and green Genoese velvet, and with carved and gilded
woodwork framing mirrors and inset paintings by Van Loo that came from an
early 18th-century Parisian *hôtel*. The atmosphere suggests a laid-back
monastery, and the tour includes a glimpse into the mattress-floored room
where the Maharishi's followers practise transcendental meditation and levi-
tation.

Nether Winchendon ☆

Outside village of Lower Winchendon, 6 m
SW Aylesbury, off A418; guided tours;
garden; *open:* most days in May and Aug BH
Sun, Mon 2.30–5.30; tel: 0844 290101

This intriguing L-shaped house with a garden running down to the Thames is
essentially medieval and Tudor, but the old building is hidden behind light-
hearted, late 18th-century gothick façades. Visitors are greeted by a screen of

wide Georgian arches, with buttressed and castellated ranges facing on to the courtyard beyond. The river front is more eccentric. Here, a pinnacled gable, three stubby towers, battlements and a mix of gothick windows and square-headed mullions are put together in a delightfully haphazard brick and stone façade, which also includes a first-floor verandah. The Georgian work melds splendidly with an array of moulded and twisted Tudor chimneys, and with a 17th-century cupola.

Nether Winchendon is still lived in by descendants of the London merchant who bought the place in 1559. Four downstairs rooms are shown. What was the Tudor parlour is now a light and airy drawing-room, lined with white linenfold panelling, with armorial glass in the bay windows and with the curly-headed profile of Sir John Daunce, who added on this room in c. 1530, prominent on the Renaissance-style carved oak frieze.

The family portraits are mostly undistinguished, but the furnishings include a unique 16th-century tapestry showing Henry VIII with a group of courtiers, a Charles I daybed and settee, and some good 18th-century pieces. For such a modest house, there is also an unusually rich collection of documents, among them a parchment road map, a ticket to the trial of Warren Hastings, the French writer Chateaubriand's passport (showing he was only 5 ft tall), and a 1771 *Boston Gazette*, offering slaves for sale.

Stowe

3 m NW Buckingham off A422; 18th-century landscape garden (NT); *open:* 2 weeks in April, and early July–early Sept, daily, except Sat and Aug BH Fri-Mon, 2–5, but check before visiting; tel: 0280 813650

This monument to Georgian self-confidence, seat of the political Temple-Grenville family, cannot be separated from its surroundings. An idealized, elysian landscape, dotted with temples, arches, obelisks and urns, envelops visitors the moment they are through the gates. The biggest eyecatcher of them all is the house, a vast classical composition dominating a dramatic vista that runs $3/4$ mile south to a Corinthian arch crowning a distant rise.

The house as it is today owes most to Richard, Earl Temple, who, between 1770 and his death in 1779, created a kind of ducal palace, and to his nephew the 1st Marquess of Buckingham, who was largely responsible for the plaster-work and painted decoration, much of it by Vincenzo Valdrè. The pediment-ed north front of 1772, with curving colonnades enclosing a vast forecourt, is impressive enough, but is outclassed by the sublime south front of 1774. Designed by Robert Adam, though with tinkering by Earl Temple's relative, the amateur architect Thomas Pitt, this honey-coloured façade, conspicuous for its lack of bedroom windows, is conceived as three elegant pavilions, linked by columned galleries and with huge windows in arched recesses lighting the principal rooms.

Sadly, both Stowe and its landscape garden must be viewed through rose-tinted spectacles. A public school since 1923, the house is inevitably scuffed and jaded, the half dozen state-rooms shown to visitors now either empty or filled with functional furniture, and well-used textbooks instead of leather-bound volumes on the library shelves. Apart from the entrance hall, with a faded painted ceiling by William Kent, the most impressive room is the elliptical saloon in the centre of the house, with a floor of grey and green-veined Carrara marble, a high, domed ceiling, and an action-packed plaster frieze of a Roman triumphal procession.

Waddesdon Manor ☆☆☆

6 m NW Aylesbury, on A41, entrance in Waddesdon village; NT; teas; grounds with aviary; *open:* Apr–mid Oct, Thurs–Sat, and Wed in Jul and Aug 1–6, Sun and BH Mon 11–6; tel: 0296 651211

The most splendid of the Rothschild mansions which sprouted in the Vale of Aylesbury in the 19th century, Waddesdon was the creation of Baron Ferdinand, grandson of the founder of the Austrian branch of the family, and great-grandson of the German financier who started the first Rothschild bank. With rosy memories of a childhood holiday in the Loire, Baron Ferdinand employed a French architect, Gabriel-Hippolyte Destailleur, to create the hugh château that now crowns a wooded hilltop, looking south over parkland to the Chilterns. With its round towers and staircase turrets, soaring chimneys and pinnacles, sculpted dormers and mansard roof, and with long narrow windows lighting the principal rooms, Waddesdon is a mélange of features lifted from Chambord, Maintenon, Blois, Anet and other Renaissance prototypes. All is in yellow Bath stone, recently cleaned to its original hardness, the long entrance front is framed by a wide avenue along the crest of the hill, and a formal fountain terrace sets off the south façade. Started in 1874, the house took 15 years to build. The top of the hill had to be levelled, water brought from 14 miles away, and all building materials hauled up by specially constructed steam tramway and teams of horses. Bare slopes were clothed with hundreds of half-mature trees.

The lavish interior recreates 18th-century France. Large, high-ceilinged reception rooms and gallery-like corridors are fitted with carved and painted panelling taken from old Parisian houses, elaborate plasterwork, and even a ceiling painting by Jacob de Wit, all creating a suitable setting for a priceless collection of furniture, carpets, paintings and porcelain. Highly crafted pieces incorporating Sèvres plaques and the finest marquetry include an inlaid and ormolu-mounted writing table made for Marie Antoinette, a huge cylinder-top desk said to have been presented to the playwright Beaumarchais by his friends, and another made for the young Louis XVIII. There are Beauvais tapestries, Savonnerie carpets made for the French Crown, including one of the 93 commissioned by Louis XIV in 1665 to cover the Long Gallery of the Louvre, almost a quarter of a mile long, and elaborately carved mirrors. And every flat surface and cabinet shows off Sèvres porcelain, clocks, snuff boxes and other *objets d'art*, among them such curiosities as an oval box carrying portraits of Madame de Pompadour's lap dogs.

In some rooms, the French theme is continued by paintings by Watteau, Lancret, Boucher and Greuze, but the pictures also include a splendid array of 18th-century English portraits, among them ten works by Reynolds, Gainsborough's *Pink Boy*, and paintings by Highmore and Romney; serene 17th-century Dutch canvases, notably Jan van der Heyden's view of Amsterdam, with tall gabled houses mirrored in a glassy canal, a game of skittles in a formal garden by Pieter de Hoogh, and works by Aelbert Cuyp, Dou, Metsu, and Terborch; two huge Venetian panoramas by Guardi; and Rubens's dream-like *The Garden of Love*, where all the men are said to be self-portraits, all the women modelled on his wife.

Tight spiral stairs lead to the long bedroom corridor on the first floor, but it is difficult to imagine anyone living among such riches, the atmosphere in the darkened rooms being more like a superbly appointed museum than a home.

West Wycombe Park ☆☆☆

At W end of village of West Wycombe, off A40; NT; guided tours depending on visitor numbers; exceptional landscape park; *open:* June–Aug, Sun–Thurs, 2–6 (weekday entry by timed ticket); tel: 0494 524411

West Wycombe is the creation of the notorious Sir Francis Dashwood, 2nd

Baronet, whose 'hellfire' caves tunnel into the prominent hill across the valley from the house. Set on the edge of a Claudian landscape, with glimpses of classical temples hidden among the trees, the house is something of an architectural curiosity. The pedimented, Palladian north façade is conventional enough, but the south front is a double colonnade, and the short east side is filled by a massive portico supported on four giant columns. This curious assemblage was the work of the little-known John Donowell, who remodelled the brick house Dashwood had inherited. For the 2nd Baronet, re-moulding West Wycombe and its park was the project of a lifetime; started in c.1739, work was still continuing on his death in 1781. Almost unaltered since, the house and its furnishings are all of a piece, a direct reflection of 18th-century taste.

Visitors see the sumptuous rooms running the length of the ground floor. There are elaborate rococo plaster ceilings, possibly by Thomas Roberts of Oxford; inset paintings of overblown, naked deities by Giuseppe Borgnis and his less talented son Giovanni; carved marble fireplaces by Henry Cheere, who gave one a plaque of cherubs warming themselves at a fire; and exquisite decorative details: delicate gold lockplates and handles, inlaid stairs and doors, with marquetry as fine as that at *Claydon House*, and painted woodwork, the red and gold patterning in the tapestry room like the decoration on fine porcelain. Gilded rococo mirrors reflect glittering chandeliers and candelabra, and from the blue drawing-room there is a mysterious, romantic view right down the house.

Connoisseurs of furniture will pick out some fine mid-18th-century French pieces, such as the two marquetry commodes by the *émigré* cabinet-maker Pierre Langlois, but Sir Francis's collection of 17th- and 18th-century Italian art, most of it acquired on numerous Continental tours, is relatively undistinguished, its highlights two luminous landscapes by Orizonte, works by Salvator Rosa and Guido Reni, and a frowning self-portrait by Artemisia Gentileschi. Sir Francis himself appears in three paintings in the dining-room, each illustrating a different aspect of his complicated character. In one he is dressed as Pope Pontius VII, in another he clasps a copy of the prayer book he produced with Benjamin Franklin, and in the third he is in oriental costume, about to down a glass of wine.

Winslow Hall

S end of Winslow, on A413 Aylesbury road; guided tours; garden; *open:* BH wkends and July, Aug, Wed, Thurs 2.30–5.30; tel: 0296 712323

A high, red-brick wall on the main road through Winslow hides this imposing, three-storey house built in 1700. Almost certainly designed by Christopher Wren, it is a symmetrical block of attractive wine-red brick, with a steeply pitched roof, pedimented main façades, and four central chimneys, an arrangement which has allowed a display of sash windows on every side. Inside, quiet panelled rooms with corner fireplaces are ranged round the central stack and reached via staircases at either end of the house, and there is one original muralled interior, painted with rather sinister garden scenes. The furnishings of the present owners include several 18th-century pieces and a collection of Chinese *objets*.

Wotton House ☆

In Wotton Underwood, 2 m S A41 between Aylesbury and Bicester, no signs; *open:* Aug–end Sept, Wed, guided tours (*c.* 75 mins) at 2 and 3.15 (Sept 2.30 only); tel: none

An inconspicuous lane from the scatter of buildings that is Wotton Underwood leads to this secretive and splendid house. Set on a low ridge, with sweeping views east over unspoilt countryside and west over a Capability Brown park, Wotton is a dignified brick and stone Queen Anne mansion, with huge urns and statues marking the roofline, giant Corinthian pilasters rising the height of the house and steps up to a pedimented central doorway. To either side are cupola-topped baroque pavilions, and the grassy entrance court is closed by a curving ironwork screen. The architect is unkown, but Wotton was almost certainly the model for Buckingham House, the precursor of the present-day palace.

While the exterior is early-18th-century, the interior, gutted by fire in 1820, is as remodelled by John Soane. All the great architect's visual tricks are here, from tantalizing vistas through round-headed arches, shallow domes and floating ceilings to restrained and unobtrusive classical friezes and a sinuous cantilevered staircase that reuses the ironwork balustrade from the old house. Huge sash windows with the thinnest of glazing bars give unbroken views over the countryside, and the shutters on the west side are pierced with holes to let in the light of the moon and the setting sun.

Wotton was brought back from a ruinous state in the 1950s by the present owner, who has furnished it with flair and panache. The main focus of the informal guided tour is the enfilade of high-ceilinged reception rooms down the west front, a sense of theatre here enhanced by the classical shop front acting as a mirror on an end wall, by the brilliantly blue service on the dining-room table, by the displays of flowers and feathers, and by a carved and gilded doge's chair.

Hertfordshire

Gorhambury ☆

On western outskirts of St Albans, entrance N side of A4147, opposite St Michael's church; guided tours; garden; ruins of Old Gorhambury (EH); *open:* May–end Sept, Thurs 2–5; tel: 0727 54051

Although only 2 miles from St Albans' urban sprawl, Gorhambury is magically cocooned by the gentle farmland of the estate. The view from the pedimented portico dominating the entrance front is still of unspoilt country, as it always has been.

Gorhambury was built between 1777 and 1784 for James Bucknall, 3rd Viscount Grimston, who needed to replace the Tudor mansion he had inherited (now a ruin in the park), and who wanted an appropriate setting for the family's pictures. These paintings, and the connections with the high-flying Elizabethan Nicholas Bacon, who built the original house, and his even more distinguished son, the lawyer and philosopher Sir Francis, are the main interest of the place. The mansion itself is a rather severe Palladian square designed by Robert Taylor, with a Victorian wing attached to the north, its most notable features two classical marble chimneypieces by Piranesi.

The tour takes visitors through the five principal rooms, each hung with portraits. The earliest include paintings of Elizabeth I and her favourite Essex attributed to Hilliard, the queen almost frighteningly old and tired, and an ambitious self-portrait by Sir Nathaniel Bacon, nephew of Sir Francis and a gifted amateur painter, who shows himself resplendent in yellow hose. The dining-room boasts Paul van Somer's portrait of the uncle, clothed in the black robes of the Master of the Rolls, while the Yellow Drawing-room – code named 'Daffodil' when the house was occupied by MI5 during World War II – is largely devoted to 18th-century works, among them Reynolds' portrait of the 3rd Viscount as a young man, with his brother and sisters, the likeness that Batoni did of James during his Grand Tour, and works by Allan Ramsay.

The Grimston and Bacon families are drawn together in the high-ceilinged, galleried entrance hall. Designed by Taylor as a cube, this impressive room is closely hung with Grimston portraits of the royal and the great of the 17th century. The black and white chequered floor came from the chapel of Sir Nicholas's Tudor house, and the brightly coloured enamelled glass that fills a couple of round-headed windows was originally installed in his father's long gallery by Sir Francis, who had a tobacco plant, a turkey and a feathered Red Indian, fresh discoveries from the New World, included among the other creatures and plants on the panes. Something of Sir Francis' intellect comes through in the library, where the books are still arranged according to his classification, the philosophy section neatly divided into 'speculative', 'divine', 'civil' and 'human'. Also in the house are photographic copies of the 1599 Quarto editions of Shakespeare's plays that were found at Gorhambury, fuel for those who believe Sir Francis wrote them himself.

Hatfield House ☆☆

In Hatfield, 21 m N London, off A1; guided tours (c. 60 mins), Tues–Sat; teas; gardens and park; *open:* late March–early Oct, daily, except Mon and Gd Fri, but open BH Mons, weekdays 12–5, Suns 1.30–5, BH Mon 11–5; tel: 0707 262823

Faced with Hatfield's grim north front, a cliff of red brick rising from an arid sea of gravel, visitors who were expecting a Jacobean prodigy house might wonder if they have come to the right place. Alas, this front has lost its heraldic beasts and other original decoration; alas, too, there is only a sideways view – from the garden – of the showy south front, with its curving Dutch gables, turreted wings and Renaissance stone centrepiece, with a loggia stretching the length of the ground floor.

Inside, spirits will lift again. Hatfield was begun in 1608 for the sickly, crook-backed Robert Cecil, 1st Earl of Salisbury, chief minister to both Elizabeth I and James I, who inherited all his father, Lord Burghley's, political acumen. The year before King James had done a swap with his minister, taking over the Cecil family's Theobald's House in exchange for what was then an old Tudor palace, the place where Henry VIII's children, Edward, Mary and Elizabeth, passed a country childhood. Cecil pulled down three wings of the palace and reused the brick in his new mansion, whose design, although principally by Robert Lyminge, was modified by the earl himself and even, perhaps, by Inigo Jones. Cecils still live here, but no subsequent generation has been as prominent as their Elizabethan and Jacobean forbears.

Visitors do a circuit of the state rooms on the first floor of the central block. The 180 ft long gallery, with its monumental marble chimneypieces, richly carved panelling and plasterwork ceiling, is largely as built, and is furnished with James II chairs, but the other rooms are more mixed, among them a 19th-century dining-room in 17th-century style and a drawing-room filled with gilded Georgian furniture. The state apartment is reached via the galleried great hall with its lavish Jacobean woodwork and 19th-century painted Italian Renaissance ceiling, and up Lyminge's splendid staircase, with the motifs of the night, a bat, a candle and a warming pan, carved on the lowest newel post and the topmost one crowned with a likeness of Cecil's gardener, John Tradescant, with his rake. The tour ends with the largely Victorian chapel and the tapestry- and armour-hung gallery created out of the loggia. Sadly, there is no hint of the eccentricities of 19th-century life at Hatfield, when the 3rd Marquess's unpredictable lighting system frequently caught fire, to be extinguished with well-aimed cushions.

Portraits from Tudor times onwards include the so-called 'Ermine' and 'Rainbow' portraits of Elizabeth I, variously attributed to Nicholas Hilliard, Isaac Oliver and others. Robert and his father appear in paintings attributed to Marcus Gheeraerts the Younger and John de Critz, there is William Wissing's intriguing picture of the 4th Earl, with the earlier portrait of the disgraced Duke of Monmouth, which the earl thought it wisest to cover up, showing through behind, and there are works by Reynolds, Beechey, Wilkie and Richmond and a few Dutch paintings, notably Joris Hoefnagel's delightful picture of Elizabethans making merry on the banks of the Thames.

Hatfield's illustrious past accounts for the young Elizabeth I's lacy garden hat and silk stockings, an enamelled and jewelled posset set which the Spanish Ambassador gave Queen Mary and Philip of Spain on their betrothal, and a selection of Tudor papers, including Lord Burghley's draft of the execution warrant for Mary Queen of Scots, much crossed out and amended.

After seeing the house, visitors can wander across to the surviving, buttressed wing of the Tudor palace, now ignominiously used for medieval-style banquets, where a viewing bay allows a glimpse of the oak and chestnut 15th-century roof.

Knebworth ☆

1 m S Stevenage, direct access off A1 (M), exit 7; guided tours on weekdays; restaurant; garden; Raj exhibition; miniature railway; park; *open:* Apr–end May, Sat, Sun, BHs, June–early Sept, Tues–Sun, then Sat, Sun only to end Sept 12–5; tel: 0438 812661

Just outside the glass and concrete of Stevenage, a grassy rise is crowned with this ebullient, turreted and battlemented High Victorian gothic fantasy, bristling with heraldic beasts and gargoyles. Strangely, the great hall wing of a genuine medieval house is hidden beneath the 19th-century alterations, with diapered Tudor brick and blocked windows visible beneath flaking stucco. But Knebworth today is entirely Victorian in spirit, and something of a shrine to Edward Bulwer-Lytton, the historical novelist and friend of Dickens who inherited the house in 1843. Not content with his mother's gentle gothicizing of the old mansion, Edward employed H. E. Kendall to create the present abandoned exterior and J. D. Crace to provide similarly unrestrained interiors.

Crace is at his most inventive in the drawing-room, with its brightly painted heraldic ceiling, richly coloured chimney-piece flanked by canopied statue niches, stained glass, heavy gothic furniture, and a crown-like chandelier. Lytton family portraits hang on the walls and also here is the 19th-century Irish painter Daniel Maclise's vision of Edward IV visiting Caxton's printing press, every historical detail painstakingly researched. The novelist is included as an armour-clad lord and Maclise's full-length portrait of him, in a pose of studied informality, hangs outside on the landing.

This climax, sadly presented without any attempt to suggest it was ever lived in, is reached through the much-altered, pine-panelled, late Elizabethan great hall, where Dickens put on some of his amateur theatricals, and up Crace's Jacobethan staircase. Heavy, rather oppressive furnishings and colour schemes tend to detract attention from portraits attributed to Gheeraerts, John de Critz, Lely, Riley and the Dutch artist van Hoogstraeten, a charming sketch by Rex Whistler showing his plan for exposing the Tudor brickwork, and an oil of the hall in the 1930s by Winston Churchill, who once proposed to the beautiful Pamela Chichele-Plowden, future wife of the 2nd Earl.

There are copies of letters from Dickens, one of them suggesting a happy ending for *Great Expectations*, and a charming note to the 2nd Earl's children from Sir Edwin Lutyens, who designed the low-key, panelled entrance hall running across the house. Bulwer-Lytton's study is re-created as he had it, with the crystal ball into which he used to gaze on a cloth-covered table, and his favourite cherrywood pipe, several feet long, but any atmosphere is destroyed by the display cases. Similarly, visitors must avert their eyes from the soulless and commercial car-park area and from the distant view of Stevenage.

Moor Park Mansion ☆

1 m SE Rickmansworth, signed from A404; some guided tours in summer; *open:* all year, except BHs, Mon–Fri 10–12, 2–4, Sat 10–12; tel: 0923 776611

The main reason for visiting what is now an excessively grand golf club is to see a handful of lavish baroque interiors. First built for the Duke of Monmouth, Charles II's illegitimate son, in *c.*1678, Moor Park was bought some forty years later by a newly rich London merchant, who commissioned Sir James Thornhill to make radical alterations. The exterior, now without its original flanking pavilions, is Palladian, with a massive pedimented portico on the entrance front. From here, visitors step straight into the astonishing two-storey hall, ringed by a galleried landing and with life-size figures reclining on the marble doorcases. Every inch is covered with exuberant paintings by Jacopo Amigoni and Francesco Sleter or high relief plasterwork, with a realistic *trompe l'oeil* dome outlined on the ceiling.

The hall is the high point of a short tour which also takes in a painted staircase and saloon, the latter possibly by Verrio for the Duke of Monmouth, and a dining-room with a more delicate, Adamesque ceiling. Clubhouse trappings and denizens are everywhere, and the landscaped park is now a rat-run of fairways and greens.

Shaw's Corner ☆

At SW end of Ayot St Lawrence, 3 m W Welwyn; NT; garden; *open:* Apr–end Oct, Wed–Sat 2–6 (closed Gd Fri), Sun, BH Mon 12–6; admission by timed ticket on busy days; tel: 0438 820307

Narrow lanes lead to the hideous, red-brick Edwardian villa at the end of a leafy village where the writer and dramatist George Bernard Shaw came to live in 1906. Set in a steeply sloping garden, with views to the countryside beyond, the house is as unattractive inside as it is out, its period furnishings almost uniformly drab. The connection with Shaw is everything, and it was the great man himself who decided to leave the place to the National Trust, moving photographs, books, pictures and other belongings here from his London house. The small rooms are full of Shaviana, from his card for the reading-room of the British Museum and theatrical relics, such as the typescript of St Joan, to photographs of his idols, friends and compatriots, among them William Morris, 'four great men rolled into one', Sean O'Casey, W. B. Yeats, Ibsen, Ghandi, and Stalin. There is a bronze bust of Shaw by Rodin and a portrait by Augustus John, who has elongated the writer's head; and there is his unnaturally tidy study, one wall lined with books, the drawers of the filing cabinet carefully labelled, and a small desk for a secretary beside Shaw's large one, his looking out on the garden, hers facing a blank wall.

This is a house of the mind, not of the senses. Only the dullest of meals could have come out of the basic, brown and yellow kitchen, and Shaw's monastic bedroom is simple to the point of austerity. If any of the ladies who pursued him so ardently in his declining years had seen this room, they would have realized their hopes were unfounded.

London

Chiswick House ☆

Between Burlington Lane and Great West Road just W Hogarth roundabout; EH; audio tour; café; extensive Italianate grounds; *open:* daily, 10–6 in summer, 10–4 in winter; tel: 081 995 0508

This pint-sized Palladian doll's house looking over the bedraggled remains of an 18th-century garden is a rich man's whimsy. Fired by what he had seen in Italy, in particular the works of the 16th-century architect Andrea Palladio, the wealthy 3rd Earl of Burlington designed his own Venetian villa, building it in the grounds of his 17th-century house at Chiswick. The earlier building has now gone, and the 3rd Earl's creation, put up in the 1720s, stands alone, its stuccoed façades dazzlingly white among all the greenery. Loosely based on Palladio's Villa Rotonda at Vicenza, it is a domed, two-storeyed square, with a slightly fussy double-armed staircase rising to the sculptural portico marking the entrance, and obelisk-like chimneys ranged along each side.

Inside, visitors see a series of small, interconnecting, virtually unfurnished rooms, some of them only a few feet across. Both floors are laid out to the same strongly geometric design, with rectangular, circular and octagonal spaces arranged round a central octagon under the dome. But whereas the lower storey is dark, plain and low-ceilinged, the principal rooms above are airy, richly decorated boxes, adorned with gilded plasterwork and inept and vacuous ceiling paintings by William Kent, one of Lord Burlington's protégés. As it is today, the villa seems wildly inconvenient and impractical, but it was never intended to be self-contained. The Earl conceived it as an adjunct to the existing house, a kind of private retreat where he could contemplate his paintings, read his books and indulge in conversation with like-minded friends. Thus, while a capacious brick-vaulted wine cellar can be seen in the bowels of the building, there is no kitchen.

The ground-floor rooms that once housed the Earl's library are now used for an exhibition on the house and gardens, but many of his paintings – royal and family portraits by Ferdinand Elle, Jan Wyck, William Aikman and Michael Dahl, and a series of scenes from classical mythology by Daniel Seiter and Sebastiano Ricci – still hang in the upstairs apartments, where they are seen against reproductions of the plush velvets – red, blue, green and canary yellow – with which these rooms were lined.

Ham House ☆☆

At Petersham, on S bank of Thames, 2 m W Richmond; NT; teas; garden; *open:* Apr–end Oct, Mon–Wed 1–5, Sat 1–5.30, Sun 11.30–5.30; tel: 081 940 1950

Overlooking a leafy stretch of the Thames, with the heights of Richmond Park at its back, is this tall, part sash-windowed, part mullioned-and-transomed house of dark red brick. Originally an H-shaped Jacobean mansion, Ham was transformed between 1672 and 1675 by the ruthless and ambitious Elizabeth, Countess of Dysart, and her second husband, the Duke of Lauderdale, whose temperament seems to have matched her own. Forming a close attachment long before the death of their respective spouses, this unattractive pair were married within six weeks of the 1st Lady Lauderdale's demise. New apartments, with sashes rather than Jacobean mullions, were built between the wings on the south front by the gentleman architect William Samwell, a row of bust-filled niches was added to the entrance façade, and the interior was refurbished with extravagant splendour.

Visitors see most of the two main floors in an extensive tour which also takes in the basement service rooms. The place is presented as it was in the

Lauderdale's time, with the remnants of the original furnishings, together with some reproductions, loans and a few later pieces, arranged according to inventories of the late 1670s and '80s. Panelled rooms, some hung with recreations of the rich yellow and crimson, black and red hangings that were once here, lead one into another, with the Duke and Duchess's four-room apartments arranged either side of the formal dining-room in the centre of the south front and their state suite, prepared for a visit by Charles II's queen, on the floor above, back to back with a set of state rooms fitted out in the 1630s by Elizabeth's father. No interior is very large, with the richest fabrics and furnishings and ceiling paintings by Verrio reserved for the intimate closets which end each range.

The Lauderdales' patronage of Dutch artists and craftsmen comes through in inset overdoor and overmantel paintings by Van de Velde the Younger, Thomas and Jan Wyck, Dirck van den Bergen, and Abraham Begeyn, and in the plain Delft tiles lining fireplaces. Silver tongs, bellows and other chimney furniture are the height of ostentation, blue and white oriental porcelain adorns mantelpieces and other surfaces, and there is some superb 17th-century marquetry, as well as cane-backed Stuart chairs, and contemporary parquet floors. Elizabeth's father was responsible for the painted and gilded great staircase with its carved balustrade, and for the compartmental plaster ceilings and decorative paintings by Franz Cleyn in the 1630s apartment, and his remodelled long gallery still runs across the house, the carved panelling with its fluted pilasters setting off 17th-century portraits in identical decorative frames. Elsewhere you can see Lely's silvery, ethereal painting of Elizabeth as a young woman, and the same artists's double portrait, done some thirty years later, of the Duke and Duchess, both hard-faced and worldly. Some of the finest and rarest fabrics, such as hangings from the state bed, are shown behind glass, and there is also a display of miniatures and other treasures, including works by Hilliard and Oliver, and a lock of hair cut from the head of Robert Devereux, 2nd Earl of Essex, on 25 February 1601, the morning of his execution.

Hampton Court ☆☆

East Moseley, on N bank of Thames, 12 m W central London; audio and guided tours of selected areas; tearoom; extensive gardens and park; open: daily, mid Mar–mid Oct, 9.30–6, mid Oct–mid Mar, 9.30–4.30 (Mon opening 10.30, and some parts closed winter months); tel: 081 977 8441

Cradled in a bend of the Thames, and almost surrounded by open parkland, is this vast red-brick palace, sprawled around three major courts and some dozen smaller yards and closes. Two quite different buildings are set back to back. The west side, with stone-mullioned, battlemented ranges framing an assertive gatehouse, and a skyline display of turrets, finials, and moulded and twisted brick chimneys, is still largely Tudor, as built from 1514 by the self-important Cardinal Wolsey and aggrandized, after the cardinal's downfall, by the equally acquisitive Henry VIII. All Henry's queens came here, the badges of two – Anne Boleyn and Jane Seymour – are carved on the building, and here his only son, Edward VI, was born. The east side, lined up with three great avenues radiating away across the park, is a serene and symmetrical baroque composition in a mix of brick and stone, built for William and Mary from 1689 by Christopher Wren. The king, who was asthmatic, needed to escape London's fog and smoke, and the flat Thames valley with its meandering river reminded him of his native Holland.

There were further changes in 1716–18 for the future George II and his consort Caroline of Anspach, William Kent did some remodelling in the 1730s, and there is more than a touch of 19th-century restoration, but it is Henry, and William and Mary, who preside here. The grassy outer courtyard, with Henry's arms emblazoned over the gateways, is Tudor, the peaceful innermost quadrangle, centred on a fountain pool and surrounded by a stone colonnade, is Wren's, and the two periods come together in the central Clock Court. On the north side, the chapel-like silhouette of Henry's great hall rises above every other range of the palace, its slender buttresses tapering into finials crowned by heraldic beasts. On the south side is an assertive classical colonnade added by Wren, the stone white against the brickwork all around.

The range damaged in the 1986 fire has been reopened, with some sixty rooms, galleries and staircases now on show. It would be easy to spend a day here, and it is certainly not a place that can be hurried through. To help visitors make sense of what they see, the authorities have divided the interior into six manageable chunks, each focused on a set of period rooms and reached by a separate entrance. Alas, the experience is a variable feast. First, few of the original contents survive. Much was sold following the execution of Charles I, and, when Hampton Court ceased to be a royal residence in the 18th century, much went to furnish other palaces. After the excitement of the exterior, visitors are too often faced with bare, meaningless rooms. Then, although Hampton Court is used to display paintings from the royal collection, including many that had belonged to Charles I, these are presented with little or no information, and are often hung so they can hardly be seen.

Henry's great hall is still immensely impressive, despite the Victorian stained glass in the windows and the polished floor, as if for dancing. Nearly 100 ft long and 60 ft high, and furnished only with Flemish tapestries that belonged to the king, it is lit to draw all eyes upwards to the sculptural, carved and gilded hammerbeam roof, on which Henry's carpenters worked round the clock, lighting the night with hundreds of candles. The gallery down which Henry's fifth queen, the adulterous Catherine Howard, ran screaming to plead with the king leads to the richly decorated chapel, a mélange of 16th-, 17th- and 19th-century work, with a blaze of blue and gold from the Tudor fan-vaulted ceiling, a carved oak reredos by Grinling Gibbons, and a *trompe-l'oeil* window by Sir James Thornhill, who took over the decoration of the Wren palace from the less-talented Verrio after the latter's death in 1707. There is a separate tour of the crypt-like Tudor wine cellars and roughly plastered, lofty Tudor kitchens, with a warming blaze in one of the huge fireplaces, and peacocks, a boar and other delicacies being prepared for a feast, and the so-called Wolsey rooms, shown unfurnished and confusingly sited in two different parts of the palace, include a tiny closet with another gilded ceiling and painted walls.

The ranges in which Henry and his queens lived were destroyed by Wren. In their place are the suites round Fountain Court created for William and Mary, with each monarch provided with a set of state rooms for audiences and receptions as well as more intimate apartments for their private lives. King and queen have their own grand staircases, hers, not decorated until the 1730s, with subdued murals by William Kent, his with a strikingly inept array of cloud-borne deities by Verrio. Of what follows, the William III rooms, newly re-created after the fire, are the most rewarding. Looking south towards the river on the first floor are the King's state apartments, a sequence of spacious, high-ceilinged rooms leading from a guard room at one end, where the whole court could mingle, via a series of audience chambers, one dominated by William's crimson canopy of state, and the room where the monarch dined in public, to the king's bedchamber, where the most trusted and privileged had access. Panelled in oak, and lit as if by candlelight from a series of glittering *torchères* down the window wall, these rooms are sparsely furnished in 17th-century style. Tudor tapestries on the walls are as William had them, overdoor and overmantel paintings by such as Rousseau and Fetti are surrounded by limewood carvings by Grinling Gibbons, with expert re-creations of those that were destroyed in the fire, the floors are bare pine as they would have been in the 17th century, the innermost rooms have painted ceilings by Verrio, and mantelpieces are crowded with some of Queen Mary's cherished collection of oriental porcelain.

The private rooms on the floor below are even more successful. A positively cosy study has William's books in tall, glass-fronted cases, one of his barometers on the wall and a plan of fortifications such as he loved to study out on the table; the dining-room, set for dessert with pyramids of cherries, meringues and crystallized fruits, is hung with Kneller's paintings of the ladies of the court which had been commissioned by Mary; and for half the year a connecting gallery is filled with the smell of overwintering orange trees.

Mary's rooms, with the private apartments looking on to Fountain Court back to back with the state rooms facing east over the gardens, are much less convincing, the best of them a tapestry-hung gallery dotted with blue and white Delftware tulip vases made for the royal couple. Several rooms were completed by Vanbrugh after William and Mary's death, with bold doorcases and chimney-pieces, and there are more murals by Verrio, but there is little in the way of furniture and the private rooms, with their early 19th-century flock papers, are positively drab. Here, and in the bare suite fitted out for George II's son by William Kent, as well as in a couple of purposeful gallery rooms, are hung paintings from the Royal Collection, none of them adequately labelled and few well lit.

Apart from the Kneller portraits, a similar array of identikit beauties by Lely, and other paintings of the English court, there is a concentration on 16th- and 17th-century works by German, Flemish and Italian artists. Although paintings are changed from time to time, visitors are likely to see Alessandro Allori's *Judith with the Head of Holofernes*, works by Tintoretto, Lotto, Palma Vecchio, Luca Giordano, Annibale Carracci and Correggio. The lucky will spot a self-portrait of the youthful Raphael, Pieter Brueghel the Elder's *Massacre of the Innocents*, set in a wintery Flemish village, works by Holbein and Joos van Cleve, Clouet's portrait of Henry VIII's rival, Francis I, and Giulio Romano's menacing study of Isabella d'Este. What is proclaimed as the palace's greatest treasure, Mantegna's sequence of panels known as *The Triumph of Caesar*, hangs alone in a former orangery, the stiff figures and two-dimensional treatment of this Renaissance masterpiece not, perhaps, as immediately appealing as many of the works in the main palace.

Kenwood ☆☆

Hampstead Lane, north London, on N edge of Hampstead Heath; EH; teas; *open:* daily, 10–6 in summer, 10–4 in winter; tel: 081 348 1286

Kenwood sits high above London, looking out towards the city over the green and leafy spaces of Hampstead Heath. There has been a house here since Jacobean times, but the stuccoed classical villa seen today was the result of Robert Adam's remodelling of the existing building in 1764–79. Consisting of a pedimented, delicately ornamented central block flanked by low pavilions, and much less grandiose than Adam's comparable creations at *Syon* and *Osterley*, Kenwood was devised as a modest country retreat for William Murray, 1st Earl of Mansfield and Lord Chief Justice, who needed to be no more than a short ride from central London. Two wings of drab yellowish brick projecting from the entrance front were additions of 1793–6 for the 3rd Earl.

The interior is principally an art gallery. Later generations of the Murrays preferred *Scone Palace* to London, and early this century most of the contents were either sold or taken to Scotland. Kenwood itself was saved by the philanthropic millionaire, Edward Cecil Guinness, 1st Earl of Iveagh, who bought the place in 1925 and left it to the nation, together with a superb collection of paintings.

Although the authorities are gradually buying back Adam's original furniture, and have acquired a set of gilded settees and stools which the architect designed for *Moor Park*, most rooms are bare and uncarpeted, with those upstairs used for changing exhibitions and collections of jewellery and shoe buckles. There is much surviving detail by Adam, including an enchanting chinoiserie fireplace, but only the apse-ended blue and gold library with a high barrel ceiling decorated with plasterwork by Joseph Rose the Younger and inset paintings by Antonio Zucchi has anything like a coherent period feel.

Elsewhere, it is the Earl of Iveagh's pictures which steal the show. Largely acquired in the late 19th century, these are headed by a late self-portrait by Rembrandt, Vermeer's *The Guitar Player*, and portraits by Hals and Van Dyck. Sea- and riverscapes include a stormy shore scene by Turner, an elegiac view of Dordrecht by Aelbert Cuyp, a typical Van de Velde, and a panorama of Old London Bridge by the rarely seen Claude de Jongh. There is a clutch of paintings by Boucher and Pater, a scattering of Italian art, and a feast of 18th-century portraits of society beauties. A couple of elegant Gainsboroughs, notably his serene Countess Howe, her pink dress barely ruffled by an approaching storm, are gathered in the former orangery, with a Van Dyck portrait of a lady of the Stuart court for company, a black page at her side. Close by is a room of mannered Romneys and Reynolds's, among them a painting of Emma Hamilton as a peasant at her spinning wheel, a plump chicken at her feet, and a likeness of the courtesan Kitty Fisher, her marmoreal skin tones perhaps reflecting the white lead she plastered on her face and which was to kill her in her twenties.

Marble Hill House

Richmond Road, Twickenham, EH; café; park; *open:* all year, daily, summer, 10–6, winter, 10–4 (closed Christmas); tel: 081 892 5115

Looking over a sweep of grass to the Thames is a stuccoed Palladian villa, with a pyramidal roof crowning the neat, three-storey façades. More country retreat than grand mansion, its rooms small and intimate, Marble Hill was built in 1724–9 for the engaging Henrietta Howard, later Countess of Suffolk, whose royal lover, the future George II, had recently given her a substantial financial settlement. Although based on a design by Colen Campbell, the final building owes as much to Henrietta's admirer Lord Henry Herbert, and to the architect builder Roger Morris. In the 18th century, Twickenham was no more than a pretty Thameside village, and there is still an illusion of country here, with views of a tree-screened *Ham House* across the water.

Inside, visitors see three floors of bare and sparsely furnished rooms. The one grand interior, reached by an impressive mahogany stair, is the Great Room on the first floor, clearly modelled on one of the state rooms at Lord Herbert's *Wilton House*. Designed as a 24 ft cube, with a lofty ceiling rising into the third storey, it is richly decorated with carved and gilded woodwork and with inset panels carrying architectural capriccios by Panini and suitable replacements for the other paintings that were once here. A stone-floored hall faces towards the river, by which most of Henrietta's visitors would have arrived, and a tight stone stair leads up to the unexpected long gallery on the third floor, with inset cupboards displaying blue and white delftware and other 18th-century porcelain. Sadly, almost all the original furniture has been lost. Apart from some capacious George II chairs with embroidery covers, and a couple of beds, the sparse period pieces here now are all too obviously space-fillers, and there are some virulently green, reproduction 18th-century wallpapers.

145
London

Osterley Park ☆

Isleworth, N of A4 (Great West Road), via
Thornbury Road; NT; teas; park; *open:*
Apr–end Oct, Wed–Sat 1–5 (closed Gd Fri),
Sun and BH Mon 11–5; tel: 081 560 3918

Cocooned within a spacious park, with belts of trees screening the spread of west
London but not, alas, the roar of traffic on the M4, is a hollow red-brick rectangle
with jaunty corner turrets. Built as a quadrangular Elizabeth mansion, Osterley
still has its Tudor stable block, but the house, while retaining its 16th-century
form, was thoroughly remodelled between 1750 and 1780, first by Sir William
Chambers and then, more importantly, by his arch-rival Robert Adam. On three
sides, regular, sash-windowed façades with roofline balustrades look out over the
park, while the east-facing entrance front is dominated by Adam's immense flight
of steps and open colonnade giving access to the raised central courtyard.

Transformed for the Child brothers, Francis and Robert, who had inherited
a fortune from their grandfather, founder of Child's Bank, 18th-century
Osterley was seen as a country retreat, intended to complement the family's
Berkeley Square house. The interior is still much as Chambers and Adam left
it, with decorative plasterwork – now restored to its original colouring – and
inset paintings by Zucchi and Cipriani setting off period furnishings, including some exquisite marquetry pieces by John Linnell. But despite its integrat-
ed Georgian interiors, Osterley is a curiously soul-less place, like a house gone
to sleep. Perhaps this is because almost all the family paintings have gone,
with only one portrait, of Robert's two-year-old daughter Sarah Anne,
remaining. Perhaps, too, it is too long since anyone lived here.

The visitor tour, embracing all the ground floor and a clutch of upstairs
rooms, is devised so that Adam's grand state apartment comes last. Starting in
the cool, stone-floored hall, the route moves into the north wing, taking in
Adam's library, with its inlaid desk and writing tables by John Linnell,
Chambers' pink and green eating-room, arranged in the 18th-century way
with the chairs against the walls and no central table, and a rather forlorn
bedroom suite, now without most of its original furniture. Chambers' finest
contribution is the sparsely furnished, 130 ft long gallery running down the
west front. The pea-green walls which once showed off paintings by Rubens
and Van Dyck now display a selection of mostly second-rate works on loan
from the V & A, but the furnishings, including delicate mother-of-pearl pagodas and sampans against the window wall, were all here in the 18th century.

The gallery is a prelude to the formal, four-room enfilade down the south
range. These interiors were for display only, with a golden drawing-room
obviously designed for special occasions leading into the ante-room hung
with rose-pink Gobelins tapestries that starts the state apartment. In the silk-
hung bedroom beyond is Adam's temple-like four poster, wreathed with artificial flowers, and the sequence ends with the Etruscan dressing-room
inspired by the excavation of Pompeii, with walls and doors painted by
Pietro Mario Borgnis with the kind of classical motifs now associated with
Wedgwood ware.

Syon House ☆☆☆

Between Brentford and Isleworth, off A315; teas; butterfly house; motor museum; extensive garden; excellent audio guide; *open:* Apr–end Sept, Wed–Sun and BH Mon 11–5, Sun in Oct, 12–5; tel: 081 560 0881

Seat of the Percys, Dukes of Northumberland, this Thames-side house only 8 miles from central London has had more than its share of history. Here Catherine Howard, Henry VIII's wanton fourth queen, waited for her execution, here the body of the king himself lay for a night on the way to Windsor, here Lady Jane Grey was pressed to accept the Crown, and here, one November night in 1605, Guy Fawkes interrupted the 9th Earl's dinner to call away his accomplice in the Gunpowder Plot.

Although now engulfed by the spread of the city, Syon is still set in a spacious park running down to the Thames, with the wooded acres of Kew Gardens giving an illusion of countryside across the river. Do not be cast down by the vast car park and its tawdry, commercialized fringe: the house stands serenely apart and, once inside, 20th-century trappings are left behind. Built in the form of a hollow square, this is a surprisingly austere place, with plain, castellated façades in yellow-grey stone, jaunty corner turrets, and box-like lodges guarding the approach. Originally a Bridgettine convent, and then a quadrangular Tudor house, Syon as it is today is largely the creation of Robert Adam, who transformed the antiquated building from 1762 for the 1st Duke. Where the outside is severe, Adam's interiors, devised within the shell of the 16th-century house, are rich and varied.

Visitors do a complete circuit of the main floor, where Adam's state rooms are wrapped like a girdle round the family apartments looking on to the courtyard. Cool decorative schemes alternate with explosions of colour. First comes the lofty classical hall, furnished only with statues and with plasterwork by Joseph Rose in the palest lilac, blue and stone; next, a rich anteroom ringed by twelve green-grey columns carrying gilded statues and with a boldly patterned, polychrome scagliola floor. An apse-ended dining-room with statue niches backed with mock red marble is again reserved and formal, a prelude to the colourful long drawing-room hung with fading red Spitalfields silk and with a coved painted and gilded ceiling looking for all the world like expensive wrapping paper. Adam's final creation, a 136 ft long gallery with views towards the river, is a delightful adaptation of the Tudor room, with delicate plasterwork in muted green and pink and medallion portraits of Northumberland ancestors going back to Charlemagne, and the tour ends in the *sotto voce* north range altered in the early 19th century.

Gilded seat furniture, mosaic-topped tables, ornate pier glasses and a delicate inlaid desk were all designed by Adam, but much of the furniture in the gallery came from the Percys' London house, and some, such as two inlaid Carolean cabinets, predates Adam's alterations. Apart from two 17th-century views of Syon and Rubens's *Diana Returning from the Hunt*, the paintings are largely portraits, among them likenesses of the 1st Duke and his wife by

Gainsborough and Reynolds, and the Stuart royal family by Honthorst, Mignard, Van Somer, Van Dyck and Lely. Most poignant is Lely's painting of Charles I with the Duke of York, executed when the king was a prisoner at nearby Hampton Court and his children were in custody at Syon.

Oxfordshire

Ardington House

In Ardington village, 12 m SW Oxford, 2½ m E Wantage, off A417; garden; *open:* May–Sept, Mon and BHs 2.30–4.30; tel: 0235 833244

Set in one of the quiet villages strung along the northern edge of the Berkshire Downs, Ardington looks out over water meadows fringing the little Lockinge Brook. Built in 1719–20, possibly by the younger Thomas Strong of Oxford, it is an imposing, symmetrically planned baroque mansion, with strongly vertical, pedimented, three-storey façades of an attractive mix of grey and red brick. Now owned by the Baring family, it is an elegantly and comfortably furnished, lived-in house. Of the few rooms shown, the most impressive is the spacious staircase hall filling the whole centre of the building, with two flights rising either side of a door to the garden and slender balusters of twisted oak, their newel posts topped with gigantic carved acorns. Much of the other carved wood and plasterwork was introduced in the 1860s, but 'the nicest dining-room in Oxfordshire', as John Betjeman called it, still has what is probably original oak panelling.

Ashdown House

3½ m N of Lambourn, on W side of B4000; NT; guided tours; woodland walks; *open:* Apr–end Oct, Wed, Sat 2–6 (closed Easter); tel: 0494 528051 (regional office)

Visiting this tall, 17th-century dolls' house set high on the Berkshire Downs is like climbing a tower. Only the staircase is shown, and, although this is splendid enough, and hung with contemporary portraits, it rises straight up to the most memorable feature of the tour, the balustraded viewing platform on the roof. From here, visitors can look out over the remnants of the woodland that once surrounded the house, and down the great avenue that still runs away to the north.

Built for the 1st Lord Craven, by the gentleman architect William Winde, Ashdown is a top-heavy, symmetrical, three-storey chalk box, its height increased by a cupola and massive chimney stacks. The portraits, several of them by Gerrit van Honthorst, show the family of Charles I's unlucky elder sister, briefly queen of Bohemia in the winter of 1619–20. The chivalrous and eccentric 1st Lord was a generous supporter of both Elizabeth and her brother, his reward this unusual collection of paintings, and the Bohemian stags' antlers that also hang on the stairs.

Blenheim Palace ☆☆☆

SW end of Woodstock, 8 m NW Oxford;
optional guided tour of state rooms; guided
tour of private apartments when Duke not
in residence (additional charge); restaurant
and café; garden and park; numerous other
attractions; *open:* mid March–end Oct,
daily, 10.30–5.30; tel: 0993 811325/811091

John Churchill, 1st Duke of Marlborough's rout of the French army at Blenheim, on 13 August 1704, gave the first serious check to Louis XIV's territorial ambitions. As a reward, Queen Anne, backed up by a grateful nation, presented her victorious general with the land and the funds for a magnificent house. The result is England's answer to Versailles, a baroque extravaganza of yellowish stone sprawled over some 7 acres, with a series of courtyards and triumphal archways forming the approach to the main house.

Right from the start, though, the building of Blenheim was hedged about with problems. The strong-willed, sharp-tongued duchess, who yearned after a red-brick house by Wren, quarrelled continually with Vanbrugh, the queen's chosen architect. Relations with the queen also soured, the Marlboroughs fell from favour, and royal payments for building operations ceased. At the lowest point, from 1712 to 1714, the Duke and Duchess took themselves abroad in a self-imposed exile. After Anne's death, they returned and the Duke finished the palace at his own expense. But he could not afford some of the most talented craftsmen. Shortly afterwards, Vanbrugh, goaded beyond endurance by the masterful Duchess, resigned, and the work was finished by his able assistant, Nicholas Hawksmoor. All things considered, it is amazing Blenheim has turned out as well as it has.

The palace is set in a glorious wooded park, with sweeping views over the islanded lake created by Capability Brown and up the slope beyond to the 134 ft Column of Victory. Vanbrugh's great entrance court is like a setting for grand opera, with a restless mélange of colonnades, stumpy towers and gateways leading all eyes inwards to the porticoed main block, and with a roofline cacophony of gesticulating statues, carved urns and military trophies. Bulbous finials perched at the corners of the towers look for all the world like giant chessmen.

Inside, visitors have two very different experiences. After a glimpse of the vast, cathedral-like hall plugging the centre of the house, walled by double arcades and with a painted ceiling by Sir James Thornhill, a couple of low-key rooms are devoted to Sir Winston Churchill, nephew of the 8th Duke, who was born at Blenheim. The birth room itself, a comfortless chamber curiously placed just off the hall, offers such relics as a swatch of the young Winston's chestnut-brown hair, a neatly darned vest which he wore as a baby, and a pink velvet siren suit. Museum-style exhibits next door include some of the revealing letters Winston sent his father from Sandhurst, and a laconic note from his housemaster at Harrow, disinterestedly reporting a case of mild concussion.

Then come the grand, formally furnished state rooms running down the south front. Most magnificent is the stone-floored, domed saloon, where the present Duke and his family dine once a year, on Christmas Day. The mahogany doors have sculptural marble surrounds, one of them by Grinling Gibbons, and murals by Louis Laguerre, showing a silent crowd looking down into the room, fill every inch of walls and ceiling. To either side are suites of lofty drawing-rooms, those to the west decorated with elaborate gilded woodwork in Louis XIV style that was added in the late 19th century, and several hung with Brussels tapestries illustrating Marlborough's campaigns, with bloody battles being conducted in serene, pastoral landscapes. There are carved marble fireplaces, ornate mirrors, florid boulle pieces with complicated inlays, a series of little bronzes, including a sentimental study of the baby 10th Duke by Fuchs, bluejohn candelabra of startling ugliness by Matthew Boulton, and a rococo, Paul de Lamerie inkstand. A hastily scribbled note on the back of a tavern bill is how Marlborough informed Queen Anne of his glorious victory.

Some striking paintings hang among all this florid grandeur. Although the Blenheim collection is not a patch on what it was, there are still a number of fine portraits, among them three canvases by Van Dyck, including a charming study of his mistress, the 4th Duke and his family by Reynolds, and works by Romney and Kneller. Also here are portraits of the willowy, gipsy-like American heiress Consuelo Vanderbilt, whose arranged marriage to the 9th Duke in 1895, when still in her teens, was designed to revitalize the Marlborough fortunes. Sargent's family group in the red drawing-room shows her with her two sons – 'the heir and the spare' – the severe black gown with sleeves lined in rose-pink satin which she is wearing chosen to echo the colouring in a Van Dyck portrait across the room.

To get the most out of Blenheim, it is best to move through the rooms at your own speed, resisting the frequent guided tours which sweep visitors rapidly through the state apartments and on into the opulently furnished, 183 ft library which ends the tour. The guides are informative and interesting, but the groups – a way of accommodating the thousands who flock here – are almost always too large for comfort, and move too fast.

Broughton Castle ☆☆☆

2 m SW Banbury on B4035, Shipston-on-Stour road; teas; garden; *open:* mid May–mid Sept, Wed, Sun 2–5, also Thurs in July, Aug and BH Sun and Mon, inc. Easter; tel: 0295 262624

This magical fortified manor of honey-coloured limestone, home of the Fiennes family for over 600 years, straddles a moated, grassy island, its only approach guarded by a 15th-century gatehouse and an equally ancient church rising out of the trees across the water. The show north front, facing the gatehouse, is a long agglomeration of steep Tudor gables, canted bays and stone mullioned-windows, with a traceried window marking the chapel at one end. An attempt at symmetry is just a 16th-century gloss on a much older building, begun by Richard Fiennes in c.1300. Inside, Broughton is a place of narrow, groined passageways, low, vaulted ceilings, worn steps and bare stone walls, but also of exuberant plasterwork, richly carved wood and stately fireplaces. Lavishly fitted out in Elizabethan times, the castle was saved from Victorian alterations by William Thomas Fiennes, 15th Lord Saye and Sele, a Regency rake who squandered the family fortune and was even forced to auction off the swans on the moat. It is still largely as it was at the end of the 16th century, despite some redecoration in a gentle gothick style in Georgian times, but the bulk of the contents had to be sold, with the swans, in 1837.

The medieval manor is buried in the east end of the present house, the undercroft of the solar wing now forming the low-ceilinged, stone-vaulted dining-room, the tiny chapel with its primitive slab of an altar still floored with medieval tiles, and the great hall, once open to the rafters, subsumed in the present entrance hall, with its huge Tudor bays cut through the earlier walls and an 18th-century plaster ceiling. The substantial 16th-century alterations emerge more powerfully on the floor above, in the rooms leading off the peach-walled, portrait-hung long gallery. In the King's Chamber, once slept in by James I, one wall is almost filled by a Renaissance fireplace in stone and stucco, probably made by the Italian craftsmen who came over in 1538 to work on Henry VIII's virtuoso Nonsuch Palace, and the great parlour has a plaster ceiling of 1599, with heavy pendants falling out of an intricate interweaving design.

Because of the sale of 1837, Broughton is not richly furnished, but there are several family portraits, including Lely's painting of Mrs Nathaniel Fiennes, mother of the indefatigable Celia, who wrote an extensive journal during her travels across England in the late 17th century. A tiny chamber at the top of the west staircase – 'a room with no ears' – is where a 17th-century William Fiennes and his co-conspirators, Pym and Hampden among them, met to plan their opposition to Charles I. From this eyrie you can step out on to the roof and look down on the intimate garden created within the ruins of the Tudor kitchens, and the tour ends in a serene and airy drawing-room, the most beautiful room in the house, where decorative Elizabethan panelling and a crested internal porch are allied with comfortable sofas and 18th-century porcelain.

Buscot Park ☆☆

On A417, between Lechlade and Faringdon; NT; tearoom; walled and water garden; *open:* Apr–end Sept, Wed–Fri, and every 2nd and 4th weekend in month, 2–6, timed entry if house crowded; tel: 0367 242094 (not weekends)

A short, uphill walk from the car park brings visitors to this quietly confident stone house, first built in the 1770s. Victorianized by an extraordinary Australian millionaire, who planted acres of sugar beet to distil into alcohol and threaded the estate with a narrow gauge railway, Buscot was returned, in the 1930s, to its former appearance. The entrance front, with a broad flight of steps up to a pedimented central bay, is much as it must have looked 200 years ago, but the two low, lantern-topped pavilions to either side were added by Geddes Hyslop, the architect who restored the house.

Inside, some Georgian features are original, among them a couple of delicate, plasterwork ceilings and an inlaid marble fireplace; others are re-creations or have been brought from elsewhere. These mostly 18th-century decorative schemes are allied with paintings and furniture collected by the financier Sir Alexander Henderson, 1st Lord Faringdon, who bought the estate in 1889, and by his son, who employed Hyslop. Between them, these two men created what is primarily a show-place rather than a home.

On show are some nine rooms on two floors, with some of the best saved until last. The two lords seem to have bought furniture to suit the house, but their taste in paintings was more catholic, embracing Old Masters, English portraits, a clutch of pre-Raphaelite canvases, and work by 20th-century artists. The latter, including a John Ward portrait of the 3rd Lord Faringdon's family and meticulous flower paintings by Mary Grierson, are unsym-pathetically hung in a bedroom with chintzy wallpaper and Louis XVI-style, tapestry-covered armchairs. Also upstairs are works by Rossetti, Watts and Millais, relegated here, perhaps, so as not to detract from the one outstanding pre-Raphaelite composition, Burne-Jones's *Legend of the Briar Rose* running round the walls of the saloon. A romantic interpretation of the sleeping beauty story, Sir Edward's richly green and blue panels are set within a continuous gilded frame, his youthful knights and ladies sprawled in a tangle of pink roses as if recovering from a wild party.

Furnished with a set of gilded Empire chairs and stools and dotted with strongly coloured oriental ceramics, the Saloon is too rich for comfort. More restful sitting-rooms show off portraits by Reynolds, a sketchy Gainsborough landscape, and a collection of 15th- and 16th-century Italian paintings, among them a charming *Rest on the Flight into Egypt* attributed to Andrea Previtali, with the holy family sitting down to a simple picnic, and Sodoma's *Madonna and Child*, with a chubby Jesus on the knee of a young girl gorgeously attired in red and green. The music room which ends the tour has two of the collection's star portraits: Rubens's painting of a proud young marchesa, her chestnut curls framed by an extravagant ruff and her body encased in the shining armour of a tight silver dress; and Rembrandt's sober study of a fair-haired young man.

Fawley Court

1 m N Henley-on-Thames, on S side A4155 to Marlow; teas July and Aug; *open:* Mar–Oct, Wed, Thurs, Sun 2–5 (closed Easter and Whitsuntide weeks); tel: 0491 574917

This red-brick William and Mary house with grounds stretching down to the Thames is a sad shadow of what it once was. The Saloon still has glorious plasterwork of *c.*1690 and there are decorative schemes from the 1770s by James Wyatt, but the whole place, now a Polish religious and cultural centre, has a strongly institutional atmosphere and offers lacklustre displays of Polish documents, arms and armour.

Greys Court ☆

In village of Rotherfield Greys, 3 m W Henley-on-Thames, E of B481; NT; tearoom; enchanting gardens; *open:* Apr–end Sept, Mon, Wed, Fri 2–6 (closed Gd Fri); tel: 0491 628529

Set on the slope of a hill, with wide views over a wooded valley, is a place of great character and charm, most visited for the enchanting garden. The house is a modest, Tudor and Jacobean building, with stone-mullioned windows in a gabled, brick and flint frontage, roughly textured in alternating bands of red and grey like some rich hanging. Unlike many Trust houses, this one is lived in and feels cosy and welcoming. Just the downstairs rooms are shown, among them a delightful drawing-room with 18th-century plasterwork on both walls and ceiling; a cluttered schoolroom in an early 18th-century wing, with a carved stone fireplace, and furnishings in richly vibrant colours; and the kitchen in the oldest part of the house, with a huge brick fireplace, heavy beams, and a rough oak staircase leading out of it.

The house stands in the north-west corner of what was once the courtyard of a fortified manor, built by Sir John de Grey in 1347. All around, forming the bones of a romantic garden, are remnants of the medieval defences and brick-built Tudor outbuildings, among them a cobble-floored building sheltering a 12th-century well and a donkey-wheel, a tithe barn, and two of Sir John's sturdy towers, one ruined, the other buttressed and battlemented. A steep climb gives a bird's eye view of garden and buildings.

Kelmscott ☆☆

At far end of Kelmscott village, 2½ m E Lechlade, off B4449; teas; garden; *open:* Apr–Sept, Wed 11–1, 2–5; tel: 0367 252486

This substantial, many-gabled old house on the banks of the Thames is where the artist, craftsman, political idealist and writer William Morris lived from 1871 until his death in 1896. Although not furnished as he had it, it is filled with his possessions, and everything about the place reflects his belief in the craft-based society of a pre-industrial age.

The house is a tall Elizabethan and Jacobean building of mellow Cotswold stone with mullioned windows and three projecting wings, like an H that has lost one of its legs, and with gutters poking far beyond the eaves to throw rainwater clear of the walls. Inside, it is restful and uncluttered, with carpets or rush matting on bare, polished boards, and colour schemes in greys, blues, green and white. Each room shows off wallpapers, embroidered and printed hangings, furniture, pottery, drawings and paintings by Morris or others of his pre-Raphaelite circle, among them Philip Webb, Burne-Jones, Rossetti and de Morgan; some furnishings are hand-crafted, one-off pieces, others were produced, from original designs, by Morris's firm.

Here are intricate embroidered hangings produced by his wife Janey and an immaculate blue-green piece which is the only tapestry he ever worked himself. Upstairs is the early 19th-century four-poster in which he was born, and his bulbous-posted Jacobean bed, while a sizeable attic displays a hand-knotted carpet in rich blues, reds and greens designed by Morris and his partner Dearle. With the possible exception of some rather rustic furniture devised by Ford Madox Brown, everything is outstandingly accomplished. More personal items include Janey's gothic jewel casket, painted with faded, elongated, medieval figures by Rossetti and the tragic Lizzie Siddall; Rossetti's battered paintbox; and Charles Fairfax-Murray's pencil drawing of Morris on his death-bed, a halo of frizzy hair round the skull-like head.

When Morris first rented the house, Rossetti shared the tenancy with him, hoping this secluded Oxfordshire village would restore a system ravaged by chloral and whisky. The most arresting pictures are his portraits of Janey; in the best-known, burnished by the rich mahogany on which it is painted, she sits pensive at a table, dark-haired in a peacock-blue dress, but more overtly sensual are the sketches of her at the age of 21, which Rossetti used as studies for the figure of the Virgin in his altarpiece for Llandaff Cathedral. No-one seeing these drawings could doubt the painter's obsession with his sitter.

Kingston House ☆

In Kingston Bagpuize, 6 m W Abingdon at junction of A415 and A420; guided tours; teas; fine garden; *open:* Apr–end Sept, Sun and BH Mon, 2.30–5.30; tel: 0865 820259

Imposing 18th-century gates by the church signal this pleasing, red-brick and stone house set in an enchanting garden. Built some time between 1670 and 1710, by an unknown but assured architect, it is a balanced, baroque composition, with low wings flanking a pedimented, three-storey central block, prominent keystones in the window arches and pedestalled urns ornamenting the roofline. A grandiose rusticated entrance looks on to the lawn that was once a fronting courtyard. Inside, well-proportioned, high-ceilinged rooms panelled in oak and pine and an impressive cantilevered staircase slot easily into the rigidly symmetrical plan.

This is an elegant, comfortable family house, with much good English 18th-century furniture but nothing much in the way of paintings. Be prepared for a brisk guided tour, conducted in a tone that may make you feel you would prefer to wander outside. Here, a Tudor terrace walk, remnant of an earlier manor, leads to a brick gazebo built over an Elizabethan cockpit.

Mapledurham House ☆

In Mapledurham village, 4 m NW Reading, off A4074 Wallingford road; tearoom; garden and water-mill; *open:* Easter–end Sept, Sat, Sun, BH Mon 2.30–5; tel: 0734 723350

Mapledurham never quite lives up to the promise of its secluded, Thameside setting, with church and village clustered outside the gates, or to the first glimpses of massive chimney-stacks, steep gable ends, diapered brickwork and picturesque, half-timbered outbuildings. Although dating from *c.*1588, the house was substantially altered in the late 18th and 19th century, when it was given the ridiculous battlemented porch, and its mostly Georgian and Victorian interiors. Descendants of the builder, Sir Richard Blount, still live in the house, but the parts shown feel largely unused.

Visitors see some eight rooms, among them the Victorian version of a Tudor great hall, the cavernous Regency dining-room and the much-altered three-room state apartment on the first floor, where a Jacobean strapwork ceiling and some fine 18th-century pieces in the saloon are overwhelmed by strident upholstery and loud-patterned wallpaper. The adjoining boudoir is more all of a piece, but the bedroom is again discordant. Most satisfying are the Tudor staircase, hung with 16th- and 17th-century portraits and adorned with another Jacobean plaster ceiling, and the light and airy chapel in Strawberry

Hill gothick, with delicate plasterwork ribs white on a grey ground. Like the Barretts of *Milton Manor*, the Blounts were staunchly Catholic, and their chapel followed hard on the Catholic Relief Act of 1791.

The paintings, too, are worth more than a glance, the long sequence of family portraits here including works by Romney, Michael Dahl and Charles Jervas, William Dobson, Paul van Somer and Cornelius Johnson. An unusually relaxed Kneller of the ill-favoured Alexander Pope recalls the poet's long friendship with the buxom Martha Blount, to whom he left the elaborately framed landscapes and mirror that now hang in the state apartment, and in the dining-room is William Larkin's enigmatic, full-length portrait of a Jacobean lady in mourning, behind her a misty, well-wooded English landscape dotted with church spires and confident brick manor houses, such as Mapledurham must once have been.

Milton Manor ☆☆

In Milton village, just off A34, 4 m S Abingdon; guided tours; teas; garden; *open:* Easter and Whitsun Sat, Sun, Mon, June–end Aug, Tues–Fri and Aug BH Sat, Sun, Mon 2–5; tel: 0235 831287

There are no great paintings or treasures to admire here, but the house is a treat, with beautifully proportioned, lived-in rooms filled with period furniture. Completed in 1663, the manor is a compact, three-storey brick box, with giant pilasters running the length of the entrance front and a high, hipped roof. Low wings either side are sympathetic extensions by Stephen Wright – one-time Chief Assistant to William Kent – for Bryan Barrett, the wealthy London lacemaker who bought the property in 1764, and Barrett also added on the outbuildings and created the lake-like ponds that set off the house.

An enjoyable tour over much of the manor is dominated by Wright's startling Strawberry Hill gothick interiors in one of the wings. The spacious, sparsely-furnished library is a gem, with a delicate gothick frieze and gentle ogee arches over the inset bookcases and the long sash windows standing out white against pale loganberry walls. Many of the shelves are filled, not with books, but with china, the subtle aubergine, pink and green colouring of a dinner service blending beautifully with the soft purple of the walls. The adjoining Roman Catholic chapel, created for Barrett at a time when practising the faith was still illegal, is less playful but similarly striking, the panelled walls vividly white and some brownish medieval glass in the windows.

Wright also redecorated the old house in Georgian style, but he kept the original symmetrical plan, with three rooms of the same size on each floor; the 17th-century plasterwork ceiling in the drawing-room, with its wreaths of oak and bay leaves; and the splendid Caroline staircase that takes up a quarter of the building. Bryan Barrett himself, a direct ancestor of the present owner, looks down on visitors, together with his parents, from a stiffly grouped portrait by Joseph Highmore in the library, and his desk sits in the entrance hall.

Minster Lovell Hall

In Minster Lovell village, 3 m W Witney, off A40; EH; *open:* Good Fri or 1 Apr, whichever earlier, to Sept, daily, 10–6; tel: 0993 775315

At one end of a pretty, thatched village is this picturesque, leafy ruin on the banks of the River Windrush. A gaunt tower, footings in the grass, and substantial remains of the great hall range are all that survive of the grand courtyard house built by the wealthy Sir William Lovell in the 1430s, with three wings opening to the water. Close by is the village's Tudor church, also financed by Sir William, and a path leads to a round stone dovecote, one of a group of medieval farm buildings that was once attached to the manor.

Nuffield Place ☆

In Nuffield village, 7 m NW Henley-on-Thames, just off A423 to Oxford; teas; garden; *open:* May–Sept, every 2nd and 4th Sun, 2–5; tel: 0491 641224

This rambling, red-brick house with slatted grey shutters, tall chimneystacks, a steeply pitched red-tiled roof – and a row of gleaming Morris Minors in the drive – was the home of the philanthropic industrialist William Morris, Lord Nuffield, who brought motoring within the reach of every man. He and his wife moved here in 1933, greatly enlarging an early 19th-century building and commissioning new furniture from Hallidays of Oxford. The comfortable period rooms are still furnished as the Morris's had them, showing how the middle-class lived in the years before World War II.

Thirties touches are everywhere: in an Art Deco clock, in a huge and bulky radiogram, in Lalique vases and in a giant, gold-handled coronation mug. Halliday's superbly crafted reproduction furniture, such as a walnut bedroom suite with drawers lined in cedar wood, is married with some genuine antiques, including softly coloured Persian carpets that still bear the marks of Lady Nuffield's dogs. Most intriguing is the industrialist's bedroom, with its worn grey carpet laid on newspaper, a light with a cracked shade roughly rigged up over the bed, and a capacious built-in cupboard filled with pliers, screwdrivers, pincers and a bevy of alarm clocks. Someone who did not know would never guess that such a quiet, unassuming house was the home of a multi-millionaire.

Rousham Park ☆☆

12 m N Oxford, off A423 at Hopcrofts Holt Hotel; guided tours (c. 30 mins); important 18th-century landscape garden; *open:* Apr–end Sept, Wed, Sun, BHs 2–4.30; tel: 0869 47110/0860 360407

Delightfully uncommercial, and still lived in by descendants of Sir Robert Dormer, the builder, Rousham is an originally Jacobean house that was remodelled in 1738–40 by William Kent, and further altered, much less successfully, in the 19th century. Built of golden stone, it sits on a wide terrace above the sluggish River Cherwell, while below, hidden from sight in a side valley, is Kent's sublime landscape garden, one of the first of its kind, laid out round a chain of ponds and cascades and with wooded vistas focused on classical temples and other features. The exterior of the house is spoiled by the hideous Victorian plate-glass windows which have replaced most of Kent's attractive octagonal panes, but the entrance front still has a 17th-century feel to it, with a dignified Jacobean porch below Kent's battlemented roofline and playful central cupola. Low, pavilion-like wings are entirely Kent, and so too are the statue-filled niches on the garden front.

Visitors are whisked through attractively furnished, portrait-hung rooms in one of the most breathless of guided tours, the whole experience so rushed that you are standing outside the front door again before you hardly know you have been inside. A welcoming, low-ceilinged hall sets the tone, its restrained 18th-century panelling setting off family portraits by Cornelius Johnson, Lely and Kneller and the Jacobean door to the porch still displaying the lead-lined musket holes through which the Royalist Sir Robert Dormer intended to frighten off any advancing Parliamentarians. Of what follows, try and linger a minute or two in the parlour, fitted out in every detail by Kent, with green panelling setting off Italian bronzes on carved brackets, a painted ceiling which he executed himself, a classical doorway in each corner (three are false), a carved marble fireplace crowned by a positively baroque over-mantel, and furniture designed by the master.

There are miniatures by Samuel Cooper (sadly difficult to see), portraits by Reynolds and Dobson, and Meissen and Nymphenburg porcelain in the white and gold drawing-room on the first floor, and the imposing former library has a high, vaulted ceiling by Kent, like the inside of an exotic tent, and exuberant rococo plasterwork added by Thomas Roberts of Oxford in 1764 framing full-length portraits. Also on show are a panelled Jacobean bedroom and a couple of uninspired Victorian rooms on the garden front, where you can compare Kent's sketch of the view over the valley with the real thing.

Stanton Harcourt Manor ☆☆

In Stanton Harcourt, on B4449 9 m W Oxford; teas on Suns and BHs; garden; *open:* Easter–late Sept, BH Mon and selected Thurs and Sun, 2–6; tel: 0865 881928

The Harcourt family's great medieval manor was largely pulled down in the mid-18th century, but the remaining fragments are romantically dotted about the garden of the present house. On one side is the late-14th-century kitchen, the largest of its kind in the country, with a lofty pyramidal roof to take the smoke from the open fire, and a spider-web of timber supporting the shutters that could be opened and closed according to the wind. Across the grass, ragged edges showing where it was once attached to the Great Hall range, is a solitary battlemented tower, with a stone-vaulted chapel on the ground floor. And the grounds as a whole enfold not only the manorial fish ponds and an arm of the medieval moat but also the ancient village church, as if this, too, belonged to the house.

The 15th-century gatehouse was remodelled and extended in the 1860s and 1950s to create the present unassuming manor, its comfortable rooms displaying the Harcourt collection of paintings, furniture, porcelain and family relics. There is a case of 18th-century Sèvres, a set of monogrammed glasses that once belonged to Napoleon, and portraits by Lely, Kneller, Mytens and Reynolds. A voluptuous landscape is attributed to Rubens, a vast seascape is the work of the younger Willem Van de Velde and his brother Adriaen, and a serene interior with a young man totally absorbed in building a card house is by the 18th-century artist Jean Chardin. There are also two lovely landscapes by Paul Sandby of the family's seat at Nuneham Courtenay, one of them a sunset-reddened vista over the wooded Thames valley.

A piece of tattered gold and crimson cloth is said to be a fragment of the standard carried by Sir Robert Harcourt at Bosworth Field in 1485, and a sliver of etched glass set out on a table was taken from the topmost room in the tower where, in 1717–18, the poet Alexander Pope worked at his translation of Homer's *Iliad*, recording the completion of the fifth volume on one of the windows.

Stonor Park ☆☆

5 m N Henley-on-Thames, on Watlington road (B480); tearoom; garden and park; *open:* Apr, Sun, BH Mon, May–Sept, Wed, Sun, BH Mon (plus Thurs in July, Thurs and Sat in Aug) 2–5.30 (BH Mons from 12.30); tel: 0491 638587

Hidden in a fold of the Chilterns, with views to hanging beech woods across the valley, Stonor has one of the most secluded and beautiful settings of any country house. At first glance, despite the rough-walled chapel with a brick campanile to one side, the place seems all of a piece, with neat rows of sash windows in a long red-brick façade, shallow wings loosely suggesting a courtyard, and a central gabled porch. But this Georgian frontage is only skin-deep, a screen thrown round a jumble of originally medieval and Tudor ranges behind. At the back, where the house burrows into the hill, the mask is more apparent, with terraced gardens falling to an all-concealing, urn-topped wall.

Stonors have lived here for 800 years, and their house has grown gradually, room on room, from a 13th-century core. Inside, the spirit is again 18th-century, with some Georgian gothick decoration, but you can sense the bones of a much older place in the curiously aligned interiors, in the library created out of the 14th-century solar, and in the arcade of a two-aisled hall exposed in an inner courtyard.

The contents are a mixed bag. There are family portraits by Kneller, John Michael Wright, Hoppner and Nathaniel Dance, some arresting Renaissance drawings, and paintings by members of the 16th-century Carracci family, including a self-portrait by the best-known, Annibale. Sales in this century greatly depleted the furniture, and some of what is here now is on loan. The best, perhaps, is in Lady Camoy's bedroom, where a William and Mary four-poster with original red-and-gold hangings is set off by three serpentine-fronted Georgian pieces. Elsewhere, you can see some heavy Regency and French Empire productions, the most hideous a shell-shaped bed of mahogany and ebony inlaid with brass, rosewood and walnut. A silvered base, supposed to represent the rippling sea, tones nicely with a suite of equally disturbing, half-animate, oyster-shell chairs.

An empty attic room in the gable high over the front door is where, in 1581, the Catholic Stonors sheltered Edmund Campion. Here the Jesuit printed his *Decem Rationes*, an inflammatory defence of the old faith which led to his torture and execution a few months later.

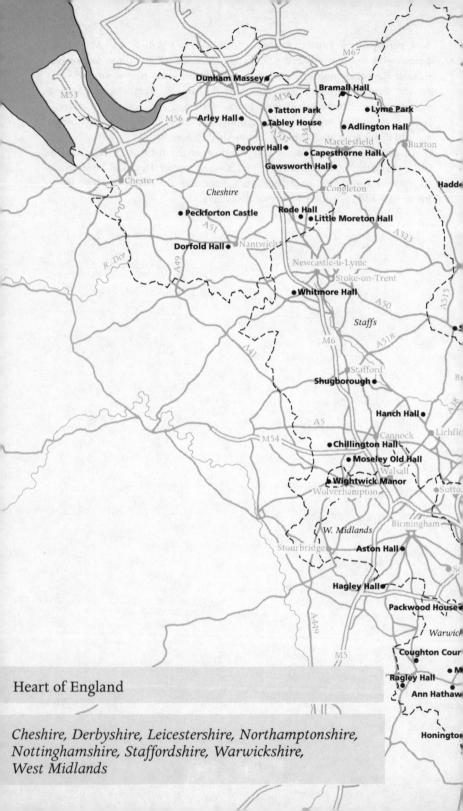

Heart of England

Cheshire, Derbyshire, Leicestershire, Northamptonshire, Nottinghamshire, Staffordshire, Warwickshire, West Midlands

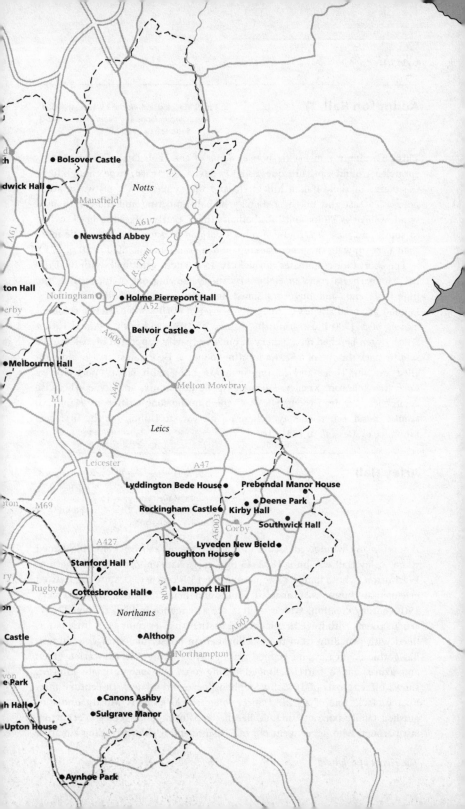

Cheshire

Adlington Hall ☆

5 m N Macclesfield, on A523; teas; wooded grounds; *open:* Good Fri–early Oct, Sun and BHs 2–5.30; tel: 0625 829206

This charmingly ramshackle house, home of the Legh family since 1315, is sprawled around a picturesque, roughly paved courtyard, large enough to be the piazza of some Italian hill town, and the venue for tea on warm afternoons. To east and north, a display of half-timbering and diamond-paned windows marks Tudor and Elizabethan ranges, partly refaced in brick, while to south and west are round-headed Georgian arcades, one now little more than a screen wall, the other backing on to a grand, pedimented front of 1750.

The short tour culminates in the lofty 45 ft Tudor great hall, with its original hammerbeam roof, an elaborate canopy curving out of the wall at the high-table end, and huge mullioned and transomed Elizabethan windows. Painted armorial shields compete with a set of stiffly posed, richly coloured murals of *c.* 1700 illustrating the history of Troy, and with a gilded Father Smith organ perched on a gallery at one end (partly supported on oak trunks said to mark the site of a Saxon hunting lodge). A Georgian staircase and panelled drawing-room and dining-room are hung with family portraits by Cornelius Johnson, Kneller, Hudson, Opie and Zoffany, and some otherwise comfortless Carolean rooms show off the hunting song written by Handel, a family friend, when he stayed here on his way to Dublin for the first performance of *Messiah* in 1751.

Arley Hall

5 m N Northwich, 6 m W Knutsford, signed from A50; guided tour (*c.* 50 mins); teas; romantic walled and yew-hedged garden; *open:* Apr–early Oct, Tues–Sun and BH Mon, 12–5; tel: 0565 777353

A solid, many-windowed Jacobean pile of diapered red brick and blackened stone, Arley Hall was built 1832–45 by George Latham for Rowland Egerton-Warburton, whose family came here in the 15th century. Despite the twisted ornamental chimneys, pinnacled gables and heraldic beasts, this is a very 19th-century creation, where visitors see a sequence of high-ceilinged, cavernous rooms with huge fireplaces and pastiche plaster ceilings. A little hall is lined with panelling from the old Elizabethan house, the outrageous library has gothic bookcases and stained glass glowing richly purple, scarlet, green and azure, and a barrel-ceilinged dining-room, the one intimate interior, shows off virginals of 1675 by Stephen Keene and a late 17th-century marquetry clock, one of a collection of longcase clocks here. Mostly undistinguished family portraits include Beechey's painting of Sir Peter Warburton, last baronet, who never went out of Cheshire and is shown reading a map of the county upside down, while upstairs, in the room where the future Napoleon III slept when he leased Arley in 1847–8, is a collection of romantic architectural watercolours by Rowland's son Piers. A gothic chapel was designed by Anthony Salvin, with one aisle by Street, and there is a 15th-century cruck barn on the way in.

Bramall Hall

3 m S Stockport, off A5102; café; park; *open:* Apr–Sept, daily, 1–5 (Sun from 11), Oct–Mar (closed Jan), Tues–Sun, 1–4; tel: 061 485 3708

On a rise in what is now a leafy public park sits one of the most substantial timber-framed houses in the north-west. Although dating from Elizabethan

and early Jacobean times, when a 15th-century core was expanded to surround a courtyard, Bramall's picturesque façades – a medley of ornamental
woodwork, finialled gables, tall, moulded brick chimneys and small-paned
casements – are partly the product of a romantic 19th-century restoration,
when some parts were entirely rebuilt, and the interior was refurbished in
antiquarian style.

In the hands of the local council since the 1930s, the house is now more
museum than home. The three surviving ranges surround a dispiriting sweep
of asphalt, and the rooms shown, on two floors of the east and south ranges,
are bare-floored, sparsely furnished and forlorn. Original features include a
decorative timber roof over the former solar, a pendanted plaster ceiling, fine
Elizabethan overmantel and striking Renaissance doorway in the first-floor
drawing-room, and some 16th-century wall paintings, notably a red and
green swirl imitating tapestry in the solar, and traces of a pre-Reformation
Passion painting in the tiny chapel. Some period furnishings are mixed with
richly carved Victorian pieces in 17th-century style and there are portraits of
the Davenport family, who lived here for 500 years, and also some fine Arts
and Crafts metalwork.

Capesthorne Hall ☆

7 m S Wilmslow, on A34; tearoom; gardens;
open: Apr, Sun, BH Mon, May, Aug and
Sept, Sun, Wed, BH Mon, June, July,
Tues–Thurs and Sun, 2–4; tel: 0625 861221

Capesthorne looks good from a distance, its long east front rising to an eventful skyline of slender turrets, curving gables and massive chimneystacks, but
close to it is revealed as a piece of romantic Victoriana, in a heavy-handed
Jacobean style. Originally created for Edward Davenport by Edward Blore,
who dressed up an existing 18th-century building in 1837, it was reconstructed only some twenty years later, to designs by Anthony Salvin, after a
fire gutted the main block, leaving the slightly sinister, blackened outline
seen today.

The tour takes in three high-ceilinged airy reception rooms, notable for
some eye-catching colour schemes, and a clutch of mostly unmemorable bedrooms. Although the spacious formal drawing-room has a splendid set of
Venetian armchairs, and there is contemporary needlework on a Jacobean
four-poster upstairs, Capesthorne is of greatest interest for Edward
Davenport's collection of Roman and Greek busts and vases, some of which
line the main downstairs corridor, and for the portraits and other paintings.

The early Italian works collected by Edward's younger brother are mostly
gone, but among the usual family portraits visitors see a brooding, sensuous,
gipsyish face that is said to be a self-portrait of Salvator Rosa, Allan Ramsay's
painting of a doe-eyed, curiously feminine Rousseau, distant vistas of Naples
by Antonio Joli, Hendrik van Minderhout's view of 17th-century Antwerp,
and a Lowry vision of the house, with the whole building tilting sideways
against a lead-white sky and a stick dog running among red-blob cows.

Dorfold Hall ☆

On A534 just S Acton village, no advance signs; guided tours (c. 30 mins); garden; *open:* Apr–Oct, Tues and BH Mon 2–5; tel: 0270 625245

A picturesque lodge by William Nesfield flags the entrance to this gabled Jacobean house of diapered red brick, with stone-mullioned windows and stacks of octagonal chimneys. The dignified entrance front is set off by a delicious courtyard, framed by restlessly zig-zagging, gabled façades. Although Jacobean in style, these whimsical compositions are 19th-century extensions joining the main block to two genuine 17th-century lodges.

The friendly unhurried tour of what is very much a family home takes in the hall running across the house and about four other rooms. The downstairs was modernized in the 18th century and is primarily Georgian, with furniture and plasterwork to match, the main features being a painting of the builder by Cornelius Johnson, portraits by Mierevelt and Northcote, and a show of Wedgwood basalt ware and turquoise Minton.

Upstairs, what was the great chamber is now an airy, barrel-vaulted drawing-room stretching across the first floor. Jacobean plasterwork adorns the ceiling, 17th-century panelling lines the walls and the chimney-piece too is original, while several pieces of period furniture include inlaid cabinets and a carved Spanish chest. Apart from the drinks table, the only modern note is a group portrait by Howard Morgan, who seems to have caught the present owners and their family at the tail end of a wild party.

Dunham Massey ☆☆

3 m SW Altrincham, off A56, M56 junction 7, M6 junction 19; NT; tearoom; garden and park; *open:* Apr–end Oct, Sat–Wed, 12–5; tel: 061 941 1025

The first view of Dunham Massey is of a long, low, 18th-century façade reflected in the waters of a wide moat. Originally an Elizabethan mansion, this sprawling, relaxed brick house is built round two courtyards, one a cobbled yard overlooked by stone-mullioned service ranges, the other now an informal garden round a fountain pool. In 1732–40, the old building was remodelled and encased in brick, to designs by the elusive John Norris. Then, in 1905, there was a thorough Edwardian restoration, with advice from the connoisseur Percy Macquoid and the fashionable Morant & Co, and from the architect J. Compton Hall, who gave the house its dormer-windowed south front, with a loose interpretation of a Jacobean centrepiece. The Georgian work was for the cantankerous George Booth, 2nd Earl of Warrington and author of a treatise advocating divorce for incompatibility; the Edwardian facelift for his descendant William Grey, 9th Earl of Stamford. Stripped of its original contents in the 19th century, Dunham Massey is a variable feast, although the 10th Earl determinedly bought back family paintings, silver and furniture when he could.

The extensive visitor tour does a complete circuit of the ranges facing on to the main court. Still of the early-18th century are the austere oak-panelled chapel, like a non-conformist meeting house, and the intimate library, with beautifully crafted models of the heavens on elaborate stands, a sculptural carved crucifixion by the young Grinling Gibbons over the mantelpiece (although this cannot be seen properly), and an array of old books, some still in their original white paper wrappers. There is also a gallery of a corridor lined with early Georgian walnut chests, but most rooms are Edwardian in flavour, among them a rather startling green and yellow drawing-room, a chintzily furnished summer parlour and an unmemorable sequence of bedrooms.

There are family portraits by Cornelius Johnson, Hoppner, Cotes, Romney and Reynolds, a darkened room shows off George Booth's early 18th-century Huguenot silver, and there are Charles II chairs, the 2nd Earl's burr walnut close stool, and inlaid satinwood bookcases by Gillow of Lancaster. A great bare space that was once the long gallery of the Tudor house is hung with Dunham Massey's most celebrated painting, Guercino's *Mars, Venus and Cupid with Saturn as Time*, and with 17th- and 18th-century views of the house by Adriaen van Diest, Knyff and John Harris the Younger, all showing the great avenues which still radiate away across the park. Most poignant is the 10th and last Earl's study, its drab carpet worn through to the floor where he forged narrow corridors between piles of books and papers.

Gawsworth Hall ☆

3 m SW Macclesfield, on A536; teas; garden; *open:* early Apr–early Oct, daily, 2–5.30; tel: 0260 223456

This modest L-shaped building, its photogenic half-timbering reflected in the waters of a moat-like pond, is the much altered and restored remnant of an Elizabethan courtyard house. The starkly black and white entrance front is pierced by a prim classical doorway and Georgian sashes, but round the corner, looking on to the little garden that was once a courtyard, is a lurching three-storey jettied bay and a show of gables and oriels, leaded casements, closely spaced studding and decorative quatrefoils. At the back, a high brick wall and grassy earthworks mark the site of an Elizabethan tiltyard and pleasure grounds, while across the water is the melancholy Georgian New Hall.

The birthplace of Mary Fitton, one of the candidates for Shakespeare's Dark Lady, Gawsworth has been brought back to life in recent years by the present owners. It is a place of small, low-ceilinged, lived-in rooms, one leading into another, and with the structure of the house showing through in exposed half-timbering and heavy roof beams. There are fragments of Elizabethan plasterwork and original carved overmantels, but these are comfortable, well-furnished interiors rather than period re-creations. A collection of mostly 19th- and 20th-century art is headed by a small-scale river scene by Turner and Constable's blackberry pickers, and there is also a portrait, attributed to Zuccaro, of Mary Fitton as a child, with her mother and younger brother.

A tiny chapel, much restored in the 19th century and with stained glass by William Morris and Burne-Jones, is on the site of a 14th-century one, built to serve a Norman house that stood on the mound to the west of the hall.

Little Moreton Hall ☆☆

4 m SW Congleton, on E side of A34; NT; optional guided tours (*c.*60 mins); tearoom; garden; *open:* Apr–end Sept, Wed–Sun, 12–5.30 (closed Gd Fri), BH Mon 11–5.30, Oct, Wed, Sat, Sun, 12–5.30; tel: 0260 272018

This giddy matchstick house is the best-known half-timbered building in England. Ringed by a moat, and set round three sides of a cobbled, weedy courtyard, it is a triumph of medieval and Elizabethan craftsmanship, its timbers arranged in all kinds of decorative motifs, the upper floors jettied over the lower, and the small-paned leaded windows displaying an extraordinary variety of patterned glazing. Two gabled, many-sided bays inscribed with the name of their creator, the carpenter Richard Dale, jostle for elbow room in a corner of the court, and a fragile and insubstantial long gallery, its timbers and windows pulled out of shape, threatens to topple the unsteady three-storey entrance range.

Built between *c.*1450 and the 1580s by three generations of the Moreton family, the hall was later let and few contents have survived. It is shown virtually unfurnished, but the place is so atmospheric this does not matter. Planned in the medieval fashion, without corridors, each room is a passage to the next, with low doorways from the court giving on to the twisting spiral staircases running between the floors. There is Elizabethan plasterwork and painted decoration, including simulated panelling in a little parlour, texts from the 1539 Tyndale Bible covering the chancel of the tiny chapel, and allegorical plaster reliefs in the 68 ft gallery.

Lyme Park ☆☆

Just outside Disley, on S side of A6, 6½ m
SE Stockport; NT; guided tours except Sun;
tearoom; gardens and park; *open:* Good
Fri–early Oct, daily, except Mon and Fri
(but open BH Mon) 2–5; tel: 0663 762023

Set on rising ground in a wild and romantic deer park, with the Pennine
moors at its back, is this grey, quadrangular gritstone palace. A self-confident
classical centrepiece on the entrance front is Elizabethan, but later alterations,
particularly by Giacomo Leoni in the 1720s, account for the sash windows,
the massive portico on the south front, and the arcaded Italianate courtyard,
with flags of pink and white stone surrounding a Renaissance wellhead.

Changes over the centuries have resulted in interiors of several periods.
A portrait-hung long gallery stretching the length of the east front is still
essentially Elizabethan, and so too, despite an early 19th-century gloss, is the
richly furnished drawing-room lined with inlaid arcaded panelling and with
the arms of Elizabeth I over the fireplace. Leoni was responsible for the
serene, high-ceilinged saloon on the south front, with natural oak panelling
encrusted with paper-thin limewood carvings thought to be by Grinling
Gibbons, while Lewis Wyatt's early 19th-century remodelling of the east
front accounts for a vaguely Jacobean library, lined with an oppressive deep
red paper, and the Carolean-style dining room with a mass of heavy
plasterwork.

Lyme lost much of its furniture when the Legh family, who had been here
since the 14th century, left in 1946. Original to the house are a scatter of walnut Queen Anne chairs and a 1760s harpsichord in the saloon, a lovely seaweed marquetry travelling chest in the long gallery, and some Charles II furnishings in two high-ceilinged chambers fitted out for a visit by the future
James II in 1676. The library has three ancient Greek tombstones, one carved
with a poignant relief of a mother and child, and other finds excavated in the
19th century by the amateur archaeologist Thomas Legh, and an outstanding
collection of late 17th- and 18th-century English clocks also came from the
family. But much else, including a group of 17th-century paintings from the
National Portrait Gallery, is on loan.

Visitors should be warned that Lyme Park is more commercial than many
National Trust properties and a popular weekend venue for the residents of
Disley, which presses close against the gates.

Peckforton Castle

Between A41 and A51, ½ m S Beeston; teas;
open: Apr–mid Sept, daily, 10–6; tel: 0829
260930

The most faithful Victorian re-creation of a medieval castle sits high on a
wooded ridge overlooking the Cheshire plain. Built by Anthony Salvin in
1844–50 for the 1st Lord Tollemache – champion athlete, father of 24, and
believer in benevolent autocracy – Peckforton is a defensible fortress of

rose-pink stone, ringed by massive walls, towered and battlemented, and with the only entrance protected by a drawbridge and formidable gatehouse.

Sadly, the picturesque distant view degenerates at close quarters into a forlorn and dusty seediness. Salvin's architecture is still as it was, with ribbed stone vaulting arching across the great hall that straddles the angle between the two main ranges, an octagonal library, and a completely circular wine cellar deep in the bowels of the building, but the huge rooms which once saw Victorian house parties are now used for wedding receptions and film sets, with no furnishings of interest and animated models of, among others, a singing verger and a headless ghost. A stone spiral stair leads up to the roof, with a wide view along the ridge towards the powerful ruined towers of 13th-century Beeston castle.

Peover Hall ☆

Off A50 at Radbroke Hall, 4 m S Knutsford, on road from Over Peover to Goostrey, no signs; guided tours (*c.* 45 mins); teas; spacious garden with theatrical topiary; *open:* early May–end Sept, Mon (except BH), 2.30–4.30; tel: 0565 722656

Set in parkland near the saucer telescopes of Jodrell Bank is this curiously irregular, three-storeyed house, faced in mellow brick, with stone-mullioned windows. While some frontages are gabled, others are squared off with a roofline parapet, as if the builder could not make up his mind. Although originally Tudor and Elizabethan, Peover has had a chequered history, and has been remodelled by the present owners, who demolished a Georgian wing and restored the place after it was used as General Patton's headquarters during World War II.

Visitors see lived-in rooms on all three floors, several of them with panelling or other features brought from elsewhere. The old kitchen, with a beamed ceiling and two massive fireplaces, has been turned into a great hall, complete with armour; a charming atticy long gallery with casement windows on three sides runs under a Tudor roof; and on the second floor is a sunny drawing-room, with a large stone-mullioned window looking down on the walled and hedged flower gardens at the back of the house. Mixed furnishings include elaborately carved beds and a massive Victorian sideboard, carved with a relief showing the signing of Magna Carta.

To the south is a brick stables block of 1654, architecturally more distinguished than the house, with mullioned windows and strapwork decoration.

Rode Hall ☆

5 m SW Congleton, off A34 and A50, between Rode Heath and Scholar Green, no advance signs; guided tour (c. 45 mins); garden; *open:* Apr–end Sept, Wed and BH Mon 2–5; tel: 0270 882961

A substantial red-brick mid-18th-century house set above a long and reedy lake is attached to a more retiring, cupola-topped Queen Anne wing, and set off by a Georgian stable block. Altered at the turn of the 18th century to designs by John Hope, and again by Lewis Wyatt in 1810, the interior is largely Regency in flavour, the few elegantly furnished, lived-in rooms on show including Wyatt's rather sombre north-facing dining-room, all mint green and black, and Hope's much more attractive library and drawing-room on the west front, the former with bookcases designed by Gillow. Home of the Baker Wilbrahams, Rode is notable for fine family paintings, including the Reynolds self-portrait given to the physician George Baker in lieu of payment during the artist's final illness, and works attributed to Beechey, Opie, Hoppner and Hudson. Gillow furniture was made specially for the house, there is a collection of teapots representing all English factories of the 18th century, and an oval, midnight-blue ante-room sandwiched between the drawing-room and library is used to display a set of gouaches and some green and orange Coalport.

Tabley House ☆☆

2 m W Knutsford, entrance on A5033, off A556; teas; *open:* Apr–Oct, Thurs–Sun and BH Mon 2–5; tel: 0565 750151

Sir John Leicester Tabley, Regency buck and friend of the Prince of Wales, was also the first great patron and collector of British art. His plan that his paintings should form the core of a national gallery was never realized, and much of the collection was dispersed on his death in 1827. But a remnant, showing Sir John's interestingly varied tastes, was saved for Tabley House, the only 18th-century Palladian mansion in Cheshire.

Designed by John Carr of York and built 1761–7, Tabley is a grand small house, the original entrance front, flanked by pavilions and with a curving horseshoe stair rising to a pedimented portico, looking south over parkland to a lake. Deep pink sandstone used for the basement storey and the portico blends uneasily with the red brickwork of the upper floors, which were originally painted grey.

Inside, visitors do a circuit of half-a-dozen rooms on the first floor (the rest of the house is given over to accommodation for the elderly), some still as designed by Carr, others as altered in the 19th century, but all convincingly re-created after Tabley's recent stint as a school and filled with the family's fine 18th- and 19th-century furniture. The drawing-room with its flowing plasterwork and a pair of George III settees either side of a green and white marble fireplace is 18th-century in spirit, the paintings hung against soft green walls here including Dobson's portrait of the first Lord Byron, his canary-yellow coat tied by an enormous red sash, and a couple of Sir John's commissions: John Martin's unearthly vision of the destruction of Pompeii, seen in a fiery glow, and Turner's view across the park on a windy day, showing the folly that still stands by the lake.

Paintings of Sir John and his descendants, including Graham Rust's arresting portrait of John Leicester Warren, the last of the line, are grouped in the dining-room, with a Lawrence full-length of the Prince Regent given pride of place over the sideboard, and the tour ends in the gallery created in 1807 out of three rooms running down the west side of the house. Hung with red damask and furnished with French-style gilded armchairs and heavy Regency rosewood sofas upholstered in deep-blue velvet, this rich interior is set off by some of the more forceful paintings in the collection, among them Ward's study of a dalmatian bitch suckling her pups and his *Fall of Phaeton* – the four white horses that were pulling the sun god's chariot shown falling, terrified, through space – two disturbing Fuselis, and Ibbetson's bull-baiting crowd scene, one of Sir John's first commissions.

A 17th-century chapel by the house, still with its original dark oak panelling and canopied pulpit, is all that remains of the old house, that once stood on an island in the lake.

Tatton Park ☆☆

3½ m N Knutsford, 4 m S Altrincham, 1½ m NE junction of A5034 and A50; tearoom; 50-acre gardens and huge park; home farm worked as in 1930s; *open:* Apr–end Sept, daily, except Mon, 12–5; tel: 0565 654822

Much visited by the denizens of Manchester, who cluster only a few miles to the north, Tatton's attractions are headed up by the great house of pinkish stone looking south over steeply falling ground to the sparkling waters of a couple of meres. Built over half a century, from 1774 to 1825, by Samuel Wyatt and his nephew Lewis, Tatton is a spare classical composition in Greek Revival style, with a pedimented portico towards the gardens, stone swags over the windows, and an arcade of pilasters running down the side of the building. Inside, Samuel's intimate rooms where the family lived from day to day contrast with Lewis' grand Regency interiors, designed for special occasions only and still with the original Gillow furniture. These two members of an architectural dynasty were working for three generations of the Egerton family, whose fortunes had been transformed by a legacy in 1758.

Lewis' lushest creations are the music room and drawing-room hung with cherry-coloured silk which start the tour, the one furnished in French style, with boulle pieces, the other in a kind of Italianate rococo, with gilded furniture carved in high relief. A show of mostly 17th-century Netherlandish and Italian paintings includes two Venetian scenes by Canaletto, Van Dyck's *Martyrdom of St Stephen*, and Guercino's richly coloured *Absalom and Tamar*. Nothing else is as ostentatious. A serene grey-green library, its size and central position reflecting the importance of the Egerton book collection, runs down the south front, with blue and white Delft ware perched on the Regency bookcases and a port decanter and various board games set out among a comfortable clutter of leather chairs, folio stands and sturdy tables.

Upstairs is a coterie of virtually untouched Regency bedrooms, furnished in mahogany and satinwood, while a combination of staircase hall and top-lit, galleried ante-room in the centre of the house produces theatrical vistas through round-headed arches and across a sequence of balustrades. Of the 18th-century house which the Wyatts remodelled, only the dining-room survives, its walls encrusted with rococo plasterwork by T. F. Pritchard, and hung with portraits by Lawrence and Beechey.

The tour ends in the extensive servants' quarters, complete with a cellar railway for carrying the coal about, and with the vast tenants' hall built on by the 4th lord in 1935, an empty aircraft hanger of a place, lined with his lordship's hunting trophies and with cases of treasures gathered in foreign parts. A guided tour of the old hall across the park introduces the realities of medieval life in a dark, rush-strewn, smoky, 15th-century great hall.

Derbyshire

Bolsover Castle ☆☆

In Bolsover, on A632 6 m E Chesterfield, 10 mins from M1, exit 29; EH; *open:* summer, daily, 10–6, winter, Tues–Sun, 10–4; tel: 0246 823349

Just north of *Hardwick Hall*, but much less visited, is the equally flamboyant house built by Bess's son and grandson, Charles and William Cavendish. Although now largely ruined, Bolsover is still stunning. Built on the site of a 12th-century fortress, it stands high on a wooded spur, with steep slopes falling away on all sides except one and with wide views west over the M1 and south along the ridge.

The house itself was built over some sixty years, from *c.* 1608, to designs by three generations of the Smythson family: Robert, who was Bess's architect, his son John and grandson Huntingdon. On the end of the ridge, four-square and battlemented like a medieval keep, is the Little Castle, a poetic Jacobean fantasy with richly decorated interiors, all now unfurnished. None of the rooms is very large, but several are ornately panelled and painted, some have been given sculptural vaulted ceilings, and many have delicately ornamented, hooded and crested fireplaces, inset with jewel-like cameos of black and coloured marbles.

Where the Little Castle is a make-believe place, the buildings further back along the ridge, which visitors see first, have a harder edge. A grassy, tree-shaded courtyard is lined, on the south side, by the impressive façade of Sir William's riding school, with its original double doors and deep stone-mullioned windows. The barn-like interior is still in use, with a floor of trampled earth and straw and an authentically horsey smell. Closing the court on the west, above a promenade along the edge of the ridge, is the range that was once a great house. Although the golden stone is now pitted, blackened and fissured and the roof has gone, this is, if anything, the most evocative part of Bolsover, with the remains of sculptural doorcases and fireplaces, elaborate stone chimney stacks and a contrast between the north end, started by Sir Charles, with its curving Jacobean gables, and the southern section completed by his son, marked by a crenellated roofline parapet and with scrolled surrounds to the upper windows. It was Sir William who built the 220 ft gallery with ten huge windows looking over the valley, its outer wall curiously embellished with cannon-like pilasters, as if guns have been bolted to the walls.

Calke Abbey ☆☆☆

9 m S Derby on A514 between Swadlincote and Melbourne; NT; tearoom; church; walled gardens and park;
open: Apr–end Oct, Sat–Wed, 1–5.30, admission by timed ticket;
tel: 0332 863822

A long lime avenue, like a cool, green tunnel, forms the approach to one of the Trust's most memorable houses. The three-storey mansion settled comfortably in a hollow in the park is an undistinguished baroque pile of 1701–4 by an unknown architect, but the contents put it in a class of its own. Since 1622 this secluded place has been the home of the Harpur Crewes, a family of reclusive, squirrel-like eccentrics who gave the house its individual character. Earlier generations, such as Sir John Harpur, 4th Baronet, who built the present house, or the two 18th-century Sir Henrys, who had a passion for the turf, seem to have been comparatively normal, but after them oddities become more pronounced. The 7th Baronet defied convention to marry a lady's maid, deliberately cut himself off from society, and communicated with his servants by letter. Even more strange was Sir Vauncey, who inherited in 1886. Rarely seen off his own land, the baronet devoted himself to building up his father's collections of birds, fossils, shells and other specimens, treated the park as a private wildlife sanctuary, and banned all cars from the estate, providing carriages from the gates for visitors. Appropriately enough, Charles Harpur Crewe, whose decease brought Calke to the Trust, died while setting mole traps in the park.

The principal rooms are still largely as they were in Sir Vauncey's time, stuffed with show-cases and other clutter. Grandest of them is the lofty, first-floor saloon, with a baroque broken pediment over the fireplace, and with the boars of the Harpur crest prominent on the ceiling. The 1841 decor and a collection of family portraits, among them Tilly Kettle's full-length painting of Lady Frances, wife of the 6th Baronet, and Lawrence's pastel of the 6th Baronet, executed when the artist was only 15, take second place to the stuffed birds and mammals and cases of dried and withered things ranged along the walls and round the billiard table in the centre of the room, in one a tableau of albino creatures – stoats, polecats, squirrels and a fox – in another a primeval crocodile skull, in a third a clutch of sea-birds. A white-and-gold late Georgian drawing-room is silted up with cloth-covered tables, cases of polished stones, and ornaments under glass domes, one of which preserves a tableau of stuffed mice, but the masculine library, apart from some equipment for making microscope slides, is conventional enough. Wall maps unravel from shelves of leather-bound books, while above the cases are ranged some of the horse paintings which are a feature of the house, including works by Gilpin, Sartorius and John Ferneley Senior.

Calke's greatest treasure, the early-18th-century state bed that was found still packed away in the box in which it had arrived, is shown in a darkened, theatrically lit closet. Hangings and coverings of Chinese silk, as fresh as the day they were made, are embroidered with brilliantly plumaged birds, gauzy butterflies, oriental figures and pagodas, each outlined in gold thread like an enamelled jewel and with tightly rolled peacock feathers used to form wings and the knots of tree trunks. Most unusually for a Trust house, visitors are also taken through untouched back quarters and decaying upper rooms, with vistas down drab, flaking corridors, glimpses of a cold, uninviting bathroom and a store crammed with oil lamps, and a plunge into a subterranean, dungeon-like kitchen and into the icy cellars opening off the central courtyard, whose rough walls show traces of a much earlier house.

Chatsworth ☆☆☆☆

On B6012, 10 m W Chesterfield, 4 m E Bakewell; tearoom; magnificent and eventful garden; park and woodland walks; *open:* late Mar–end Oct, daily, 11–4.30; tel: 0246 582204

In the broad valley of the Derwent, a pastoral oasis among the Derbyshire peaks, is the kingdom of Chatsworth, a place of wooded hills, of fountains and cascades, of verdant meadow and rolling parkland. At its heart, on a gentle slope above the river, is the Versailles-like palace of the Dukes of Devonshire, one of the largest and most important houses in Britain. Although its form, with four tall ranges round an internal courtyard, preserves the skeleton of the Elizabethan mansion built here by Bess of Hardwick and her second husband, Sir William Cavendish, Chatsworth as it is now is largely a creation of the late 17th and early 19th centuries. From 1686, with the help of William Talman and Thomas Archer, the lst Duke gradually rebuilt the old house, creating the sculptural baroque façades – all giant fluted pilasters, urn-studded rooflines and huge windows with prominent keystones – that lord it over the valley. Then, just over 100 years later, the charming and extravagant 6th Duke doubled the size of the place by commissioning Jeffry Wyatville to add the long north wing which extends like an outstretched arm towards the car park.

Both landscape and buildings are on the grandest scale. In the garden, 5 miles of footpaths take in waterworks and crags engineered by Joseph Paxton and long beech-hedged walks, while the tour of the house involves walking a third of a mile and up and down some 160 steps. There is nothing remotely cosy here, but these ornate interiors, designed for show, are in a class of their own, and still, despite the depredations of death duties, filled with one of the greatest private collections of furniture and art. More than this, there is a strong sense of a discerning overall intelligence, with the highest standards maintained despite often overwhelming visitor numbers.

A suitably intimidating and almost processional approach – down a marble-floored corridor, through a vast painted hall and up a great stone staircase
– leads to the five-room 17th-century state apartment filling the second floor
of the south front. The visual equivalent of cream chocolate, these rooms are
almost uncomfortably opulent, with richly coloured, tempestuous mythological scenes by Verrio and Laguerre painted on the lofty ceilings, and walls
hung with gilded and embossed leather or lined with mellow panelling
encrusted with Grinling Gibbons-style swags of fruit, flowers and game.
These lush boxes set off a rich assortment of furnishings. Some, such as the
Mortlake tapestries, a silver chandelier and Coromandel lacquer cabinets, are
also 17th-century, others, such as gilt side tables by William Kent, a boulle
gem cabinet and bilious green malachite pieces, or a tester bed that belonged
to George II, are later imports, while a procession of mostly 17th-century
paintings includes a charming child portrait by Cornelis de Vos, a *trompe
l'oeil* violin apparently hanging on the back of a door by Jan van der Vaart,
cabinet paintings by Teniers the Younger and Adriaen van Ostade, a blue-
green landscape by Jan Brueghel, and scenes from classical mythology by
Lely and Luca Giordano.

Past the almost unaltered 17th-century chapel, painted by Verrio, Laguerre and Ricard, lined with more richly carved panelling and boasting a reredos of pink and grey veined alabaster, come the 6th Duke's apartments. There is only a glimpse of the long library which he created out of the Elizabethan gallery, with its gilded and stuccoed Restoration ceiling, and a wash of sofas and low lights like an exclusive club. But the tour ends with Wyatville's dining-room and gallery in the north wing, the former with a gently arched, gilded and coffered ceiling like the lid of an enormous trunk, the latter filled with idealized neo-classical nudes by Canova and his contemporaries reflecting the 6th Duke's passion for sculpture. However tired by this point, do not rush through these rooms in search of a cup of tea, for here, paradoxically, are some of the finest paintings in the collection. Full-length portraits by Mytens and Van Dyck hang on the silk-lined walls of the dining-room, while in the gallery, hung almost on top of the way out, are Sebastiano Ricci's *Presentation in the Temple*, two strongly contrasting portraits by Frans Hals, and Rembrandt's searching painting of an aged eastern potentate.

The historic collections are being augmented by the present duke, whose purchases of modern art include a bronze war horse by Elisabeth Frink in the gardens, and Lucian Freud's bleak portrait of his mother. For an extra charge, visitors can also sometimes see a set of Regency bedrooms on the site of the apartments used by Mary Queen of Scots, who was briefly a prisoner here between 1570 and 1581. No trace of the tragic queen remains, and these rooms are principally of interest for some fine portraits by Reynolds, Mercier, Ramsay and others, including a likeness of William Kent by Benedetto Luti.

Eyam Hall

Off A623 in Eyam village, just west of church; parking in village car park; guided tours only (*c.* 40 mins); tearoom; *open:* end Mar–late Oct, Wed, Thurs, Sun and BH Mon, 11–4.30; tel: 0433 631976

Built in 1671, only a few years after the plague reduced the population of the village by 80 per cent, Eyam Hall is a sturdy, weatherworn H-shaped house of dark millstone grit, with a later kitchen wing added to one side. Still lived in by descendants of the builder, it is a modest place of unexceptional, low-ceilinged rooms, many of them with Victorian fireplaces and other alterations, and hung with stiff family portraits. Some of the furniture, such as the high-backed settles and chests in the stone-flagged hall, has been here since the 17th century, and a sparsely furnished little room is lined with fragments of 15th- and 16th-century tapestry, used like wallpaper.

Haddon Hall ☆☆☆

2 m SE Bakewell, 6¹/₂ m N Matlock on A6; tearoom; garden; *open:* Apr–end Sept, Tues–Sun and BH Mon 11–6 (closed Suns in July and Aug); tel: 0629 812855

On a craggy wooded spur above the Wye sprawls an atmospheric double-courtyard house. Walking down from the gatehouse on the main road and over the stone bridge across the river, visitors can savour a view of battlemented grey walls, and of the great north-west tower guarding the entrance. Beyond is a sloping, roughly paved courtyard surrounded by weathered, unco-ordinated ranges with mullioned windows and stone doorways, and with a flight of steps descending boldly from an upper apartment.

Built over several centuries, with Jacobean embellishments to medieval and Tudor work, Haddon slept for 200 years during the 18th and 19th centuries when the Manners family, Dukes of Rutland, abandoned it in favour of *Belvoir Castle*. As a result, the original house has survived largely unaltered, apart from some sympathetic restoration by the 9th Duke in the early years of this century. In an extensive tour, visitors see sparsely furnished rooms in three ranges, some graciously panelled and with painted or plasterwork ceilings and decorative friezes, others much more simply finished, with exposed timber framing or stonework. All are very bare, the only furnishings a couple of Tudor and Stuart portraits, a fine range of 16th- and 17th-century chairs and a few tapestries, all that was left after a fire in 1925 destroyed some sixty hangings.

The kitchens still have their meal arks and dole cupboards for storing food, troughs for holding water, and ranges of pitted and scratched tables and dressers, one so worn that a hole has been etched through the wood. A little chapel with its own entrance in a corner of the outer court is one of the oldest parts of the house, with a Norman pillar and font and walls covered with muted medieval paintings, among them three grinning skeletons and a lovingly depicted St Christopher, fish leaping at his feet. A pristine marble effigy to the 9th Duke's elder brother, who died just after his ninth birthday, is dazzlingly white among all the old wood and stone.

The tour ends in the finest room in the house, the 110 ft long gallery lined with silvery arcaded panelling of 1603 and lit by windows on three sides. The only modern touch, Rex Whistler's dreamy view of Haddon painted over the fireplace, seems perfectly in tune with a set of 17th-century embroidered chairs and the ribbed plaster ceiling, and the whole room is tinged by a watery light from the ancient glass in the two great bays overlooking the terraced garden high above the Wye. While a ball to celebrate her sister's wedding was at its height in the 1560s, the heiress Dorothy Vernon is said to have slipped away through the garden to elope with her lover, John Manners, running to meet him down the long flight of steep stone steps which still plunges to a narrow packhorse bridge across the river.

Hardwick Hall ☆☆☆☆

6¹⁄₂ m W Mansfield, approach from M1 (exit 29) via A6175; NT; tearoom; garden; park and woodland walks; Old Hall (EH), exterior only; *open:* Apr–end Oct, Wed, Thurs, Sat, Sun, BH Mon 12.30–5 (sunset if earlier); tel: 0246 850430

The formidable Bess of Hardwick, Countess of Shrewsbury, crowned a life of social advancement by building the Elizabethan prodigy house that sits high on a ridge overlooking the M1. Symmetrical and compact, with huge windows filling every inch of wall, Hardwick is a glittering lantern of a house, with Bess's initials – ES for Elizabeth of Shrewsbury – defiantly cresting the six slender towers which project boldly on every side, their outlines shifting and regrouping as you walk round. Just outside the forecourt is the evocative ruin of Bess's first building enterprise, Hardwick Old Hall, used to accommodate the servants when the new house was finished. Probably the work of the talented Robert Smythson, who was also responsible for *Longleat*, Hardwick was begun in 1590, when its indomitable chatelaine was already in her sixties. Just a few weeks earlier, her situation had been transformed by the death of the Earl of Shrewsbury, her estranged fourth husband, who had left her one of the richest women in England. The Countess moved in seven years later and lived on here until her death, in 1608.

Like no other Elizabethan house in England, Hardwick has survived not only unchanged but with its original contents largely intact. In the 18th century, Bess's Cavendish descendants, the Dukes of Devonshire, preferred their nearby palace of *Chatsworth*, and by the 19th Hardwick's antiquarian atmosphere was appreciated for what it was and subtly enhanced by the 6th Duke, who enriched the house with tapestries, portraits and furnishings from the family's other properties.

The visitor route rises slowly to Bess's state apartments on the second floor. Atmosphere is everything, the succession of spacious, sparsely furnished, tapestry-hung rooms often being so dark, despite the windows, that details vanish in the gloom. There are carved doorcases; flamboyant chimneypieces of pink and grey alabaster; plaster overmantels carrying the stags of the Hardwick crest, their horns made of real antlers; tables covered with precious carpets; richly carved Elizabethan furniture; and a wealth of 16th- and early-17th-century needlework: velvets embroidered with gold and silver thread, patchworks made from medieval copes and vestments, and intricately worked cushion covers, most of them now framed like pictures.

The skeleton of the house is the great processional stone staircase which climbs relentlessly upwards, joining the lofty great hall on the ground floor with the grandest interiors high above. A final twist brings visitors into the airy High Great Chamber, lit by walls of glass, still with its original painted frieze above the 16th-century Brussels tapestries and with the table made to celebrate Bess's marriage to the Earl of Shrewsbury in the window bay, its top inlaid with playing cards and board games, musical instruments, and even with the music for a four-part motet. Next door is the 162 ft long gallery, with chairs and stools covered in faded crimson velvet and tapestry-lined walls thickly hung with portraits of Bess's family and Tudor and Stuart royalty. Here is Bess as an old woman, with flaming red hair above a worn face, here are likenesses of the bull-faced Sir William Cavendish, the father of her children, of her third spouse, the ascetic-looking William St Loe, as well as of the Earl of Shrewsbury, and here too is a rich, stylized portrait of Elizabeth I, with white face, bejewelled hair and a gorgeous dress embroidered with sea creatures. Most memorable is the portrait of the philosopher Thomas Hobbes, tutor to the 2nd and 3rd Earls of Devonshire and a family friend, who died at Hardwick in 1679. Painted three years before his death, when Hobbes was 88, the picture shows a wispy-haired and sunken-cheeked old man, but the eyes burn with intelligence.

Kedleston Hall ☆☆

5 m NW Derby, off A52; NT; tearoom; garden and park; *open:* Apr–end Oct, Sat–Wed, 1–5.30; tel: 0332 842191

This domed and porticoed great house, like a setting for a national art collection, sits half-way up a grassy slope, framed by trees on the skyline behind and looking out over a shallow, lake-filled valley. Known as one of the greatest works of Robert Adam, Kedleston was in fact begun in 1759 by Matthew Brettingham and James Paine, whose vast, 300 ft north front, with curving quadrant corridors connecting the central block to pavilions either side, greets visitors as they come down the drive. In contrast to this piece of mainstream Palladianism, Adam's south front, built without the planned pavilions, is almost baroque in its restlessness, with a windowless, columned centrepiece that looks as if the house has swallowed a triumphal arch and a horseshoe stair picking up the curves of the dome.

Built for Nathaniel Curzon, lst Lord Scarsdale, Kedleston was always intended to be a show-place, with the central block given over to a display of paintings and sculpture that was open to visitors from the start. Then, as now, the family lived in one of the pavilions. The result is a series of principal rooms that are still largely as Adam conceived them, with original decoration and furnishings, but a complete lack of warmth.

Adam's vast hall and saloon run through the house, linking the north and south fronts. Reflecting the 18th-century fascination with classical Greece and Rome, these top-lit, sparsely furnished spaces were inspired by the architecture of the ancient world, the one ringed by giant columns of reddish-brown alabaster and copies of antique statues like a Roman courtyard, the other a huge domed rotunda based on the Pantheon, with doors, paintings and even furniture following the curve of the walls. The rooms either side are more cheerful, with plaster ceilings by Joseph Rose picked out in a medley of pastels or, in one case, in strong mustard yellow and maroon, and with a mix of family portraits and 17th-century Italian and Flemish paintings often still in their original arrangement. To the east, a relatively sober library and music room flank a showy drawing-room, with alabaster surrounds to the windows and doors and long settees so encrusted with carvings of merfolk that they seem to be sprouting gilded warts and carbuncles. To the west is a four-room state apartment notable for a canopied bed, ornate mirror and other pieces carved with palm fronds, and for the view from the windows of the little, late-13th-century church, all that remains of the medieval village swept away by Curzon and Adam.

There are charmingly informal portraits of the lst Lord and his wife by

Arthur Devis and Nathaniel Hone, while the Italianate landscapes, still-lifes and religious works with which Lord Curzon covered his walls include a compelling portrait of an old man by Ferdinand Bol, one of Aelbert Cuyp's golden landscapes, and Salomon Koninck's shadowy *David before Nebuchadnezzar*, where the yellow-robed prophet is like a beacon of light in the darkness. Also on show is a glittering assemblage of enamels, brasswork, silver, textiles, bronzes and other treasures brought back by Marquess Curzon of Kedleston, the most distinguished member of the family, who was Viceroy of India from 1899 to 1905.

Melbourne Hall ☆☆

In Melbourne village, 9 m S Derby, entrance by parish church off road to Wilson; guided tour (c. 45 mins); tearoom; garden; parking by church; *open:* Aug, daily, except first three Mons, 2–5; tel: 0332 862502

Melbourne Hall's show façade, a pedimented stone frontage with rows of orderly sash windows, has its back to the village, looking east over a sweep of grassy terraces. Like the chunky wings framing the former courtyard on the south side of the house, this is a Georgian addition to a much older building. Once, when the Scottish border was wild and lawless, the bishops of Carlisle had a palace here, using the Norman church that still stands beside the house as their cathedral, and their old residence was partly re-used in the U-shaped, Jacobean house built by Sir John Coke which forms the basis of the present hall.

The ravishing garden, with its fountain pools, statues by Van Nost, and a gilded wrought-iron arbour by Robert Bakewell of Derby, like a cage for some monstrous bird, is Melbourne's best-known attraction, but the house is just as rewarding. Passing by descent through the Coke, Lamb and Kerr families, Melbourne has a notable collection of portraits and other paintings and an accumulation of fine 17th- and 18th-century furniture, while a colourful array of residents includes Lord Melbourne, Queen Victoria's first Prime Minister, and his unstable wife Lady Caroline Lamb, known for her involvement with Byron.

The guided tour does a circuit of the ground floor, starting in the conservatory-like room built over what was once the courtyard. Despite the hint of grandeur about the exterior, this is a modest place, lived-in and comfortable. The long dining-room, once the great hall, still has a Jacobean flavour, its 17th-century panelling hung with portraits by Lely, Dahl, Kneller and Hudson, and with Cornelius Johnson's sharp-eyed likeness of old Sir John, and high-backed Charles II and William and Mary chairs pushed back against the walls. On the Regency table are a set of gilded 17th-century Venetian finger bowls, inset with garnets and cornelians, and a sideboard shows off a monstrously heavy oak cheeseboard, one of the many presents which Queen Victoria gave her adored Lord Melbourne.

A spacious blue-walled drawing-room, with Chippendale-style mirrors and bird paintings by de Hondecoeter and others, has a formal touch, but the much-used study and pink-walled library are positively cosy, the one hung with strong portraits by the present Lady Kerr, the other showing a William and Mary walnut cabinet, a self-portrait by Kneller, sketches attributed to Gainsborough and Rembrandt, and two works by Jacopo Bassano, one a nativity scene, the other of Moses striking the rock, with an array of tubs, bowls and pitchers to collect the precious water. A version of Holbein's well-known portrait of Thomas More dominates the hall, and also here are a little painting of the poet John Keates as a child, standing stiffly on guard outside his sick mother's bedroom, and three drawings of babies sketched by Lady Caroline, two of whose children were still born, the third mentally retarded.

Sudbury Hall ☆☆

In village of Sudbury, 6 m E Uttoxeter, off A50; NT; museum of childhood; tearoom; garden; *open:* Apr–end Oct, Wed–Sun and BH Mon (closed Gd Fri) 1–5.30 (or dusk); tel: 0283 585305

At the end of a red-brick village stands one of the most eccentric houses of Charles II's reign. The creation of George Vernon, who seems to have acted as his own architect, Sudbury is a dour E-shaped mansion with stone-mullioned windows in walls of diapered red brick and a flamboyant two-storey stone porch. This old-fashioned exterior, curiously finished off with a hipped roof and a cupola, as if Vernon had suddenly become aware of the latest architectural fashions, is allied with magnificent interior decoration by the finest London craftsmen of the day, some of it not completed until 30 years after the house was started.

The visitor tour starts with the sparsely furnished principal rooms. A low-key, portrait-hung hall leads to Sudbury's astonishing staircase hall, with fluid plasterwork framing inset paintings of half-clothed deities by Louis Laguerre, a pierced pine balustrade by Edward Pierce carved with acanthus leaves and giant blossoms, and with baskets bursting with pomegranates and other fruits on the newel posts, and an architectural doorway at the foot of the stairs. There is more work by Pierce and Laguerre in the saloon, where carved woodwork frames a series of full-length family portraits, and the adjoining drawing-room has festoons of game and fruit by Grinling Gibbons over the chimney-piece. The most individual plasterwork, by Robert Bradbury and James Pettifer, is upstairs, where an old-fashioned 138 ft long gallery has been decorated with caricatures of Roman emperors and with an exotic menagerie, including a group of cavorting grasshoppers, bursting from foliage wreaths and panels on the ceiling.

These are rooms to parade through. On the east side of the house are a more intimate panelled study and sitting-room and a dining-room set with delicate Sèvres porcelain and family silver. Furnishings throughout are sparse or non-existent, but there is an exceptional 17th-century Flemish cabinet, painted with biblical scenes, and Vernon portraits adorn almost every room, among them works by Lawrence, Hoppner, Vanderbank, Kneller and John Michael Wright, whose painting of George Vernon, resplendent in a yellow coat, stands out among the formal, stylized poses in the saloon.

Leicestershire

Belvoir Castle ☆

7 m W Grantham, between A607 and A52; café; garden; woodland trail; regimental museum of 17th/21st Lancers; *open:* Apr–end Sept, Tues, Thurs, Sat, Sun and BH Mon 11–5 (6 Sun and BH Mon); tel: 0476 870262

Like a medieval assault force, visitors to Belvoir must scale the steep, wooded slopes of the limestone outcrop on which the castle stands. A stiff 15-minute walk reveals a romantic, 19th-century vision of a Norman fortress, a confection of bulging towers, battlements, splayed and buttressed walls, and chimney stacks disguised as turrets. Far from medieval windows give the game away, but this grandiose yellow-stone building is dramatic enough, particularly when seen from a distance.

Designed by James Wyatt, the castle was begun in 1801 for John Henry Manners, 5th Duke of Rutland, soon after the young man's 21st birthday. When Wyatt died in 1813, only two fronts had been finished, and then, in 1816, a fire swept through the interior. Much of Belvoir as it is today is the work of the family chaplain, the Rev. Sir John Thoroton, who, backed up by Wyatt's three sons, picked up the pieces.

The rooms on show are all grandiose and showy. The Rev. Thoroton, whose ecclesiastical leanings emerge only too clearly, was responsible for the gothic fantasy of an entrance hall and for the cloister-like ballroom, but a gilded, mirrored saloon with decoration by Matthew Cotes Wyatt transports visitors to France. French clocks stand on the Italian marble mantelpieces, genuine Louis XIV panelling lines the walls, gilded chairs and sofas stand stiffly around, and a painted ceiling offers Wyatt's version of the story of Jupiter and Juno, with a confusion of naked bodies, flying draperies and swirling clouds helping to disguise a tale of passion, jealousy and revenge. One of the few rooms to escape the fire was Wyatt the Elder's 131-ft long gallery on the south-west front, with a huge bay bulging out into the castle's one round tower. Lined with pedestalled marble busts by Joseph Nollekens, hung with sickly pink 18th-century Gobelins tapestries and gilded mirrors, and with doors of inlaid maplewood, this is a period piece.

Apart from the portraits by Reynolds, Jervas and Hoppner lining the ballroom, the best of the paintings are displayed in a top-lit, crimson-walled gallery. Although the fire destroyed some of the finest, there is still a notable array here, including a portrait of Shakespeare's friend the Earl of Southampton by Cornelius Johnson and an aggressively posed Henry VIII attributed to Holbein. There are three of Gainsborough's romantic views of rural life, a domestic interior by Jan Steen, a mannered set of religious paintings by Poussin, the best of them a Last Supper imagined as a Roman banquet, with the disciples sprawled on couches, miniatures by Hilliard, Cooper and Oliver and various family portraits, among them J. J. Shannon's dreamy canvas of the beautiful, red-haired Lady Violet Manners, wife of the 8th Duke. Next to the gallery is the suite used by the Prince Regent when he visited Belvoir. Sadly, the narrow corridor leading to the bathroom, with a curved recess to accommodate the royal stomach, is not on view.

Lyddington Bede House

By St Andrew's church in Lyddington, 6 m N Corby, 1 m E A6003; EH; *open:* Easter or 1 Apr–30 Sept, daily, 10–6; tel: 057282 2438

An octagonal gazebo standing high above the village street like a stone sentry-box flags this medieval treat, the surviving wing of a 14th-century bishop's palace. A long, buttressed façade of warm local limestone looks across to the village church, a row of handsome mullioned and transomed windows on the first-floor lighting the spacious unfurnished room with a delicately carved wooden cornice that was the bishop's great chamber. Downstairs is a warren of tiny, bare rooms, created when the former palace became an almshouse in 1600.

Stanford Hall ☆

At Stanford, 7¹⁄₂ m NE Rugby, off B5414; guided tour (*c.* 45 mins); teas; motorcycle museum; garden and grounds; *open:* Easter Sat–end Sept, Sat, Sun, BH Mon and Tues following, 2.30–6; tel: 0788 860250

The Braye family's stately William and Mary house sits in idyllic open park-land on the west bank of the Avon. Built over some forty years, Stanford Hall was begun in 1697 by William Smith of Warwick, who was responsible for the lovely, sash-windowed south front faced in soft grey sandstone. The place was finished off by his brother Francis, who designed the more deferential brick and ironstone stables.

There are many good features, from original panelling, brass door furniture and Francis's flamboyant inlaid staircase to some delightful, black and yellow 18th-century coal scuttles. And there is a mixed collection of family paintings and furniture, including a Dutch wardrobe and a marquetry clock made for the house in the 1690s.

Apart from the lofty, salmon and gold ballroom made out of the original entrance hall, with a show of Stuart portraits that once belonged to Bonnie Prince Charlie's brother, Henry, Cardinal Duke of York, most rooms are intimate, if slightly forlorn. A cosy library shows off family documents, including William Smith's building estimate (for some £2150), and there is an attractive blue-green drawing-room, hung with portraits and furnished with a Queen Anne bureau and gilded Venetian chairs. A case of Jacobite relics shows off the cardinal's crucifix and rosary and in the stables is a replica of the fragile flying machine in which the pioneering Lt Percy Pilcher was killed in the park in 1899.

Northamptonshire

Althorp ☆☆

6 m NW Northampton, on A428, 6 m from M1 exit 16; guided tours (c. 45 mins) except on busiest days; tearoom; garden; *open:* Gd Fri–Easter Mon and daily in Aug, 1–5.30, plus some other days in season; advisable to check before visiting; tel: 0604 770209 (answerphone), 770006 (estate office)

For anyone with a serious interest in a house and its contents, visiting Althorp is a frustrating and disappointing experience. The house itself is surprisingly plain, with two long wings framing a severe Palladian frontage and the whole, with its unrelieved rows of sash windows, encased in drab, grey-white brick. This pallid composition, with just a grassy sward separating it from the tawny-brown stone of a virile stable block, is in fact a remodelling of a Tudor and Jacobean house, whose brick and stone façades are hidden behind Henry Holland's late 18th-century mask.

Holland was responsible for remodelling much of the interior too, but his work has been overlain by the heavy Victorian hand of MacVicar Anderson and by more recent decorative schemes, with an opulent designer gloss to them. Then, although the interior is stuffed with the Spencer family's treasures, the guided tour is too fast and selective for any real appreciation, and visitors are required to peer into rooms from the door, their way barred by wicker dog gates.

The tour starts promisingly enough in a lofty, 18th-century hall, designed to take the huge Wootton hunting canvases which cover the walls and with a stuccoed ceiling by Colen Campbell. Beyond, what was the Tudor courtyard is filled by a gloomy, galleried saloon, the unusual Stuart staircase here, with a grand lower flight branching into two, allied with a closely-hung sweep of Spencer and royal portraits, the more recent including striking paintings of the 6th and 7th Earls by William Orpen and Augustus John.

There is a glimpse of the three-room enfilade which Holland created down the west side of the house, with a quietly formal drawing-room furnished with 18th-century mahogany pieces and hung with portraits by Rubens sandwiched between a Regency library and a flamboyant interior in Barbara Cartland pink. Visitors glance, too, into MacVicar Anderson's grandiose dining-room built on in 1877, with a Snyders still-life over the fireplace flanked by two Salvator Rosas, and into various upstairs rooms. In one, the long oak-panelled gallery, two portraits by Van Dyck must be admired from a distance of 115 ft; in another, visitors are invited to view Titian's painting of his mistress through a crack in the door. Elsewhere, you may catch sight of a fine William and Mary walnut cabinet flanked by silver-gilt cushion mirrors, and you can walk into the room filled with gilded, formal furniture made by James 'Athenian' Stuart for the Spencer's grand London house, including two tripod candelabra and an extravagantly decorated mirror, with a swag of flowers falling across the glass.

Aynhoe Park

In village of Aynho, 6 m SE Banbury on A41; guided tours; garden; *open:* May–Sept, Wed, Thurs 2–5; tel: none

Surprisingly, this stately house is built almost on top of the village street, the gates opening straight on to a great courtyard framed by pedimented buildings on three sides. The house looks all of a piece, but in fact several hands have been at work here. An originally Jacobean mansion, still partly visible on the park front, was remodelled and enlarged in 1710–14 by Thomas Archer, who added the flanking pavilions, and then again, in 1805, by Sir John Soane. Aynhoe is now divided into apartments, and visitors see only the public rooms on the ground floor. Apart from Archer's oak staircase inlaid with walnut, these are largely as altered by Soane, whose subtle curves, gentle vaults and shallow apses enliven the elegant enfilade down the south front, with aligned double doors giving a vista from the orangery at one end to the library at the other. Portraits of the Cartwright family who lived here for 350 years and some sympathetic furnishings add greatly to the charm of these rooms.

Boughton House ☆☆☆☆

3 m N Kettering, off A43; free-flow tour of ground floor, guided tours of first-floor state apartment (c. 50 mins, advance booking advisable); tearoom; park walks; *open:* Aug, daily, 2–5; tel: 0536 515731

This magical house, sprawled round seven courtyards, and surrounded by the remnants of great avenues and a formal water garden, grew from a monastic manor. At the back are low two-storey ranges, but the front, which visitors see first, is a palatial affair, grafted on to the older building in the 1690s by the cultivated Ralph, lst Duke of Montagu. Some time ambassador to Louis XIV and fired with an enthusiasm for all things French, the duke contrived to make Boughton look like a grand château, with a long classical colonnade, dormers in a mansard roof, and elegant windows divided by slender pilasters. A pedimented, off-centre archway gives entrance to a large open courtyard, closed on one side by a domed stable block. Boughton is still largely as it was in the 1st Duke's time, filled with a rich accumulation of furniture, paintings and other treasures, many of them acquired during his ten-year stint in Paris, and decorated with mythological ceilings – a succession of scantily clothed deities in improbable situations – painted by Louis Chéron.

The main tour does a circuit of the principal rooms set round Fish Court, now a green and white garden. Apart from the baroque staircase hall painted with *trompe l'oeil* reliefs and sculptures and the lofty great hall, where Chéron's painted barrel ceiling, the most colourful of his creations, hides an original hammerbeam roof, Boughton is a succession of intimate panelled rooms, like a series of precious boxes filled with good things. Everything is strikingly well-preserved: furnishings are still in their original covers, tapestries are unfaded, and some 16th-century carpets seem in mint condition. The French accent is continued with ornate Louis XIV pieces, among them a little desk with a sparkling mother-of-pearl border made for Versailles, and perhaps presented by the Sun King himself, writing tables inset with Sèvres porcelain plaques, boulle kneehole desks and a marquetry commode, while a show of porcelain is headed up by a pair of Meissen swans swimming among gilded rushes that were made for Madame de Pompadour. There is English furniture here too, notably some Charles II chairs still covered in their original green and red velvet and a couple of tables of c. 1690 by Gerreit Jensen, and there are such rarities as Carolean glass candlesticks, and a table and mirror of oriental design specially made for the Duke.

And then there are the paintings. A long run of family and royal portraits is headed up by works by Honthorst, Batoni and Gainsborough and by John de Critz's unforgettable painting of Shakespeare's patron, the Earl of Southampton, imprisoned in the Tower, a companionable pussy-cat at his side. The francophile Duke was responsible for numerous flower paintings by Monnoyer, brought to Boughton when his London house became the British Museum, but a crop of Old Masters has a more Italian and Spanish accent, among them a luminous, richly coloured Holy Family by Garofalo, a menacing El Greco, an equestrian portrait of Henry IV by Taddeo Zuccaro, and a heavy-eyed young man in a plumed hat by Annibale Carracci. The lime-green drawing-room is hung with some forty or so grisaille sketches of his contemporaries by Van Dyck, although few can be seen properly, and a gallery-like passage shows off a collection of Dutch and other 17th-century works, including a crowded shipping scene by Aelbert Cuyp, a view of the Thames by Samuel Scott, and some charming domestic interiors.

The way out is through the lst Duke's unfinished east wing, with 17th-century construction techniques laid bare, and those who are still unsated can, for an extra charge, have a guided tour of the first-floor state apartment. Fitted out for a visit by William I, this sequence of high-ceilinged, painted and panelled boxes offers more of the same, the most startling sight here being the glittering, mint fresh, gold, blue and red upholstery on a Charles II settee.

Canons Ashby ☆☆

At Canons Ashby on B4525
Northampton–Banbury road; NT: tearoom;
garden and park; *open:* Apr–end Oct,
Wed–Sun and BH Mon (closed Gd Fri)
1–5.30 (or dusk); tel: 0327 860044

Built round a cobbled courtyard, Canons Ashby is rustic, unpretentious and delightfully haphazard. Home of the Dryden family from the 16th century until 1981, the house is a Tudor and Elizabethan manor with Jacobean and early Georgian embellishments. Some windows are sashed, others stone-mullioned casements, some walls are of rendered brick, others of rough rubble spotted with moss and lichen, while the garden front, with its off-centre stubby tower, is faced in stone. The only attempt at grandeur is the bravura baroque doorway that was once the main entrance. Splendid gate piers crowned with lions, pinnacles or stone urns dot the walled and terraced gardens which drop away to the north, and close by is the truncated west end of a huge medieval priory church, built for the community of Augustinian canons which gave the house its name.

A great hall fills the west range, but this was self-consciously medievalized in the 18th century. More atmospheric is the sequence of interconnecting rooms looking on to the garden, with a broad oak staircase of the 1630s leading to the former great chamber on the first floor. The most splendid room of the Jacobean house, this has a domed plaster ceiling, with a positively malevolent central pendant, and one wall is almost filled by a painted chimney-piece, its mouldings and friezes now cracked and warped. Two small panelled rooms carry the faded remains of Elizabethan painted decoration, in one case with a frieze of improving moral inscriptions such as 'he displeases many who pleases himself too much'.

Sparse furnishings include an intriguing 17th-century bracket clock set into the wall of the stone-floored Tudor kitchen, with a cupboard on the stair behind giving access to the works, and some fine 18th-century pieces, among them a delicious set of Queen Anne chairs embroidered with flower-filled, blue and white Delft pots. Among the family portraits lining the dining-room is a likeness of the poet John Dryden, a close relative of the family, but there is nothing tangible to connect Canons Ashby with the Elizabethan poet, Edmund Spenser, who was a cousin and frequent visitor.

Cottesbrooke Hall ☆☆☆

Cottesbrooke village, 9 m NW
Northampton, off A50; guided tour (*c*. 40
mins); teas; garden; *open:* Easter, May and
Aug BHs, late Apr–late Sept, Thurs 2–5.30;
tel: 060 124 808

Thought to be the original of Jane Austen's Mansfield Park, Cottesbrooke is a
stately Queen Anne house of red brick and grey stone, possibly by Francis Smith
of Warwick, with a central block connected by gently curving screen walls to
lower pavilions either side. Corinthian pilasters rise the height of the house to an
urn-topped roofline, and the original front door, now opening on to a formal garden, is crowned by a dignified broken pediment. Wooded parkland drops away
from the house, with vistas through the trees to a couple of lakes, a three-arched
classical bridge – introduced by Robert Mitchell when he turned the house
round in the 1780s – and the spire of Brixworth church, 3 miles to the south-east.

Inside, spacious, high-ceilinged 18th-century interiors, some with Mitchell's
Adamesque plaster decoration, set off an exceptional collection of sporting paintings assembled by James Buchanan, Lord Woolavington, in the late 19th and early
20th century, as well as period portraits, 18th-century furniture, and French,
English and oriental porcelain. In an information-packed but necessarily selective
tour, visitors are taken in through the west pavilion, down the quadrant corridor,
sumptuously lined with tapestries and china cabinets, and round the principal
floor. Everywhere, sporting paintings dominate. Some are studies of prize-
winning animals, some of racehorses at full stretch, some hunting scenes. Some
are meticulously exact, others anatomically bizarre. Among work by Wootton,
Sartorius, Morland, Sawrey Gilpin, Agasse, J. F. Herring, John Ferneley and
others are several Ben Marshalls, some of them with pink-tinged, feathery Monet
skies, a surreal Stubbs of the champion racer Gimcrack, a couple of Henry and
William Barraud's panoramic meet paintings, in which one brother is said to have
done the horses, the other their riders, and some delightful sketches of hounds by
Alfred Munnings, one showing a pack feeding round a trough, tails in air. Such
riches tend to dominate in a house which also offers a library with a gently curving Chippendale desk and a strongly lit self-portrait by Wright of Derby, and a
coolly green and white staircase hall, with fluid rococo plasterwork that is in fact
made of papier mâché and a delicious Queen Anne walnut settee at the foot of the
stairs. And in the bow-windowed drawing-room are conversation pieces by
Zoffany and Devis and a delicate 17th-century Flemish architectural cabinet with
receding perspectives crafted in tortoise-shell, ebony and ivory.

Deene Park ☆☆☆

8 m NW Oundle, 6 m NE Corby, on A43;
teas; lovely garden; *open:* June, July, Aug,
Sun 2–5, and Easter, May and Aug BH Sun
and Mon, 2–5; tel: 078 085 278

This picturesque and individual house grew slowly over the centuries. At its core is
the intimate paved courtyard surrounded with Elizabethan and Jacobean ranges

that was once the heart of a medieval quadrangular house, but to the south, looking outwards over grassy terraces and a narrow lake, is a long battlemented and turreted Georgian façade, the result of extensions and remodelling in the later 18th century. And the most intriguing feature is a now-blocked Elizabethan bay window on the east front, with little Ionic columns forming the mullions between the lights.

Home of the Brudenell family, later Earls of Cardigan, since 1514, Deene Park is a beautifully presented, lived-in house. Entered from the courtyard through an Italianate, two-storey porch is the stone-floored, Elizabethan great hall, spanned by an improbably perfect hammerbeam roof, lit by a bay filled with heraldic glass, and with a smoke-blackened Renaissance fireplace brought from elsewhere in the house. A sturdy oak staircase of c.1610 leads up to a suite of Tudor and Elizabethan rooms, among them a bedroom lined with linenfold panelling and the tapestry-hung former great chamber looking into the courtyard, furnished with Charles II and William and Mary pieces and decorated with a lovely plasterwork ceiling of c.1600.

Quite different are the high-ceilinged, airy, late-18th-century rooms along the south front. A pink-walled, cluttered library cum boudoir shows off Reynolds' severe portrait of the stiff-backed Lady Mary Montagu, wife of the 4th Earl; a formal, French-style blue and pink drawing-room has a couple of intricately inlaid Carolean tables by Gerreit Jensen; and the orange-walled Regency dining-room is hung with Ferneley's paintings of the 7th Earl's hunters and with de Prades' romanticized vision of the Charge of the Light

Brigade, with the Earl, dashing in a glittering gold breastplate, to the fore. The head of the chestnut charger who carried him is preserved, tastefully arranged on artificial grass, in a glass case in the hall outside, and here too is a portrait of the alluring, gipsyish Adeline, with whom he fell in love at the age of 60, scandalizing Victorian society. Elsewhere are portraits by Honthorst, Lely, Thomas Hudson and William Larkin, and J. M. Wright's painting of the frail and proud lst Earl, painted in 1658 after several years' imprisonment during the Civil War.

Kirby Hall ☆☆

4 m NE Corby, off unclassified road to Deene, signposted from main Corby–Oundle road; EH; *open:* all year, summer, daily, 10–6, winter, Tues–Sun 10–4; tel: 0536 203230

The only noise here the chatter of birds, this secluded, romantic ruin of gold-tinged stone is more atmospheric than many a much visited country house. From the approach road, it looks deceptively intact, its long west façade crested with ornate, gently curving gables, and paired Tudor chimneys silhouetted against the sky. Only close to, do you notice the roofless walls and the glassless windows. Kirby's heyday lasted just over a century, from 1570, when it was started by Sir Humphrey Stafford, to 1706, when the last owner who cared about it died.

An intriguing mix of the conventional and the wildly innovatory, of the domestic and the foreign, Kirby was built to a medieval plan, its ornamentation is French, Dutch and Italian, and the house is unusually symmetrical for its date. At its heart is a spacious, grassy courtyard. The arresting entrance range, with its pedimented windows, balconies and open loggia, was added in the late 1630s, but the other wings, marked by giant, fluted pilasters, are 16th-century. A flamboyant Renaissance porch, embellished with columns, colonettes, a voluptuous gable and an ornate balcony, leads into the great hall range and the south wing, the only part that is now roofed. Visitors can wander inside, through the lofty, galleried hall with its plasterwork barrel ceiling, and up the grand stone staircase leading to the floorless shell of the long gallery.

Lamport Hall ☆

In Lamport village, 8 m N Northampton on A508; teas; garden; *open:* Easter–end Sept, Sun and BH Mon, also Thurs in July and Aug, 2.15–5.15; tel: 060128 272

Gradually evolved over 300 years, Lamport Hall is a variable feast. Passers-by on the A508 see a long and graceful, sash-windowed façade, with a rusticated centrepiece of 1654–5 by John Webb, Inigo Jones' right-hand man, sandwiched between wings by Francis Smith and his son William of the 1730s and 40s. Like much of the interior, the other fronts are largely 19th-century; the one to the north, facing the stump-towered village church, is an uncompromisingly ugly composition of 1861 by the Scottish William Burn.

Home of the Ishams from 1560 until 1976, Lamport is still full of family furniture and paintings, including portraits attributed to Mierevelt and Cornelius

Johnson, but is now administered by a trust and has an impersonal feel. The best is downstairs, along the west front. In the centre is Webb's exuberant, sparsely furnished, lofty hall, lit by a double row of windows, decorated with three-dimensional 18th-century plasterwork featuring the swan of the family crest and profiled medallion heads, and hung with portraits advertising the family's Stuart allegiance. An elegant library remodelled in 1819 is a period piece, with classical busts ranged along the pilastered bookcases and early 19th-century furniture. At one end is Carlo Maratta's portrait of Sir Thomas, 3rd Baronet, whose extensive Grand Tour in the 1670s yielded the fleshy mythological and religious paintings which are such a feature of the house, among them works by Gimignani, Brandi, Guido Reni, Sebastiano Ricci and a tubby infant Christ by Van Dyck. Preserved under a dome is a pot-bellied, weather-worn Victorian garden gnome, one of the earliest of his kind and the only survivor of the troop which once perched on the gigantic rockery.

Lyveden New Bield

4 m SW Oundle, signed from A427, final access on foot $^1/_2$ m along farm track; NT; *open:* all year, daily; tel: 083 25 358

Approached along an unfenced, one-track road bordered by huge, hedgeless fields, this unfinished stone shell is seen crowning a low ridge, its glassless windows blank against the sky. Begun in 1594 by the courageous but foolhardy Sir Thomas Tresham, determined to declare his newly embraced Catholicism, the house, more lodge than mansion, is built as a cross. Its walls are carved with the instruments of the Passion and with a long Latin inscription glorifying Our Lady, while a play with numbers in the design brings in further references to Salvation, the Godhead and the Tresham coat of arms. Strange that this folly has survived so long; strange, too, that the country around still echoes the desolation created by Tresham when he depopulated the village here.

Prebendal Manor House

In Nassington, 6 m N Oundle, no signs; guided tours (c. 35 mins); teas on Sun; *open:* June–end Aug, Wed, BH Mon, and Sun in July and Aug 2–6; tel: 0780 782575

This small house set slightly back from the road opposite the village church incorporates the remnant of a 13th-century manor. Apart from the medieval porch with its weathered carved heads, the sash-windowed frontage looks unexceptional enough, but round the back are two round-headed windows and a lovely Norman door, and the much altered interior still has a sequence of 13th-century stone arches and the beetle-grazed timber roof that once spanned the great hall. The original solar block is now just outlines in the garden, but the manor is still set off by part of a former lodgings range, a square stone dovecote and a fine 18th-century tithe barn. The informal guided tour concentrates on building history.

Rockingham Castle ☆☆

2 m N Corby, off A6003; teas; garden; *open:* Easter Sun–end Sept, Sun, Thurs, BH Mon and Tues and Tues in Aug, 1.30–5.30; tel: 0536 770240

This eyrie of a house sits high on a steep escarpment, with wide views over a scatter of steepled villages in the rural Welland valley. For 400 years a royal castle, Rockingham is still walled, and approached through a drum-towered 13th-century gateway. Beyond is a wide, grassy court surrounded on three sides by gabled Tudor and Jacobean ranges of warm local stone. The ruinous old castle was turned into a comfortable residence by Edward Watson, who leased it from the Crown in 1544. It was bought outright by his Jacobean grandson, who started the long gallery wing, and altered again in the 1840s by Anthony Salvin, who added the conspicuous battlemented tower to the west front. Charles Dickens, a frequent visitor, put on some of his theatrical productions here, dedicated *David Copperfield* to the Watsons, and based Chesney Wold in *Bleak House* on the castle.

The short tour mixes remnants of the old house with 19th-century and more recent interiors, ending with a steep climb to the battlements of Salvin's tower. Past the medieval cobbled 'street', lined with brew house and laundry, and through the old kitchens, is what was the Tudor great hall, hung with 16th-century portraits and with some contemporary furniture, but much restored. There is a glimpse of a cool, green and white Edwardian library and then it is upstairs to the unashamedly Victorian, 90 ft long gallery, lined with a bold gold and green paper, hung with heavy red curtains and furnished with inviting deep green sofas and inlaid French pieces.

A long run of family portraits includes works by Dobson, Lely, Angelica Kauffmann, an early Reynolds, a group of children by Zoffany, and Ben Marshall's atmospheric painting of four Watson brothers hunting in Rockingham park. Juxtaposed is a small and disparate collection of modern canvases, among them a disturbing Stanley Spencer, a child portrait by Augustus John, an angry, tormented Christ, monkey-like daubs by Barbara Hepworth and a version of Sickert's *Ennui,* of a couple who have long exhausted any interest in each other.

Southwick Hall ☆

In Southwick village, by church, 3 m NW Oundle, no advance signs; collection of bygones and Victorian and Edwardian costume; teas; *open:* Easter, May and Aug BH Sun and Mon, and Wed, early May–late Aug, 2–5; tel: 0832 274064

This rambling building of local limestone set at one end of a quietly pretty village has gradually evolved over some 600 years. On the south front, a gabled Elizabethan range with generous stone-mullioned windows is attached to a stubby medieval tower, one of the remnants of the 14th-century house, but the 18th-century west wing is a delicious exercise in Strawberry Hill

gothick, and the east side of the house is a rebuild of 1870. Inside, visitors see a series of modest, unexceptionally furnished, mostly 18th-century interiors, including an airy room that was once the great hall and the barrel-ceilinged, panelled bedroom that was the solar. Upper rooms in the south tower, reached by a worn spiral stair, look tired and unloved, although the former chapel still has its original traceried windows and altar niche, and there is a view over the trees from here to the octagonal lantern of Fotheringhay church. Most welcoming is the cosy little parlour with a big west-facing bay and a shell-headed, porcelain-filled niche; most memorable the stone-vaulted medieval undercroft to the tower, with a two-headed green man carved on the central boss.

Sulgrave Manor ☆

In Sulgrave village, 7 m NE Banbury, signposted from A422; guided tours; refreshments; living history days; *open:* Mar–Dec, daily (except Weds) 10.30–5.30 (4 in Mar and Oct–Dec); tel: 0295 760205

This unassuming, stone-built, L-shaped manor was the ancestral home of George Washington, first president of the USA, whose great-grandfather emigrated from England to Virginia in 1656. Of the substantial house built by the wealthy wool merchant John Washington in *c.* 1560, only part survives; one wing is a Queen Anne addition, another a sympathetic 1920s extension in Tudor style. Most of the contents were acquired piecemeal after massive restoration early this century, but the furnishings are all in period and the guided tour, which takes visitors over the older parts of the house, is well done.

Still 16th century in character are the sparsely furnished, stone-floored great hall and the chamber open to the roof above, fitted out with richly carved oak pieces and an Elizabethan four-poster. The early-18th-century rooms are cosier, among them a panelled parlour, with chocolate cups ready on a table and a spinet in the corner, two tiny Queen Anne bedrooms and a splendidly equipped kitchen, with curtains to draw round the fire to increase the draught. In these rooms, only a painted chair and a portrait by the American artist Gilbert Stuart connect the house with George Washington, but there are more personal relics in a little museum, among them the president's brown velvet coat, saddlebags and liquor case.

Nottinghamshire

Holme Pierrepont Hall

5 m E central Nottingham, follow signs to National Water Sports Centre and continue a further mile; teas; enchanting courtyard garden; *open:* June, Sun, July, Sun and Thurs, Aug, Tues, Thurs, Fri, Sun 2–5.30 and Easter, late May and Aug BH Sun, Mon, Tues 2–6; tel: 0602 332371

Quietly slumbering beside a slender-spired church is this remnant of a once-grand Tudor and Stuart house, with brick ranges set round a butterfly-rich garden in the former courtyard. A shadow of its former self, and recently brought back from the brink of final decay, Holme Pierrepont is an informal unpretentious kind of place, with the owners in attendance. The entrance range, with its Tudor brickwork and three-storey towers flanking the central arch, is the oldest part. Here, two surprisingly spacious ground-floor rooms evoke 17th-century Dutch interiors, with sturdy oak furniture and brass candlesticks seen against bare brick walls, heavily beamed ceilings, and portraits attributed to Vanderbank and Kneller, while one of the bedrooms upstairs has an arch-braced, 15th-century timber roof. The still unrestored north range across the courtyard is a Victorian rebuild, but the east wing is a meld of 17th- and 18th-century work. A sunny long gallery recently created on the first floor has a big bay overlooking the garden, an Elizabethan stone door-way, and some 18th-century pieces, but the overall effect is spoilt by utilitarian tables set for tea and a display of souvenirs. Beyond, a gracious Jacobean staircase leads back to the courtyard, with portraits by G. F. Watts looking down on rough oak treads and a carved pine and elm baluster with baskets of flowers on the newel posts.

Newstead Abbey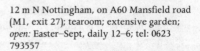

12 m N Nottingham, on A60 Mansfield road (M1, exit 27); tearoom; extensive garden; *open:* Easter–Sept, daily 12–6; tel: 0623 793557

This vast rambling building created out of an Augustinian priory was briefly the home of Lord Byron, whose family lived here for 300 years. By the time

Byron inherited, in 1798, the courtyard house created by a Tudor ancestor was fast becoming a ruin, and in 1817 mounting debts forced him to sell. Much of what you see today is the result of restoration in an antiquarian style by his old schoolfriend Colonel Thomas Wildman, who commissioned John Shaw to create the mock-Tudor entrance front with its huge stone-mullioned windows and pinnacled porch.

Still standing is the beautiful 13th-century west front of the abbey church, with pinnacled buttresses, canopied statue niches, and a gaping hole where once was a huge traceried window. The church behind has gone, but the abbey cloisters lie at the heart of the house, the stone-vaulted walkways now looking out on to a little garden and a beast-encrusted, gothic fountain. The chapter house was transformed into the Byron chapel, now brightly painted, and beneath Shaw's evocation of a medieval great hall is a stone-vaulted 13th-century undercroft, filled with Byron monuments.

All this emerges on the extended tour, which takes visitors through a rabbit warren of galleries and state rooms on many different levels, and into a 19th-century suite devoted to the family of W. F. Webb, the African explorer and friend of Dr Livingstone who bought the house in 1860. There are some 16th-century painted overmantels, an early-18th-century ceiling and some period furnishings, but it is the Byron connection which makes the place. A collection of papers and manuscripts includes some of the letters the poet wrote to his patron Elizabeth Pigot, pouring his thoughts out in a manic stream and underlining almost every other word. Also on show is the brass collar worn by his beloved dog Boatswain, now buried beneath a grandiose classical memorial in the ruins of the church; his wedding ring; and his individual toothpick, fashioned as a tiny sword in a silver sheath. An ornate boulle cupboard inlaid with brass and pewter in the rather cavernous saloon is the piece from which Byron used to produce his skull drinking cup; his

bedroom has the pompous four-poster he used when at Cambridge; and one of the rooms has been set up as his study, with his wine coolers standing in the windows, his crucifix hanging on the wall, and a bottle of port and a wine glass ready on the table. A pile of his leather-bound books is topped off by another grinning skull.

Staffordshire

Chillington Hall ☆

8 m NW Wolverhampton, 2 m S Brewood (poorly signed); guided tour (c. 30 mins); 4-m walk round temple-fringed, Capability Brown lake; *open:* May–mid Sept, Thurs, also Easter and May BH Suns and all Suns in Aug, 2.30–5.30; tel: 0902 850236

This imposing, smoke-blackened, red-brick house looks east over sheep-grazed parkland towards the tower blocks of Wolverhampton. The two-storey entrance façade, with a pedimented portico supported on streaky grey columns of local Tunstall stone, is part of a rebuilding of 1786–9 by Sir John Soane, but round the side is a busier, many-windowed almost baroque frontage of 60 years earlier, probably the work of Francis Smith of Warwick. Here, two floors miraculously become three, with the join cleverly disguised by Soane's false-windowed 'towers' on the corner of the house. This 18th-century work for Peter Giffard and his grandson Thomas replaced the family's Tudor courtyard mansion.

The brief and uninspired guided tour concentrates on Soane's high-ceilinged, comfortless main rooms, decorated with bold, unyielding plaster-work in a severely classical style, hung with family portraits, including two by Batoni, and furnished with some pieces specially made for the house, among them a massive sideboard and formal settees and chairs upholstered in gold. Soane at his most experimental contrived the oppressive, mausoleum-like domed saloon on the site of the Tudor great hall. Lit only from above, it is dominated by a pastiche baronial fireplace, and hung with a huge Snyders canvas of a boar hunt. Light-hearted plasterwork decorates the early 18th-century staircase hall and the welcoming, south-facing morning room in the baroque wing.

Hanch Hall

4 m NW Lichfield, on B5014; guided tour (c. 60 mins); tearoom; teapot and doll collections; garden; *open:* mid Apr–end Sept, Sun, BH Mon 2–6; tel: 0543 490308

Although developed from a Tudor hunting lodge, Hanch Hall is predominant-ly 18th- and 19th-century. The south front is a pleasing, brick-and-stone, Queen Anne façade with a central pediment, but round the side and looking on to the courtyard at the back are curved gables, a pierced stone parapet, a staircase tower and other Victorian additions in Jacobean style. The interior, restored and refurnished by the present owner, is similarly mixed. A friendly, extensive tour takes in a fragment of a kingpost roof and a couple of low-ceilinged, panelled interiors that could well be 16th-century, but the Jacobean staircase with its carved newel posts and pierced balustrade is a Victorian pastiche, and the south-facing reception rooms are largely furnished in a period-less stylistic mix, including pieces and portraits on loan from the local council, and with a shaggy goatskin carpet covering the floor of the elegant, cream-coloured drawing-room. Most disconcerting of all are the hideous wax figures found propped up in chairs and stretched out on the four-posters.

Moseley Old Hall ☆

4 m N Wolverhampton, S of M54 between A449 and A460 (access from south-bound A449 only); NT; optional guided tour (c. 60 mins), teas; re-created 17th-century garden; *open:* Apr–end Oct, Wed, Sat, Sun, BH Mon, and Tues in July and Aug, 2–5.30; tel: 0902 782808

Seeing Moseley for the first time, with its Victorian casements and façades of dark red brick, and with the M54 only yards away, it is difficult to believe this is the house where the Whitgreave family hid Charles II for two nights in September 1651, following the Battle of Worcester. But there are star-shaped Elizabethan chimneys, and once inside it is clear the present façade has been slapped on to a much older, timber-framed house. Faltering imaginations are helped by modest, dimly lit rooms, mellow panelling, cracked and wood-wormy timbers and undulating floors, and by the atmospheric warren of attics divided by massive Elizabethan chimney stacks. Inside, too, the noise of traffic fades away.

The lengthy and optional guided tour is an uneasy mix of Civil War narrative and general social history. Visitors follow the route Charles took, coming into the house through the silvery old garden door, and climbing the narrow back stair to the room where he rested. The four-poster bed on which he lay is still here, and the hide where he crouched when Cromwell's men came to the house is beneath a trapdoor in a cupboard by the fire. From a little room over the porch, now fitted up as a study with desk and beeswax candle, Charles watched the remnants of his army struggling back north, and John Huddleston, the Whitgreave's resident priest, took the king up to the simple chapel on the third floor, since prettified with a barrel vault. There are a few historical documents, such as a bill offering a £1,000 reward for the capture of the king, but most of the solid 17th-century furniture is not original.

On the third night Charles stole away through the garden gate, disguised as a serving man. He never returned to Moseley, but in 1685, as he lay dying, it was John Huddleston who received him into the Catholic faith and gave him the last rites.

Shugborough ☆

6 m E Stafford, on A513; audio tours; tearoom; garden and park; rare breeds farm; museum of 19th-century life; *open:* late Mar–end Oct, daily, 11–5; tel: 0889 881388

A long drive flanked with brackeny woodland on the slopes of Cannock Chase suddenly opens out into a grazed park. There is a glimpse of a column to the left, and of a triumphal arch stalking across a hill to the right, and then the house itself appears, a long, grey building set low by the River Sow, with bowed wings attached to a three-storey central block. A massive portico runs right across the central façade, while at the back a huge Regency bay, tied down by pretty trellised verandahs on either side, projects towards the river. Seat of the Ansons, Earls of Lichfield, this rambling place, and the eyecatchers that dot garden and park, are both creations of the 18th century, when Thomas Anson's fortunes were transformed by his brother George's capture of a Spanish treasure galleon. A modest William and Mary house was remodelled in the 1740s by Wright of Durham, with more alterations, in the 1790s, by Samuel Wyatt, while in mid-century James 'Athenian' Stuart produced the copies of classical monuments which make Shugborough so memorable.

A tour of much of the ground floor and a bedroom suite upstairs takes in interiors by Wright and Wyatt – the former with light-hearted, rococo plasterwork, the latter in a more grandiose style – as well as comfortable, essentially 20th-century sitting-rooms still in use by the family. In one wing is Wright's sombre dining-room, hung with Nicholas Dall's huge canvases of classical ruins, the only colour in the blue, white and gold ceiling; in the other is his intimate, welcoming library, its two halves divided by a low arch and the busts above the bookcases including a likeness of the 1st Countess holding a rabbit. In between come Wyatt's red drawing-room and saloon, the former with Adamesque plasterwork by Joseph Rose the Younger on a high, gently arched ceiling, gilded chairs and sofas made for the room, and marquetry and ormolu-mounted Louis XV and XVI pieces introduced after most of the original contents had been dispersed in a sale; the latter a bare gallery of a room with mirrors on the end walls endlessly repeating the yellow scagliola columns down each side.

To the rump of the 18th-century picture collection – Reynolds' portrait of the rotund Admiral George, two huge biblical canvases bought as Guido Renis, an enchanting landscape by Zuccarelli, and Dall's views of house and park – have been added 19th-century sporting paintings and a series of animal drawings by Landseer. And there are relics of the gallant admiral, among them the sword he took from the captain of the Spanish galleon, and porcelain and painted mirrors he brought back from China.

Whitmore Hall ☆

Off A53, behind Whitmore church, 4 m from Newcastle-under-Lyme, no signs; guided tour (c. 30 mins); grounds; *open:* May–Aug, Tues, Wed, 2–5.30; tel: 0782 680478

Looking down a double lime avenue towards the church is a Carolean frontage of red brick and stone, with rows of sash windows, and massive chimney stacks rising from a hipped roof. This façade was slapped on to a half-timbered Elizabethan house in 1676, but the interior seen today is 18th- and 19th-century, some of it the result of rebuilding after a fire in 1880 destroyed what was left of the old hall.

Home of the Mainwaring family since the 16th century, Whitmore has sadly lost most of its original furniture, but there is a run of portraits, including some attributed to Marcus Gheeraerts the Younger, a Lely and a rare double portrait by Michael Dahl. The short visitor tour takes in the classical central hall and the main rooms to either side, among them a lovely long drawing-room decorated in soft green and cream and furnished with painted Hepplewhite chairs and a William and Mary walnut cabinet, and a room called after the colourful Admiral Rowland Mainwaring, who did the initial sketches for a dramatic painting of the Battle of the Nile by Luny, showing the French flagship going up in flames on the night of 1 August 1798.

The only remnant of the Elizabethan house is a small and sturdy Tudor stable block by the side of the steep, beech-shaded drive, the unaltered interior still with its original pebble floor and wooden stalls decorated with pendants and lozenges.

Anne Hathaway's Cottage ☆

At Shottery, 1¼ m W Stratford upon Avon, off A422 and A439; teas; garden; *open:* all year, weekdays, 9–5.30, Sun, 10–5.30 (shorter hours Nov–Feb); tel: 0789 292100

This sizeable cottage climbing a gentle slope away from the road is almost too pretty to be true, its old-world charm enhanced by a colourful, pint-sized garden. Timber-framed, with walls that are partly white-washed, partly bare brick, it is lit by tiny latticed casements and topped off by a thatched roof that looks as if it is slowly oozing over the walls. Anne Hathaway, Shakespeare's future wife, was born here in 1556, into a well-to-do yeoman family whose house was well above the average. The simple rooms, opening one into another, are still furnished with Hathaway pieces, but most are later than the time of William and Anne. Only a carved four-poster, the kitchen table, and the worn settle on which the couple are supposed to have done their courting are Elizabethan. Like all the places connected with the bard, the cottage is vastly overvisited, but it still has atmosphere, despite the fact the hamlet is now effectively part of Stratford.

Arbury Hall ☆☆☆

2 m SW Nuneaton, off B4102, few advance signs; guided tours (*c.* 60 mins); tearoom; gardens; *open:* Easter Sun–end Sept, Sun and BH Mon 2–5.30; tel: 0203 382804

Arbury is a spectacular example of 18th-century gothick set in romantic wooded grounds. The creation of Sir Roger Newdigate, 5th Baronet, who also started the Oxford poetry prize that bears his name, the house is a remodelling of an Elizabethan courtyard mansion, its pointed windows and pinnacled and battlemented roofline a delicious contrast to the late-17th-century red-brick stable block with its curving Dutch gables and a pedimented doorway designed by Christopher Wren.

The interior is in a class of its own. Uninhibited plaster fan vaulting and lacy tracery, with chandeliers hanging from delicate pendants, reaches a crescendo in the saloon, which is modelled on Henry VIII's chapel at Westminster Abbey, and in the lofty dining-room created out of the Elizabethan great hall, with copies of antique sculptures arranged in canopied niches round the walls, and a kind of aisle-like arcade on the garden side. Sir Roger's architects, each bolder than the one before, were his near-neighbour Sanderson Miller, William Hiorn of Warwick, and Henry Keene, surveyor to Westminster Abbey, their work, completed in 1805, spanning a period of some fifty years.

Newdegates still live here (the family name has reverted to its original spelling) and the half-dozen rooms shown, most of them opening off the cloister-like vaulted passage running round the Elizabethan courtyard, are hung with a long sequence of portraits and filled with an accumulation of treasures. Jacobean oak furniture in the dining-room is set off by Elizabethan and Stuart portraits, among them John Bettes' icon-like painting of the ageing Elizabeth I, and a sumptuously attired Mary Fitton, one of the candidates for the Dark Lady of Shakespeare's sonnets. Elsewhere are a village scene by Ruisdael, with steep red-tiled roofs round a tall church tower, Mercier's *Card Players*, an unlikely John the Baptist by Reynolds, and portraits by Lely, Romney, Hudson, Mary Beale, Dahl, Knapton, Hoare, and Arthur Devis, who has captured Sir Roger self-consciously seated at a desk in his new library. There are some good marquetry pieces, a Renaissance cabinet dated to 1628–33 that belonged to Archbishop Laud, and a number of stools charmingly embroidered by Sir Roger's first wife, Sophia, who made a joke of her untidiness by depicting playing cards, a fan and other objects that she was wont to leave lying about.

The tour starts in an unaltered 17th-century chapel, with plasterwork fruit and foliage by Edward Martin on walls and ceiling and delicate contemporary brasswork on the door, and it ends in the Elizabethan long gallery running down the north front, now used to display some of the accomplished sketches and watercolours which Sir Roger did on his Grand Tour.

Baddesley Clinton ☆☆

5 m SE Solihull, off A4141 Warwick road; NT; entry by timed ticket on busy days; tearoom; garden; *open:* March–end Oct, Wed–Sun and BH Mon (closed Gd Fri), 2–6 (Oct 12.30–4.30); tel: 0564 783294

Just beyond the clutches of Birmingham, on the edge of a remnant of the Forest of Arden, is this romantic, moated old house, its brick and stone ranges rising sheer from the water. A two-arched brick bridge leads to a battlemented gatehouse with a great Elizabethan window above the entrance; beyond is a tiny courtyard garden, the effect of wisteria against stone, half-timbered gables and the view over the moat to the north rather spoilt by a summer display of garish bedding plants.

Although dating back to the 15th century, and with a moat 200 years older, Baddesley Clinton is largely the work of a remarkable Elizabethan, Henry Ferrers, who built the south range and remodelled the interior. Sympathetic 18th- and 19th-century additions and alterations have done nothing to destroy the charm of the place, and Ferrers' descendants lived on here into the 20th century.

The interior is a series of atmospheric panelled rooms, with elaborately carved Elizabethan overmantels and richly coloured armorial glass put in by Henry Ferrers. Sadly, fine period furniture that used to be here was sold in the 1970s (some of it ending up in nearby *Packwood House*), and there is now an entirely appropriate, but mostly rather plain collection of 17th- and 18th-century oak pieces, some of them with 19th-century embellishments. A series of romantic Victorian portraits, some with the house as misty backdrop, are the work of Rebecca Dulcibella Orpen, wife of Marmion Edward Ferrers, who lived at Baddesley in a curious *ménage à quatre*, with Rebecca's aunt Georgiana and her youthful husband Edward Heneage Dering. The story goes that Dering had approached Georgiana for the hand of her niece, and that the lady had accepted him for herself, the young man being too gallant to disabuse her. Certainly, only a year after the deaths of their respective spouses, Rebecca and Edward married each other.

Visitors see most of the east and south ranges, including the airy barrel-ceilinged great parlour in the gatehouse where Rebecca and Georgiana used to set up their easels, now a cool, empty, rush-matted space with light reflected from the moat playing on the walls. In the west range, the oldest part of the house, a tiny oratory is a reminder of the Ferrers' adherence to the Catholic faith. In October 1591, when anti-Catholic mania was at a height, seven priests and two or three of their flock scrambled down the garderobe shaft beneath the simple cross here to hide in the medieval drain that is visible through a glass panel in the kitchen floor, while the house above was searched for several hours.

Charlecote Park ☆

5 m E Stratford upon Avon, 6 m S Warwick, on N side B4086; NT; tearoom; garden and park walk; *open:* Apr–end Oct, daily, except Mon and Thurs, 11–1, 2–5.30; tel: 0789 470277

The young Shakespeare is said to have been brought before Sir Thomas Lucy of Charlecote for poaching deer, and to have taken his revenge, years later, by caricaturing the squire in *The Merry Wives of Windsor*. With its gabled, red-brick façades, octagonal turrets, tall chimneys and stone-mullioned windows, Charlecote still looks 16th-century, but in fact the house was largely rebuilt and the interior remodelled, in Elizabethan revival style, between 1829 and 1867. Only the delicious rose-pink gatehouse, a range of Tudor outbuildings, with a fully equipped brewery, and the splendid Renaissance stone porch carrying the arms of Elizabeth I are as originally built. Even the surrounding deer park, laid out on low-lying meadows fringing the Avon, is not as Shakespeare knew it, having been landscaped by Capability Brown.

The 19th-century work was carried out for George Hammond Lucy and his wife Mary Elizabeth, initially with advice from the antiquarian Thomas Willement and Jeffry Wyatville's pupil Charles Smith, latterly with the help of the architect John Gibson. A sequence of large, high-ceilinged, rather gloomy rooms are hung with boldly patterned wallpapers, ornamented with ribbed and pendanted Jacobethan plaster ceilings and brilliantly coloured armorial glass, and filled with the Lucys' carefully assembled furniture, some pieces genuine antiques, others 19th-century interpretations of Elizabethan style.

There is 16th-century glass in the windows of what was the great hall, but the beamed ceiling is painted plaster, the floor is a chequer of Italian red and white marble, and the furniture includes a huge alabaster bowl by Pisani with doves perching on the rim, bought in Florence. Elsewhere there are suites of ebony furniture, some of it dating from the 17th century, *pietra dura* cabinets, and a hideous carved sideboard, with a central plaque showing cherubs playing at farming. A long run of Lucy portraits, from Elizabethan times onwards, includes works by Cornelius Johnson, Batoni, Gainsborough and Raeburn, and two ovals painted on copper by William Larkin. Sadly, the Old Masters that used to hang in the amber-walled drawing-room have mostly been sold, and there is only the rump of the collection here now.

Coughton Court ☆

2 m N Alcester, on E side A435; NT; teas; garden; river walk; *open:* Easter weekend, Sat and Sun in Apr and Oct, 1.30–5.30; May–end Sept, daily, except Thurs and Fri, 1.30–5.30; tel: 0789 762435

Coughton's star feature is a thrusting gatehouse of *c*.1530, calling to passers-by on the main road with a lantern-like show of glass, octagonal corner turrets and a battlemented roofline. Behind, framing a little courtyard, are gabled and half-timbered ranges. This Tudor and Elizabethan house was begun by George Throckmorton in the early 16th century, but is much altered, with the family paying dearly for a strong allegiance to Charles I and the Catholic faith. Repaired after a bombardment during the Civil War, the house was again damaged in 1688, when it was attacked by a Protestant mob and the east wing that once closed the courtyard was destroyed. Later changes account for the stuccoed gothick façades either side of the gatehouse and for the loss of the moat. Rising out of trees next to the house is the ancient parish church, while just beyond, as if advertising the faith which cost them so much, is the Catholic chapel built by the family in 1853.

The tour starts in the three-storey gatehouse, where visitors can climb a spiral stair to the roof and look out over the gently rolling country round about. The first-floor oriel room where a group of ladies waited anxiously for news of the Gunpowder Plot is now a stiff little drawing-room, but the chamber above, with a priest-hole hidden beneath a turret alcove, is more atmospheric. In the much-altered south wing, a cavernous saloon once did duty as a chapel, and a large dining-room is lined with a mix of Tudor and Jacobean panelling. Family treasures include an embroidered early-16th-century cope of purple velvet, one of the many chemises in which Mary Queen of Scots is said to have been beheaded, and the dole gate from Denny Convent, whose last abbess, in 1539, was a Throckmorton. Family portraits, many of them hung on the Georgian stairs, include works by Cornelius Johnson, Lely, Batoni and two strongly contrasted paintings by Nicolas de Largillière, one of a primped and preened Sir Robert, 4th Baronet, with a shining breast-plate over his coat, the other a more dignified study of his aunt, who was an abbess.

Farnborough Hall ☆

W side Farnborough village on road to
Avon Dassett, 6 m N Banbury; NT; rose
garden and terrace walk; *open:* Apr–end
Sept, Wed and Sat 2–6; tel: 0684 850051
(regional office)

The Holbech family's mellow 18th-century house looks out over the wide
Warmington valley, with the ridge of Edgehill rising in the distance. Built of
warm brown stone, with gently pedimented doorcases, rows of sash windows
and a balustraded roofline, and with charming rococo decoration in the principal rooms, Farnborough was remodelled by William Holbech II in 1745–50
to provide a setting for the sculpture and paintings he had acquired in Italy.
Holbech's architect was almost certainly his near neighbour Sanderson
Miller, and the plasterwork was most likely by the Yorkshireman William
Perritt.

Visitors step into a Palladian hall. Classical busts, some antique, others
18th-century, sit half in, half out of a ring of oval niches, with a curly-headed
Marcus Aurelius dominating a company of Roman emperors and goddesses, a
marble floor echoes the design of the ceiling and an Italianate landscape is
inset over the chimney-piece. The dining-room, the best interior in the house,
was devised to take views of Rome and Venice by Panini and Canaletto. There
are only poor copies here now, but these are framed by delightfully light-
hearted plasterwork, incorporating a violin here, a pair of snub-nosed dogs
there, and there are also 18th-century chairs and side tables. The staircase,
with a plasterwork wreath of fruit and flowers ringing a domed skylight and
more niche-framed classical busts, is similarly engaging, while the cluttered,
book-lined library, the only other room to be seen, has a Regency feel about
it. Outside, there are shell-decorated rainwater heads on the early-18th-
century west front, and a glorious grassy terrace walk punctuated by classical
temples and an obelisk stretches three-quarters of a mile along the shoulder of
the valley.

Honington Hall ☆

In village of Honington, 10 m S Stratford
upon Avon, $\frac{1}{2}$ m E A3400; no advance
signs; guided tours (*c.* 30 mins); garden;
open: June–Aug, Wed, BH Mon 2.30–5; tel:
0608 661434

No-one knows who designed this charming red-brick, Caroline house, set
above lawns running down to the River Stour. Tall brick chimneys rise from a
hipped roof, sash windows flank the central doorway, with its baroque broken
pediment, and busts of Roman emperors lean out of medallion-like niches. All
is symmetrical and assured. A little stone church, also of the late 17th century,
is half-hidden in the trees to one side, and a curving, screen wall conceals a rustic stable court of mellow limestone, with an octagonal dovecote in the yard.

The great surprise is the lavish Italianate plasterwork dating from

The Heart of England   206

mid-18th-century alterations. The brief informal tour of the lived-in down-stairs rooms starts in the lemon and white hall, decorated with languid classi-cal maidens impersonating the arts, cherubs representing the elements and puzzled lions dangling ornamental swags wherever they could be fitted in. And it ends in the astonishing domed saloon rising through two floors that was added to the garden front. Designed by the gentleman architect John Freeman, this extraordinary piece of one-upmanship, now picked out in pastel blue and white, is a rococo extravaganza, with light-hearted repre-sentations of the elements and seasons (water is a shaggy spaniel among the bullrushes) climbing the dome to a brooding central canvas.

Mary Arden's House

Wilmcote, 3½ m NW Stratford upon Avon, between A422 and A34; refreshments; *open:* all year, weekdays, 9.30–5, Sun 10.30–5, shorter hours Nov–Feb; tel: 0789 293455

The childhood home of Shakespeare's mother, still in a rural setting, is a half-timbered Tudor farmhouse facing across a grassy square to barns and cow-sheds in a pleasing mix of grey stone, weathered red brick and silvery oak. The house is one-room deep, and modestly furnished with simple Elizabethan and Jacobean pieces intended to conjure up a 16th-century lifestyle, although none of the contents was here in Mary Arden's day. Probably, too, the house was without its bare and atticy bedrooms when she knew it, with the main room open to the roof. Shakespearean echoes are faint indeed, and the farm is now allied to a countryside museum, and approached through a commercial entrance complex.

Packwood House ☆

11 m SE Birmingham, off B4439, 2 m SE Hockley Heath (M42 exit 4, M40 exit 16); NT; yew topiary garden; *open:* Apr–end Sept, Wed–Sun and BH Mon 2–6; Oct, Wed–Sun, 12.30–4.30; tel: 0564 782024

This modest Elizabethan house with prominent gables and massive chimney stacks seems all of a piece, its small, panelled rooms filled with gleaming 16th- and 17th-century oak and walnut furniture and hung with tapestries. But in fact Packwood is a 20th-century creation. Left ruinous at the end of the 19th century, the house was rescued from 1905 by the cultivated Graham Baron Ash, son of a wealthy industrialist, who devoted years to replacing leaded casements, acquiring period panelling, fireplaces and even oak floors from other demolished buildings, and building up a collection of suitable furniture. Not content with this, Baron Ash, as he liked to be called, converted an old brick barn into a Great Hall, inserting an oriel window, using the hay rack in a balustraded gallery, and linking it to the main house with an Elizabethan-style long gallery.

Packwood shows what can be done with taste and money, and the fine collection of antiques displayed here is still as arranged by Baron Ash, who built up each room as if it were a painting. The place seems self-consciously neat and trim, but this is how he had it, hating any untidiness. Several pieces were acquired from *Baddesley Clinton*, just two miles away, among them a long refectory table and an ornate Charles II cupboard inlaid with mother-of-pearl. Others, such as the oak bedstead said to have been slept in by Margaret of Anjou before the battle of Tewkesbury in 1471, or a fireplace from Stratford which might have warmed Shakespeare, were bought for their associations.

The old house, its drab brown render hidden behind wisteria and magnolia, is set off by an enchanting Carolean garden, complete with pavilions, by a decorative Restoration stable block in mellow red brick, and by ornamental gates.

Ragley Hall ☆☆

2 m SW Alcester, on A435; tearoom; garden and woodland walks; *open:* mid Apr–late Sept, daily, except Mon and Fri (but open BH Mon), 12–5; tel: 0789 762090

Boldly crowning a ridge, with a long grassy ride dipping into the valley below, is this imposing, many-windowed Restoration house of pale grey stone. Begun in 1680 by Robert Hook, whose only surviving building this is, Ragley was not completed for another 50 years, and was altered in the 1780s by James Wyatt, who added the extraneous portico on the entrance front. Inside, a baroque layout with stairs at either end of the building and strong cross axes is allied to largely 18th-century decoration, some, by James Gibbs, in the rococo style of the 1750s, some betraying Wyatt's heavier hand.

Seat of the Seymours, Marquesses of Hertford, whose Tudor forbear became the third wife of Henry VIII, the house is now primarily a show place. Central focus of the high-ceilinged state rooms down the west front is Wyatt's opulent crimson and gold saloon, furnished with gilded Louis XVI pieces and a show of oriental jade, and hung with Cornelis van Haarlem's *Raising of Lazarus* and other 17th-century religious works. More restful is the adjoining leaf-green sitting-room, with its rococo ceiling, gay Chinese

Chippendale mirrors above inlaid French commodes, and several portraits by Reynolds and Van Loo. A Regency-flavoured yellow and white dining-room has a display of late-Georgian silver, a state bed surmounted by a flourish of feathers was made for the future Prince Regent when he visited Ragley in 1796, and an east-facing breakfast room, with a carved pearwood overmantel of 1756, has horse paintings by Wootton.

The high point of the tour is the baroque great hall set across the house, with a froth of plasterwork by Gibbs picked out in pink, white and grey and the only furnishings the wooden settees and chairs made for the room in 1756, pushed back against the walls in period style. Among all this 18th-century finery the modern art on the stairs comes as rather a shock. Ceri Richards's raw streak in the north hall is almost painful; Graham Rust's frescoes on the south stairs are gentler and more in the spirit of house, with some witty detail, but his temptation scene on the ceiling has come straight from a children's picture book.

Upton House ☆☆

On A422, 7 m NW Banbury; NT; tearoom; terraced, valley garden; *open:* mid June–end Oct, Sat–Wed inc. BH Mon, 2–6, entry by timed ticket at peak times; tel: 0295 87 266

Upton is an art gallery masquerading as a country house. Although the core of the place dates from the 17th century, and a baroque broken pediment crowns the entrance front, Upton was transformed in the 1920s by the 2nd Viscount Bearsted, son of the founder of the Shell organization, who wanted somewhere to display his collection of paintings and 18th-century English and Continental porcelain. The interiors created by the architect Percy Morley Horder are discreetly luxurious, unobtrusive spaces, with nothing showy to detract attention from what is on the walls, while the bays he added to either side of the existing house merely unbalance the two main façades, creating compositions that are much too long for their height.

Nobody comes here for the architecture or the atmosphere. The porcelain, too, although excellent of its kind, is something of an acquired taste, with cabinets filled with snuff bottles, or displays of delicately modelled figures from the Chelsea, Bow, Derby, Worcester and Liverpool factories. The paintings are another matter. The range is enormous, including works from the 14th to the 19th century and representing Continental as well as British art. The quality is consistently high, with masters such as El Greco, Brueghel, Holbein, van der Weyden and Bosch all represented, and there is an interestingly varied mix of subject matter, from intense early religious works to sentimental portraits by Greuze, a Venetian view by Canaletto, and a dramatic landscape by Jacob van Ruisdael, with sun breaking through cloud.

The paintings are grouped like with like. Portraits by Romney, Beechey, Raeburn and contemporaries are clustered round the stairs, sporting paintings, including three strangely naive rural scenes by Stubbs, are in the dining-room, 16th- and 17th-century Dutch paintings are shown in the sunny long gallery looking on to the garden – the only room which seems self-consciously grand – and the earliest works, of the 14th, 15th and 16th centuries, are hung in the subterranean gallery created out of a squash court which comes near the end of the tour. Here is a company of haloed, stylized figures, many of them gorgeously attired in robes of scarlet and gold, Brueghel's monochrome *Death of the Virgin*, lit by the radiant figure in the bed, and some minutely observed backgrounds, such as the Flemish red-brick house which frames Jan Provost's pregnant Virgin, or the botanically correct dandelions, irises and nettles flourishing around a 15th-century St Jerome.

Warwick Castle ☆

SW edge of Warwick, M40 Jc. 15; tearoom; gardens; *open:* all year, daily, except 25 Dec, 10–5.30 (4.30 Oct–Feb); tel: 0926 495421

Sold by the 8th Earl in 1978 to Madame Tussaud's, Warwick Castle is a crowd-pulling, money-making business, which combines the genuinely old with waxwork theatricals. Built on a sandstone bluff overlooking the Avon, with panoramic views across the river, the castle consists of a vast grassy courtyard surrounded by a many-towered medieval curtain wall, with a range of 17th- and 18th-century apartments against the east side. At the south end, partly climbed by the enclosing wall, is the high grassy mound that once carried a Norman keep.

Two tours are on offer. The first is a conventional trip through the Charles II state apartments, arranged like a string of beads at one end of the thoroughly Victorian, armour-filled great hall. A long drawing-room is lined with cedarwood panelling of the 1670s and furnished with wide-bodied 18th-century chairs; the state bed presented by George III is set off by Delft garden tapestries of 1604, all fountains, arbours and balustraded steps; and there are some lovely rococo girandoles, 16th-century Italian chests, and a Dutch marquetry table, but the whole presentation is so artificial that nothing seems quite real. Most of the castle's finest paintings went before the Tussaud's takeover, and the 17th-century portraits attributed to Lely, Van Dyck, Kneller, Holbein and Michael Dahl are mostly copies or studio productions.

A separate entrance gives access to Tussaud's *tour de force*: a re-creation of a house party in 1898 when the Earl and Countess of Warwick entertained the Prince of Wales. The Victorian interiors, with their fringed lampshades, roaring fires, huge flower arrangements and crowded surfaces, have been lovingly re-created, and peopled with realistic waxworks in period dress. Suitable sound effects accompany the fruity alto entertaining guests in the drawing-room, a maid endlessly runs a bath, and a discreet butler pours drinks in the prince's bedroom.

Those who are eager for more can climb some 200 steps in a tour of the ramparts, visit the armoury and the dungeon, and take in two rooms furnished in 17th-century style in the Watergate Tower, where Sir Fulke Greville, who took over what was almost a ruin from James I, came to a violent end.

Aston Hall

2 m N Birmingham city centre, signed from
Aston exit off A38(M); grounds; *open:*
Apr–end Oct, daily, 2–5; tel: 021 327 0062

One of the last great Jacobean houses sits stranded, like some beached whale, among the sprawl of Birmingham, close by Aston Villa football ground. Built for Sir Thomas Holte from 1618 on what was then a prominent rise above the road to Lichfield, Aston Hall is an impressive U-shaped house of diapered red brick and stone, with a skyline of curved Dutch gables and ogee-capped tur-rets. On the east-facing entrance front, two long wings reach out towards the turret-like lodges squaring up the courtyard. Beyond, where there should be green fields and rolling hills, the view is brutally cut short by a section of ele-vated motorway.

Although the hall has lost most of its original contents and is now in the hands of the local corporation, the interior is not as bleak and soulless as many such places. Several 17th-century features survive and most rooms have been sensitively furnished with period pieces, while a scatter of Holte portraits gives a semblance of authenticity. In an extensive tour involving all three floors and all three ranges, the best comes first. From the panelled, stone-floored great hall, a Jacobean stair carved with swan-necked sea-horses leads up to rooms with original strapwork ceilings, splendid fireplaces of stone, alabaster and marble, and friezes moulded in high relief with mythical beasts and ancient warriors. Most impressive is the 136 ft long gallery run-ning the length of the west front, with an undulating floor, faded tapestries on arcaded panelling, and a light dusting of cane-backed Charles II chairs.

Hagley Hall ☆☆

At Hagley, 3 m S Stourbridge, between
A491 and A456; guided tours (*c.* 60 mins);
teas; *open:* early Jan–end Feb, daily except
Sat, 2–5, also Easter, late May and Aug BH
Sat, Sun, Mon, 2–5; tel: 0562 882408

Tucked beneath the wooded humps of the Clent Hills is a four-square Palladian house of lichen-stained pink sandstone, set high enough to enjoy sweeping views south and west over the rolling Worcestershire countryside. Designed by the gentleman architect Sanderson Miller for the 1st Lord Lyttleton, and built 1756–60, Hagley is imposing rather than beautiful, its main feature the four stumpy corner towers topped with pyramidal caps. A double staircase leads up to the principal floor, discreet pediments mark the main façades, and behind, overshadowed by the house, is the parish church which Miller also rebuilt, its spire mingling curiously with Hagley's prominent chimneys when seen from the right angle. The interior, marked by rococo plasterwork by Francesco Vassali, is relatively modest. Descendants of the 1st Lord still live here, but much was lost in a fire in 1925. The rooms seen on the friendly, informal tour are partly original, partly as skilfully restored; a couple are clearly still used by the family, others are now primarily showpieces or venues for functions.

Visitors walk straight into the stone-floored, lemon and white, 18th-century hall, with copies of antique statues of Mercury, Venus and other classical deities paired with Vassali's plaster medallions of the same gods as children. The monumental stone chimney-piece, with a relief signed by the stuccadore above, is held up by carved Herculean figures, every muscle strained and taut, and there are busts of Rubens and Van Dyck sculpted by Michael Rysbrack. A barrel-arched lobby encrusted with plaster blossoms by Vassali opens into the equally flamboyant, sparsely furnished saloon, with plaster festoons signifying music, painting, the chase and other suitable interests setting off portraits by Wootton, Ramsay, Richard Wilson, who is much better known for his landscapes, and an unusually alert Batoni.

To one side of this hall-saloon axis are the cosy, red and gold library, furnished with comfortable sofas and armchairs and with a painting of Alexander Pope and a portrait by Sir Joshua Reynolds among the pictures hung above the bookcases, and a little panelled room with a robust Elizabethan overmantel saved from an earlier house and an impressive reproduction strapwork ceiling on the barrel vault. Here are two works by Van Dyck, including a painting of three desolate women mourning the crucified Christ, and one of Van Rymerswaele's many versions of a couple of wrinkled misers counting their coins.

More formal rooms on the other side of the house include an unaltered 18th-century drawing-room designed round a set of Soho tapestries, and with paintings by James 'Athenian' Stuart inset in the plasterwork on the ceiling; an 85 ft gallery divided by screens of fluted columns and hung with 17th-century portraits; and the crimson and gold dining-room, with a Charles II tapestry showing a formal equestrian exercise. There is furniture designed by Adam and Chippendale, a Louis XVI bureau, exuberant rococo pier glasses carved with swan-necked ho-ho birds, and a ghostly musician is said to sometimes haunt the drawing-room. Visitors may be shown the basement grotto, but, sadly, they cannot wander in the park, with its ruined castle, obelisks and other eyecatchers.

Wightwick Manor ☆☆☆

3 m W Wolverhampton, off A454; NT; admission by timed ticket; guided tours (*c.* 60 mins); garden; *open:* end Apr–end Dec, Thurs and Sat 2.30–5.30, also open, ground floor only, BH Sun and Mon (no tour); tel: 0902 761108

Wightwick is a unique period piece. A rambling, many-gabled, half-timbered house put up in two stages at the end of the 19th century, it is filled with furnishings and fittings by William Morris and Co and with paintings by the pre-Raphaelites and their circle. More overgrown Tudor cottage than stately home, Wightwick was built for the local paint and varnish manufacturer Samuel Theodore Mander by Edward Ould. The earlier half, dating from 1887, is relatively restrained, but the east wing, added in 1893, is flamboyant and richly decorated, with ornately carved bargeboards, elaborately patterned half-timbering and twisted brick chimneys. This division persists inside, where modest, family rooms at one end contrast with the large and showy great parlour, billiard room and dining-room built for entertaining at the other.

Wallpapers, hangings and upholstery designed by Morris, softly curving light fittings by Benson, fireplace tiles in rich greens and reds by William de Morgan, and stained glass by Kempe, all chosen for the house by the Manders, mix harmoniously with their Flemish tapestries and Persian rugs, and with William and Mary pieces, such as the walnut chairs lining the hall, or a seaweed marquetry cabinet. And the house has been greatly enriched by the late Sir Geoffrey and Lady Mander, who presciently added to the collection in the pre-war years, when pre-Raphaelite art was unfashionable.

Visitors are taken over the ground floor, and can then wander at leisure through bedrooms and nurseries, and down to the cream and brown kitchen. The lofty parlour open to the roof is Ould's version of a galleried great hall, with a deep inglenook fireplace, a wide window bay, and a plaster frieze showing Orpheus charming the animals. Dark green wall hangings were designed by Dearle, Morris's associate; there are brass chandeliers by Benson, a huge Morris chesterfield, books from Morris's Kelmscott Press, and an array of blue and white oriental porcelain, while on the walls is Burne-Jones's surreal *Love among the Ruins* and Watts's painting of the beautiful Mrs Nassau Senior, sister of the Thomas Hughes who wrote *Tom Brown's School Days*.

Elsewhere you can see Rossetti's and Holman Hunt's composite portrait of Janey Morris, a self-portrait by Millais, paintings of Christina Rossetti by her brother, including a caricature of her in a rage, and works by Ford Madox Brown. There is little of the 20th century here, apart from Felix Topolski's portrait of Lady Mander, all controlled energy.

Cambridgeshire, Essex, Lincolnshire, Norfolk, Suffolk

Gainsborough

Lincoln

A158

Doddington Hall

Gunby Hall

Skegness

Aubourn Hall

Lincs

A17   A15

Fulbeck Hall

Boston

Belton House

Grantham

Woolsthorpe Manor

Grimsthorpe Castle

A1

Stamford

Burghley House

Peterborough

Elton Hall

Cambs

Holkham Hall

A148   Cromer

Felbrigg Hall

Houghton Hall

Blickling Hall

Sandringham

King's Lynn

R. Ouse

A1065

Beeston Hall

Norwich   Gt Yar

Oxburgh Hall

Norfolk

A136

A140   A143

Somerleyton

A134

A11

A17

Huntingdon

Euston Hall

Wingfield Colle

Suffolk

Anglesey Abbey

Bury St Edmunds

Haughley Park

A45

Ickworth

Otley Hall

Cambridge

Little Hall, Lavenham

Kentwell Hall

The Priory, Lavenham

Wimpole Hall

Melford Hall

Ipswich

A134

A12

Felixstowe

Audley End

A604

Castle House

Gosfield Hall

Colchester

A120

Layer Marney Tower   **Shalom Hall**

Essex

St Osyth Priory

Clacton-on-Sea

Chelmsford

A12

M11

M25

Ingatestone Hall

Brentwood

A127

Southend-on-Sea

Cambridgeshire

Anglesey Abbey ☆☆

In village of Lode, 6 m NE Cambridge on B1102; NT; tearoom; extensive garden, with weather-boarded mill; *open:* late Mar-mid Oct, Wed-Sat 1.30-5.30, Sun and BH Mon (entrance by timed ticket), 1–5.30; tel: 0223 811200

Despite its name, Anglesey Abbey is a 20th-century creation. Both the house of *c.*1600 and its surroundings were transformed from 1926 by the wealthy Huttleston Broughton, 1st Lord Fairhaven, who rebuilt what was by then a shadowy ruin and carved a palatial garden out of the unpromising fens, planting hundreds of trees and creating long grassy vistas enlivened by classical urns and sculptures. Of the Augustinian priory founded here in 1135, all that remains is the stone-vaulted monk's parlour, now a dining-room, and the walls of the chapter house range. From the south, the abbey looks like an attractive Jacobean manor, with stone dormers breaking the roofline and stone-mullioned windows, but hidden away behind are Lord Fairhaven's modern extensions, added on to house his growing collections of paintings, furniture, tapestries and other treasures.

Softly lit, sumptuously furnished rooms have a timeless feel, the treasures filling them ranging from a glittering cope to a self-portrait by Canaletto, from jewelled crucifixes to a lush Tahitian landscape by William Hodges. What is here is so diverse that it is difficult to know what the 1st Lord really liked. There are fragile flowers of porcelain and amethyst, bluejohn urns and obelisks and other precious, artificial trinkets; there is a whole congregation of carved saints from almost every country in Europe; and there is furniture by Kent, Flitcroft and Chippendale. Some juxtapositions are exactly right; others jar.

And then there are the paintings, many of them displayed in the purpose-built galleries designed by Professor Richardson in the 1950s. Canvases by Munnings and Wootton are reminders of Lord Fairhaven's sporting interests, and an affection for the town where he lived as a child accounts for the gallery hung with views of Windsor. But who could acquire a dozen repetitive moonlit scenes by the Pethers, a sentimental Landseer, a clutch of Etty nudes *and* two of the most exquisite Italianate landscapes Claude ever painted?

The largest room is the lofty library built on in 1938, lit by huge mullioned and transomed windows and lined with bookcases made from the piles of Rennie's Waterloo Bridge, demolished four years before. Kneehole desks and comfortable sofas stand on a soft green carpet, there are jade elephants, carved angels and Gainsborough's inlaid paint box on display, and one wall is filled by Constable's impressionistic view of the Thames, with George IV embarking on the royal barge in one corner.

Burghley House ☆☆

1 m SE Stamford, just off A1; guided tours
(c. 1 hr), except on Sun, 1-5, and BHs; teas;
open: Apr-early Oct, daily, 11–5 (closed one
Sat in Sept for horse trials); tel: 0780 52451

A gently rolling landscape park sets off the grandiose Elizabethan house created by William Cecil, 1st Lord Burghley, Chief Minister and Lord High
Treasurer to Elizabeth I. Built over 30 years from 1555, the great man acting
throughout as his own architect, Burghley is a glittering stone palace, with
huge mullioned windows, a bold strapwork parapet and a display of tall
chimneys and ogee-capped turrets. A four-storey gatehouse leads into the
central courtyard, where a soaring clock tower seems to have strayed from a
nearby church. Descendants of Cecil's eldest son, the 1st Earl of Exeter, have
lived here ever since, while his younger son, Robert, founded another
dynasty of Cecils at *Hatfield*.

If you can, take time to walk round the outside of the house – or rather, as
much of it as you are allowed to see – before going inside, as this will help to
make sense of the interior. If you can, too, go to Burghley on a Sunday afternoon, when you are allowed to wander at your own pace. Visitors do a complete circuit of the first floor, seeing some twenty richly furnished rooms
crammed with paintings and other treasures, but the guided tour is a breathless scamper, with no time to appreciate more than a fraction of the 400 or so
pictures on view.

Where the outside is still largely Elizabethan, the interior reflects remodelling in the late 17th century by the 5th Earl of Exeter, who hired the extravagant and demanding Antonio Verrio to paint the baroque ceilings and
murals – a profusion of scantily clad deities in improbable situations – which
are such a feature of the five-room state apartment; divided the long gallery
in the west wing into five closet-like rooms; commissioned lovely plasterwork
ceilings from Edward Martin; and brought back an outstanding collection of
Italian art from a series of Continental tours, including works by Luca
Giordano, Carlo Dolci, Carlo Maratta and Filippo Lauri. He also hired Jean
Tijou to supply the glistening golden gates leading into the courtyard and
had one room painted by Verrio's rival, Louis Laguerre.

This Restoration grandeur, much of it adorning rooms of very modest
dimensions, is allied with equally rich furnishings, many of which were
acquired by later generations. There are 17th-century tapestries, Carolean
and Georgian state beds, 18th-century serpentine chests of drawers and marquetry pieces, pagodas of mother-of-pearl, and stepped corner fireplaces displaying 17th-century Japanese porcelain. Panelled and damask-lined walls
are closely hung with family portraits, the 5th Earl's Italian paintings and
later acquisitions, among them works by Gainsborough, Lawrence and
Thomas Hudson; Kneller's portrait of Verrio; a luminous Virgin and Child by
Orazio Gentileschi, executed on copper, with our Lady unusually depicted in
a saffron-yellow dress; two huge flower paintings by Giuseppe Recco;
Brueghel the Younger's *Rent Day*, with papers and accounts spilling from

shelves and counters as the peasants queue up to pay their dues, and a still life by Hermann van der Mijn. The first William Cecil stares out of a suitably imposing portrait by Marcus Gheeraerts.

The tour starts in the Elizabethan kitchen, with its high stone vault, and ends in the 1st Lord's great hall, reached down a staircase painted with Verrio's version of Hell, and rising through two storeys to a double hammer-beam roof.

Elton Hall ☆☆☆

6 SW Peterborough, on A605; guided tour (*c.* 60 mins); tearoom; garden; *open:* May BH Sun and Mon, July, Wed, Sun, Aug, Wed, Thurs, Sun and BH Mon 2-5; tel: 0832 280468

From the east, coming down the lime avenue leading off the A605, this substantial L-shaped house looks like a cross between a French château and a grand hotel, with long windows below pedimented dormers, but from the garden to the south it is a gothick fantasy, a long panorama of light-hearted towers and turrets, pointed windows, battlements and pinnacles, with a genuine medieval gatehouse at one end blending harmoniously with the later work. Of the original Tudor mansion, only the gatehouse tower and a stone-vaulted undercroft remain, while the Jacobean house built here by Sir Thomas Proby was extensively remodelled in the late 18th and 19th centuries, with several interiors created by Henry Ashton for Granville Proby, the 3rd Earl of Carysfort, in the mid 1800s.

Most flamboyant of Ashton's interiors is the high-ceilinged, white-and-gold French drawing-room, with a huge bay to the gardens, its gilded chairs covered in Beauvais tapestry and two exquisite Louis XV parquetry cabinets standing out from an assemblage of 18th- and 19th-century pieces. Slightly overwhelmed by all the glitz are portraits by Allan Ramsay, Romney and Hoppner, and several by Reynolds, who was a friend of the family, among them a wild-haired sketch of himself and his unfinished painting of the courtesan Kitty Fisher (considered unsuitable in Victorian times and banished to the housekeeper's room). A gothick octagon next door is lined with cabinets filled with Sèvres porcelain, while some of the best of a fine collection of paintings hang two and three deep in a cavernous 19th-century dining-room, its traceried gothic windows copied directly from those that once lit the medieval chapel. Here are portraits by Van Dyck and Lely, flower paintings by Monnoyer, landscapes by Hobbema and Poussin and 15th- and 16th-century Italian and Flemish religious paintings, among them Girolamo Genga's *Virgin of Mercy*, with an adoring multitude sheltering under our Lady's voluminous green cloak.

In the adjoining anteroom, a misty pink landscape by Gainsborough sits uncomfortably with Constable's much quieter study of Dedham Vale, and elsewhere are a delightful Millais portrait of the 5th Countess, in a close-fitting bottle-green habit, an unreal classical fantasy by Alma-Tadema painted on marble, and Henry O'Neill's vision of soldiers departing for India at the time of the mutiny, shawled women on the quay reaching up to the men on the ship. Appropriately, a prayer book that belonged to Henry VIII, and some of Sir Thomas Proby's meticulous accounts, are shown in the intimate library in the old tower. Alas, the guided tour, although by no means short, allows no time to linger.

Wimpole Hall ☆

8 m SW Cambridge, off A603; NT; tea-room; home farm with rare breeds; park; *open:* late Mar-end Oct, Tues, Wed, Thurs, Sat, Sun, 1–5, BH Sun and Mon, 11–5; tel: 0223 207257

Although built of warm red brick, Wimpole is an unwelcoming barracks of a place, fronted by an arid sweep of gravel. This is the largest house in Cambridgeshire, with a 270 ft frontage and with substantial wings flanking a three-storey central block. Once a compact Jacobean house, it was altered by James Gibbs, for Edmund Harley, 2nd Earl of Oxford, in the early 18th century; by Henry Flitcroft, for the 1st Earl of Hardwicke, on his purchase of Wimpole in 1740; by John Soane, for the 3rd Earl, in the 1790s, and lastly, and least successfully, by H. E. Kendall, for the 5th Earl, in the 1840s, whose additions, now largely demolished, extended the house to twice its present size. Where the outside, if austere, seems largely all of a piece and 18th-century in spirit, the inside is diverse, with work of all periods.

Wimpole's furnishings are noticeably sparse. After a chequered history, during which most of the contents were dispersed, the house was restored and refurnished by Rudyard Kipling's daughter Elsie, who, with her husband

Capt. George Bambridge, bought the estate in 1938. The couple's approach to their palace seems to have been sensibly pragmatic, the comfortable, intimate rooms where they lived from day to day contrasting with the sparsely furnished grand interiors.

The extensive visitor tour takes in some twenty rooms, many of them rather dark and with generally subdued colour schemes. The 50 ft library that Gibbs designed to take Lord Harley's great collection of books, the finest of its day, still fills one of the wings, with decorative plasterwork on the high coved ceiling and a castor-borne pulpit giving access to the upper shelves. At one end is Soane's more light-hearted extension, a delightfully feminine book room with projecting cases supporting elliptical arches, and Soane was also responsible for the T-shaped yellow drawing-room, its apse-like inner end toplit from a positively ecclesiastical dome, and for the cold and sinister plunge bath, with a double staircase sweeping down to a tiled pool capable of holding 2,199 gallons. Nothing is what it seems, with stone painted to appear as wood, plaster walls lined to look like stone. Illusion of a different kind pervades James Gibbs's baroque chapel on the south-east corner of the house. This barn of a room is painted with *trompe l'oeil* murals by Sir James Thornhill, with gesticulating figures representing the four Doctors of the Church leaning restlessly from deeply shadowed niches.

The few paintings here now include sporting and animal pictures by John Wootton, some of them featuring beasts from the menagerie kept by the 2nd Earl of Oxford, a few Yorke family portraits, and works by Arthur Devis, Tilly Kettle and Tissot.

Essex

Audley End ☆☆

1 m W Saffron Walden, on B1383; EH; audio tour; restaurant; collection of wagons and agric machinery; miniature railway; garden and park; *open:* Gd Fri or 1 Apr, whichever earlier, to end Sept, Tues–Sun (except BHs) 1–5.45; tel: 0799 522399

The kind of place that makes unsuspecting drivers swerve off the road with delight, Audley End still looks like the Jacobean palace it once was, with a broad sward sweeping up from the River Cam to an array of stone-mullioned windows, turrets topped with gilded weather vanes, and massive chimney stacks. All is symmetrical, self-conscious and assured, with Renaissance porches flanking the huge windows lighting the great hall and a pierced parapet hiding the roof. Imposing as it is, this block of a house is all that remains of a much larger, double-courtyard mansion built in 1605-15 by the rapacious, high-flying, Thomas Howard, 1st Earl of Suffolk, James I's Lord Treasurer.

After this build-up, the interior may disappoint. First, apart from a couple of ceilings and chimney-pieces, most of the Jacobean detail has been replaced by later decorative schemes. Rooms designed by Robert Adam for the 1st Lord Braybrooke, who inherited in 1762, are a treat of a different kind, but are only partly furnished, while the predominant 19th-century interiors, created by the 3rd Lord, are a definitely mixed bag. It is best to linger in the handful of jewels among the thirty or so rooms on show, and to hurry through the rest.

The tour begins and ends in the 1st Earl's impressive, portrait-hung great hall, a richly carved Jacobean oak screen at one end echoed in double arches of stone by Vanbrugh at the other, with staircases and passages leading enticingly off. Then comes the Adam suite along the south front, where an uncomfortably low-ceilinged dining-parlour, decorated in apple green to merge with the lawns outside, leads into two drawing-rooms, one with a fluid plasterwork ceiling and deep pink silk on the walls, the other, like a jewel casket turned inside out, with delicate painted decoration by Biagio Rebecca. Another 18th-century addition, but by a quite different hand, is the entrancing chapel, designed in the most light-hearted Strawberry Hill gothick by one John Hobcraft. Slender cluster columns support delicate gothick vaulting, the plasterwork white on a pale coffee ground, a dais-mounted throne sits halfway down the room, and the family galley is warmed by a delightfully insouciant fireplace.

The Jacobethan 19th-century rooms, mostly on the second floor, are gloomier and heavier. Apart from the book-filled library, with a walnut-veneered Broadwood grand that was once played by Chopin, and the 18th-century state bed, most of the interest here is in the paintings, among them portraits by Lely and Beechey, a terrifying likeness of the aged George III, and works by Van Goyen and Canaletto, although several canvases are difficult to see.

All comes together in the light and airy Saloon which ends the tour. Full-length family portraits are inset in the gilded, 18th-century panelling, sea monsters cavort on a Jacobean plaster ceiling, and in the centre, as if waiting for Lord Byron, is a vast Victorian ottoman, at least 12 ft square, all plush red velvet and plump tasselled cushions.

Castle House ☆

Just outside Dedham village, 7 m NE Colchester; small garden; *open:* May–early Oct, Wed, Sun, BH Mon, and Thurs and Sat in Aug, 2-5; tel: 0206 322127

The pink Georgian villa where Sir Alfred Munnings lived from 1919 until his death in 1959 is now devoted to a display of the controversial and outspoken artist's work. Although the main rooms still contain the Munnings' furniture, the house is primarily a gallery, decorated and carpeted throughout in plush anonymity. There are several of the racehorse paintings which made Munnings famous, but also a large collection of early works, done before his nose was to the grindstone of lucrative commissions. These pictures, many of them executed in his twenties, show

how varied his talent was, his mastery of portraiture and landscape, and his uncanny ability to convey light, movement and the nuances of class.

Gosfield Hall

At Gosfield, $2\frac{1}{2}$ m SW Halstead, no advance signs: drive leads off A1017 through village; *open:* May–Sept, Wed, Thur, 2-5 (guided tours); tel: none

Built round an enchanting courtyard garden, complete with fountain and magnolias, Gosfield has developed from a quadrangular 16th-century house. One range, all diapered red brick, pinnacled gables, mullioned windows and tall chimneys, is still Tudor, pierced by a gateway arch and with a narrow panelled gallery running the length of the top floor. The rest of the house has been substantially remodelled. The east range has a baroque entrance hall, with a ceiling painting attributed to Thornhill, while the 18th-century south and north wings contain a lofty ballroom with floor to ceiling mirrors and a library with a deep window bay towards the lake. Gosfield is now divided into private apartments, and the tour, which takes in the public rooms only, is primarily of architectural interest.

Ingatestone Hall

Down Station Lane, Ingatestone, 6 m SW Chelmsford, no advance signs; tearoom; garden; *open:* Easter-end Sept, Fri-Sun, plus Wed and Thurs in high season, 1-6; tel: 0277 353010

A startlingly red gatehouse range with a clock tower over the central arch leads into a large grassy courtyard, partly walled in yew. On the far side are three wings of the Tudor courtyard house built here by Sir William Petre, Secretary of State to Henry VIII, Edward VI and Mary Tudor. The mellow brick walls, crow-stepped gables and tall chimneys are original, but most of the stone-mullioned windows, too large and precise to be the real thing, date from a major restoration after World War I.

For long divided into apartments, the house is again lived in by the Petre family, but the much-restored interior is disappointing. A low-ceilinged, panelled drawing-room looking south over the gardens shows off two portraits by Stubbs, one of the portly 9th Lord out hunting, the other of the elegant 10th Lord on a well-bred chestnut, greyhounds by his side. There are glimpses into priest-holes, and a spiral stair leads up to a pine-panelled Georgian interior, and to the 95 ft, portrait-hung long gallery. This should be the highlight of the tour, but the furnishings are too mixed and the room too cluttered, with a row of glass cases displaying estate documents and family relics. There are paintings attributed to Cornelius Johnson and Romney, and a portrait of Arabella Fermor, from whom the 7th Lord stole a lock of hair, setting off the family feud which prompted Alexander Pope's *Rape of the Lock*. Some may find the tranquil garden, with its smooth lawns and a tree-shaded walk by a long canal, more rewarding.

Layer Marney Tower ☆

6¹/₂ m SW Colchester, 1 m S B1022, off road from Tiptree to Layer Breton; *open:* Apr-Jun and Sept, Sun, Thurs 2-6, Jul, Aug, Sun-Fri 2-6, BHs 11-6; tel: 0206 330784

A narrow lane off an insignificant byroad leads to one of the most startling buildings in East Anglia. The north front, seen first, is relatively plain, with two long brick ranges flanking a towered entrance, and you must go through the central arch into the garden to enjoy one of the great façades of Tudor England. Here, the tower thrusts skywards in hexagonal eight-storey turrets and a display of diapered and moulded brickwork. Two huge Tudor windows over the arch are mullioned, transomed and framed in carved terracotta and a frieze of plump terracotta dolphins and shells crests the turrets. Built in the early 1520s, at the same time as *Hampton Court*, this tower was the creation of the high-flying Henry, 1st Lord Marney, who planned it as the entrance to a courtyard mansion that was never completed. The use of terracotta, which had only recently been introduced into England, was an Italianate touch such as only a sophisticated courtier would have been able to command.

Visitors can see what was once a range of buttressed Tudor stables, now converted into a long gallery, and the little brick church where Lord Marney is buried. You can also climb to the roof of the tower, via a depressingly drab staircase and exhibition room, and an impressive barn to the east of the house is used to show rare breeds of farm animals.

St Osyth Priory ☆☆

St Osyth, off the B1027 to Clacton-on-Sea; gardens; *open:* Easter weekend, then May-end Sept, Sun-Fri, 10.30-12.30, 2.30-4.30; tel: 0255 820492

On the flatlands edging the Colne estuary is an atmospheric, partly ruined jumble of buildings marking the site of a once-great priory. The precincts are guarded by the abbey's immense Tudor gatehouse, its walls banded in flint and stone and empty statue niches flanking the central arch. Beyond, across a vast sweep of grass like an unused cricket pitch, is the L-shaped, red-brick house that evolved from the abbot's lodgings, with a twelve-light oriel window over the main entrance, decorative Tudor chimneys, and a modest Georgian wing jutting out to the west. Just a stone's throw away are the picturesque ruins of the hall and domestic ranges built by the Tudor high-flyer Lord D'Arcy, who acquired the priory after the Dissolution, and his impressive, four-storey, flint and stone tower, with a steep spiral stair leading to the roof. A tiny vaulted chapel at the foot of the tower is the oldest part of the complex, dating back to the 13th century.

Inside the priory, cosy Georgian rooms contrast with the cavernous mock-medieval Victorian interiors created in a major restoration of 1866, when the big sunny drawing room on the first floor acquired its ribbed and painted ceiling and carved gothic doorways. Treasures on display include a section of carved panelling from the abbey, a set of mahogany Chippendale chairs and a tiny Roman bronze no more than 18 in high that was dug up at Colchester just a few miles to the north. The biggest draw, though, is the paintings, in particular a number of works by Stubbs. Here is his triptych-like *Sampson*, with three views of a jet-black stallion on the one canvas, and the life-size portrait of the rearing chestnut *Whistlejacket*, so big that the floor had to be lowered to get the canvas in. The animal is being proudly watched both by his owner, the 2nd Marquis of Rockingham, in a painting by Sir Joshua Reynolds, and by Stubbs himself, in a portrait by his friend Ozias Humphrey.

Shalom Hall

7 m SW Colchester at S end of Layer Breton, on E side of Tolleshunt D'Arcy road; guided tour; *open:* Aug, Mon-Fri 10-1, 2.30-5.30; tel: none

A high brick wall flags this small, unsigned, late Georgian house. Inside, comfortable family rooms are hung with some exceptional paintings, including

Essex

four Gainsboroughs – one a quizzical, smiling self-portrait – works by William Beechey, Romney and Patrick Nasmyth, and 17th-century portraits.

Lincolnshire

Aubourn Hall ☆

In Aubourn village, off A46, 7 m S Lincoln; guided tour (c. 40 mins); garden; *open:* July, Aug, Wed, 2-6, and two Suns in June; tel none

This compact, L-shaped brick house overlooking a canalized stretch of the Witham is attributed to John Smythson and thought to date from c. 1628. There are traces of diapering on the entrance façade, regular stone-mullioned windows, and a dignified stone doorcase. Inside, this is a place of small panelled rooms, some of them with original brick-backed fireplaces.

The most striking feature of the informal guided tour, which takes in rooms on all three floors, is a delicious Jacobean staircase with a strapwork balustrade, finialled newel posts, and dog gates carved with fierce canine heads. There is some fine 18th-century furniture, including examples of Dutch and English marquetry, and the lemon-walled drawing-room on the south-east corner of the house has a show of French pieces and child-size samples. Joshua Reynolds' painting of a son of the family at his books, and a fantasy landscape by Jan Griffier, with sailing ships clustered below a many-spired town and a wall of mountains in the distance, stand out from the mostly run-of-the-mill portraits and a set of 20th-century architectural capriccios.

Belton House ☆☆

3 m NE Grantham, on A607; NT; tearoom; garden, park and lakeside walk; *open:* Apr-end Oct, Wed-Sun and BH Mon (closed Gd Fri) 1-5.30; tel: 0476 66116

Rising from a pancake-flat park on the banks of the Witham is a giant dolls' house of honey-coloured stone. Four-square and symmetrical, with shallow wings framing the pedimented main façades, dormers in the hipped roof and a crowning cupola, Belton is every inch the confident Caroline house. Probably designed by the gentleman architect William Winde, it was built in 1685–9 for Sir John Brownlow, grandson of the Elizabethan lawyer who bought the estate, and Brownlow descendants lived here until Belton came to the Trust. Although some of a rich accumulation of furniture, porcelain, silver and pictures has been sold, almost everything of importance remains.

The extensive tour takes in some twenty rooms on two floors. Ornate plaster ceilings and rich panelling embellished with Grinling Gibbons-style limewood carvings in the principal rooms suggest these are 17th-century interiors, but in fact much of the Restoration-style decoration dates from the late 19th century, when Belton was sensitively restored. These Caroline rooms contrast with a few classical interiors by James Wyatt, who was called in in 1776, with his nephew Jeffry Wyatville's more opulent work of 1809–20, and with a comfortably 20th-century bedroom.

Visitors enter Belton as they have always done, up the grand steps leading to the sparsely furnished, marble-floored hall on the south front. This is the first of the formal 17th-century rooms, back to back with the more colourful but similarly bare saloon looking north over the garden. To the east are Wyatville's tapestry room and red drawing-room, the former lined with 18th-century Mortlake hangings and furnished with Louis XV pieces, the latter, hung with crimson damask, showing off a brilliantly blue, 17th-century lapis lazuli cabinet on a gilded stand. To the west, more bare interiors – one hung with rare 17th-century tapestries – lead to the almost unaltered chapel, a sombre, well-like room rising through two storeys to a splendid plasterwork ceiling by Edward Goudge. A carved baroque reredos is painted to look like marble, silver Stuart sconces glisten on the panelling, and an early 16th-century Madonna and Child in the family gallery is surrounded by the finest carving in the house. Wyatt designed the impressive first-floor library, with delicate plasterwork on a gentle barrel vault, while his blue bedroom shows off an exceptional early 18th-century burr walnut bureau and a state bed over 16 ft high.

Family portraits amassed over three centuries hang in almost every room, among them works by Lely, Wissing, Riley, Closterman and Kneller, Hudson, Dahl and Mercier, Reynolds and Romney, Watts and Frank Salisbury, and Lord Leighton's enchanting study of the young Lady Adelaide, wife of the last Earl. There is a cluster of mostly 17th-century Flemish and Italian cabinet works, and one room is devoted to three giant bird paintings in garden settings by de Hondecoeter. The porcelain, ranging from late 17th-century Imari ware to early 19th-century Sèvres and Meissen, is similarly scattered through the house, but the silver, much of it acquired in the 18th century when one of the family was Speaker of the House of Commons, is gathered in a darkened corridor.

Doddington Hall ☆☆

In Doddington, 5 m W Lincoln on B1190, signposted from A46; teas; garden; *open:* Easter BH Mon, then May-Sept, Wed, Sun, BH Mon 2-6; tel: 0522 694308

Doddington entices passers-by. A short avenue leads to a red-brick gatehouse with curving Dutch gables, while beyond, over the wall of the courtyard, can be seen the stone-mullioned windows and cupola-topped turrets of a three-storey Elizabethan mansion. Reputed to be by Robert Smythson, architect of *Hardwick* and *Longleat*, this too is of warm red brick, with stone dressings, a high parapet hiding the roof and strongly angular, symmetrical façades. The interiors, though, are largely mid 18th century, the result of a major refurbishment carried out by Sir John Delaval, who inherited the estate in 1749.

Visitors see rooms on all three floors, gradually progressing up the

impressive 18th-century staircase that rises through the north end of the house. Intimate, cosy interiors, such as the tapestry-lined Holly Room, with contemporary red-and-yellow crewelwork hangings on the 17th-century four-poster, contrast with the three long rooms set one above the other in the centre of the building. The hall is a little bleak, the drawing-room cluttered and museum-like, the best of the three the sparsely furnished, 96 ft long gallery filling most of the top floor, its windows looking west over the formal walled garden to an avenue of Lombardy poplars running into the fields. Round-headed alcoves in the lemon-yellow walls are filled with oriental porcelain and Sir Joshua Reynolds' portrait of John Delaval's sister Sarah, with her husband and son, dominates the end wall. Another Reynolds, of John's elder brother Sir Francis, heir to *Seaton Delaval*, hangs on the stairs, and the small collection of portraits also includes works by Lawrence, Lely, Dahl and Sargent.

Intriguingly, Sarah, the last of the Delavals, left the house to her lover, Capt. George Jarvis, rather than to her grieving husband, and it is the Jarvis family who live here now. Relics of the gallant captain include his tasty cure for gout, a concoction of raisins, fennel, coriander, saffron and rhubarb steeped in brandy.

Fulbeck Hall ☆

At village of Fulbeck on A607, 14 m S Lincoln; teas in July; garden and nature trail; *open:* Easter, May and Aug BH Mon, most of July, daily, 2–5; tel: 0400 72205

Gold-tipped, 18th-century gates mark the entrance to the Fane family's pleasing sash-windowed house of yellow-grey stone standing high on Lincoln Edge, with views west over a deeply rural landscape. Ornamented with plain pilasters and elaborate keystones, Fulbeck dates from 1733, but was altered in the late 18th century, when the substantial bow with wrought-iron balconettes was pushed out to the north, and then again in Regency times, when the original ground floor was enlarged. At the back, a charming Elizabethan service wing, like a row of cottages, is all that is left of an earlier house.

Just a few rooms of the lived-in interior are shown. Still early-18th-century in feel is the pine-panelled, stone-flagged hall, with a round-headed arch giving on to the staircase. Everything else is later. A masculine, green-walled dining-room running out into the bow is hung with sporting paintings; a pretty drawing room, with walls painted turmeric yellow and deep bays to south and east, shows off several pieces of delicate, inlaid furniture, a view of Old Northumberland House by Samuel Scott, and a rambling, repetitive letter from the octogenarian Duke of Wellington, protesting his lack of a relationship with Lady Georgina Fane, then in her fifties and trying to revive a long-dead attachment. Upstairs is a piece of fun, a recreated tent room hung with swathes of a bold yellow and grey, Laura Ashley stripe.

Grimsthorpe Castle ☆☆

4 m NW Bourne on A151, off A1; tearoom; garden; park; *open:* Easter Sun and Mon, late May–mid Sept, Sun and BH Mon 2-6; tel: 0778 32205

This great quadrangular house sits on the crest of a low rise, with sweeping views over serene 18th-century parkland. Each façade is different. A wide oak avenue forms a suitably grand approach to Vanbrugh's baroque north front of 1724-6, with its arched windows, corner towers, huge Doric columns, urn-topped roof-line, and sweeping entrance court, centred on a vast stone basin. From the yew-hedged formal gardens to the south, Grimsthorpe is all Tudor gables and chimney stacks, with a rough medieval tower at one end, while on the west is a prim, early-19th-century, gothick façade by Henry Garling, with chimneys disguised as slender turrets. Originally a medieval castle, in 1512 Grimsthorpe was transformed into a Tudor courtyard mansion by Charles Brandon, Duke of Suffolk. Then, in the 18th century, the 2nd Duke of Ancaster, whose family have lived here since the time of Henry VIII, commissioned Vanbrugh to turn it into a baroque palace, but the great architect died and money ran out with only one range completed.

A tour embracing all four ranges starts in Vanbrugh's lofty stone- and marble-floored hall, with double arcades screening the staircases to either side, and *trompe l'oeil* statue-filled niches by Sir James Thornhill on the fireplace wall. Then it is into the east range, where Vanbrugh's gloomy and cavernous dining-room is succeeded by the three intimate 18th-century state rooms created in one of the oldest parts of the castle, and seen with curtains drawn and lights low. The perfunctory guide leaflet does little to raise enthusiasm for the fine rococo plasterwork framing portraits attributed to Van Dyck, Ramsay, Reynolds and Hudson, and for fireplaces carved by Henry Cheere, one of them sporting a relief of Androcles and the lion. The furnishings are a mix of English and Continental pieces, among them Chippendale mirrors, flamboyant Venetian glasses, 17th-century Flemish cabinets of tortoiseshell and ebony, and two huge French writing tables, topped with elaborate, gilded clocks. In the south and west ranges, visitors are confined to the gloomy, gallery-like corridors looking on to the central courtyard, with just glimpses into a couple of bedrooms and an array of family portraits, including works by Lely, Kneller and Lawrence, and an arresting de Laszlo of the raven-haired wife of the 2nd Earl, providing the main interest. It is a relief to emerge into the coolly beautiful Chinese room, with its delicately vaulted window bay, and into the light and sunny chapel, with a frivolous wineglass pulpit, a large Venetian window in the north wall and white plasterwork on pale coffee walls.

Gunby Hall ☆

7 m W Skegness, on S side of A158, entrance on a roundabout; NT; garden; *open:* Apr–end Sept, Wed, 2–6; tel: none

This prim, red-brick Queen Anne house, with regimented rows of sash windows and a brick parapet hiding the roof, seems out of place in such a rural and remote corner of England. Inside, the few rooms on show are modest and homely, their main interest – apart from a fine collection of clocks and 18th-century glasses – the paintings and other treasures illustrating past connections.

The Massingberd family who built Gunby in *c.*1699 and lived on here until World War II seem to have been adept at acquiring colourful acquaintances and relations. Tennyson, who used to come over from his parents' home a few miles away, is remembered in a signed scrap of poetry; Edward Lear, another family friend, is represented by a drawing of bird-haloed palm trees; and a portrait by Holman Hunt recalls connections with the Pre-Raphaelites.

Even more intriguing are the treasures associated with Dr Johnson which came to the Massingberds through marriage. In the drawing-room is Reynolds' portrait of 'Lanky' Bennet Langton, close friend of the good doctor, who used to read the *Dictionary* to his family at breakfast while an attendant combed the girlish locks shown falling over his arm. Boswell himself appears in a sketch by Bennet's son, his double chin and pronounced paunch to the fore, a cane clasped behind. And visitors who ask can see Langton's copy of the *Life of Johnson*, its flyleaf inscribed 'From his very faithful and obliged friend, The Author'.

Woolsthorpe Manor

In village of Woolsthorpe, 7 m S Grantham, $\frac{1}{2}$ m NW Colsterworth, 1 m W of A1; NT; *open:* Apr–end Oct, Wed–Sun and BH Mon (closed Gd Fri), 1–5.30; tel: 0476 860338

Isaac Newton was born on Christmas Day, 1642 in this otherwise unexceptional, stone-built, early-17th-century house. The modest, low-ceilinged rooms with their deep-set, stone-mullioned windows and whitewashed walls are sparsely furnished with period pieces, none of which belonged to the scientist's family. Although Newton left Woolsthorpe for Cambridge in 1661, one of his most fertile periods was when he returned to the village in 1665 to escape the plague. The upstairs room he used as a study displays a third edition of his monumental *Principia Mathematica*, and a panelled closet filling one corner, like a room within a room, is set up to demonstrate one of the experiments he conducted here, how white light can be broken into a rainbow of colours. A rough drawing of a church on the kitchen wall, one of several graffiti in the house, may, or may not, have been scribbled by Newton as a boy.

Norfolk

Beeston Hall ☆

11 m NE Norwich, on S side A1151; teas; lake walk; *open:* late Apr–mid Sept, Fri, Sun and BH Mon, plus Wed in Aug, 2-5.30; tel: 0692 630771

Beeston is a small gothick house of great charm prominently placed on the crest of a rise, with castellated and pinnacled façades unusually encased in a veneer of gleaming, pearly-grey flint. Built in the 1780s for the Preston family, who have been here since the Civil War, and possibly designed by William Wilkins the Elder, Beeston's architecture is its most notable feature. The tour of the ground floor takes in three or four well-proportioned, lived-in Georgian rooms, with some subdued gothick detail in the hall and library and a scatter of family portraits. Souvenirs of the Russian Revolution and a dedication in a Glazunov ballet score are fruits of the 6th Baronet's diplomatic career, and there is also an 18th-century model of the house.

Blickling Hall ☆☆☆

1½ m NW Aylsham, on B1354; NT; restaurant; garden; park and woodland walks; *open:* late Mar–end Oct, Tues, Wed, Fri, Sat, Sun, BH Mon (closed Gd Fri) 1-5; tel: 0263 733084

The winding back lane from Aylsham gives no hint of this splendid, double courtyard Jacobean mansion. Suddenly, round a corner, there it is, with gilded vanes glinting on ogee-capped corner turrets, curving Dutch gables, massive chimney stacks and a spread of mullioned and transomed windows in walls of red brick and stone. Low, cottagey service wings run forward on either side. Of the medieval and Tudor house that once stood here, only the moat remains, a dry ditch corseting the later building.

Built from 1616 for the wealthy lawyer Sir Henry Hobart, Blickling was designed by Robert Lyminge, who drew heavily on his work at *Hatfield House*. Inside, despite 18th-century alterations by the Norwich architect Thomas Ivory, his son and nephew, and some later changes, much Jacobean detail survives. Sir Henry's descendants, Earls of Buckingham and Marquises of Lothian, continued to live here until the house came to the Trust, and the family's portraits and furnishings, including a Reynolds and two full-length Gainsboroughs, still fill the rooms.

The extensive visitor tour, which takes in almost twenty rooms, leads up to the state apartment on the first floor. Across the curiously cramped outer courtyard is the great hall, filled with Lyminge's bravura staircase and hung with full-length portraits of the Georgian 1st Earl's friends and political allies. Three rather dark ground-floor rooms include a comfortable chocolate and cream drawing-room displaying the family's Canaletto, of Chelsea from the Thames. Then it is upstairs, down a subdued corridor and into a sunny turret bedroom, furnished with a four-poster hung with green and red 17th-century crewelwork hangings and a Chippendale dressing table, and with delicious, flower-encrusted Meissen porcelain in the adjoining bathroom.

The finale begins with the south drawing-room on the opposite corner, with its stripped pine Jacobean chimney-piece, rich plaster ceiling, and 18th-century sofas upholstered in rose pink silk to match the masquerade dress worn by the 1st Earl's sister in a portrait by Michael Dahl. The suite that follows includes the 18th-century state bedroom, still furnished as described in the 1793 inventory, with rococo mirrors, serpentine-fronted chests and Mytens' portrait of Sir Henry, portentous in fur-trimmed robes, and the similarly formal Georgian reception room that adjoins it. A huge tapestry of Peter the Great here was presented to the personable 2nd Earl by Catherine the Great during his three-year stint as ambassador to St Petersburg.

The high point is Sir Henry's 125 ft long gallery, lit by six great windows to the garden and with the most individual of the Jacobean ceilings, with witty panels illustrating the five senses. A library since the mid 18th century, when the 1st Earl inherited some 10,000 books from a distant cousin, it has the feel of an ancient university. Richly coloured stained glass was the work of John Hungerford Pollen, and this pre-Raphaelite artist was also responsible for the deep painted frieze, full of rabbits, owls, toadstools and other country motifs. Some of the rarest books, such as a copy of the Bible written in the dialect of the Massachusetts' Indians, are on display.

Felbrigg Hall ☆☆

2 m SW Cromer, entrance off B1436, signposted from A148 and A140; NT; restaurant; walled garden; woodland and lakeside walks; *open:* late Mar–end Oct, Mon, Wed, Thur, Sat, Sun 1.30–5.30, BH Mon 11–5; tel: 0263 837444

Set in an extensive wooded park, with wide views over sheep-grazed meadow to the lake hidden in a hollow below the house, is an architectural curiosity, home of the Windham family for some 500 years. Visitors arriving hotfoot from the car park are faced with the showy Jacobean south façade designed by Robert Lyminge in 1624, with its stone-mullioned windows, central two-storey porch, tall brick chimneys, and a pierced roofline parapet proclaiming GLORIA IN EXCELSIS DEO. Just round the corner, though, Felbrigg becomes a well-mannered, William and Mary house, with rows of sash windows framed in warm red brick and dormers in a hipped roof. This west front was added by William Samwell in the 1680s, only 50 years after the earlier work: within a lifetime, building styles had been transformed.

The principal interiors leap forward another 50 years, to 1749, when the engaging William Windham II commissioned James Paine to create suitable settings for the paintings he had collected on an extensive Grand Tour. Beyond the Victorian gothic Great Hall, with its heavy bookcases and lumpy ceiling, are William's three state rooms: the lilac and white dining-room, with light, rococo plasterwork by Joseph Rose, and the much richer, scarlet-walled drawing room and cabinet, both of which have virtuoso 17th-century ceilings by Edward Goudge, with pheasants, woodcock, plover and other local birds fluttering among a display of flowers and fruit. The paintings, with their undulating gilded frames, are still as Windham arranged them. In the drawing-room, a pair of huge sea-battles by Van de Velde the Younger, all billowing smoke and tattered, cannon-rent sails, face across the room to two views of London by Samuel Scott. The adjoining cabinet is crammed with pictures in the 18th-century manner, with another vast Van de Velde and other Dutch marine paintings mixed in with a couple of stylized flower pictures and numerous Italian landscapes and classical ruins – 26 gouaches and 7 oils – by Giovanni Battista Busiri.

The best is seen first. Upstairs is a splendid gothic library, all dark pinnacled bookcases and leather-covered armchairs, but the bedrooms have little of interest, apart from Humphry Repton's caricature of the politician William Windham III, arms flung wide in a passionate speech.

Holkham Hall ☆☆☆

2 m W Wells, off A149; tearoom; museum of bygones; garden; magnificent park; beach; *open:* late May-end Sept, Sun-Thurs, 1.30-5, Easter, May and Aug BH Sun, Mon 11.30–5; tel: 0328 710227

This sprawling Palladian house set low in a hollow forms the centrepiece of a gently rolling wooded landscape of wide vistas and huge skies, one of the most sublime parks in England. Built of unyielding, yellowish-grey local brick, Holkham is impressive rather than beautiful. Wings project from all four corners of the central block in a restless, in and out composition like a series of loosely connected pavilions, with pediments and Venetian windows ornamenting almost every bay.

Started in 1734 and not completed until some twenty-five years later, Holkham was the creation of Thomas Coke, later 1st Earl of Leicester, who returned from an extended Grand Tour in 1718 determined to build a fitting setting for the art and sculpture he had amassed abroad. His chosen architect, whom he had met on his travels, was the young William Kent. The influence of Kent's patron Lord Burlington and the Palladian movement accounts for the ascetic exterior; inside, as at *Houghton* nearby, where the interior is also Kent's work, all is richness and opulence. Walls hung with crimson velvet and damask, domed and coffered ceilings, gilded plasterwork and sculptural marble fireplaces set off custom-made furniture and one of the richest private art collections in England.

The visitor tour takes in the 12 state rooms that fill the first floor of the central block. Designed to show off Coke's treasures, these apartments, still as they were in the 18th century, were never intended for everyday living. A theatrical marble hall thrusts into the heart of the building, with a great flight of steps spilling down between fluted columns of pink alabaster and walls lined with statue niches. More classical sculpture, a mixture of athletic male nudes and decorously draped women, furnishes the apse-ended, 105 ft gallery running down the west side of the house. Along the south front, with views over Holkham's Versailles-like formal garden and the park beyond, Coke's paintings take over. The hang in the opulent saloon half-way down has recently been returned to its 1750 arrangement, with restless, richly coloured mythological canvases by Chiari and Procaccini overpowering Rubens's quieter Holy Family, imagined beneath a palm tree, and Van Dyck's portrait of the dashing Duc D'Aremburg.

More Old Masters and family portraits are grouped in the rooms to either side, among them classical landscapes, bird paintings by Hondecoeter, and portraits by Gainsborough and Batoni of the young Thomas William Coke, 'Coke of Norfolk', who inherited the house in the late 18th century, the one in rich autumnal browns and ochres, the other showing the young earl in a masquerade costume. What should be the climax of the sequence, a room lined with landscapes by Claude, Nicolas and Gaspard Poussin, Salvator Rosa and Vernet, is marred by the fact many of the canvases are difficult to see, but there is something rather moving in having a view of the park from here that matches anything on the walls. Small, richly furnished rooms on the east front, some tapestry-hung, make up the bedrooms and dressing-rooms of the State Apartment. Apart from the Genoa velvet bed hangings, the most strik- ing feature here is Bastiano di Sangallo's copy of a lost Michelangelo cartoon, a confusion of naked, heavily muscled bodies like a study in anatomy.

Houghton Hall ☆☆☆

13 m NE King's Lynn, off A148; tearoom; model soldiers collection; park; *open:* Easter–late Sept, Sun, Thurs, BHs, 2-5.30; tel: 0485 528569

Sir Robert Walpole, 1st Earl of Orford, Britain's first Prime Minister, needed a regional power base to support his parliamentary career. The house built on his Norfolk estate from 1721, the work of Colen Campbell and James Gibbs, was designed to impress. Set in a vast deer park with avenues radiating out in all directions, it is a mixture of Palladian elegance and baroque flamboyance. Campbell's Italianate main block, with the principal floor raised above a rusticated basement, a balustraded and urn-studded roofline, and an ornate pediment on the main front, is lifted by the cupola-topped domes at each corner added by Gibbs. Low colonnades curve out to subdued service pavilions either side and only yards away, and almost as magnificent as the house, is the four-square, quadrangular stable block of 1733–5, the soft brown local stone with which it is faced contrasting nicely with the golden sandstone brought from Yorkshire for the house. Sir Robert was as passionate about hunting as he was about architecture and politics, taking his guests to inspect their mounts before church on a Sunday.

There are still horses and ponies in the stables, and the first-floor state rooms are still largely as fitted out by William Kent, with painted ceilings, lavish use of plaster, mahogany and marble, and gilded furniture upholstered in the original green and red velvets. All is for show, the rooms for everyday living being elsewhere. The two grandest interiors sit back to back across the centre of the house. On one side is Kent's cube-shaped, galleried stone hall, rising 40 ft to a coved ceiling, with pedimented doorways and carved chimney-pieces by Michael Rysbrack, and decorative plasterwork by the Italian duo Artari and Bagutti, who have peppered the cornice with chubby cherubs. Double doors open to the similarly large and lofty saloon, its walls lined with crimson Genoa velvet, and door cases and seat furniture richly gilded.

The tour of the state rooms proceeds through seven more interiors, most of them much smaller, but all richly decorated and furnished. The dining-room has service alcoves set in a wall of purple and grey Carrara marble; a dressing room is hung with unique Mortlake tapestries woven with portraits of the Stuart kings; and one of the bedchambers has Kent's monumental state bed, hung with green velvet and with a headboard devised as a huge shell. A late-18th-century chinoiserie bedroom with handpainted wallpaper of the most brilliant blue, delicious rococo mirrors and oriental porcelain in Chippendale corner cupboards, and the Regency white drawing-room, with its lacquered bureaus, and delicate Louis XV tables topped with purple amethyst and Sèvres porcelain, are both in the spirit of the earlier work.

Only the paintings are not what they were. There are family portraits by Reynolds, Wootton, Van Loo, Kneller, Zoffany and Sargent, and a theatre interior by the young William Orpen, but the magnificent collection of some 120 Old Masters amassed by Sir Robert was sold by his eccentric and impecunious grandson, the 3rd Earl, to Catherine the Great and now hangs in the Hermitage in Leningrad. The Empress, round and grey-haired like a benevolent granny, presides over the saloon in a portrait which she gave to the earl. She is smiling gently, as well she might. Sadly, what was perhaps Houghton's most memorable painting, a still-life in shades of white by Jean-Baptiste Oudry, was recently stolen.

Oxburgh Hall ☆☆

Oxborough, 7 m SW Swaffham, on S side
Stoke Ferry road, E of A134; NT; tearoom;
garden and woodland walk; *open:* late
Mar–end Oct, Sat-Wed, 1.30–5.30
(from 11 BH Mon); tel: 036 621 258

Built right at the end of the Middle Ages, when, even on what was then a remote island in the Fenland marshes, men could think of comfort and display rather than defence, Oxburgh is a piece of early Tudor showmanship. A three-arched bridge leads across a wide moat to a virtuoso gatehouse, seven storeys high, battlemented and turreted, its walls marked by decorative brickwork and stone-mullioned windows lighting the principal chambers. The rest of this courtyard house, its brick ranges rising directly from the water, is similarly romantic, but several apparently Tudor features, such as the sturdy tower at one corner, the fanciful oriels jettied out over the moat, the crenellated roofline and the twisted terracotta chimneys, were part of J. C. Buckler's extensive alterations of 1835–70 for Sir Henry Bedingfeld and his son, when a simpler silhouette was made more eventful.

Inside, too, the tower is the only part which is genuinely old, most of the rooms on show being decorated and furnished in a romantic Victorian style, with much carved woodwork. Most pleasing is the long, low-ceilinged library, hung with sparkling, boldly patterned wallpaper and with an intricate overmantel made up of medieval fragments from Continental churches. Sadly, although Bedingfelds have lived here since the early 15th century, there are only a couple of family pictures, most of the rest having been dispersed in a sale in 1951. The tower, though, is everything it should be, with a brick-floored chamber once slept in by Henry VII, a priest's hole secreted behind a former garderobe, and a spiral staircase crafted of brick, with the banister moulded in the thickness of the wall and a continuous barrel vault twisting from top to bottom. From the battlements, you can look down on steeply pitched roofs and decorative chimneys and out over the heavily wooded, deeply rural Fen country.

Just before the tower, a darkened room displays Oxburgh's greatest treasure, green velvet hangings carrying embroidered panels worked between 1569 and 1584 by Mary Queen of Scots and Bess of Hardwick, whose husband had been entrusted with guarding the queen. As important is the carved Flemish altarpiece of *c.*1515–25 in the little 19th-century brick chapel beyond the moat, and faded and beautiful Renaissance terracotta screens adorn the Bedingfeld chantry chapel in the half-ruined church by the car park.

Sandringham ☆

8 m NE King's Lynn, signposted off A149
and A148; restaurant; garden; country
park; *open:* mid Apr-end Sept (but closed
for three weeks Jul-Aug), Mon–Sat, 11-4.45,
Sun 12–4.45; tel: 0553 772675

The Queen's private country residence looks like a well-endowed convalescent home. Overlooking an ornamental lake and tree-studded landscaped lawns is a tall, angular building of brick and stone in a heavy-handed Jacobean style, built by A. J. Humbert for the future Edward VII between 1867 and 1870. A low gabled wing, faced in thin slabs of dark brown stone and with attractive curved gables, was added in 1892.

A 10- to 15-minute walk through the grounds brings visitors to the yew-hedged courtyard on the entrance front. About half a dozen rooms on the ground floor are shown, most of them fussily furnished, with chocolate-box portraits of the royal family by H. von Angeli, Winterhalter, Edward Hughes and others. A 19th-century version of a great hall, fitted out with comfortable sofas and chairs and with family photographs on every surface, leads into the less relaxed interiors running down the south front. Here is a long, cream-and-white drawing-room, with decorative plasterwork on both walls and ceiling and panelling inset with family portraits and panels of cavorting cherubs. Formal painted furniture, blue Sèvres vases on the mantelpieces and some ornate tables add a French flavour, and the room is lined with cabinets displaying glittering enamelled silver given by the Russian Imperial family, 18th-century Worcester porcelain, and precious objects of jade, amber, rock crystal and quartz. In the mint-green dining-room next door is a dessert service decorated with sentimental animal paintings by Landseer and the tour ends in the cavernous ballroom added on in 1883.

An array of guns, paintings of royal yachts, and statuettes of racehorses in a corridor demonstrate the royal interest in sport, while the museum in the former coach houses displays a sorrowful collection of antlered heads and leopard and tiger skins, bagged during big-game hunting in Africa and India before World War II. Less controversial is the array of royal gifts, among them silver coffee pots from Arabia and a bag made of Kiwi feathers, and the family's cars, including a child-size replica of James Bond's Aston Martin made for Prince Andrew.

Suffolk

Euston Hall ☆☆

At Euston, 3 m SE Thetford, on A1088; tearoom; garden; *open:* early June-late Sept, Thurs, 2.30-5, also one Sun in Jun and Sept; tel: 0842 766366

The main reason for visiting Euston Hall is to see a superb collection of portraits, among them several Van Dycks, a sumptuous Lely or two, and works by Mytens, Mignard, Wissing, Reynolds and Nathaniel Dance. The house itself is a remnant, all that is left of a much grander mansion built round three sides of a courtyard for the Earl of Arlington in 1670-6. Subsequently altered by Matthew Brettingham, who faced the whole building in red brick, it was largely destroyed in a fire in 1902. What you see today is the north wing, which faces across a spacious grassy court to Brettingham's stable block of 1750-5.

The paintings celebrate the judicious marriage which the Earl arranged for his daughter Isabella, who was betrothed, at the tender age of five, to the 1st Duke of Grafton, illegitimate son of Charles II and Barbara Villiers. Dukes of Grafton have lived in the house ever since, their ancestry drummed into them by the Stuart portraits on almost every wall, the 17th-century equivalent of the family photograph album.

In the cavernous dining-room are James I and his wife by Van Somer, Henrietta Maria by Van Dyck and the Earl of Arlington himself, the scar of a Civil War injury proudly emphasized by a black patch on his nose. On the way in, there are an unusually informal Van Dyck of Charles I and Lely's portraits of Charles II and Barbara Villiers, he haggard and tired, she depicted as the penitent Magdalen, loose-haired and with a single rope of pearls at her throat.

Upstairs, on the rectangular top-lit landing curiously known as the Square, the paintings have been arranged with some wit. Here is Barbara again, but her prettier rival, Nell Gwyn, is relegated to an adjoining corridor, and the real black sheep of the family, the effeminate and dissipated Duke of Orleans, who may or may not have helped to poison his wife, Charles II's favourite sister Henrietta, is tucked skilfully into a corner, almost out of sight. As an antidote to all these formally posed Stuarts, seek out J. J. Shannon's portrait of the present duke's grandmother, her clear blue eyes suggesting something of her former beauty. And for admirers of Stubbs there is his painting of the 3rd Duke's mares and foals, with Nathaniel Dance's portrait of the 3rd Duke himself, Prime Minister when only in his thirties, hanging close by.

Across the garden is the little parish church, its airy 17th-century interior still retaining the pulpit of 1676, carved with roses and pomegranates, box pews and other original fittings.

Haughley Park

4 m NW Stowmarket, signed on A45 near Wetherden; guided tour (*c.* 30 mins); garden and woodland walk; *open:* May-Sept, Tues 3–6; tel: 0359 40205

This imposing, E-shaped, redbrick house with pinnacled crow-stepped gables dates from 1620, but the garden front was rebuilt with Georgian bays in the early 19th century, and most of the interior has been recreated after a fire in January 1961 gutted all but the south end. Visitors see a few comfortable, well-furnished, lived-in rooms on a tour that concentrates on the 1820s rebuild. Apart from the solid, 'Jacobean' staircase copying the original, and the fine Regency fireplace brought here from a London house, the main feature of Haughley is the collection of 16th- and 17th-century Dutch and Flemish paintings, among them portraits by Honthorst, a flower painting by Verelst, and an animated Last Supper, with the disciples shown as the labourers they were. There are also Venetian scenes by the local painter Alfred Stannard.

Ickworth ☆☆

In Horringer, 3 m SW Bury St Edmunds, on W side of A143; NT; audio guide; teas; garden; park and woodland walks; *open:* Apr, Oct, Sat, Sun, BH Mon 1.30–5.30; May-end Sept, Tues, Wed, Fri, Sat, Sun, BH Mon, 1.30–5.30; tel: 0284 735270

Ickworth could well be a mausoleum for some long-forgotten East Anglian king. A 600 ft frontage is dominated by a huge domed rotunda, like a proto-type for the Albert Hall, from which single-storey corridors curve gently out to substantial wings on either side, one a major house in its own right. Not royalty, but a prince of the church was responsible for this unique building. Started in 1795, it was the creation of the genial and eccentric Frederick

Hervey, 4th Earl of Bristol, Bishop of Derry, holder of the richest see in Ireland and a passionate traveller and collector, who gave his name to a trail of Hotels Bristol across Europe. Built to designs by the Italian architect Mario Asprucci the Younger, and intended to display the Bishop's considerable purchases of paintings and other treasures, Ickworth was unfinished when the 4th Earl died in 1803, in a peasant's outhouse in Italy – from where his coffin was shipped back to England labelled as an antique sculpture – and most of his acquisitions were captured by the French during Napoleon's Italian campaign of 1798.

The rooms visitors see echo the Earl Bishop's original plan, but the decorative schemes date largely from the 1820s, when the 5th Earl finished off his father's house, and the wide-ranging collection of paintings, furniture, silver and porcelain is a legacy of several generations of the Hervey family, many of whom were as colourful as the Earl Bishop. The tour focuses on the four vast, high-ceilinged, rather forbidding rooms filling the ground floor of the rotunda. Across the garden end, like the segment of an orange, is the half-moon library, with screens of yellow scagliola columns concealing its curious shape, a mix of French, Georgian and Regency furniture, and an intriguing conversation piece by Hogarth. A formal drawing room is hung with full-length portraits by Gainsborough, Romney, Lawrence, Kauffmann and Reynolds, and a theatrical, marble-floored hall running into the centre of the house is the setting for sculptor Flaxman's colossal *The Fury of Athamas*, with a blank-eyed, frenzied figure about to dash out his infant son's brains in an agony of despair.

Some of Ickworth's greatest treasures are reserved for the corridor arms. One shows off the family silver, and the intimate smoking room half-way down the other is hung with the cream of the paintings, including a dramatically lit portrait by Titian, Velazquez's painting of the six-year-old son of Philip IV of Spain, a huge hound sleeping by his side, and an unknown boy, set against a richly embroidered hanging, by Carlo Ceresa. Also here is a charming, fresh-faced self-portrait by Madame Vigée-Lebrun, commissioned by the 4th Earl himself. No wonder he smiles out at us from the painting she did of him in Naples in 1790.

Kentwell Hall ☆

N end of Long Melford, off A134, 3 m N Sudbury; re-creations of Tudor life; tearoom; walled garden; re-created timber-framed buildings; *open:* Easter, May and Aug BH weekends, 11-6, Apr-mid June, Sun, 12-5, mid June-mid July, Sat, Sun 11-5, mid July-late Sept, daily, 12-5; tel: 0787 310207

People come to Kentwell not for fine furnishings and paintings – of which there are none – but to enjoy a disarmingly informal family house, to admire the heroic restoration programme, or to experience the popular re-creations of Tudor life. Seen from a distance, framed by the splendid lime avenue which runs almost a mile from the gates, Kentwell seems to be a miraculously preserved Tudor mansion. Like *Long Melford* just down the road, this is a tall, three-armed, red-brick house set round a spacious courtyard, with delicious octagonal turrets on the ends of the wings, a three-arched bridge over a wide moat, and a square brick dovecote on the edge of the water. Closer inspection reveals Georgian and 19th-century windows in among the diamond-paned casements and other changes which suggest something of the massive internal alterations, the most drastic of them carried out by Thomas Hopper in the 1820s.

Visitors can wander at will through rooms on three floors, including a gallery-like attic silted up with an accumulation of trunks, baskets and other clutter, the children's bedrooms, and a 20th-century interpretation of a Roman bathroom. Hopper's grand reception rooms are all on the ground floor, among them a heavy-handed Jacobethan dining-room and great hall, the latter with a plasterwork hammer-beam roof and simulated panelling, now showing distinct signs of wear, the former with illusionist strapwork decoration aggressively picked out in red and gold and an alarming scarlet table. Most endearing is the sunny, classical library filling the end of the east wing, with a rising tide of books and papers overwhelming every surface and a pale pink Knole settee in front of the marble fireplace.

Little Hall, Lavenham

On E side of Lavenham market place; *open:* Gd Fri–mid Oct, Wed, Thurs, Sat, Sun, BH Mon 2.30-5.30; tel: 0787 247179

This tiny, timber-framed building squashed up against a Georgian hotel is a traditional hall house dating from the 14th century. Visitors are shown three minute furnished rooms and a bare attic dormitory created out of the top half of the Great Hall, with original soot-blackened beams in the crown-post roof.

Melford Hall ☆

In village of Long Melford, E side of A134, 3 m N Sudbury; NT; garden; *open:* Apr and Oct, Sat, Sun, BH Mon 2–5.30, May–end Sept, Wed, Thurs, Sat, Sun, BH Mon 2–5.30; tel: 0787 880286

One of two Elizabethan houses in an architecturally rich village, Melford Hall is more of a piece than the rival *Kentwell Hall*, with tantalizing glimpses of ogee-capped, finialled turrets and an octagonal Tudor summer house over the buttressed red-brick wall bordering the road. The gatehouse is a romantic 19th-century addition, but the hall itself, rebuilt on medieval foundations for the wealthy local lawyer William Cordell some time between 1554 and 1578, is little changed, with three brick wings embracing a courtyard and a display of polygonal turrets and decorative chimneys.

While the hall still looks largely Tudor, the interior was remodelled in the mid 18th century and again, between 1813 and 1820, by Thomas Hopper.

There are some Cordell family portraits, and a marvellous estate map of 1580, with fields peopled by happily grazing rabbits, but most of what is on show relates to the sea-faring Hyde Parker family, who came here in 1786. Apart from Hopper's classical staircase, with a single flight climbing between screens of Ionic columns, nothing, either, is very grand, partly because several of the principal rooms were gutted by fire in 1942.

The showiest interior is Hopper's double library; the larger part, designed all of a piece, has bookcases, tables and armchairs of oak inlaid with yew and walnut and is hung with paintings by Dominic Serres of the gallant Admiral Sir Hyde Parker's naval battles. The man himself, in a portrait by Romney, presides over the smaller octagon, and there is also a charming sketch of his girlish, 14-year-old grandson, who was lost with his grandfather in a ship-wreck in the East Indies in 1783. Next door is the panelled blue drawing-room, hung with 17th- and 18th-century Dutch paintings, while upstairs you can see the little room where Beatrix Potter, cousin of the present baronet's grandmother, always slept when she came to Melford. There are several of her meticulous water-colours, and the blue-bonneted, Paisley-shawled model for Jemima Puddleduck.

Otley Hall ☆

10 m N Ipswich, ¹/₄ m NE Otley village, down Hall Lane (by Methodist church); teas; garden; *open:* Easter Fri–Mon, late May and Aug BH Sun and Mon, 2-6; tel: 0473 890264

This moated 15th-century manor, a picturesque array of gables, diamond-paned casements, undulating red-tiled roofs, and decorative Tudor chimneys, is one of the most desirable of Suffolk's timber-framed houses, tucked away down a narrow lane. Thought to be the remnant of what was once an H-shaped building, the house is now like an ungainly T, with a stubby hall wing attached to cross ranges running east and west. On some walls the closely set half-timbering and brick infill is exposed; others are plastered, with a flowing vine-leaf frieze ornamenting the only jettied façade.

Charming, handwritten notes direct visitors round some half-dozen, lived-in rooms on a tour that leaves an impression of sloping floors, dark and battered woodwork, roughly plastered passages, and logs piled up by brick-backed fireplaces. Apart from the galleried, two-storey kitchen created in the earliest part of the house, the most impressive interior is the single-storey hall, now a welcoming sitting room, with a continuous wood-mullioned window filling the north wall, the skeletal remains of a screen at the west end, a floor of yellow, 18th-century bricks, and massive ceiling beams moulded and grooved like stone. The adjoining dining-room is lined with linenfold panelling, and upstairs there are fragments of fresco decoration.

The Priory, Lavenham

In Water Street, Lavenham; restaurant; tiny garden; *open* Apr-Oct, daily, 10.30-5.30; tel: 0787 247417

One of the many photogenic timber-framed houses funded by Lavenham's medieval cloth trade, the priory was rescued from decay by the present owners and is still under restoration. Visitors see the rooms used by the family, with some uncompromisingly modern furnishings as well as exposed beams and remains of Elizabethan wall paintings.

Somerleyton Hall ☆

5 m NW Lowestoft off B1074, signposted from A143 Great Yarmouth road; tearoom; garden; miniature railway; *open:* Easter Sun–end Sept, Thurs, Sun, BH Mons, and Tues, Wed in July, Aug 2-5; tel: 0502 730224

This High Victorian extravaganza in the reddest of brick and dull brown stone is a stylistic mélange built round three sides of a courtyard. The pinnacled and columned three-storey stone porch looking over the garden is an Elizabethan pastiche, but the dormer windows could have come from a Loire château, while a stumpy Italianate campanile-cum-water tower on one side of the house is balanced by a pepper-pot clock tower over the stable arch on the other.

Curving Dutch gables on the ends of the wings are part of the original Jacobean house, transformed in 1844-51 for the railway and building magnate Sir Morton Peto. Sadly, Sir Morton over-reached himself and only 10 years later was forced to sell his new house, and the works of art he had collected, to another *nouveau-riche* industrialist, the carpet manufacturer Sir Francis Crossley, 1st Baron Somerleyton, whose descendants have lived here ever since.

Visitors approach through the gardens laid out for Sir Morton, with glasshouses by Joseph Paxton, a yew maze by W. A. Nesfield, lawns shaded by specimen trees, and urns and other stone ornaments by the magnate's architect, John Thomas, who was primarily a sculptor. After this build-up, the interior, with only a few rooms shown and as much 20th- as 19th-century décor, may seem something of an anti-climax, but Sir Morton's paintings are still here and visitors are given a warm welcome. The pictures mirror 19th-century taste, ranging from Guido Reni's introspective *Simeon with the Infant Jesus* and a double portrait of Rembrandt and his wife Saskia by Ferdinand Bol, one of the master's pupils, to a sentimental Landseer and a pair of specially commissioned seascapes by Clarkson Stanfield. There is some Jacobean panelling, made from oaks grown in the park, and a self-important domed entrance hall, walled in polished marble and carved wood, floored with Minton tiles, and furnished with a hippopotamus-foot umbrella stand and a pair of huge polar bears, two of the 57 shot by Lord Somerleyton and his companion on an Arctic expedition in 1896. Alas, a domed winter garden of glass and iron was pulled down in 1914, its site now marked by a sunken garden.

Wingfield College ☆

At village of Wingfield, 7 m E Diss, signposted off B1118; tearoom; garden; *open:* Easter Sat-late Sept, Sat, Sun, BHs 2-6; tel: 0379 384505

Just yards away from Wingfield's cathedral of a church is what appears to be a long, low Georgian house, with an oversized central pediment and Venetian windows. Small 18th-century rooms flank the tiny hall, but at the back, projecting into the garden, is a timber-framed great hall, open to the roof, a blocked-up Tudor window is visible in the cosy kitchen, and many other clues suggest all is not what it seems. In fact, Wingfield's Palladian façade has been grafted on to a much older structure, all that remains of the college founded here in 1362 by Sir John de Wingfield, friend of the Black Prince, who also provided for the building of the collegiate church. Unravelling past history is what a visit to Wingfield is all about, and afterwards you can go into the church and see the tombs of Sir John and his descendants, the de la Poles, with splendid effigies in stone, wood and alabaster. Be warned, though, that this surprising place, reached only through a confusing web of narrow lanes, is not easy to find.

vd, Dyfed, Mid Glamorgan, South Glamorgan, Gwent,
nedd, Powys, Gloucestershire, Hereford and Worcester,
pshire

Holyhead

Penrhyn Castle
Plas Newydd
Bangor
Caernarfon
Bryn Bras
Betws-y-Coed
Gwynedd

Llandudno
Abergele
Bodrhyddan Hall
A55
M56
Bodelwyddan Castle

Tower
Chester
Clwyd
Wrexham
A5
Erddig

Chirk Castle

Pwllheli
Shropshire
M6

hiw
Dolgellau
R. Severn
Shrewsbury
Weston Park
Boscobel House
M54
Machynlleth
Attingham Park
Powis Castle
Welshpool
Benthall Hall
Acton Round Hall
Upton Cressett Hall
A483
A458
The Moat House
Gregynog
A4091
Newtown
Wilderhope Manor
Shipton Hall
Dudmaston

Aberystwyth
Walcot Hall
Stokesay Castle
Birmingham
Powys
A49
Kidderminster
Harvington Hall

Croft Castle
Berrington Hall
Witley Court
A487
R. Wye
Leominster
Lower
Brockhampton
M5
Hanbury Hall
Burton Court
Builth Wells
Kinnersley Castle
Elgar's Birthplace

Dyfed
Moccas Court
Dinmore Manor
Worcester
Hereford and Worcs
Little Malvern
Court
Snowshill Manor
Brecon
Eastnor Castle
Sufton Court
Carmarthen
A40
Hellen's
M50
Stanway House
Sezincote
Sudeley Castle
Glos
west
Tretower Court
Whittington Court
Castle
A470
Littledean Hall
Hardwicke Court
ke
Gloucester
Merthyr Tydfil
Woodchester Park
Mansion
Swansea
Mid Glam
Gwent
Berkeley Castle
Owlpen Manor
A470
Llancaiach Fawr
Chavenage
Castell Coch
Penhow Castle
M4
Tredegar House
A433
S. Glam
Cardiff
Bristol

Clwyd

Bodelwyddan Castle ☆☆

Just off the A55, near St Asaph; audio tour
(*c.* 60 mins); Victorian portraiture
exhibition; tearoom; gardens; *open:* mid
Apr–end Oct, daily, except Fri, 10.30–5
(open Fri in July and Aug); tel: 0745 583539

Cresting a rise well back from the coast, with a view east to the undulating
ridge of the gentle Clwydian hills and north, over the slender spire of St
Asaph church, to the sea, is this rambling, playful castle of gleaming white
limestone. Created for the Williams family by the architects Welch and
Hansom (he of the cab) in the 1830s, Bodelwyddan's outward show of
chunky towers, slender turrets and battlements is wrapped around a much
older house, with two tall 17th-century chimneys disguised by a massive arch
on the north front.

A girls' school for 60 years, Bodelwyddan has recently been rescued by the
local council, with re-creations of 19th-century interiors matched with period
paintings from the National Portrait Gallery. Although it would be difficult to
imagine anyone actually living in the castle as it is now, Bodelwyddan has
none of the dispiriting soullessness that afflicts many council-owned properties: strongly coloured period wallpapers, voluminous curtains and bold carpets in the nine rooms on show make a vibrant appeal to the senses and the
thin scatter of furniture lent by the V & A includes designs by E. W. Godwin
and Waterhouse, and a forceful Biedermeyer sofa with wooden arms.

Beyond the tiled and stencilled entrance hall, with its fake armour of ceramic and wood, and the long corridor hung with a selection from G. F. Watts's fifty or so portraits of the eminent figures of Victorian England (some now long forgotten), rooms are arranged both thematically and chronologically, leading slowly backwards. In the so-called dining-room, with its heavily fringed, lilac and gold drape curtains, brilliant red Turkey carpet and assorted potted palms, the pictures are of political figures and social reformers from the later 19th century, among them a watchful Arthur Balfour by Alma-Tadema, and Sargent's Joseph Chamberlain of 1896, an unimpressive figure with red-rimmed, watery eyes. A billiard room is devoted to sporting portraits and cartoons from *Vanity Fair*; a yellow-walled drawing-room to musicians, dandies and women; a library, its shelves filled with *trompe-l'oeil* books, to writers and thinkers, among them Carlyle by Millais, the claw-like hands unfinished, and Watts' furiously scribbling Sir Anthony Panizzi, chief librarian of the British Museum. Last comes an almost 18th-century sculpture gallery, with slender plaster vaulting painted to simulate stone, and extraordinary gothic curtain pelmets, used by the school for amateur theatricals. Here are a couple of portraits by Lawrence and a display of idealized and characterless neo-classical marbles by the North Wales sculptor John Gibson.

Bodrhyddan Hall ☆

Signed off B5151, just east of Rhuddlan; guided tours, *c.* 60 mins; tearoom; garden; *open:* June–Sept, Tues, Thurs 2–5.30; tel: 0745 590414

Bodrhyddan is a series of houses, with later façades wrapped round what has gone before. The impressive west front facing down the drive, with an assertive centrepiece rising to a curved Dutch gable, is a Queen Anne revival façade of 1873-4 by William Nesfield, its trim lines of brick and stone, tidy windows, and a fringe of neatly clipped yews dramatically set against a scree-etched ridge rising in the distance. On the south side, facing down a grassy ride to the original gate piers, is a remnant of a William and Mary front in mellow red brick, its entrance of 1696 now forming a garden door, while at the back, looking on to the garages designed by Sir Clough Williams Ellis, are an Elizabethan stone gable and a column-flanked Renaissance doorway, now leading into a cellar.

For centuries, Bodrhyddan has been the home of the Conwys, hereditary keepers of the round-towered 13th-century ruin at Rhuddlan just down the road. Family portraits and an eclectic mix of treasures are displayed in some half a dozen rooms as varied as the exterior. The 19th-century panelled entrance, with a show of mostly Civil War armour, gives on to a long, low-ceilinged room that was the great hall, with an inglenook fireplace by Nesfield. Upstairs there is a white and gold drawing room dominated by two of the most flamboyant fireplaces in Britain, with huge rococo mirrors above an assemblage of carved 16th- and 17th-century panels illustrating the life of Jesus. Former bookshelves are filled by a show of oriental and Continental porcelain, and the room is furnished with painted, wheelback Hepplewhite chairs.

The paintings, mostly assembled in a spacious dining-room added on in the late 18th century, include works attributed to Hogarth, Vanderbank, Reynolds, Ramsay, Michael Dahl and Arthur Devis, a hound with a jaunty tail by Stubbs, and two portraits dated 1696, of the teenage Duc d'Anjou and Duc de Berry by Detroy. A vividly decorated altar set of painted Cantonese enamel was looted from Spain during the Peninsular War, some mummy cases were brought back from Egypt by returning honeymooners in 1836, and on the stairs is Nesfield's rebus window, telling the story of poor Cock Robin.

Chirk Castle ☆☆☆

20 m NW Shrewsbury, off A5 ½ m W Chirk village; NT; tearoom; garden; park walks; *open:* Apr–late Sept, daily, except Mon and Sat, but open BH Mon, 12–5; Oct, Sat, Sun, 12-5; tel: 0691 777701

Chirk still looks like a castle. The long drive from the baroque entrance gates – a froth of ironwork touched with gold – suddenly reveals a brooding mass on a crest to the right of the road, with drum towers bulging out of a high curtain wall. This protective carapace, begun in 1295 as one of Edward I's chain of border fortresses, enfolds domestic ranges facing inwards on to a courtyard. The west side is still 14th-century, with stark and bare medieval rooms built within the thickness of the walls and linked by a worn spiral stair, and with a cave-like dungeon 30 ft below ground. The grand rooms created for the Myddelton family since 1595 are all in the north and east ranges, the former a composite of 18th- and 19th-century work by Joseph Turner of Chester and Pugin and Crace, the latter Jacobean.

Visitors go in through Pugin's pseudo-medieval, armour-hung, stone-floored hall. Beyond, a Georgian staircase carved out of one of the towers leads to an enfilade of state rooms with Adamsque decoration and a show of 17th- and 18th-century portraits, including two rare works by Peter Tillemans and others by Dahl and Allan Ramsay. Some heavy Renaissance colouring on the coffered ceilings – gold, wine red and banner-blue – is a Pugin touch. In the middle is the stiff and formal saloon, with dull gold walls showing off a set of Mortlake tapestries and Lelyesque royal portraits, and with 17th-century Florentine cabinets against the walls and stiff-backed settees and chairs by Ince and Mayhew round the fire. Bubbly, Dresden-style candlesticks provide some light relief, and there is an exquisitely inlaid harpsichord by Burkat Shudi. A panelled, 100 ft long gallery running the length of the east range plunges back into the 17th century, its sparse fittings including Carolean silver sconces, a show of high-backed Restoration chairs and the inlaid ebony cabinet which Charles II gave Sir Thomas Myddelton in 1661, its silver-encrusted interior painted with scenes from the life of Christ. Charles I slept in a room off the gallery in September 1645, but none of the furnishings here now is of his time.

Erddig ☆

2 m S Wrexham, off the A525 or A483/ A5152; NT; tearoom; formal garden and park; *open:* Apr–end Sept, daily, except Thurs and Fri (but open Gd Fri), 12–5 (tapestry and Chinese rooms shown Wed and Sat only); tel: 0978 355314

The approach along the crest of a beech-shaded scarp gives glimpses of a pedimented stone front looking west to the moorland ridge of the Long Mountain, but this austere classical façade, added in 1772-3 by James Wyatt, is no clue to the house. Behind, and facing on to the garden, is a late Stuart building of warm red brick, lengthened in a similar style in the 1720s. This is an unassuming, inward-looking place, with modest, rather dark rooms leading one into another. Home of the mildly eccentric and unambitious Yorke family for some 250 years, it is full of a rich accumulation of belongings, the finest of which were acquired by the prosperous London lawyer who bought the house in 1716. But the presentation is low-key and needs affectionate understanding.

Visitors are taken to the house through a series of service courtyards surrounded by 18th- and 19th-century brick outbuildings, with evocative smells coming from the still-used stables and bakery. The house tour climbs from basement to attics. Some rooms are frankly dreary, among them the classical dining-room remodelled by Hopper in 1826, with yellow scagliola columns against peppermint green walls, and the funereal drawing-room. Others, such as a tapestry-hung room furnished with silvered gesso chairs, are intimate period pieces. There is much original Stuart panelling, a mixed bag of family portraits, including works by Gainsborough, Cotes and Kneller, and an early-18th-century state bed embroidered with multi-coloured birds, although these are difficult to see from behind the glass screen that now keeps visitors at a distance. Some of the finest 18th-century pieces – walnut chairs with original upholstery, gesso girandoles and carved gilt pier glasses – are part of a general clutter in the long saloon.

Also on show are the spacious and airy attics where the servants slept, with views of trees and grass from casement windows, and there is an unusual sequence of servants' portraits hanging in the basement. To the west of the house, prominent grassy heaps flag the now abandoned coal mine that almost destroyed Erddig. A passionate plea to the authorities from Philip Yorke III is one of the key exhibits in the little museum, and another side of this cultivated man comes through in a series of hilarious reports written when he was courier for a holiday company.

Tower

1 m SW Mold, off B5444 Nercwys road; guided tours; *open:* 30 days a year between Easter and Aug BH; tel: 0352 700220

Visitors are treated to a friendly, informal tour of this modest family house, which take its name from the stubby, early-Tudor tower at one end. The place was much altered in the 19th century, when the main range was given its battlemented, mock-Tudor frontage, but there are still some ancient features to be seen, including the remains of a Jacobean staircase.

Dyfed

Picton Castle ☆☆

4 m SE Haverfordwest, off A40; guided tours (c. 60 mins); tearoom; woodland garden; *open:* Easter Sun and Mon, mid July–mid Sept, Sun, Thurs 2–5; tel: 0437 751326

Looking south over the remote, wooded estuary of the Eastern Cleddau is a massy battlemented building of rough, pinkish-grey stone, home of the Philipps family since the 15th century. Developed from a castle built here in c. 1300, Picton was extensively remodelled in 1749-52, possibly by James Gibbs, when the large sash windows were put in, and again in c. 1800, when the keep-like block was added to one end. Four towers were converted into the gently bulging bays that rise the height of the building to north and south.

A relaxed and informative guided tour takes visitors over the principal rooms on the first floor. What was the medieval great hall is now an airy, high-ceilinged drawing-room lit by long, round-headed windows on both sides, with 18th-century decoration picked out in white and grey on dusky pink, a Snetzler organ of c. 1750 on the gallery at one end, and a marble fireplace by Henry Cheere, one of four in the castle, carved with frowning, bearded caryatids. Family portraits include works by Hudson and two autumnal Graham Sutherlands of the present owners, and there is a show of porcelain.

Strong colour schemes in the Regency wing – a dining room in blue-green and white, and a coral-walled drawing room – set off a severe portrait of Elizabeth I, possibly by Antonio Mor, horse pictures by Wootton, a stormy beach scene by Morland, and James Stark's elegiac *Rabbiting in Windsor Forest*. These paintings are mixed with a memorable and varied collection of modern art, including Augustus John's watercolour of the gipsyish, raven-haired 'Dorelia', a treescape by Kyffin Williams, all green and brown flames against an azure sky, the Canadian artist F. B. Taylor's Lowry-like skating scene, with a ribbon of energetic figures among matchstick trees, and Felix Topolski's drawing of Augustus John, a crazed spiderweb of lines making up a staring, aged face. Out in the castle courtyard is the Graham Sutherland Gallery (open Apr–Sept, daily, except Mon), a reflection of the artist's friendship with the Philipps family and of his deep love of Pembrokeshire. Most of the works on show were painted in Wales, but also here are examples of Sutherland's portraits and of the dainty, pastoral etchings in the style of Samuel Palmer with which he started his career.

Mid Glamorgan

Llancaiach Fawr

On B4254, off the A470 north of Cardiff; guided tours (*c.* 60 mins); café; small garden; *open:* all year, Mon–Fri, 10–3.30, Sat, Sun 10–4.30; tel: 0443 412248

Now in the hands of the local council, this rough-walled, semi-fortified Tudor manor is presented as it might have been in 1645, during the Civil War, when its most famous owner, Colonel Prichard, entertained Charles I to a meal. Visitors are conducted over the house by characters in period dress who pretend to be family servants, imparting a mix of social history and invented gossip in a strangely repetitive Jacobean patter. The tour takes in all three floors, proceeding from a stone-floored kitchen with herbs hanging from the beamed ceiling to the little room known as Colonel Prichard's study high under the roof, with a pigeon loft in one wall and a tiny window looking out over the porch. Most rooms have rough whitewashed walls and bare floors, and are sparsely furnished with a range of reproduction pieces, from solid benches and stools to a carved highbacked chair and tester beds. In the parlour, panelled in oak in the 1620s at the same time as a grand new staircase was put in, there is even a Welsh harp and a lute. The place has been much restored, with an ugly modern stair inserted in the north-east corner, and the presentation is entertaining rather than convincing. More for children than adults.

South Glamorgan

Castell Coch ☆

At Tongwynlais, 5 m NW Cardiff, off A470 to Merthyr Tydfil; Cadw; woodland walks; *open:* Apr–late Oct, daily, 9.30–6.30; late Oct–end Mar, Mon–Sat, 9.30–4, Sun 2–4; tel: 0222 810101

It is difficult to take Castell Coch seriously. Rising out of beech woodland above the gorge-like valley of the Taff is a pint-sized Walt Disney castle, with three conical turrets, chunky wooden walkways clinging to the sharply curved curtain wall, a defensive entrance with drawbridge, portcullis and murder holes, and a dungeon. Built between 1875 and 1891 for the enormously wealthy 3rd Marquis of Bute, it was designed by William Burges as a kind of gothic weekend retreat. The massively thick walls follow the outlines of a 13th-century fortress, but no medieval castle ever looked like this.

The main rooms, reached by a slippery outside stair from the tiny courtyard, have sensuously rich painted and stencilled decoration, but the oak furniture is comfortless and functional, with not a cushion, carpet, or piece of soft upholstery to be seen. The most splendid rooms sit one above the other in one of the towers. Below is a rib-vaulted, glittering octagonal drawing-room ringed by a kind of Moorish arcade. The green and gold murals, inspired by illuminated manuscripts, show wild creatures disporting themselves among branches hung with golden pomegranates, apples and pears; butterflies encrust the gilded ribs of the vault; and the door cases are carved with fat caterpillars, plump snails and twisting lizards. Above, at the top of a tight spiral stair, is Lady Bute's circular bedroom, with a red and gold oriental-style divan marooned in the middle of the floor, panels of mirror glass in the dome above, and walls painted with athletic, voyeuristic monkeys. Little castellated turrets hold the water for the washstand, and a cupboard is a manic chequerboard of red, gold and blue. After all this, the low-key kitchen, with cheery blue and white china on the dresser and a scrubbed table, is quite a relief.

Gwent

Penhow Castle ☆

On A48, half way between Chepstow and Newport; choice of audio tours; limited parking; *open:* Gd Fri–end Sept, Wed–Sun and BHs, and daily in Aug, 10–6, Oct-Easter, Wed 10–5; tel: 0633 400800

A small Norman keep, one of six that defended Chepstow against the Welsh, dominates a picturesque huddle of buildings crowning a steep promontory above what was once the main road into Wales. Despite the drawbridge across a rock-cut ditch, and the high curtain wall closing the tiny paved courtyard, Penhow is more house than fortress, with modest gabled ranges attached to the 12th-century tower. A rough-walled medieval and Tudor wing has a steep spiral stair rising to a great hall on the first floor and stone-mullioned windows, but across the yard is a late 17th-century house built directly onto the curtain wall, with sash windows in apricot-washed walls and a shell-headed doorway leading onto a terrace above the cliff. All is intimate, small-scale.

Once the seat of the St Maur or Seymour family, who became Dukes of Somerset, by 1714 Penhow was let as a farm and all but the 17th-century rooms became grain stores and chicken runs. It was bought by the present owner in a ruinous state in 1973 and is being gradually restored. The main walkman tour (*c.*60 mins) takes visitors into all three ranges and, by way of a narrow stair in the thickness of the wall, up to the roof of the keep, where there is a view east to the Severn suspension bridge. The re-created older rooms feel more like a film set than the real thing, with a black rug thrown over the 'medieval' bed in the tower, arrays of brass candlesticks, and a couple of gothic pews and other theatrical flourishes. A panelled parlour and dining-room in the Restoration wing are more convincing.

Tredegar House ☆☆

Visitors approach Tredegar from the back, past a couple of brick barns and other outbuildings, with no hint of the 17th-century grandeur which makes this place such a treat. Before taking a tour, go round to the front, where a symmetrical brick and stone façade, with a baroque central doorway, huge, stone-mullioned windows and carved stone ornaments, looks north-west across a double courtyard and up a broad oak avenue that disappears over a hill in the distance. Although the vista is now bisected by the M4, and the grounds are a public park, this frontage of 1664-72 is still a thrilling sight. Behind, facing on to the internal courtyard, is the one surviving range of the original grey stone Tudor house.

Seat of the Morgan family, lords of Tredegar, for 500 years, the house is now being restored by the local council after a recent stint as a school. The breathless guided tour, with no time to linger, takes in some thirty rooms of various periods, most of them very sparsely furnished and with only a few pieces that belong to the house. An enfilade of well-proportioned, panelled 17th-century state rooms across the main front, each grander than the one before, culminates in a glittering room on the corner of the house, with an original stucco and painted ceiling and grained pine panelling rich with gilded decoration. Inset paintings, one of them a copy of a Titian Venus, another a version of Rubens' *Judgment of Solomon*, are endearingly amateur, and there are blue and purple Delft tiles lining the fireplaces. A second enfilade on the upper floor has been spoilt by later alterations, but there is a bold 17th-century plasterwork ceiling here, and a much rarer survival, a tiny closet lined with expensive cedar panelling. A dressing-room has been furnished according to a 17th-century inventory and there are some fine William and Mary and 18th-century pieces, among them a cabinet inlaid with tortoiseshell, ebony and ivory that is original to the house.

The tour starts with a couple of 19th-century interiors and finishes with the servants' hall and the housekeeper's room fitted out with spice drawers in the old Tudor wing. In between is a suite of rooms furnished to conjure up Tredegar's Indian summer in the 1930s, when the eccentric Evan, 4th Viscount, entertained on a lavish scale. Here is Augustus John's portrait of his mother, and a painting of Evan hangs in the room in which he used to dabble in black magic, assisted by Aleister Crowley, 'the wickedest man alive'.

Gwynedd

Bryn Bras

4½ m E Caernarvon, off A4086; tearoom; woodland garden and walk to viewpoint; *open:* end May–end Sept, daily, except Sat, 1–5 (mid July–end Aug, 10.30-5); tel: 0286 870210

At the northern end of the deep cleft of the Llanberis Pass, picturesquely set against a wooded hill, and with a stream plunging through the gardens, is this toy fort of a place, its matchstick turrets of rendered brick and the partly ivy-smothered castellations best seen from a distance.

Created in 1830–5 for a local attorney, Bryn Bras is on a much more modest scale than nearby *Penrhyn,* which was built at the same time. Part is now let as holiday apartments, and visitors see just a few lived-in ground-floor rooms along the east-facing entrance front. There are a couple of massive slate fire-places, a neo-Norman hall and some arresting stained glass, such as the large, round-headed 1920s windows featuring scarlet Welsh dragons, but few con-tents of interest. A corn sheaf crest and the motto *Deo Faventes* seen on the newel posts of the stair, in glass, and on the bridge to the former stables, recall the castle's pre-war heyday, when it was owned by Duncan Elliot Alves, the oil magnate and friend of Lloyd George.

Penrhyn Castle ☆☆☆

1 m E Bangor, at Llandegai on A5122; NT; audio tour; doll collection; industrial railway museum; tearoom; garden and grounds; *open:* Apr–end Oct, daily, except Tues, 12–5 (from 11 July and Aug); tel: 0248 353084

Strung out along a low ridge sandwiched between Snowdonia and the sea is an array of battlemented walls, towers and turrets, the whole vast complex, built of finely jointed local limestone, leading up to the splay-walled keep that rises 115 ft at the southern end. Designed by Thomas Hopper for G. H. Dawkins Pennant, who inherited the estate and a prodigious fortune from a distant cousin, and built 1820-40 by local craftsmen, Penrhyn is in a class of its own. This is a castle which could surely withstand a siege, but its severity is tempered by torch-like turrets and by deep-set romanesque windows, some with graceful columns dividing the lights, others with zigzag ornament or moulded arches. Everywhere there is a subtle interplay of curves and angles, and of advancing and retreating surfaces.

Inside, it is the stuff of nightmares. Everything is larger than it needs to be, and there is a manic edge to the rich, unrelentingly repetitive Norman and Celtic decoration of the principal rooms. Then, nothing is quite what it seems: plaster is grained to look like wood or painted to resemble stone, furniture is made of slate, and a cunningly placed mirror doubles the length of a cloister-like corridor. Hopper himself designed much of the furniture, from the heavy tables on cluster-column legs in the library to a chunky wardrobe and bed-side tables topped with polished limestone.

Visitors step into a lofty hall like a badly converted cathedral, with soaring Norman arches incised with bands of abstract ornament and lacy capitals to the columned piers. All is stone, the only colour from pulsating stained-glass windows. Hopper's Norman ornament reaches a climax on the staircase, with slender columns tracing blank arcades on the inner wall and dazzlingly white plasterwork around the lantern high above. Among the repeated motifs are disconcerting details: a half-moon of hands over a door, a leggy spider on a capital, and grimacing faces, some gap-toothed, some with pointed ears, some barely human.

The main rooms, on show to the public from the start, were never meant to be used every day. The family lived in the keep, where visitors see some almost intimate bedrooms, with barrel-arched ceilings, restful blue and green William Morris wallpapers, and stunning views. The lengthy tour ends in the dining-room and morning-room, their deep red walls hung with family por-traits and the Spanish, Italian and Dutch paintings collected by the 1st Baron Penrhyn in the mid 19th century. Here are serene riverscapes by Van der Neer, a rustic peasant scene by Teniers, a Canaletto of the Thames at Westminster, with the abbey prominent in the distance, and Palma Vecchio's Holy Family, with saints gathered round like kindly relatives. The English portraits, including works by Romney and Ramsay, are outclassed by Rembrandt's powerful, black and white image of a merchant's middle-aged wife, handkerchief clutched in her rather manly hands. Henry Hawkins' painting of Penrhyn slate quarry, source of the family fortunes, with ant-like men dropping on ropes down cliffs of bare rock, is relegated to a corridor.

Plas Newydd ☆☆

Anglesey, on A4080, off A5 at W end Britannia bridge; NT; tearoom; garden overlooking Menai Straits; *open:* Apr–late Sept, daily, except Sat, 12–5, Oct, Fri and Sun, 12–5; tel: 0248 714795

A downward path steepening into steps descends to this long, creeper-clad house looking east over the Menai Straits to the ridges of Snowdonia. A strange Janus of a place, on one side Plas Newydd is gothick, with huge traceried windows, while on the other square-headed sashes fill three bays projecting towards the sea, the only unifying thread the little ogee-capped, octagonal turrets punctuating both façades. Originally Tudor, Plas Newydd was remodelled in three stages in the 18th century, most dramatically by James Wyatt and Joseph Potter in the 1790s, and then again in the 1930s for the 6th Marquess of Anglesey, who commissioned the Rex Whistler mural for which the house is best known. Inside, work by Wyatt and Potter in schizo-phrenically different styles is allied with comfortable pre-war furnishings and striking colour schemes introduced by Lady Marjorie Manners, wife of the 6th Marquess.

Facing up-slope are the lofty gothick hall and music room, with delicately vaulted ceilings and traceried doors. Carved stucco and wood simulate stone capitals and bosses and a medieval-style gallery, and walls are plastered to look like stone. Apart from some fine portraits, including one of the Tudor founder of the family fortunes and others by Lawrence and Hoppner, these are large, empty spaces, their lack of colour a marked contrast to the cheerful reception rooms on the other side. Here, Wyatt and Potter worked in a classi-cal idiom, with marble fireplaces carved by Richard Westmacott the Elder and chaste plaster friezes. The colour schemes, though, are Lady Marjorie's. An octagon room is strongly red and white, the drawing room, hung with huge pastoral landscapes by Balthasar Ommeganck, has leafy green sofas on a rich blue carpet, and upstairs is Lady Marjorie's prettily feminine, pink and white bedroom fitted out with advice from Sybil Colefax, with pink ribbon threaded through the snowy counterpane, a muslin-hung kidney-shaped dressing-table, and pink cushions on a chintzy daybed.

A portrait by Sir James Shannon shows Lady Marjorie in a golden Egyptian head-dress, and there are paintings of the 6th Marquess and his family by Rex Whistler, whose wide-ranging talents are demonstrated in an exhibition of his work. His mural, filling one wall of the dining-room, is a 58 ft panor-ama over a mountain-girt, choppy green sea bordered by Renaissance cities. It is full of delightful detail, from a small boy stealing apples and women gos-siping to weeds between the paving stones of the quay in the foreground and the figure of the artist himself sweeping up leaves in a long colonnade, while the strong colours make the view from the window seem almost insipid.

Plas-yn-Rhiw ☆

On S coast of Lleyn peninsula, 12 m SW Pwllheli, signed off B4413 to Aberdaron; NT; cottage garden; *open:* Apr-late Sept, daily, except Sat 12–5, Oct, Sun, 12–4; tel: 075 888 219

Dug into a steep and sheltered hillside at the far end of the remote Lleyn peninsula, with wide views over the sandy crescent of Porth Neigwl and across the sea towards the mountains of Snowdonia, is an unremarkable three-storey house of rough grey stone, with a Georgian frontage, complete with genteel verandah, hiding a much older building behind. Inside, the small, low-ceilinged rooms are shown as they were furnished by the determined Keating sisters, Eileen, Lorna and Honor, who bought the property just before World War II, rescued it from dereliction, and lived on here until their deaths. A wind-up gramophone, early gas stove and other details convey a period atmosphere, but there is something rather touching about the narrow beds covered with patchwork quilts, the smart shoes and fur stoles which would have been so out of place here, and about the careful watercolours and tiny woodcuts which reflect Honor's early ambition to be an artist. Unusually for the Trust, there is no guide to the contents, and visitors must consult the stewards about anything that catches their eye.

Powys

Gregynog

Near village of Tregynon, 5 m N Newtown, off B4389; walks in extensive grounds; *open:* early Jun–end Sept, Mon–Sat, guided tours at 11 and 3 (advisable to check); tel: 0686 650224

Set amidst sweeping lawns walled by belts of trees is this 1840s pastiche of a gabled Elizabethan manor, with moulded and painted concrete simulating half-timbered façades. Turned into something of a centre for the arts by the Davies sisters, who bought the place after World War I and set up the Gregynog press here, the house is now attached to the University of Wales. The short guided tour takes in a handful of public rooms, one of them lined with ornate Jacobean panelling retained from the old hall. The Davies sisters' collection of Impressionists has mostly gone, but a large sitting-room still shows off a couple of busts by Rodin, Augustus John's *Zoe* and a still-life by Matthew Smith, and visitors can also see the functional music room used for a yearly festival that involved such luminaries as Sir Adrian Boult.

Powis Castle ☆☆☆

On A483 1 m SW Welshpool; NT; tearoom; exceptional gardens; *open:* Apr–end Oct, daily except Mon and Tues (but open BH Mon, and Tues in Jul and Aug) 12–5; tel: 0938 554336

Balanced on a narrow rocky ridge high above Welshpool is a towered and battlemented keep of rough pink sandstone. Despite the array of mullioned and transomed windows, and the luxuriant terraced garden descending in great leaps below the castle, with huge domes of yew oozing over the retaining walls, Powis still looks like a medieval fortress, one-time stronghold of a dynasty of Machiavellian Welsh princes.

The interior has been remodelled over the centuries by the Herberts, Lords and Earls of Powis, who acquired the castle in 1587. The one Elizabethan survival is an enchanting T-shaped long gallery with meadow flowers and a menagerie of weird and wonderful beasts depicted on the plaster ceiling and frieze, *trompe l'oeil* panelling carrying original brass sconces and early family portraits, a Tompion clock, and a show of unassertive sculpture that includes a spitting marble cat from classical Rome. At either end are Powis's two 17th-century interiors: a baroque staircase painted with half-clothed deities by Verrio and his pupil Gerard Lanscroon; and the formal Versailles-like state bedroom, with an ornate four-poster set back behind a carved balustrade in a tapestry-lined alcove, silvered gesso furniture, and inset paintings of extra-ordinary ineptness.

The rest of the state apartment is a sequence of large, high-ceilinged, rather dark interiors, their strange shapes moulded by the configuration of the original castle, with Jacobethan plasterwork and panelling created by G. F. Bodley in the early years of this century. These rather oppressive Edwardian rooms show off fine Carolean and 18th-century French and English furniture, including some marquetry pieces and a couple of oyster-veneered cabinets, and the family's paintings and other treasures: portraits by Reynolds, Romney, Gainsborough and Batoni, Isaac Oliver's freshly coloured miniature of the Jacobean 1st Lord Herbert, a richly caparisoned horse held by attendants in the background, and Bellotto's moody panorama of Verona, with a little chapel and a fleet of watermills moored out in the glassy river.

Nathaniel Dance's full-length painting of Clive of India is a reminder that many of the finest contents came here after his son married a daughter of the house. In the range against the medieval curtain wall flanking the entrance court, beyond a ballroom created by T. F. Pritchard in the 1770s, is a museum devoted to the treasures brought back from India by the 1st and 2nd Lords: boxes of sandalwood and rosewood inlaid with ivory, enamelled hookahs studded with rubies, emeralds and diamonds, a brilliantly coloured cotton tent, and a tiny golden tiger snatched from the throne of Tipu Sahib, Sultan of Mysore.

Tretower Court ☆

10 m NW Abergavenny off A479; Cadw; *open:* Apr–late Oct, daily, 9.30–6.30, late Oct–end Mar, Mon–Sat 9.30–4, Sun 2-4; tel: 0874 730279

In the valley of the Usk, where the river cuts south-east between the Black Mountains and the Brecon Beacons, is this defensive medieval house of rough pink and grey stone. Facing on to a spacious walled courtyard are two long low ranges; the north wing, with an open gallery giving access to the upper floor, dates from the 14th century, while to the west a dignified 17th-century façade with a classical doorway disguises what is essentially an early Tudor building. High walls with covered first-floor walkways ring the other sides of the court, and the way in is through a two-storey gatehouse, with a gothic postern gate beside the vaulted main passage.

Visitors can wander over every inch of the building, sharing bare unfurnished rooms with the birds that dart in and out. Internal partitions have gone, a Tudor oriel is a reconstruction, but the place is full of period detail,

from stone archways and trefoil-headed lights to unglazed, shuttered openings, and the decorative timber roof over the stone-floored great hall, with
moulded and carved beams held together by pegs. Just a few yards north-
west, crowning a mound, is the ruined Norman keep that once guarded the
route through the mountains, and which the more civilized house replaced.

Gloucestershire

Berkeley Castle ☆☆

10 m SW Stroud, 15 m NE Bristol, off A38;
guided tours (c. 75 mins); tearoom; garden;
open: Apr–Sept, Tues–Sun, BH Mon 11–5
(Apr and Suns 2–5), Oct, Sun 2–4.30;
tel: 0453 810332

Mentioned in Shakespeare's *Richard II*, and the place where, in 1327, Edward
II was imprisoned and murdered, this great lump of castellated, pink-grey
stone commanding the wide Severn valley, with the remains of a circular
Norman keep rising above a buttressed curtain wall, still looks every inch the
fortress. Lining the protective carapace, like the soft flesh within the shell,
are the castle's living quarters, a series of mostly 14th-century ranges facing
on to an inner courtyard. There have been changes and improvements since,
particularly in the early years of this century, when several of the windows
were modernized, and the castle was embellished with doorways and
chimney-pieces brought from some abandoned French château, but the original structure is essentially unaltered. Berkeley is now a house rather than a
fortress, but there is nothing cosy or manageable about it, and the medieval
skeleton shows through in rough, unplastered walls, stone arches, frequent
changes of level, and the lack of any logical plan. Visitors see a confusing
warren of interconnecting rooms: some are tiny, others light and well-
proportioned, but all have the feeling that the castle has the upper hand and
several are chill and comfortless.

Although the Berkeley family have lived here for over 800 years, the contents on show are not as rich as the castle's long history and associations
might suggest. There are royal and family portraits, among them works by
Paul van Somer, Edmund Ashfield, Gainsborough, Lely, Hoppner and Mary
Beale, and several canvases showing members of the family in their distinctive canary-yellow hunting coats. Seascapes by Van de Velde the Elder
feature ships commanded by members of the family and there is also a pastoral scene by Stubbs, with a groom watering a grey and a chestnut, and a
landscape by Salomon van Ruysdael. A mix of furnishings includes
Hepplewhite saddleback chairs and other Georgian pieces, Flemish tapestries
and scarlet Tudor hangings.

Apart from the great hall, with its high saddle roof and painted screen, and
the hexagonal stone-floored kitchen, spanned by radiating 15th-century timbers, the most memorable interior is the morning-room created out of what

was once a chapel. This serene, tapestry-hung chamber, lit by graceful traceried windows, still has its medieval painted decoration, with a frieze carrying lines from a translation of the Book of Revelation done by the castle chaplain in 1387. The room where Edward II was murdered is blurred by later
alterations, but you can still peer down the terrifying, well-like dungeon,
28 ft deep, where less exalted prisoners were thrown to die.

Chavenage ☆

2 m NW Tetbury, signed from A46 and
B4014; guided tours (c. 45 mins); *open:*
Easter Sun, Mon, May–end Sept, Thurs,
Sun and BH Mon 2–5; tel: 0666 502329

A narrow by-road leads to this E-shaped Elizabethan manor of rough
Cotswold stone, with long, gabled wings embracing a little courtyard, a
stone-tiled roof spotted with lichen and moss, and a wall of glass lighting the
hall to the left of the porch. This entrance frontage, finished in 1576, is
delightfully asymmetrical, with traceried and trefoil-headed windows made
of stonework from a local priory.

A relaxed guided tour by the present owner, whose family came here in
1894, takes visitors over the south side of the house, the mostly low-ceilinged
and intimate rooms of the original building contrasting with a cavernous
Edwardian ballroom running along the back and a lofty late 18th-century billiard room hung with copies of Italian paintings. The great hall still has its
carved screen at one end, a splendid fireplace of *c.* 1680, its stonework inset
with cameos of polished black marble, and medieval stained glass, probably
from the priory, in the three-tier window. Elsewhere is some Elizabethan
panelling carved with lively figures representing the arts and sciences (medicine is portrayed by a snake charmer) and two intimate tapestry-hung bedrooms recall the time of the Civil War, when the then owner, Colonel
Nathaniel Stephens, was visited by Cromwell and persuaded to throw in his
lot with the parliamentarians. Legend has it that a phantom coach driven by
the headless monarch himself turned up to collect the colonel at his death – a
fate said to await every lord of the manor – and the ghost of a hooded monk is
said to haunt the tiny chapel in the garden, its pinnacled tower originally an
18th-century gothick folly.

Hardwicke Court

W side A38, 5 m SW of Gloucester, 3 m N
Whitminster, via unmarked drive just S of
turning to Hardwicke church; garden;
open: Easter Mon–end Sept, Mon, 2–4;
tel: 0452 720212

This atttractive, stone-faced, late-Georgian house looking east over parkland
to the Cotswolds was built by Sir Robert Smirke, architect of the British
Museum, in 1816–17. The hall and three main rooms are shown, all of them
comfortable, lived-in interiors, hung with family portraits by Kneller, Opie

and Dahl and with one of Gainsborough's romantic, idealized village scenes. Of the grand Elizabethan house that once stood here, only one arm of the moat survives, incorporated in the garden.

Littledean Hall

At Littledean on A4151, 12 m W Gloucester, signposted from A48; garden; *open:* early April–end Oct, daily, 10.30–5.30; tel: 0594 824213

Although historically interesting, with a medieval, possibly Saxon, hall underlying an originally Jacobean house and the outlines of a Roman temple in the garden, this is an unrewarding place to visit. The 19th-century gothic north front is a positively sinister concoction of gables and stone-mullioned windows, and the few bare rooms on show, despite some 17th-century panelling and a carved Flemish overmantel, are chill and dispiriting.

Owlpen Manor ☆

3 m E Dursley, off B4066, 1 m E Uley, signed down lane off village green; tiny terraced garden; *open:* Apr–end Sept, Tues, Thurs, Sun and BH Mon, 2–5.30; tel: 0453 860261

A twisting lane from Uley leads up a steep-sided valley to a picturesque huddle of buildings. Dug into the wooded north slope of the combe is a small gabled manor of Cotswold stone, with a tiny church poised immediately above, and a walled and terraced garden, complete with gazebo and blowsy yews, running down to the brook. A mill crowned by an 18th-century cupola sits beside the stream.

The manor is L-shaped, with a Tudor hall and Jacobean parlour tacked onto an originally 15th-century east wing, and a few narrow Georgian sashes contrasting delightfully with the old stone mullions. Largely abandoned from the mid-18th century, Owlpen stood empty until rescued and restored in the 1920s by the Arts and Crafts disciple Norman Jewson.

Visitors are shown five cluttered, lived-in rooms in the long south wing, where a few Arts and Crafts pieces blend easily with 17th- and 18th-century furnishings. In the centre is the one-storey hall, with a six-light window to the garden, a polished stone floor put in by Jewson, and a grand classical doorcase with fluted pilasters leading into a tiny Georgian parlour, its panelling painted in elegant greys and a shell-headed niche by the fireplace. A low-ceilinged, oak-panelled Jacobean parlour at the west end of the range gives access to a broad newel stair leading up to the former great chamber and solar, the first hung with rare painted hangings that have always been in the house, the latter with a view down-valley to the Iron Age hillfort above Uley. Fluid paintings by Frank Moss Bennett and etchings by the more accomplished F. L. Griggs show the house as it was before restoration, and plasterwork rabbits, a hedgehog and a stern-faced owl above the doors of the hall are by Jewson and his mentor, Ernest Gimson.

Sezincote ☆

On A44, just east of Bourton on the Hill
(lodge is S side of road at bottom of hill);
guided tours (*c.* 30 mins); exotic water
garden; steep uphill walk back to car park;
open: May, June, July, Sept, Thurs, Fri,
2.30-6; tel: none

Sezincote is in a class of its own. Visitors get a hint of what is to come on the
trek across the garden, where sacred Indian bulls sit on the parapet of a little
bridge and a sinister, three-headed snake slithers up a tree trunk beside the
path. Set looking over a wooded, intensely English landscape is an exotic,
two-storey bungalow, built of golden stone, with pint-sized minarets studding the corners, and a bulbous copper dome like a pale green onion erupting
from the roof. Peacock-tail arches hood the first floor windows, a deep,
bracketed cornice marks the roofline, and wrought-iron balconies suggest a
villa by the sea. The finishing touch is a long, arcaded gallery-cum-conserva-
tory which curves gently out behind the house, ending in a pinnacled, octagonal pavilion. Built for Sir Charles Cockerell, an East India Company nabob,
Sezincote was designed by his brother, Samuel Pepys Cockerell, and finished
in *c.* 1805. S. P. Cockerell had never been to India, indeed had hardly been

abroad, but he had expert advice from the artist Thomas Daniell, who had spent nearly a decade in the east.

Alas, there is nothing exotic, or even very memorable, about the interior. Visitors see what were the three main reception rooms on the first floor, two of them now fitted out as bedrooms, and the former billiard room, now decorated with modern murals of Indian scenes. Most impressive is the grand, top-lit staircase beneath the dome. Most interesting are five views of Sezincote by Daniell, one of them said to commemorate a visit by the Prince Regent, for whom, in 1815, Nash designed the similarly exotic, but more vulgar Brighton Pavilion.

Snowshill Manor ☆☆

In centre of Snowshill, 3 m S Broadway; NT; terraced garden; *open:* Apr and Oct, Sat, Sun, 11–1, 2–5, Easter wkend, May–end Sept, Wed–Sun and BH Mon 11–1, 2–6; tel: 0386 852410

This stone-built Cotswold manor in the centre of an unspoilt village contains the extraordinary collections assembled by the eccentric Charles Paget Wade, who bought Snowshill in a ruinous state in 1919 and devoted the rest of his life to restoring it, filling every nook and cranny, every ledge and windowsill, with thousands of finely crafted objects.

Visitors wander through a warren of tiny rooms and passages, with steep and narrow stairs leading from ground floor to attics. As is immediately clear, Wade was no unthinking magpie. A craftsman himself, he relished anything of good workmanship and design, arranging like with like and accruing richly coloured Continental and eastern pieces – scarlet tent bags, blue and white porcelain, red lacquerwork – to give some vibrancy to his dark interiors. Each room is different, each unexpected, and each evocatively named, from the toy-filled Seventh Heaven to the bicycle-stacked Hundred Wheels under the roof, where early machines are suspended from the beams. In one, there is a cluster of Chinese cabinets, Japanese clocks, and gleaming golden buddhas; another is devoted to nautical objects and curious instruments, such as spindly-armed models of the solar system; and a third is filled with a silent company of musical instruments, arranged like an orchestra, or serried ranks of shuttles and spinning wheels. There is a menacing, theatrically-lit display of Samurai armour, all grimacing masks and staring eyes, while in among the main displays are such everyday objects as travelling medicine chests, a delicate glass device to diffuse candlelight, and a collection of truncheons and fire buckets.

A couple of panelled bedrooms look almost normal, but this is not a house for living in. Mr Wade would install his guests among all these ghosts, but he himself lived in the cottage in the garden, where visitors can see his cluttered kitchen-cum-living-room, primitive bathroom and galleried bedroom reached by an outside stair. Here, Wade's theatricality comes through in gilded censers swinging from the beams and in the huge crucifix on the end gable.

Stanway House ☆☆☆

5 m SW Broadway, off B4077; garden;
open: June–Sept, Tues, Thurs, 2–5;
tel: 038 673 469

Who could not fall in love with Stanway? A bend in a narrow, leafy lane suddenly reveals a delicious, many windowed, Jacobean gatehouse, its curving
gables topped with scallop shells, fluted columns and a pediment framing the
archway, and rabbits and birds carved on the gates. Over a high wall are tantalizing glimpses of the gables, chimneys and licheny stone-tiled roofs of a
cluster of buildings, all in golden Cotswold stone, while a steep wooded hill
rising behind the house is crowned with a gloriously purposeless pyramid.

This magical manor house, cheek by jowl with a little church and a 14th-
century tithe barn, is built in the form of an L. A long, west-facing hall range
of c.1580 is attached to a shorter south wing finished in c.1640, with a
flamboyant strapwork parapet crowning its heart-stoppingly beautiful, mag-
nolia-clad façade.

Owned by the Earl of Wemyss and lived in by his son, a descendant of the
Tracy family who were here in the 16th century, this unpretentious, secluded
place could hardly be more different from *Gosford House*, the Earl's grand
Scottish seat. Furniture and paintings accumulated over centuries are displayed in cluttered, hugger-mugger, lived-in rooms and shown with humour
and endearing touches of eccentricity. And then, the house itself keeps
intruding: in the little flights of steps which carry the south wing gently
uphill, in a warped and worm-eaten oak staircase, in a stone arch dating back
to c. 1510, and in curiously varied window levels.

Entering through the kitchen quarters, visitors emerge in the tapestry-hung,
stone-flagged great hall, its screen now hidden behind stuccoed Doric columns
but the lantern-like window bay still filled with green- and yellow-tinged old
glass and a long shuffleboard table of c.1620 down one side. Beyond is the
south wing, where a crowded drawing-room is half-filled by two exotic
Chinese Chippendale day beds, their canopies hung with gold bells and painted
with brilliantly plumaged birds and flowering foliage. These unique curiosities,
as if awaiting the entourage of a sultan, upstage portraits by Romney and
Raeburn, a couple of classical compositions featuring sparsely-clad beauties by
Lagrenée, and two early 19th-century Broadwood pianos. Elsewhere, in a tour
that takes in a couple of bedrooms as well as most of the ground floor, visitors
see a William and Mary seaweed marquetry cabinet, Sheraton chairs, charcoal
drawings by Sargent and a fine portrait by Francis Cotes. The way in passes
through the audit room, where tenants still pay their quarterly rents in person,
and where one wall is hung with a charmingly naive 18th-century view of the
house, showing the cascade that once thundered down the hill below the pyramid; and in the exit corridor is a piece of panelling carved with the names of
the three young sons of an 18th-century Tracy, one of whom only got as far as
inscribing 'Ant' before he was discovered. Stanway also boasts a thatched
1920s tennis pavilion, seen on the approach from the cark park.

Sudeley Castle ☆☆

Just outside Winchcombe, 6 m NE
Cheltenham, off B4632, well signposted;
restaurant; garden; *open:* Apr–end Oct,
daily, 12–5; tel: 0242 602308

The medieval and Tudor castle that once stood here, used as a base by Prince
Rupert, Charles I's dashing nephew, during the Civil War, was slighted by
the Parliamentarians. The ruins of the banqueting hall, a roofless, heavily
buttressed stone barn, and an exuberantly pinnacled, 15th-century honey-
stoned chapel, form picturesque backdrops to the romantic garden, but the
rambling, castellated courtyard house with huge stone-mullioned windows is
largely as created by Sir George Gilbert Scott for the Dent brothers, who
bought the estate in 1837 and whose descendants are still here. Sir George
also gave the chapel its 19th-century interior and the canopied marble effigy
of Catherine Parr, Henry VIII's sixth queen, who outlived the king, married
again, and died at the castle in 1548, five days after giving birth to a
daughter.

Inside, Sudeley both excites and disappoints. Visitors are shown a succession of modest, largely 19th-century rooms on the east side of the castle, with
nothing grand or impressive about any of them. What is in them, though, is
well worth seeing, as the Dents set out to acquire contents worthy of the
place. Some of the treasures reflect Sudeley's past history, among them
Catherine Parr's prayer book, with her signature and a note from Henry VIII
inside; and mementoes of the Civil War, such as a silk waistcoat said to have
belonged to Charles I, and his inlaid dispatch box, captured at the Battle of
Naseby in 1645. Others, such as the 16th-century Sheldon tapestry illustrating Adam and Eve's expulsion from Paradise, and the Aubusson hangings
that once belonged to Marie Antoinette, are just prized for what they are.
Particularly outstanding are the paintings, among them two chubby infants
by Van Dyck, a domestic scene by Jan Steen, a ruined water mill by Jacob
van Ruisdael, all crumbling thatch and foaming water, a rather dark Claude,
and two dreamy Turners, one an improbably romantic vision of the lake at
Stourhead, with classical temples perched on a steep Mediterranean coast, the
other a misty view across the Thames of Horace Walpole's *Strawberry Hill;* it
was at a sale of works of art from this gothick villa that the Dent brothers
obtained many of the castle's most prized possessions.

Whittington Court ☆

4½ m E Cheltenham, just off A40 on road
to village; garden; *open:* 4 weeks in Apr and
Aug, 2–5; tel: 0242 820218

Whittington is an intriguingly lop-sided house, as if an E-shaped Elizabethan
mansion had been chopped in half. Nobody knows whether the missing west
end fell down or was never built, but what is left combines a gabled remnant
of the 1580s with a more expansive Jacobean wing. To one side are mellow
farm buildings, which include a lichen-spotted 17th-century barn. A tiny,

originally Norman church stands just feet away on the other, and two arms of a former moat are weedy ditches in the garden. Inside, generous stone-mullioned windows light comfortable, lived-in rooms. The oak staircase of 1657 still has its original dog-gate, three classical stone chimney-pieces are features of the Jacobean wing, and the now-subdivided long gallery looking out over the church is approached through a pair of grand classical arches with massive keystones that are much too self-important for such a modest place. The owners and their family stand in each of the rooms shown, bombarding visitors with information.

Woodchester Park Mansion ☆

5 m SW Stroud, off B4066 at minor road to Nympsfield, use public car park for Nympsfield long barrow and Coaley Peak; optional guided tour (c. 60 mins); refreshments; open: Apr–Oct, 1st wkend in month and BH Sat, Sun, Mon, 11–4; tel: 0453 860531

A minibus shuttles visitors to the mansion from the Nympsfield road, but it is more exciting to walk. From the ivy-smothered gates, a narrow muddy track plunges into a deep wooded valley. After a mile or so, the trees fall back round a sweep of rough pasture, and there, tucked right against the valley wall, appear the gabled façades and glassless windows of one of the strangest houses in England. The dream of the eccentric and ardently Catholic William Leigh, who had the place designed as a kind of domestic monastery, round a courtyard, Woodchester was begun in 1856, but abandoned, unfinished, ten years later.

It is still as it was then, its fascination stemming partly from incompleteness, partly from the idiosyncratic gothic designs of the 21-year-old architect, Benjamin Bucknall, pupil of Charles Hansom, who made everything he could – fireplaces, door surrounds, skirting, gutters and even the bath – of creamy Cotswold stone. The west front, seen first, is unexceptional, but round the corner is a show of huge mullioned and transomed windows, aggressive gargoyles, and closely-set buttresses. The east range is dominated by the chapel, with its flamboyant tracery, and gutters in the courtyard are supported by fluttering stone owls.

Inside, while fireplaces and door frames are in place, floors are still missing, walls are unplastered, and visitors can look up 50 ft to the timbers of the roof. More eerie is the sense the workmen have only just gone: 19th-century scaffolding is still in place, and a 30-ft ladder leans against a wall. Stone vaulting was planned for all the principal rooms, but only the ceilings of the drawing-room and chapel were ever completed, the latter with beautifully carved bosses pinning the delicate ribs.

The mansion is slowly being restored, but expect windows to be boarded up and floors inches deep in bird droppings. Much of the servants' wing is now given over to colonies of bats, which emerge at night to feed on the insects of the pastures.

Hereford and Worcester

Berrington Hall ☆

3 m N Leominster, on W side A49; NT;
tearoom; walled and woodland garden;
open: Apr–end Oct, daily, except Mon
and Tues (open BH Mon, closed Gd Fri),
1.30–5.30 (4.30 Oct); tel: 0568 615721

A four-square, compact Georgian mansion faced in dull red sandstone, Berrington was built between 1778 and 1783 by Henry Holland, Capability Brown's son-in-law, for Thomas Harley, who made a fortune supplying the British army with pay and clothing. Sold by Harley's descendant, the 7th Lord Rodney, in 1901, Berrington was then owned by the Cawley family until it came to the Trust in 1957. Few of the original contents are still here, and, more than many Trust properties, it has the feel of a museum piece. Apart from the well-stocked laundry room and the prettily tiled dairy in the stable yard, it is also something of a connoisseur's house, with features of primarily specialist interest.

One of Berrington's main attractions is Holland's lavish internal decoration, from the black, white and green-grey marble flooring the entrance hall and panelled doors of Spanish mahogany to the azure blue scagliola columns in the boudoir and the light-hearted lantern lighting the staircase. All the principal rooms are adorned with pastel-coloured Adamesque plasterwork, and with medallion paintings and grisaille panels by Biagio Rebecca, whose pink-tinged banquet of the gods in the dining-room has the deities feasting at a cloud-borne, curiously empty table.

In contrast with this Georgian elegance, much of the furniture is French, from a collection with no connections with the house. Thus, the white panelled, stiffly arranged drawing-room displays inlaid, serpentine-fronted, Louis XV commodes, a French piano of *c.*1900, and a boulle writing desk. Berrington's former owners are glimpsed only occasionally. The dining-room is hung with Luny's action-packed paintings of Admiral Rodney's great sea-battles, and portraits and other mementoes in the two modest rooms devoted to the Cawley family include a poignant 1908 photograph of the 1st Lord Cawley setting off for the hunt with his four sons, three of whom were to lose their lives in World War I.

Burton Court

3 m W Leominster, signposted from A44;
tearoom; tiny garden; *open:* late May BH to
end Sept, Wed, Thurs, Sat, Sun, BH Mon
2.30–6; tel: 054 47 231

This lived-in, family house on the site of an ancient manor is primarily a Regency villa with later alterations, notably the Tudor-style entrance front with a bold, two-storey stone porch that was added by Sir Clough

Williams-Ellis in 1912. Behind is Burton Court's one surprise: a medieval great hall, rising to an early 14th-century timber roof and with a carved Jacobean overmantel of 1654. This room, like most of the others on show, is used to exhibit items from the present owner's costume collection, embracing oriental as well as Regency and Victorian dress. There is little to excite a visitor who is not interested in these displays.

Croft Castle ☆

5 m NW Leominster, signposted from A49 and A4110; NT; park walks; *open:* Easter Sat–Mon, May–end Sept, Wed–Sun and BH Mon 2–6, also wkends in Apr and Oct, 2–5; tel: 056 885 246

Croft Castle stands in the glorious country of the Welsh Borders below a 1000-ft ridge crowned by an Iron Age hillfort. Built as a hollow square, with walls of rough weathered stone and slender corner turrets, Croft dates back to the 14th and 15th centuries, but has been much altered since. Massive remodelling in the 18th century, notably by Thomas Farnolls Pritchard, gave the castle its symmetrical Georgian south front, the delightful gothick bays flanking the entrance and its civilized interiors, while earlier improvements account for some Jacobean stone-mullioned windows. A tiny Tudor church standing only yards away is treated like an unusual garden building, with a girdle of lavender and roses.

The tour takes in the panelled hall, a 1913 dining-room in classical style, and the sparsely furnished Georgian reception rooms. Sadly, much of Pritchard's decorative detail has been lost, but there are still a couple of fluid plasterwork ceilings, some 18th-century panelling, and the enchanting coffee and white gothick staircase, with cluster columns for newel posts and crocketed arches outlined in plaster on the walls. A mix of furniture ranges from early oak tables and chairs in the hall to fine William and Mary walnut pieces, such as an oyster-veneered work box on barley-sugar legs, and the spiky gothick chairs in the gallery-like corridor framing the courtyard. A small show of family portraits includes an early, russet-toned Gainsborough of the sweet-faced girl who married the 3rd Baronet, a brace of de Laszlos, an Arthur Devis of a very English couple out for a stroll by the River Hoogly in India, and some works by Lawrence, who was a close friend of a Croft cousin.

Dinmore Manor

S of Hope under Dinmore, 6 m N Hereford, signposted off A49; garden; *open:* all year, daily, 9.30–5.30; tel: 0432 71322

Come here to enjoy Dinmore's setting, high above a deep wooded valley, and the panoramic views, but have no expectations of the house. There was a medieval monastery here, but the cloisters embracing the garden, with virulent stained glass in the traceried windows, date only from the 1930s, as does the pastiche of a galleried medieval hall. Nothing else of the rambling gabled manor is shown; of much greater interest is the simple, rough-walled, 14th-century chapel in the garden.

Eastnor Castle ☆☆

On A438, Hereford–Tewkesbury road, 2 m E Ledbury; tearoom; grounds and deer park; *open:* Easter–end Sept, Sun, BH Mon, also Mon–Fri in Aug, 12–5; tel: 0531 633160

Eastnor is an early 19th-century vision of a medieval castle, built by Robert Smirke for the 1st Earl Somers and dramatically sited above a deep valley, with views to the Malvern hills. Battlemented walls with strongly projecting corner turrets trace out a square building of vast proportions, with a stubby tower rising from the centre like a truncated cathedral spire and a huge *porte-cochère* half filling the gravelled forecourt. The lichen-streaked yellow-grey stone is softened by a blanket of Virginia creeper, fiery red in autumn, but even so only a megalomaniac could have dreamt up such a place.

The cavernous state rooms, with decorative schemes of the 1840s and '60s by the arch-gothicist Augustus Welby Pugin and the lesser-known George Fox, more than match the promise of the exterior. The great hall rising 60 ft into the tower is furnished as a comfortable Edwardian drawing-room, but the low lamps, grand piano and deep red sofas cannot overcome the pervading chill, the painted walls, marbled columns, and round-headed arches suggesting the castle has swallowed a romanesque basilica. Lavish decoration reaches a climax in Pugin's drawing-room. A family tree is painted above the fireplace, the blue and gold arch of the ceiling springs from a burst of gilded fan vaulting, heavy gold pendants hang like stalactites, and Pugin's heavy and uncomfortable gothic furniture is set off by richly coloured, 17th-century Brussels tapestries. The 63 ft library is similarly rich, with Flemish tapestries hanging above bookcases of Italian walnut inlaid with box.

Although what is on show has been thinned by death duties over the years, there is still a notable collection of armour, and some splendid paintings, including Romney's portrait of Sir Charles Cocks, 1st Baron Somers, with his drink-swollen nose, the same artist's picture of the languid 1st Earl, builder of the castle, and works by Kneller, Lely and Michael Dahl, and by the family's close friend G. F. Watts, whose full-length portrait of the 3rd Countess is a study in grey. Some of the most interesting pictures alas, not easy to see, hang in the cold state bedroom, among them an action-packed Last Supper attributed to Jacopo Bassano, and a baptism ascribed to Tintoretto.

Elgar's Birthplace ☆

Broadheath, 3 m W Worcester, off A44; garden; parking at Plough Inn; *open:* May–Sept, daily, except Wed, 10.30–6, Oct–Apr, 1.30–4.30, closed mid Jan–mid Feb; tel: 0905 333224

This tiny, red-brick cottage with views to the Malvern Hills is the place, above all others, which influenced the music of Edward Elgar. The composer was born here in 1856, on a day when the 'bees were humming, and all the earth was lovely', and although the family moved back to Worcester when he was two, to be near his father's expanding music shop, they continued to come to Broadheath for the summer.

Three minute rooms and a broad landing are packed with exhibits illustrating the great man's professional and private life, from manuscripts and corrected proofs of his works to photographs of his beloved dogs and sketches drawn to amuse his daughter, among them a pipe-smoking dragon. His desk is here, and such things as the baton with which he conducted the first performance of *The Apostles*; his music is a constant background, and in the garden is his octagonal thatched summerhouse, brought here from his last home.

Hanbury Hall

4½ m E Droitwich, 1 m N B4090, 1½ m W B4091; NT; tearoom; garden; *open:* Apr–end Oct, Sat, Sun, Mon 2–6; tel: 0527 821214

This serene house, with long sash windows in brick and stone façades and a jaunty cupola crowning the hipped roof, is one of the most satisfying of buildings. Built by the barrister Thomas Vernon towards the end of the 17th century, it is typical of those thrown up by the gentry all over England after the Restoration of Charles II. Sadly, the interior does not match the promise of the outside. Many of the original furnishings have gone, the few rooms shown being largely fitted out from bequests, and Hanbury is also being used for the Trust's experiment with corporate entertaining, with little tables arranged in what was the drawing-room.

Then, Hanbury's showpiece, the grand staircase painted by James Thornhill in 1710, is something of an acquired taste. Drawing the eye up from the monochrome gloom of the entrance hall, with its dark brown panelling and *trompe l'oeil* ceiling domes, the stair glows with colour and imagination, but the baroque treatment, with a confusion of deities on the ceiling and the story of Achilles round the walls, is very much of its time. There are more ceiling paintings in the showy dining-room, where Vernon portraits are hung thickly against yellow damask and where a robust Victorian table – for the entertaining – shows off the family dinner service. Most satisfying is a white-panelled bedroom, furnished with walnut and marquetry pieces and hung with 17th-century Dutch and English flower paintings.

Harvington Hall ☆

3 m SE Kidderminster, ¹/₂ m from junction A448 and A450; teas; garden; *open:* Mar–end Oct, daily, except Gd Fri, 11.30–5.30; tel: 0562 777 267

Narrow lanes lead to this picturesque, red-brick manor squashed into a corner of a grassy, moated island. A remnant of a quadrangular Elizabethan house, Harvington partly surrounds a tiny courtyard, with a low gatehouse range separating the compact north tower, rebuilt in *c.*1756, from the many gabled, L-shaped main block, with its sandstone-mullioned windows and soaring chimneys. Although long unlived in, the dusty rooms on show either bare or very sparsely furnished, this is an atmospheric place. Once owned by the Roman Catholic Pakingtons, who housed their priests here, it is full of ingenious hiding places from the era of religious persecution, the best of them thought to be by the renowned Jesuit builder Nicholas Owen, while past neglect has preserved Elizabethan wall paintings and other original features.

Visitors see all three floors of the main block, a warren of little rooms divided by lath-and-timber partitions, with walls and ceilings pulled out of shape, and confusingly varied floor levels. Former family rooms on the first floor, including a barrel-ceilinged withdrawing-room, boast Elizabethan panelling and some pieces of original furniture, but the best of Harvington is on the third floor. Here, under the roof, are two chapels, the walls of the smaller running with red and white tears symbolizing the blood and water of the Passion, the larger with a hide where vestments and altar plate could be bundled away. In a closet-like room reached by its own flight of steps is Owen's most ingenious hide, with an entrance only 10¹/₂ in wide behind a pivoting beam.

Hellen's ☆

Opposite church in Much Marcle village, off A449, Ross-Ledbury road; guided tours (*c.*90 mins); *open:* Easter–early Oct, Wed, Sat, Sun, BH Mon 2–6; tel: 0531 84440

This remote, unspoilt house is a modest, T-shaped brick manor, all that remains of a once larger building, with a cobbled courtyard folded between a stubby, mid-15th-century range and a longer Charles I wing. An angular staircase turret projects into the courtyard, and a splendid octagonal brick dovecote in the garden is emblazoned with its date, 1641, and the initials of its builders. There have been some alterations since the Civil War, with a few Georgian sashes inserted among the diamond-paned, stone-mullioned windows, but Hellen's escaped any drastic 19th-century improvements.

More than this, apart from the decades either side of World War II, the house has been lived in by descendants of the original builder, and is rich in family stories. Here, Roger Mortimer, murderer of Edward II, is said to have brought the beautiful French queen with whom he hoped to seize the Crown, imprisoning the king in nearby *Berkeley Castle* a few days later; here, the story goes, a Catholic monk sheltered by the family was chased from room to room by Cromwell's men, to be cornered and murdered in the chamber that had been decorated, a century earlier, for a visit by the Catholic Mary Tudor; and a Hellen's daughter who became lady-in-waiting to Charles II's shy young queen, Catherine of Braganza, was given the seductive portrait that is said to have persuaded the king to commit himself, and that now hangs, appropriately enough, on walls hung with gilded Spanish leather.

Intimate panelled rooms in the Jacobean wing, one of them lit by mirrored, silver sconces, contrast with the rough-walled galleried hall in the medieval remnant, with a huge, hooded fireplace. Upstairs, visitors are shown sad Hetty's room, where a child of a much later generation was locked up for 30 years after returning in disgrace from an unsuitable elopement; a rope to the bellcote on the roof goes up through the ceiling, and the French silk coverlet on the four-poster is embroidered with delicate wild flowers.

Kinnersley Castle

4 m W Weobley, on A4112; guided tour (*c.*35 mins); *open:* Aug, daily, except Tues, 2–4, and some other days in season; tel: 0544 327407

This L-shaped, gabled Elizabethan house of rough red sandstone with small-paned, stone-mullioned windows and massive Tudor chimneys is built round a five-storey medieval tower, possibly a remnant of an earlier quadrangular building. Although once again in private hands after many years as a home for the elderly, Kinnersley still has an institutional feel, and the drab, sparsely furnished interior is of interest only for its original fittings. There is a splendid plaster ceiling in the former solar, and some equally fine overmantels and panelling, while the staircase in the tower has a rare tailor's table at the top, built to make use of the drop over the upper flight. The guided tour takes in rooms on all three floors and ends with an optional climb to the roof, from where it is just possible to make out the faint outlines of a former moat.

Little Malvern Court

Little Malvern, 3 m S Great Malvern, on A4104, no advance signs; guided tour (*c.*35 mins); garden; *open:* late Apr–late Jul, Wed, Thurs 2.15–5; tel: 0684 892988

Looking east over the Severn, with the wooded slopes of the Malvern hills swelling up behind, is a little group of buildings marking the site of a medieval Benedictine priory. The red-tiled house, with silvery, half-timbered gable ends attached to congenial 18th- and 19th-century extensions, developed from what was the monk's refectory. Close by is the buttressed tower of the priory church, and the garden running along the contours of the hill is laid out round a chain of former stew ponds.

Sadly, what is on show does not live up to the promise of the setting. A stunningly concise tour concentrates on the first-floor hall that was the refectory. Although much altered, this spacious room still has its original 14th-century roof timbers, is appropriately furnished with some 17th-century pieces and hung with a few interesting paintings, notably Paul Delaroche's sombre *Lord Strafford on His Way to Execution*, with the disembodied hands of Archbishop Laud coming through a window to bless the doomed figure kneeling below. Otherwise, there is a glimpse into a chapel created in a gable end and of the neo-Jacobean dining-room in the addition by Joseph Hansom, he of the cab.

Lower Brockhampton ☆

2 m E Bromyard, on A 44 Worcester road; NT; estate walks; *open:* Apr–end Oct, Wed–Sun and BH Mon (closed Gd Fri), 10–5 (4 in Oct); tel: 0885 488099

A single-track road plunges ever downwards through the Brockhampton estate to this seductive, half-timbered, late 14th-century manor-house set on

a moated grassy island in the depths of the valley. Its timbers, cut from the oak woods that still flourish all around, are silvery with age, tall chimney stacks rise above an undulating roof, and a timbered gatehouse, its upper floor jettied out over the lower, straddles the moat at a drunken angle. Inside, visitors see the roughly furnished, stone-floored, galleried great hall rising to the roof and a 17th-century parlour, and there are the ruins of a medieval stone-built chapel to the north of the moat. Those who take the park walk will see the red-brick Georgian house on the shoulder of the valley which replaced the manor.

Moccas Court ☆

13 m W Hereford, on S bank of Wye, approached from B4352; gardens; river walk; *open:* Apr–Sept, Sun 2–6; tel: 098 17 381

Set in a sublime park on the banks of the Wye, with grassy terraces falling to the river, is an austere red-brick box built in 1775–81 by the local architect Anthony Keck. Inside, a couple of well-proportioned reception rooms with restrained Georgian decoration are a prelude to an enchanting circular drawing-room based on designs by Robert Adam that fills a bow on the river front, its walls hung with delicately painted French wallpaper, the ceiling gently domed and the inlaid mahogany doors, the overmantel mirror and the floor-length windows all following the curve of the room. As impressive is the top-lit, oval stairwell rising through the centre of the building. The drawing-room is shown empty, and the sympathetic furnishings elsewhere were introduced by the present owner, who has restored both house and park.

Sufton Court

4 m E Hereford off B4224, just N Mordiford on road to Dormington; guided tour (*c.* 40 mins); *open:* 14 days in May and latter half of Aug, 2–5.30; tel: 0432 870268

Set high above the Wye valley, with panoramic views over the river and into Wales, is a severe classical box built by James Wyatt in the 1790s. The old house which he replaced still sits further up the valley, tucked under the hill. The owners' informal tour takes in a few airy, high-ceilinged ground-floor rooms, with restrained classical decoration. Most of the furniture from the old house has gone, but there is some Georgian silver and a Spode dinner service to be seen, and there is a show of accomplished watercolours of the Mediterranean and elsewhere by a 19th-century member of the family.

Witley Court

10 m NW Worcester on A443; EH; *open:* all year, summer, daily, 10–6, winter, Tues–Sun, 10–4; tel: 0299 896636

A rough, unmade-up road leads to the ghost of a grandiose Italianate

Victorian mansion, its vast rooms now filled with weeds and saplings, and a grassy ramp where once there were steps. Giant, columned porticoes by John Nash dominate the principal façades, one looking on to the entrance court, the other staring out over the shadow of a formal garden, where there are still domed temples and an immense sculptural fountain. Rising over the house, and half-embedded within it, is a baroque church, with gilded plasterwork framing ceiling paintings by Antonio Bellucci and stained-glass windows brought here from the demolished palace of the 1st Duke of Chandos. The organ case, too, came from the Duke's chapel, but the instrument on which Handel played, and for which he composed his Chandos anthems, was rebuilt in the 19th century.

Shropshire

Acton Round Hall ☆

Just W Acton Round village, 6 m NW Bridgnorth, no advance signs; garden; guided tours (c. 45 mins); *open:* May–Aug, Thurs 2.30–5.30; tel: 074631 203

Set high on the hill above Acton Round village is this dignified, four-square early 18th-century house by the Smith brothers of Warwick, with dormer windows in a steep hipped roof and stone pilasters and pedimented doorways against brick façades. Largely uninhabited for 200 years, the house is little altered, with well-proportioned panelled rooms leading off a stone-floored hall.

The interior may come as a surprise. The setting is 18th-century, but the contents reflect the enthusiasms of the present owner, whose tastes are individual. The hall is ringed with ceremonial halberds and suits of armour, while a stuffed monkey clings to the chandelier overhead. Tusked and antlered heads line the stairs, one of them swinging open to reveal a drinks cabinet, and a soft-eyed giraffe peers down from the upper landing. There is much for lovers of kitsch to enjoy, such as a parody of an 18th-century console table carved with grinning devilish faces, like a prop from a Ken Russell film. The owner's highly personal tour also takes in a splendid William and Mary state bed, and there are a number of fine 18th-century French clocks.

Attingham Park ☆

4 m SE Shrewsbury, on N side of old A5, now B4380; NT; tearoom; park walks; *open:* early Apr–end Sept, Sat–Wed, 1.30–5, BH Mon 11–5, Oct, Sat, Sun, 1.30–5; tel: 074 377 203

Attingham's immense 400-ft, grey-stone frontage, with curving colonnades running out from a three-storey central block to pavilions either side, was designed to look good from the bridge across the River Tern half a mile away, and to conceal the old brick house left standing behind. Designed in 1782 by George Steuart for the 1st Lord Berwick, this south façade is an austere classical composition, ornamented only with a giant portico and plain pilasters.

Despite later changes by Nash, the interior is still largely as devised by Steuart, with a set of 'masculine' apartments on the west side, most of them decorated in rich deep reds, balanced by a corresponding suite of 'feminine' rooms to the east, with delicate 18th-century plasterwork and painted decoration, and a predominance of pastel colours. Sadly, most of the original furnishings went in a 16-day sale in 1827, and the largely Regency pieces here now reflect the Italianate tastes of the 3rd Lord, who was ambassador in Naples. Similarly, the paintings are a mixed bag, with some works of character among the rump of the 2nd Lord's great collection.

Attingham is a connoisseur's house, appealing to a range of specialist interests. There are important examples of the work of Angelica Kauffmann, from marble plaques and ceiling roundels based on her designs to the three paintings dominating the drawing-room, one of them a rather moody portrait of the 2nd Lord, the other two strongly coloured mythological subjects. There is some exquisite decorative detail, including a painted circular boudoir and a floor inlaid with rosewood, satinwood and mahogany; and a display of mostly late 18th- and 19th-century family silver, with several pieces by Paul Storr, can be seen in the bowels of the building. Although the best of the paintings have gone, the toplit red-walled picture gallery, added on by Nash in 1805–7, still has Mediterranean landscapes by the Italophile Jacob Philipp Hackert, one of them showing the partially excavated ruins of Pompeii, and the Dutch painter Schalken's dramatic, candlelit portrait of William III, while elsewhere you can see Salvator Rosa's *Christ and the Money Changers*, and Sickert's shimmering blue portrait of the 8th Lady Berwick.

Benthall Hall ☆

Off B4375, 1 m NW Broseley, 4 m NE Much Wenlock; NT; garden; *open:* Apr–end Sept, Wed, Sun and BH Mon 1.30–5.30; tel: 0952 882159

The Benthall family's modest Elizabethan house still looks as it did in the 16th century, with stone-mullioned windows in a gabled and bayed sandstone frontage, and a show of moulded brick chimneys. Inside, comfortable, lived-in rooms are lined with Jacobean panelling and furnished with a mix of 17th- and 18th-century pieces, only a few of which are original to the house. A Jacobean staircase carved with the leopard and lion of the Benthall crest leads up to an airy first-floor sitting-room in what was the great chamber, but the high point of the short tour is the pink and dove-grey sitting-room on the south-west corner of the house, where ornate carved panelling is matched by an extravagant plaster ceiling and a frieze of improbable animals. Mostly 20th-century family portraits include works by Glyn Philpot, and there are examples of local pottery, including the blue and white imitation Willow Pattern made at the 18th-century Caughley works.

Boscobel House

8 m NW Wolverhampton, on unclassified road between A41 and A5; EH; $^1/_2$-hourly guided tours during most of day; tearoom; garden; *open:* summer, daily, 10–6, winter (closed Jan), Tues–Sun 10–4; tel: 0902 850244

Boscobel is the best-known of the houses that sheltered Charles II after the rout of his army at Worcester in 1651, but do not expect to find much of the 17th century here. The three-storey, half-timbered hunting lodge which Charles saw became a farm and is much altered, with stucco hiding the Jacobean half-timbering and sashes with traceried glazing replacing the original casements. And it is now presented as it was in the 19th century, when the Evans family restored it in a romantic antiquarian style. So, the panelled parlour is furnished with a cloth-covered table, potted plants and a chintzy *chaise-longue* and settee, and there are Victorian grates and washstands in the bedrooms. Outside is a picturesque cobbled farmyard, surrounded by mostly 19th-century brick buildings.

Boscobel must be taken as it is. It sits high, with panoramic views west to the Clee Hills, and with imagination the well-wooded, quietly rural landscape can be turned into the forest Charles saw. Most atmospheric is the bare-floored attic where he is said to have paced up and down, watching anxiously for traffic on the road, while in a field a few yards beyond the garden is a ragged oak, said to be a descendant of the one in which he hid.

Dudmaston ☆

4 m SE Bridgnorth, on A442; NT; tearoom; garden and lakeside walk; *open:* Apr–end Sept, Wed, Sun 2.30–6; tel: 0746 780866

Gloriously set, with grassy terraces falling to a long lake and views to rolling hills, Dudmaston is an undistinguished mongrel of a house. Originally an assured brick mansion built between 1695 and 1701 by Sir Thomas Wolryche, whose descendant, Lady Rachel Labouchere, still lives here, its classical lines have been marred by unsympathetic alterations in the 1820s, and by the heightening of the south wing some ten years later. Visitors anticipating the usual National Trust experience must adjust their expectations too. There is a fine portrait-hung panelled hall, furnished with 17th-century walnut chairs and a long oak and elm refectory table, and an elegant airy library on the west front is shown as a comfortable sitting-room, with glowing Dutch flower paintings on the walls and soft green and pink upholstery. But most of the rooms shown are either picture galleries or devoted to wordy displays on the Darbys of Coalbrookdale, the father of computing, Charles Babbage, and the naturalist and photographer Frances Pitt, all of whom are connected to the family.

Then, too, the art collection is focused on 20th-century sculpture and largely abstract paintings – all doodles, blobs and angular constructions – bought by Sir George Labouchere since the 1950s, many of them by artists he knew personally and acquired on his diplomatic postings. A stint in Madrid is reflected in a sombre group of Spanish paintings, including a couple of works by the Catalan Tàpies, while the bow-windowed former dining-room and an adjoining panelled closet show off a Kandinsky doodle painting, a couple of geometric Ben Nicholsons, a spiky bull drawn by Lynn Chadwick, and small bronzes by Hepworth and Henry Moore. Here again, colours are muted. The only gaiety is in an impressionist pastel by Guillaumin and an expressive Matisse of the head of a girl, and in Arp's relief of a seductive pair of lips in the library. There is a room devoted to meticulously observed botanical paintings, from the work of Redouté and Ehret to Mary Grierson and Pandora Sellars, and another hung with 18th- and 19th-century topographical watercolours, among them two strongly coloured cameos by Edward Lear and some pictures of places in Shropshire, including a painting of Dudmaston by Moses Griffith, and works by Devis and Sandby.

The Moat House

8 m S Shrewsbury, E side Longnor village, access lane signed on open days; guided tour (c. 45 mins); *open:* Apr–Sept, Thurs, late May and Aug BH Mon, 2.30–5; tel: 0743 718434

This modest, half-timbered house dating from c. 1390 sits on a grassy, moated island dotted with the humps and bumps of former outbuildings. The owners' enthusiastic guided tour concentrates on the building and its history, with much of the time spent looking round the outside. Notable features include ancient silvery beams honeycombed with death-watch beetle, an original wood-mullioned window, the great limestone chimney stack put in in Elizabethan times, when the hall was floored over, and the decorative timber roof that now graces an upper room, with rare carved wooden masks that are thought to represent the builder and his wife.

Shipton Hall ☆

In Shipton, 6 m SW Much Wenlock, at junction of B4376 and B4368; guided tour (c. 30 mins); garden; open: Easter-end Sept, Thurs, BH Sun and Mon 2.30–5.30; tel: 074 636 225

A gabled Elizabethan manor of local stone with moulded brick chimneys, Shipton Hall sits in a natural hollow high above a walled and terraced forecourt, with a medieval dovecote perched above the house and a pedimented stable block further down the hill. A four-storey tower like a truncated campanile marks the curiously off-centre porch, and round the back, looking on to a trio of Elizabethan fish tanks, is a Georgian extension of 1769 by Thomas Farnolls Pritchard, who also gentrified much of the old house.

Visitors see some half-dozen, lived-in rooms on two floors, with some original oak panelling and a few leaded Tudor windows among the later sashes. The hall and staircase, decorated with rococo plasterwork, are all Pritchard, the first with an innovative firebox made at Ironbridge and busts in broken pediments over the doors, the latter with a large gothick window looking north up the hill. A dining-room made out of the old kitchen is lined with panelling brought from elsewhere, a rose-pink drawing-room running out into a deep bay has a show of florid Continental porcelain, and the wooden overmantel in the Georgian library-cum-music-room is carved on one side with a pile of books, on the other with a lyre and flute. All rooms on the front of the house look out over unspoilt rolling countryside, with just one half-timbered house marking the site of old Shipton village, moved so as not to spoil the view.

Stokesay Castle ☆

1 m S Craven Arms, off A49; EH; refreshments; garden; open: summer, daily, 10–6, winter, Wed–Sun, 10–4; tel: 0588 672544

Just off the busy A49, in a green valley framed by wooded ridges, is a unique survival, a fortified 13th-century manor. Guarding the approach across a now-grassy moat is a half-timbered, Elizabethan gatehouse, its upper floors jettied out over the lower, and decorative carving around the archway and on the corner posts. Beyond, a grassy courtyard fronts the main house, with a gabled and buttressed hall and solar range sandwiched between two towers. That to the north, with its lancet windows and battlements, looks properly defensive, but the south tower, a warren of little rooms stacked one on another, has a homely, half-timbered top storey carried out over the moat on wooden brackets.

Built by Lawrence of Ludlow, a wealthy wool merchant, who bought the property in 1281, Stokesay has been little changed, apart from some sympathetic 19th-century and later restoration to repair decades of neglect. Visitors can wander through the unfurnished, rough-walled rooms of the main building, one floored with medieval tiles, another with a hooded 13th-century fireplace. The 52 ft hall rising to a medieval timber roof is seen in the dim light filtering through crudely shuttered, unglazed windows, with birds darting in and out. Only the solar, with its richly carved Flemish overmantel and 17th-century panelling, suggests any degree of comfort.

Upton Cressett Hall

4 m W Bridgnorth, signed off A458 just S Morville; guided tours (c. 40 mins); garden; *open:* May–end Sept, Thurs, 2.30–5; tel: 074 631 307

The narrowest of lanes runs two miles or so west from the Bridgnorth road to an isolated clutch of buildings set high on the side of a steep-sided valley. Two banks of twisted brick chimneys, first seen silhouetted against the sky, mark the hall itself, with a long gabled frontage of diapered red brick looking east over the combe. Across a stretch of turf, its archway lined up with the front door, is a gabled and turreted brick gatehouse, while just to the north, on the other side of a deep grassy ditch marking the former moat, is a tiny Norman church of rough, warm sandstone, with a medieval oak porch, weatherboarded bellcote and richly-carved chancel arch. Originally a 14th-century timber-framed manor, the hall was extended in the 15th century and remodelled and encased in brick in Elizabethan times, when the gatehouse was built. Now partly demolished, it consists of a truncated great hall wing attached to a long cross range; some windows are the old stone mullions but many have been altered, and the south front, facing the gatehouse, has been given Georgian sashes and a classical front door.

Visitors see all three floors of the gatehouse, where some Elizabethan plasterwork ceilings and overmantels survive, and four lived-in, sympathetically furnished rooms in the main house. The kitchen has a 13-foot fireplace, the drawing-room boasts 16th-century panelling, while upstairs, reached by a warped Tudor stair of solid oak, is the upper half of the medieval great hall, open to the roof and spanned by massive timber arches.

Walcot Hall

Unmarked drive goes off S from B4385 by Powis Arms pub on E edge of Lydbury North, 3 m SE Bishop's Castle; *open:* BHs in season, May, Sun, Wed, Fri; Jun, Wed, Fri; July and Aug, Sun; Sept, Wed, 2.15–4.30; tel: none

A long lime avenue leads up to this austere, porticoed, red-brick house looking out over a lake to the whale-back hump of the Long Mynd. Walcot owes its classical simplicity to Sir William Chambers, who remodelled an existing house in 1760 for Clive of India. Alas, the interior has been much altered since, and the Clive family paintings and furniture removed to *Powis Castle.* Alas, too, the ground-floor rooms shown by the present owners are offered without a word of explanation. The 18th-century-style staircase is a modern pastiche, the oak panelling in the library is also 20th-century, but the sunny cluttered drawing-room on the south-east corner of the house still has its original Chambers plaster ceiling, picked out in white and pale green, while across the paved courtyard, no longer attached to the rest of the building, stands the cavernous ballroom built by Clive's son.

Weston Park ☆☆

On A5 at Weston under Lizard, 3 m N M54, Junction 3; tearoom; gardens; park; *open*: Easter week, May–mid June and early Sept, Sat, Sun, mid June–end Aug, daily, except Mon, Fri (daily in Aug), 1–5; tel: 095276 207

Seat of the Bridgeman family, Earls of Bradford, this dignified brick and stone Restoration house with panoramic views south over the rolling Shropshire countryside is the centrepiece of a 1,000-acre landscape park, with a wooded lake behind the house focused on James Paine's Palladian bridge and a vista along the ha-ha to his Temple of Diana. The mansion itself was designed in 1671 by the then mistress of the house, Lady Wilbraham, who gave Weston its show front, with gently curving pediments over the end bays and a stone centrepiece.

Visitors do a circuit of eight or so rooms on the ground floor, all of which were extensively remodelled in the 18th century and again between 1860 and 1890 by the 3rd Earl, who roofed over an internal courtyard and moved the entrance from south to east. An ugly Victorian *porte-cochère* opens into the elegant classical hall that was once the library, the horse paintings by Ferneley here heralding the outstanding art collection for which the interior was substantially re-arranged in recent years.

A classical, apse-ended drawing-room shows off a quartet of Lely beauties, among them a painting of Lady Wilbraham herself, whose satin dress inspired the fresh green and white colouring of the room. To one side is the comfortable, tobacco-tinged Victorian library, with portraits by Constable, Romney, Reynolds and Hoppner above the bookcases and Riley's painting of the wily, saturnine Sir Orlando Bridgeman, Charles II's Keeper of the Privy Seal, over the fireplace. To the other is the formal French sitting-room created by the 3rd Earl, its walls hung with late-18th-century rose-pink Gobelins tapestries that were originally made for a bedroom, and for which the doorcases here have had to be altered. The toplit billiard and smoking rooms with which the 3rd Earl covered the courtyard are now devoted to a gallery-like show of Dutch cabinet pictures and Italian works, among them a splendid two-dimensional council of war by Leandro Bassano, seascapes by Vernet, a dramatic Salvator Rosa landscape and Gerrit Dou's tiny portrait of an old woman with an hour glass. There is a Stubbs here too, and the lofty Victorian dining-room with portraits hung against pink silk damask shows off Van Dyck's painting of Sir Thomas Hanmer, thought by the diarist John Evelyn to be one of the Dutchman's finest works.

The star of the collection, Holbein's portrait of the smooth-faced Sir George Carew, who went down with the *Mary Rose*, is one of a show of early portraits in the little breakfast room that ends the tour, other notable paintings here including works by Mor, Clouet, Van Somer and Johnson, and a bullish head by Thomas de Keyser that is thought to be a portrait of the influential Dutch theologian Hugo Grotius. More prosaic treasures include gossipy, indiscreet letters written by the septuagenarian Disraeli to the 3rd Countess of Bradford, referring to Queen Victoria as 'The Faery', and the stuffed remains of the yellow parrot which he gave to the countess and which performed the extraordinary feat of producing an egg a day for 23 days before expiring on the 24th.

Wilderhope Manor

7 m SW Much Wenlock, $\frac{1}{2}$ m S B4371; NT; waymarked walks; *open:* Apr–end Sept, Wed and Sat, 2–4.30; Oct–Mar, Sat only 2–4.30; tel: 069 43 363

This tall, gabled house of rough local limestone dug into the south-facing slope of a secluded Shropshire valley was built in the late 16th century, possibly by the same mason as the nearby *Shipton Hall*. Large mullioned and transomed windows look out across the valley, banks of red-brick Elizabethan chimneys rise above the lichen-yellow roof, and a little pediment floats above the projecting porch. Inside are stone fireplaces, old plank doors, an original spiral stair, each tread a solid block of wood, and four ornamental plasterwork ceilings, where a variety of stylized motifs, haphazardly arranged as if by an uncomprehending child, include the initials ES and FS for the builders Francis and Ellen Smallwood. What was the great hall, with a huge 18-light window, has the only surviving Elizabethan fitting, a rack for 13 bows, over the fireplace. Otherwise, the place is now a youth hostel, fitted with bunk beds and other functional furnishings.

North-west England

Cumbria, Greater Manchester, Lancashire, Merseyside

Naworth Castle ●

Carlisle

A69

A595

A6

● Hutton-in-the-Forest

Cockermouth

Penrith

● Mirehouse

Keswick

● Dalemain

A66

Whitehaven

A66

Cumbria

A591

M6

A685

Dove Cottage ● ● Rydal Mount

● Townend

Brantwood

Windermere

Muncaster Castle ● ● Hill Top

Kendal

Sizergh Castle ●

● Levens Hall

A590

Kirkby Lonsdale

Holker Hall ●

● Leighton Hall

Morecambe

Lancaster

A6

Lancs

Browsholme Hall ●

● Chingle Hall Gawthorpe Hall

Blackpool

M55

Burnley

Preston

● Samlesbury Hall Towneley Hall

M65

A680

A646

Hoghton Tower ●

Blackburn

Meols Hall ●

● Astley Hall

Southport

● Rufford Old Hall

● Turton Tower Rochdale

Smithills Hall ● Hall-i'-th-Wood

A565

A59

M61

M62

M58

Wigan

Bolton

Bury

A580

Oldham

M63

Manchester

Merseyside

St Helens

M62

Liverpool

Widnes

Stockport

Birkenhead

M53

R. Mersey

M56

Speke Hall ●

Brantwood

2¹/₂ m S Coniston, on E side Coniston Water, signed from village; tearoom; estate walks; *open:* mid Mar–mid Nov, daily, 11–5.30, mid Nov–mid Mar, Wed–Sun, 11–4; tel: 05394 41396

John Ruskin, artist and radical thinker, bought this ungainly, top-heavy dinosaur of a house, sight unseen, in 1872. He was 53, a rich man, and riding high on his reputation as an authority on painting and architecture. Brantwood then was not as ugly as it is now. Built as a sizeable cottage in 1797, it had been extended once, but it was Ruskin who added the third storey, to accommodate the family of his niece Joan and her painter husband Arthur Severn, who increasingly became his keepers, and he extended his purchase in other ways too, starting with the octagonal turret room off his bedroom.

Visitors should not expect too much. After Ruskin's death in 1900, the Severns began steadily to sell his collection of art treasures, books and manuscripts, and that there is anything here at all is entirely due to his disciple, J. H. Whitehouse, who bought back as much as he could, culminating with the house itself in 1932. Brantwood has been much altered since Ruskin lived here, and is now largely an art gallery, with sparsely furnished rooms hung with watercolours and sketches by the great man and his friends and contemporaries, including some of the careful architectural drawings for *The Stones of Venice*, and a portfolio of his alpine views, and two portraits of Rose de la Touche, 29 years his junior, with whom he was infatuated. Only the dining-room and Ruskin's bedroom have any atmosphere, the former with the sage's leather-upholstered chairs round a long table and family portraits on duck-egg blue walls, the latter still with William Holman Hunt's study of a peach and a bunch of grapes over the fireplace, as Ruskin had it, but sadly without his collection of 20 Turner watercolours.

For an understanding of the man, the house is less important than its setting. Behind Brantwood wooded slopes rise steeply to open fells, while before it the ground drops away sharply to Coniston Water, with views to the rugged hills across the lake.

Dalemain

3 m SW Penrith on A592; teas; yeomanry and countryside museums and agricultural bygones; garden; *open:* Easter Sun–early Oct, daily, except Fri and Sat, 11.15–5; tel: 07684 86450

At the hub of a vast estate extending up on to the fells is this unpretentious and attractive house, home of the Hasell family since 1679. The long south front, of smooth, pearly pink sandstone, is a Georgian wing of 1735, but behind, backing on to a tiny internal courtyard, is a much older façade of rough grey stone, an altered mishmash of medieval and Elizabethan work with stone-mullioned windows and a former pele tower at one corner. The house is approached across a cobbled yard, past a huge 16th-century barn and a fragment of the old curtain wall.

The tour starts in the Georgian wing, where a sequence of comfortable, intimate rooms, one panelled with oak from the estate, another decorated with hand-painted, golden-brown Chinese wallpaper and a carved rococo chimney-piece, show off portraits by Zoffany and Devis and some fine 18th-century furniture, including a delicately painted table, Chippendale-style chairs, and a mulberry bureau bookcase. The rooms in the old house, some now altered beyond recognition, are more mixed, but a stone spiral stair leads to a tower chamber with a Tudor plaster ceiling and period furniture, and the stone-walled medieval hall, now the tearoom, has a 1550s beamed ceiling. There are displays of family glass and porcelain and mementoes of the formidable Lady Anne Clifford, whose secretary was a Hasell.

Dove Cottage ☆

$\frac{1}{2}$ m SE Grasmere village, off A591; guided tours; *open:* daily, 9.30–5.30 (closed mid Jan–mid Feb); tel: 05394 35544

This tiny, white-harled cottage dug back into the hill above Lake Grasmere was the home of William Wordsworth and his sister Dorothy from 1799–1808. It is now the centre of the Lake District's flourishing Wordsworth industry, with relics, writings and portraits of the poet and his circle on display in the adjoining museum.

Knowledgeable guides take visitors over the house, bringing alive what are now bare and cheerless rooms but which once, particularly after Wordsworth's marriage to Mary Hutchinson in 1802, must have been bursting at the seams. The few sparse furnishings include the poet's writing chair, four-poster bed and longcase clock; the room where his three young children slept is still lined with newspaper as the Wordsworths had it; and downstairs there is the panelled parlour where ale was dispensed to passing travellers when the cottage was the Dove and Olive Bough Inn. Dorothy's 'domestic slip of mountain', as she called the precipitous garden, runs up steeply behind to the Wordsworth's summerhouse, the only place now, because of later building, from which there is a view of the lake.

Hill Top ☆

In hamlet of Near Sawrey, 2 m S Hawkshead; NT; cottage garden; *open:* Apr–end Oct, Mon–Wed, Sat, Sun and Gd Fri 11–5; tel: 05394 36296

Behind the village pub, a long strip of garden with fruit and vegetables in tidy rows leads up to the modest farmhouse bought by Beatrix Potter, creator of Peter Rabbit, in 1905. Only a few years later Beatrix married a local solicitor and moved to a larger house across the valley, but Hill Top was kept on as

a studio and private bolt hole, and as a symbol of her escape from the stultify-
ing London regime of her parents. Favourite china, books, and furniture were
left here, and her will gave instructions that nothing must be changed.

This shrine to one of the best-loved of children's authors is a typical local
farmhouse with rough-cast walls, slate roof and cosy, low-ceilinged rooms.
The little porch leads straight into a stone-flagged kitchen with horse brasses
over the range, a rag rug on the floor, and blue and white china on the
dresser. There is a tiny panelled parlour to one side, and upstairs are a couple
of bedrooms and the rather bleak extension where Beatrix wrote, with
gloomy landscapes by her brother Bertram on the walls. Her clogs and straw
hat are out in the kitchen, her pottery and knick-knacks are everywhere, and
the homely furniture she originally had is mixed with some grander pieces
acquired after her mother died. For those who know the books, the real
delight is seeing how she incorporated Hill Top and the village in her illustrations, reproducing the grandfather clock and dresser in one painting, the
stairs in another, the view over the valley or a local crossroads in a third.
Sadly, only one of her watercolours is still in the house.

Holker Hall ☆

$^1/_2$ m N Cark-in-Cartmel on B5278, 4 m W
Grange-over-Sands; tearoom; motor
museum; gardens and park; *open:* Apr–end
Oct, daily, except Sats, 10.30–4.30; tel:
05395 58328

Holker Hall is dominated by its west wing, a restless, thrusting, vaguely
Tudor composition with pinnacled gables, bold chimneys, a cupola-topped
tower, and large stone-mullioned windows. Built by Paley and Austin following a fire in 1871, this piece of High Victoriana is attached to a remnant of
the old house, with some 18th-century work hidden behind a subdued
Jacobethan façade of the 1840s.

The old wing is the private family home of the Cavendishes, former Dukes
of Devonshire, who inherited Holker in the 18th century. The new wing is
what visitors see, with large, high-ceilinged reception rooms opening off the
long hall running the length of the ground floor, and a similarly spacious,
gallery-like landing giving access to bedrooms above. Sumptuous fittings
include fireplaces of Derbyshire alabaster in the booklined library, original
red silk on the walls of the drawing-room, and ribbed plaster ceilings and
carved panelling echoing the style of the exterior.

The furnishings are the kind of eclectic and cluttered mix that the
Victorians loved. In the drawing-room, comfortable sofas covered in a virulent stripe rub shoulders with painted Hepplewhite chairs, inlaid French and
Dutch pieces and a Chinese Chippendale table on cluster-column legs; elsewhere are Venetian chandeliers and marble-topped tables, while the bedrooms show off a collection of rustic carved wardrobes from northern France,
elegant serpentine-fronted commodes, and William Morris-designed fabrics,
as well as some rescued Tudor and Jacobean woodwork.

Although many paintings were lost in the fire, and others have been sold, there are portraits here by Hoppner, Reynolds, Wissing, Sargent and Richmond, a stormy Vernet seascape, atmospheric shadowy church interiors attributed to Neefs, works by David Teniers the Younger and Poussin, landscape sketches in heavy pencil by Gainsborough, and a painting of a young man wrapped in a black cloak that is said to be a self-portrait by Van Dyck. And in the library is the microscope of Henry Cavendish, the 18th-century scientist who discovered the density of the earth and the properties of hydrogen and whose name lives on in the Cavendish laboratory at Cambridge.

Hutton-in-the-Forest ☆☆

6 m NW Penrith, on B5305 (M6 exit 41); guided tours *(c.* 45 mins); teas; garden and woodland walk; *open:* Easter–end Sept, Thurs, Fri, Sun, BH Mon 1–4; tel: 07684 84449

Set in woodland on the edge of an extensive park is this intriguing, L-shaped house framing two sides of a long courtyard. Facing down the court, to a distant view of the Pennines, is a cool baroque frontage of the 1680s by the local Edward Addison, a synthesis of broken pediments, urn-studded roofline and grand centrepiece. Built of the palest limestone, this elegant façade is framed, like the filling in a sandwich, between castellated blocks of rough red sandstone, one a pele tower dating from the mid-14th century, built when Cumbria was a lawless frontier zone and Scots raids an ever-present danger, the other a gothick mass with a romantically turreted skyline, one of many 19th-century additions by Anthony Salvin and George Webster of Kendal. Looking across the court, over terraced gardens falling away to a lake, is a long wing of the 1630s, with a gallery above an arcaded loggia. Although an engraving of 1707 by Kip clearly shows a matching wing on the other side of the forecourt, this seems never to have been built.

Inside, the extensive Victorian restoration shows in heavy, Jacobethan ribbed ceilings and some rich William Morris wallpapers and fabrics and Arts and Crafts fittings. The varied tour takes in rooms of all periods, from a stone-vaulted hall at the base of the pele tower to the cluttered High Victorian drawing-room, with Hepplewhite-style Gillow furniture upholstered in a loud Regency stripe and artificial flowers under glass domes. There is still a feel of the 17th century in the gallery, lined with ornately carved oak pieces, and in the long hall behind the 1680s front, with its original panelling, Charles II walnut chairs and contemporary staircase, the balustrade carved with sprawling, child-sized cupids.

The house is still lived in by descendants of Sir Richard Fletcher, who bought the place in 1605. A long run of family portraits includes works by Mary Beale and Romney, and an enchanting family group by Hogarth, appropriately presiding over an unexpected, coffee and cream 18th-century interior, with rococo plasterwork attributed to Joseph Rose the Elder and sparse Chinese Chippendale furnishings.

Levens Hall ☆☆☆

5 m S Kendal, on A6; steam collection; tearoom; topiary garden; park walk; *open:* Apr–end Sept, Sun–Thurs 11–5; tel: 05395 60321

Framed by an ancient topiary garden, the huge yew shapes like giant chessmen, Levens is a tall gabled house of rough grey stone, with stone-mullioned windows. The medieval pele tower which originally stood here survives only in a vaulted undercroft, and the hall as seen today is largely Elizabethan, fitted out with oak panelling, carved overmantels and plaster ceilings, and furnished with a rich accumulation of Stuart and Georgian pieces and a varied collection of paintings and other treasures. Passing by descent since 1700, when the young heir's gambling debts forced him to sell the estate to his first cousin, Col. James Graham, it is a beautifully kept, lived-in house, combining comfort with show.

Of the five downstairs rooms open to visitors, the most striking is the panelled drawing-room on the north-east corner of the house. The ribbed plaster ceiling, columned Renaissance overmantel and huge windows are the backdrop to William and Mary settees and walnut and cane chairs, to one of those Carolean mirrors with bevelled edges designed to reflect the light, to a set of rococo walnut *torchères*, and to a delicious table with double twists in the spiral legs. The colonel and his wife appear in portraits by Lely, and there is a copy by Rubens of a painting of Anne of Hungary, clutching her little dog. The carpeted Elizabethan hall, only one storey high, has a plaster hunting frieze, dotted with hounds and deer and a unicorn or two, and there are two early Madonnas here, one a stylized icon, full of saints with gilded haloes, by the 15th-century Bicci di Lorenzo, the other by the 16th-century Pieter van Aelst, with a glimpse of a green and hilly landscape through an open window. A dining-room lined with embossed and gilded Cordoba leather contains some of the family silver and two bulbous Elizabethan buffets, the oldest pieces in the house, while a clutch of small, *sotto voce* bedrooms are devoted to a show of mostly 18th-century needlework and a set of watercolours by Peter de Wint, who came to Levens in the early-19th century to teach its heiress to paint. Display cases show off such treasures as Beau Brummel's snuff box, an Isaac Oliver miniature painted on a ring, and a Sèvres chocolate service in green and gold, and the 17th-century staircase is hung with some Old Master sketches and drawings, among them an undignified back view of a cherub by Van Dyck, birds by Brueghel the Elder, and a wild-haired gladiator by Tiepolo.

Mirehouse ☆

4½ m N Keswick, on A591; teas; garden and woodland and lakeside walks; *open:* Apr–Oct, Sun, Wed, and Fri in Aug, 2–5; tel: 076 87 72287

In the hands of any other family, this modest, undistinguished house, superbly set on the edge of Bassenthwaite lake with the fells rising steeply behind, would be of little interest. But this was the home of John Spedding and his sons Tom and James, friends of Wordsworth, Tennyson, Carlyle and other luminaries of the day, all of whom have contributed to an impressive display of literary mementoes. The house itself, inherited by John Spedding in 1802 and still lived in by his descendants, is a much extended 17th-century lodge, with Georgian bays flanking the entrance front, and some 19th-century reception rooms.

Of the rooms shown to visitors, only a couple feel lived-in, notably the intimate dining-room in the Georgian wing; and the four-square music room of 1851, hung with portraits by Romney and Hudson, a harbour scene by Abraham Storck, Francesco Longhi's Holy Family, and a tiny Constable, of storm clouds gathering over Hampstead Heath. The others are devoted to museum-like displays. There are James's sketches of Tennyson, one showing a curly-headed, beardless figure, the other of the poet forlorn in a potting shed, there is Julia Margaret Cameron's sepia photograph of the bard, wild-haired and dishevelled, and there are numerous letters and papers: careful communications from Carlyle and the geologist Sir Charles Lyell, poems by Southey and Wordsworth, and material which James accumulated in his life-long study of Francis Bacon.

Muncaster Castle ☆☆

1 m SE Ravenglass on A595; walkman tour (c. 45 mins); tearoom; gardens; owl centre and nature trail; open: end Mar–end Oct, Tues–Sun and BH Mons 1–4; tel: 0229 717 614

Set high above Eskdale, this mock castle of pinkish granite looks down on the river winding in great loops to the sea, and across the valley to the Scafell massif, ridge upon ridge fading gently into the distance. Solid and self-important, Muncaster has grown from the pele tower built here in c. 1325, with substantial remodelling at the end of the 18th century by John Pennington, 1st Lord Muncaster, and then again in 1860-4 by Anthony Salvin for the 4th Lord, when the house acquired its chunky, battlemented outline.

Guided by the entertaining audio tour, visitors see a series of large, high-ceilinged, mostly panelled rooms, hung with a long accumulation of family portraits (Muncaster has passed by descent since the 13th century), and enriched with carved woodwork, including an armoured German saint of 1520 and ornate Tudor overmantels brought here from elsewhere. The general effect is heavy and dark, but the barrel-vaulted drawing-room which Salvin created out of a courtyard is lighter in feel, with plasterwork white on grey and a classical chimney-piece, portraits attributed to Lely, Kneller, Reynolds and Lawrence on the walls, and a sprinkling of delicate Louis XV tables and a William and Mary oyster-veneered cabinet on rich Turkish rugs. A dining-room lined with green and gold leather shows off ornate silver made for the house by Paul Storr and a Gainsborough copy of a Titian done for a bet, while upstairs, reached via Salvin's curious gothic staircase with lancet openings to the hall, is a sequence of tapestry-hung bedrooms furnished with bulbous four-posters and other 16th- and 17th-century pieces.

Visitors can see a silver-gilt copy of the glass bowl known as the Luck of Muncaster, said to have been given to a 15th-century Sir John Pennington by Henry VI, sporting paintings by Ferneley and Munnings, and some Elizabethan needlwork panels illustrating stories from the Bible, the excesses of Sodom and Gomorrah conjured up by gently amorous couples in a leafy garden. A dressing-room suggests things shoved hastily out of sight, but the most lived-in interior is the octagonal galleried library, something like a book-lined chapter house, on the site of the medieval kitchens, with sofas round the fire, and some William and Mary chairs and card tables and perhaps even a sleeping dog hidden among the general clutter.

Naworth Castle

12 m E Carlisle, off A69; tearoom; open: Easter wkend–end Sept, Wed, Sun and BHs, and Sat in July, Aug, 12–5; tel: 06977 41156

Naworth's battlemented and towered façades, approached through a ruinous gatehouse, rise high above a little burn curling round its walls to north and east. The remains of Lanercost Priory are deep in the valley below, and beyond is the glorious border country traversed by Hadrian's Wall. Built of rough grey stone, with startlingly pink, stone-mullioned windows, this Tudor courtyard house, seat of the Howards, Earls of Carlisle, is half castle, half great mansion. An early 14th-century tower, one of those built against the Scots, marks the south-west corner, but most of the rest dates from the 1520s. Sadly, all but one range was gutted by fire in 1844, and Naworth today is as reconstructed by Anthony Salvin. Sadly, too, many of the original contents were removed early this century to *Castle Howard*, and there is a depleted air about the place.

Visitors see some five rooms in the east and south ranges, including a tiny panelled library and chapel, enriched with medieval woodwork, that were created in the south-east tower as part of 17th-century improvements. With views over the private walled garden and down onto the burn, this is the most atmospheric part of the castle. A 78 ft great hall, the largest in the north of England, rises to Salvin's medieval-style timber roof; the only furnishings, apart from a quartet of aggressive heraldic beasts and a couple of Elizabethan portraits, are a set of 16th-century Gobelins tapestries acquired by the 5th Earl at the time of the French Revolution. A sad library, now the shop, is another barn of a room, with a huge blank space destined for Burne-Jones' never-completed mural of Arthur in Avalon. Only the elegantly furnished, green-panelled drawing-room, hung with portraits by Kneller, Lely and Van Somer, feels remotely lived in.

Rydal Mount

Between Ambleside and Grasmere off the A591; garden; *open:* Mar–end Oct, daily, 9.30–5, Nov–Feb, daily, except Tues, 10–4; tel: 05394 33002

No-one would visit this unexceptional, drably furnished place if it were not for the fact Wordsworth lived here for the last forty years of his life, from

1813 until 1850. The house, rendered a creamy yellow, is a 16th-century farm cottage swollen into a polite residence, with two of the tall cylindrical chimneys characteristic of traditional Lakeland architecture. It is now owned by one of Wordsworth's descendants, but most of the original contents have gone. There are a few personal relics, among them the poet's inkstand and leather dispatch box, and his settee covered in black leather, and some family portraits, including Henry Inman's painting of William as an old man, a charming watercolour of the poet's daughter Dora, who died of consumption in her early forties, and Dorothy at the age of 62, her clear gaze giving no hint of the mental illness that would shortly engulf her.

Visitors see some half-dozen rooms, including the attic study added in 1838, but the greatest pleasures are the views of the fells from every window and the 4-acre garden which Wordsworth created, with its terrace walks and vistas over Rydal Water and Windermere.

Sizergh Castle ☆☆

3½ m S Kendal, NW of A590/A591 interchange; NT; tearoom; garden; *open:* Apr–end Oct, Sun–Thurs, 1.30–5.30; tel: 05395 60070

A gentle slope leads visitors into a gravelled court embraced by long low wings with huge, tiered chimneys, undulating, mossy roofs and a mix of stone mullions and sashes. At the far end is an intriguingly varied façade, with an 18th-century gothick frontage sandwiched between a medieval pele tower and a gabled Elizabethan block. Basically dating from the 14th, 15th and 16th centuries, Sizergh was given a facelift in *c.* 1770, when the great hall range next to the tower received its Georgian veneer.

Apart from the unconvincing, fireplace-less 18th-century drawing-room, with portraits by Kneller, Romney, Dahl and Wissing on cool green walls and an uncomfortable scatter of ebonized furniture, the interior is largely Elizabethan and earlier. A tour of the first and second floors takes in a series of intimate, oak-panelled rooms with ribbed ceilings, carved overmantels dated between 1563 and 1575, and even some linenfold from the time of Henry VIII. Most satisfying are the dining-room hung with Stuart portraits, an echo of the family's devotion to the cause, and the adjoining drawing-room, with some inlaid French pieces among the worn and comfortable sofas and more 17th-century works on the walls, including a portrait by Lely. Elsewhere are some walnut Queen Anne chairs, a horse painting by Ferneley, and – in the gloomy, stone-floored entrance hall with its Tudor fireplace – some blue and white, early 18th-century Delft jugs.

More medieval in spirit is the rough-walled room open to a timber roof on the second floor of the tower. Furnished with a Jacobean refectory table and Elizabethan benches and chairs, this room is still lit by some trefoil-headed, three-light 15th-century windows and has its original adze-hewn floor. Next door is what was Sizergh's finest Elizabethan interior. The room still has its 16th-century plaster ceiling and frieze and original four-poster, but all but a fragment of the Renaissance panelling inlaid with poplar and bog oak that once lined the walls is now in the Victoria and Albert Museum.

Townend ☆

3 m SE Ambleside, at S end Troutbeck village; NT; *open:* Apr–end Oct, Tues–Fri, Sun and BH Mon 1–5, or dusk if earlier; tel: 053 94 32628

One of the more secluded Lakeland valleys shelters this substantial, L-shaped, yeoman farmer's cottage dating back to the 16th century, once the centre of an 800-acre estate. A 17th-century barn sits just across the road and Townend itself, curiously built downslope, is a place of rough, lime-rendered walls and small oak-mullioned windows, with tall cylindrical chimneys rising from the stepped and mossy roof. Inside, a series of dark, low-ceilinged rooms, some flagged in slate, others with rag rugs on bare wooden floors, are filled with the sturdy furnishings accumulated by the Browne family, who were here for over four centuries. Some carved and dated pieces, such as the four-poster bed and cradle in the main bedroom, are authentically 17th-century, others were created by the last George Browne, who died in 1914. A manic wood-carver and joiner, he embellished everything, from chairs to clock cases, and contrived a Heath Robinson set of fitted cupboards and drawers in the kitchen, incorporating a longcase clock in their midst. All is down-to-earth, with hams hanging in the huge kitchen chimney, earthenware pottery in the pantry, and charmingly naive studies of sheep by the local William Taylor Longmire on the walls. And over the kitchen, reached by a tight oak staircase, are the tiny rooms where the servants slept.

Greater Manchester

Hall-i'-th'-Wood

2 m NE Bolton town centre, off A58; *open:* Apr–Sept, Tues–Sat 11–5, Sun 2–5; tel: 0204 301159

No wood now surrounds this forlorn relic caught within the web of Bolton. An asphalted approach through a housing estate suddenly turns to cobbles and there is a glimpse of the black and white, half-timbered east wing, its façade elaborately patterned. This is the earliest part of the hall, dating from c. 1500. A relatively subdued extension in local stone was an Elizabethan improvement, and then, in 1648, a clothier's son added the thrusting porch and the stone-mullioned and finialled south-west wing. Divided into tenements for much of the 19th century, and stripped of its panelling, the hall was rescued, refitted and furnished by the philanthropic 1st Lord Leverhulme, who bought the house in 1899.

Now in the hands of the local corporation, this is a sad and lifeless place. Small low-ceilinged, panelled rooms are furnished with a good collection of

17th-century oak pieces, including handsome, high-backed chairs, and a finely carved chest and cupboard, but the hall feels like the museum it is. Strangely, it was here Samuel Crompton developed his spinning mule, the little collection of relics on show including the violin which he played in a local orchestra, putting the fees towards tools and materials for his invention.

Smithills Hall

2 m NW central Bolton off A58; grounds; *open:* Apr–Sept, Tues–Sat, 11–5, Sun and BH Mon 2–5; tel: 0204 841265

In wooded grounds on the lower slopes of Smithills Moor, with deep, rhododendron-choked ravines cutting it off on two sides, is a sprawling gabled building. Much of the Tudor-style architecture is the result of 19th-century remodelling and extension, but the eastern end, where ranges of blackened sandstone and silvery half-timbering frame three sides of a grassy quadrangle, dates back to the 14th century. Visitors see the medieval great hall open to a timber roof and both floors of the adjoining solar wing, together making up what was once an L-shaped manor. A spacious parlour with moulded ceiling beams and linenfold panelling carved with profiled medallion heads is a 16th-century addition, but the stone-built chapel on the end of the range, badly damaged by fire in 1856, has been largely rebuilt, with only some Tudor heraldic glass and carved angels to suggest what has been lost.

In the hands of the local corporation since 1930, Smithills is more museum than home. The rooms are appropriately furnished with stout 17th-century chairs, tables and chests, but only a couple of pieces belong here, and the place as a whole, clearly much restored, is soulless.

Lancashire

Astley Hall

Astley village, NW outskirts of Chorley off A581; café; park; *open:* Apr–end Oct, daily, 11–12, 1–5, Nov–Mar, Fri, Sat, Sun 11–12, 1–4; tel: 0257 262166

In the middle of what is now a public park stands a house of some character. A self-important Jacobean frontage with huge displays of glass filling two octagonal bays and a roofline balustrade hides a modest Elizabethan house behind, with low, half-timbered ranges around an intimate, stone-flagged court. A south wing is a 19th-century addition, as is the drab brown render hiding the Stuart brickwork.

Inside, much period detail remains, from the arcaded oak panelling painted with heroic figures, such as Tamerlane and Francis Drake, in the lofty hall, and some astonishingly bold Jacobean plaster ceilings, to the crude but vigorous 17th-century staircase and an atmospheric long gallery undulating the length of the third floor. But visitors must contend with the deadening hand of the local corporation that now owns the place. Part of the house is used as a local museum and art gallery, and an institutional red carpet leads from room to room.

Browsholme Hall ☆☆☆

5 m NW Clitheroe, off B6243; guided tours (*c.* 30 min); teas Aug only; lakeside walk; *open:* Easter wkend, late May BH wkend, July, Sat, Aug, Sat, Sun and BH wkend, 2–5; tel: 0254 826719

On the edge of the Forest of Bowland is an unpretentious, three-storey Tudor and Elizabethan house, home of the Parker family since 1507. Short gabled wings frame a long façade of pinkish sandstone and paired fluted columns make up a lively classical centrepiece. Although Browsholme has lost its fourth storey, and some of the mullions have been replaced by sashes, it still looks all of a piece, with an unassertive 18th-century wing tucked away on the east side. For so modest a house, the contents are surprisingly rich. Sturdy 17th-century chests, chairs and cupboards have always been here, and each generation has clearly squirrelled things away, but much was acquired in the early 19th century by the antiquarian Thomas Lister Parker, who assembled no fewer than 14 paintings by Northcote, patronised Turner, Romney, Callcott and Buckler, and employed Jeffrey Wyatt to create a lofty classical drawing room in the west wing so he had somewhere to show his art collection, shortly afterwards adding on a grandiose dining-room. These two Regency interiors contrast with the intimate panelled rooms of the old house.

Guided tours by members of the family start in the cluttered, stone-floored hall, with walls hung with a motley collection of armour, guns, antlered heads and curiosities. A little panelled library has low bookshelves supported by pew ends, some Jacobite relics, and a couple of charming portraits attributed to Devis, and upstairs a series of south-facing, interconnecting bedrooms leads off a cosy drawing-room panelled in *c.* 1700 and filled with a collection of 18th-century pieces, including an unusual rococo chair. The paintings are concentrated in Wyatt's red-walled drawing-room and the dining-room, the former dominated by Luny's *Battle of Trafalgar* and Callcott's copy of a stormy seascape by Turner that was once in the house, the latter by a whole row of Northcotes which includes a likeness of the dignified old man who was the last Keeper of the Forest. Also here is a splendid portrait by Batoni, with his signature and the date, 1773, inscribed on the head of the sitter's gold-topped cane, a Lely pastel of Oliver Cromwell, and works by Hudson and Romney, while in a passage outside is the autumnal watercolour of Browsholme which Turner painted in 1799.

Chingle Hall

Just W Goosnargh, S of B5269 (inconspicuous sign); guided tours (*c.* 45 mins); *open:* Apr–Oct, Mon–Sat, 12-4, Sun and BHs 10–5; tel: 0772 861082

For some, Chingle Hall is an extending experience. This small moated house dating back to medieval times, its brick façades now hidden beneath white render, is known for all kinds of paranormal occurrences, from strange scents and doors that have a will of their own to the appearance of a ghostly monkish figure.

Alas, such manifestations do not appear to order. But all visitors can count on an enthusiastic and entertaining tour of the small, bare rooms, several of which contain pointers to the hall's other claim to fame, as a stronghold of the Catholic faith and probable birthplace of John Wall, executed at Worcester in 1679 and one of the last English martyrs. There are several priest and document hides around the house, and the little, stone-floored room where Mass was celebrated has a shelf to indicate the altar and a hole in the floor for concealing vestments and plate.

Gawthorpe Hall ☆

Off A671, on eastern outskirts of Padiham; NT; tearoom; garden; *open:* Apr–end Oct, daily, except Mon and Fri (but open Gd Fri and BH Mon) 1–5; tel: 0282 778511

A long lime avenue from Padiham leads to this strongly vertical Elizabethan house on the banks of the Calder, with a peaceful view of distant hills. Built for the Shuttleworth family between 1600 and 1605, and attributed to the great Robert Smythson, Gawthorpe is a compact, three-storey block, its blackened sandstone walls broken by bays rising the height of the house and by a spread of mullioned and transomed windows. All this is original, but the thrusting staircase tower and bold chimneys rising high above the house are by Sir Charles Barry, who restored Gawthorpe in 1850–2 for the eminent Victorian educationalist Sir James Kay-Shuttleworth.

The few furnished rooms on show have been fitted out to capture this 19th-century heyday, with original plaster ceilings and woodwork allied to gothic pieces made for Sir James and to re-creations of the rich wallpapers, curtains and carpets supplied by Pugin and Crace. A cluttered drawing-room lined with inlaid arcaded panelling of 1603 is awash with pot stands, hung with tasselled leaf-green curtains and a sugary Venetian chandelier, and dominated by Pugin and Crace's octagonal central table, its inlaid top invisible under a spread of photographs, boxes and other *objets*. A 70 ft long gallery running the length of the second floor still has its Elizabethan plaster ceiling and overmantel, but a display of 17th-century portraits, some of the thirty or so on loan from the National Portrait Gallery and including likenesses of Pepys, Purcell and the playwright Thomas Killigrew, is hung against an uncompromisingly bold, gold and brown Pugin paper.

In contrast to the Victorian rooms, much of the house is now devoted to displaying the textile collections built up by Rachel Kay-Shuttleworth in the 1950s and 60s. There are some Jacobean needlework panels and Georgian embroidered waistcoats, but much of what is here is 19th- and 20th-century, including some dazzling *art nouveau* pieces, glittering stoles, lacy infants' clothing, intricate quilts and the inevitable samplers.

Hoghton Tower ☆☆

5 m E Preston, on A675; guided tour (*c.* 40 mins); teas; dolls house collection; garden; *open:* Easter Sat, Sun, Mon, then Suns to end Oct, plus Tues, Wed, Thurs in July and Aug and most BHs, 2–5; tel: 025 485 2986

A wide grassy approach, straight as an arrow, leads half a mile uphill to this atmospheric and intriguing Tudor house, crowning a 560 ft spur of the Pendle Hills, with a precipitous drop behind. Low ranges of dark grey stone with mullioned windows surround two sloping courtyards: the outer, entered through a castellated gatehouse, is as spacious as a town square and divided by a splendid 17th-century gateway; the inner is more intimate, with a fan of steps spilling down from the great hall range. Created by Thomas Hoghton in 1565, the house was substantially restored, in an antiquarian style, in *c.* 1700, when the outer court took on its present form, and again in the last three decades of the 19th century, with help from Paley and Austin of Lancaster and R. D. Oliver of London.

Visitors do a circuit of the principal rooms looking onto the inner court, penetrate the Piranesian service tunnels built in Victorian times and venture into the Tudor well house. The galleried great hall, where James I knighted the Sir Loin of beef on 17 August 1617, has a splendid screen of *c.* 1700 and the original refectory table, but the panelling and ribbed ceiling are 19th century. Other interiors, mostly small, panelled rooms opening one into another, are similarly mixed. There are a couple of original stone fireplaces, and baroque panelling and some painted decoration survives in what was the early 18th-century state apartment, but a ballroom on the corner of the house, with two monumental limestone chimney-pieces, a ribbed ceiling and some genuine Elizabethan panelling, is a Victorian invention. There is some good 18th-century furniture, including a made-up state bed using Jacobean marquetry, but no paintings of note, apart from two Buckler watercolours of the house. Sadly, the most splendid contents were destroyed in a fire while in store and Hoghton has also lost its porcelain, while an intrusive modern bar and glimpses of stacking chairs, evidence of Hoghton's popularity as a function venue, do nothing for the atmosphere.

Leighton Hall ☆☆

2 m W A6, through village of Yealand Conyers; guided tour (*c.* 60 mins); teas; garden and nature trail; eagles and falcons flown; *open:* May–Sept, Sun, BH Mon and Tues–Fri, 2–5 (Aug 11.30–5); tel: 0524 734474

Coming down through the park, there is a view of a playful gothick façade, pinnacled, battlemented and turreted, gleaming white against a distant vista of the Lakeland hills. This limestone frontage dates from *c.*1822, when a much older house was remodelled. At one end is a prim conservatory, at the other a sympathetically styled Victorian wing added by Paley and Austin in 1870, while what looks like a chapel, with a traceried window below a cross on a gable end, is in fact just a false wall screening the stables.

Leighton Hall's main claim to fame, apart from the matchless setting, is that it was bought by the grandson of Robert Gillow, and is full of pieces produced by the furniture firm he founded. The house itself is a smallish, lived-in place, with modest, comfortable rooms. Apart from the hall, with a stone staircase curving gracefully upwards behind a three-arched screen carried on cluster columns, the interior is only gently gothicized. The dining-room, toplit from a spiderweb dome and with 18th-century landscape paintings inset in the panelling, has a prototype expanding Gillow table, and spoon-back Gillow chairs; a double drawing-room and library with a big bay towards the hills shows off some delicate, inlaid Gillow pieces and is closely hung with cabinet paintings, among them a couple of Guardi's Venetian scenes, a shipwreck by George Morland, a tiny Poussin, a dark autumn landscape by Richard Wilson and a Rubensque flute player by Jordaens; and the tour ends in a music room in the Victorian wing, with a portrait of a dark beauty by Luke Fildes on the end wall.

Meols Hall ☆

Northern edge of Southport, opposite botanic gardens, signed from A565; garden; *open:* mid July–mid Aug, daily, 2–5; tel: 0704 28171

Meols Hall sits on the edge of the old village, looking out over a flat reclaimed expanse that was once a vast mere, with the ridge of the Pennines a blur in the distance. A gabled wing dated 1695 is attached to a trim, self-important, four-square brick box, with a parapet hiding the roof. It could well be early-18th century, but in fact, although Meols is built round a mid-17th-century core, the house as it is today was largely reconstructed in 1960–4 by Col. Roger Hesketh, who inherited the remnant of a family collection and the old hall, and remodelled one to take the other, also building on an apparently late-Georgian wing. There are some Jacobite relics, notably what is said to be a fragment of the old coronation regalia that disappeared during the Civil War, and some painted 18th-century furniture, but the main reason for visiting Meols is to see the paintings.

A large Regency-style library, furnished with comfortable sofas and a grand piano, was added on to take James Ward's lifesize painting of an Arab stallion, and an equally huge mahogany bookcase. Portraits by Allan Ramsay here are matched in the intimate rooms to either side by works by Highmore, Reynolds, Romney and Lawrence, and by a family group set in a shadowy sepia interior by Arthur Devis. There are classical landscapes by Poussin and Orizonte, hunting scenes by Tillemans, an entombment by Salvator Rosa and one of Jan Brueghel's characteristically small-scale, richly coloured, biblical landscapes, with a diminutive Christ surrounded by a growing multitude and blue hills fading into the distance.

Rufford Old Hall ☆

In village of Rufford, on E side A59, 7 m N Ormskirk; NT; tearoom; garden; *open:* Apr–end Oct, daily, except Fri, 1–5; tel: 0704 821254

Set in leafy grounds beside the sluggish Leeds and Liverpool canal is an interestingly varied L-shaped house. One arm is a black and white, half-timbered Tudor great hall, with small-paned lattice windows and a generous, five-sided bay, 10 ft deep, marking the high-table end. Wooden pegs holding the structure together protrude from the walls by a good inch, as if the timbers had grown thorns. This impressive fragment is all that remains of the manor built here by Sir Robert Hesketh some time between 1523 and 1541. A west wing has entirely disappeared, apart from indentations in the grass, while the east wing, reconstructed in 1662, is now a modest red-brick Carolean range. Rufford was altered again in 1821, when the rooms in the angle of the L were rebuilt and given a black and white façade, partly done in cement.

The Tudor hall, sparsely furnished with 17th-century chairs and a scattering of armour, is the high point of the tour. A large, stone-floored space, 46 ft long by 22 ft wide, it rises 18 ft to a rustic version of an ornate timber roof, with now-battered angels marking the main beams. At one end, the wall curves out to form a canopy over the high table; at the other is a movable screen of black bog oak, carved with unrestrained abandon and crested with three twisted and etched pinnacles. Most of the other rooms are 19th-century, the best of them a drawing-room running across the house, lined with a bold wallpaper in the deepest yellow, cluttered with sofas, oriental vases, cloth-covered tables and potted palms, and with a peephole to the hall.

Samlesbury Hall

Samlesbury, 5 m W Blackburn, on A677; teas; *open:* all year, Tues–Sun, 11.30–5 (4 in winter); tel: 025481 2229

This curious, L-shaped building precariously jutting out into the main road is a heavily restored remnant of a medieval and Tudor moated courtyard house. The earliest brickwork in Lancashire, of c.1540, faces one side of the long south wing, but the other façades are half-timbered, with aggressive black and white frontages. Visitors see much of the interior, including the galleried chapel that was originally a separate building, and the great hall in the earliest part of the house, open to a timber roof and with an oriel bay at the high table end. But conversion to an inn and a school in the 19th century followed by massive restoration means little of the original plan or fabric remains, and the gallery-like room under the roof of the south wing is now used to sell antiques, books and bric-à-brac.

Towneley Hall

1 m SE Burnley, on A671; cafe; park; *open:* all year, Mon–Fri, 10–5, Sun 12–5; tel: 0282 24213

Towneley Hall is a sombre, U-shaped house with a steep and verdant ridge at its back but a prospect of Burnley across the now-public park. Although dating from the 15th century, the hall was massively remodelled in the 18th century and again, between 1816 and 1820, by Jeffrey Wyatt – later Sir Jeffry Wyatville – who gave the place its castellated and turreted façades. Sold to the local council in 1902 as an empty shell, it is now a museum and art gallery, with a mix of furnished rooms and more formal displays. There is an early-17th-century long gallery running the length of the south-east wing, a baroque hall with plasterwork by Francesco Vassali and Martino Quadri, and a couple of airy, high-ceilinged Regency reception rooms. Of Charles Towneley, the 18th-century dilettanti and connoisseur whose collection of antique marbles is now in the British Museum, there is hardly a trace, apart from Zoffany's portrait showing him surrounded by classical sculpture and the exquisite early-16th-century carved Flemish altarpiece which he installed in the first-floor chapel.

Turton Tower

5 m N Bolton, on B6391; grounds; *open:* May–Sept, Mon–Fri, 10–12, 1–5, Sat, Sun 1–5, Mar, Apr, Oct, Sat–Wed, 2–5, Nov, Feb, Sun 2–5; tel: 0204 852203

Thickly wooded grounds conceal the stocky pele tower and half-timbered extensions that make up this modest L-shaped house. Although the pele tower dates back to *c.* 1420, and the wings are originally Elizabethan, Turton as it is now owes most to the Kay family's romantic restoration in the 1830s and '40s. Rooms were given 17th-century style ribbed plaster ceilings, Jacobean panelling and ancient stained glass were brought from elsewhere, and the exterior was enlivened with added half-timbering and other picturesque details. Now in the hands of the local council, it is a lacklustre and spiritless place, with a mix of furnished rooms and more formal displays.

Merseyside

Speke Hall ☆

On N bank of Mersey, off A561 on W side Liverpool airport, follow airport signs from M62; NT; tearoom; garden and woodland walk; *open:* Apr–end Oct, daily, except Mon (open BH Mon), 1–5.30; end Oct–mid Dec, Sat and Sun 1-4.30; tel: 051 427 7231

Sandwiched between Liverpool airport and a rash of factories is this unlikely survival. Set low round a cobbled, weedy courtyard, and approached across a now-grassy moat, are the gabled, strongly black and white, half-timbered ranges of a modest Tudor and Elizabethan manor. Built over a hundred years from 1490 by three members of the Norris family, the exterior is pleasingly diverse, but the courtyard façades are all of a piece, with continuous bands of diamond-paned, wood-mullioned casements.

The interior is largely as it was in 1868, after the house had been bought by the Watt family and leased to the shipping magnate and patron of the arts, F. R. Leyland. Small, rather dark rooms, some panelled, others hung with early William Morris papers, are furnished with mostly Victorian pieces, with much carved and stained oak in an antiquarian style, and a scattering of carpet-seated chairs, cloth-covered tables and potted palms. The 16th-century comes through strongly only in the stone-flagged great hall, with its Flemish Renaissance panelling carved with medallion heads and a crude gothic chimney-piece, and in the adjoining parlour, where a splendid overmantel is carved with three generations of the Norris family, including all Sir William's 19 children, and a Jacobean plaster ceiling has panels of fruit, nuts and flowers sculpted in high relief. Upstairs, a squint giving a view of the gatehouse and a ladder to a hide in the roof are reminders of the time when Catholic priests were sheltered here.

The approach is heart-sinking, but the hall, screened by belts of trees, seems to shrug off its surroundings. To the south it is sheltered by a high grassy bank, like some prehistoric earthwork, with views across the glistening waters of the Mersey from the top.

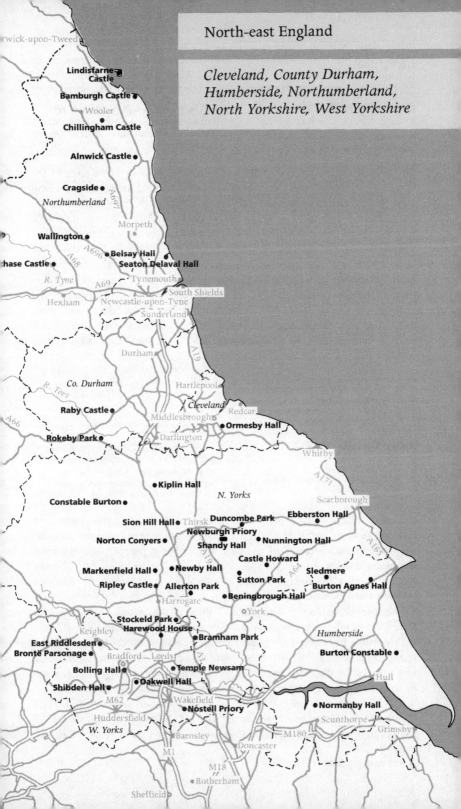

North-east England

Cleveland, County Durham,
Humberside, Northumberland,
North Yorkshire, West Yorkshire

rwick-upon-Tweed

Lindisfarne
Castle

Bamburgh Castle ●

Wooler

Chillingham Castle ●

Alnwick Castle ●

Cragside ●

Northumberland

Wallington ●

Morpeth

Belsay Hall ●
Seaton Delaval Hall ●

hase Castle ●

R. Tyne

Tynemouth

Hexham

South Shields

Newcastle-upon-Tyne

Sunderland

Durham

Co. Durham

R. Tees

Hartlepool

Raby Castle ●

Cleveland

Middlesbrough

Redcar

Rokeby Park ●

Darlington

Ormesby Hall

Whitby

Kiplin Hall ●

N. Yorks

Scarborough

Constable Burton ●

Sion Hill Hall ●

Thirsk

Duncombe Park ●

Ebberston Hall ●

Newburgh Priory ●

Norton Conyers ●

Shandy Hall ●

Nunnington Hall ●

Castle Howard ●

Markenfield Hall ●

Newby Hall ●

Sledmere ●

Ripley Castle ●

Allerton Park ●

Sutton Park ●

Burton Agnes Hall ●

Beningbrough Hall ●

Harrogate

York

Humberside

Stockeld Park ●

Keighley

Harewood House ●

Bramham Park ●

East Riddlesden ●

Brontë Parsonage ●

Bradford — Leeds

Burton Constable ●

Bolling Hall ●

Temple Newsam ●

Hull

Shibden Hall ●

Oakwell Hall ●

Wakefield

M62

Huddersfield

Nostell Priory ●

Normanby Hall ●

Scunthorpe

W. Yorks

Barnsley

M180

Grimsby

Doncaster

M1

M18

Rotherham

Sheffield

Cleveland

Ormesby Hall

3 m SE Middlesbrough, W of A171; NT; tearoom; garden; *open:* Apr–end Oct, Wed, Thurs, Sat, Sun, BH Mon, Gd Fri 2–5.30; tel: 0642 324188

This plain Palladian cube of yellowish sandstone sits in a green oasis in the spread of Middlesbrough, with high-rise flats glimpsed above the screening trees. Built for the Pennyman family in the 1740s, perhaps by their relative, the gentleman architect Col. J. Moyser, Ormesby is a place of no pretensions, whose original contents went in a sale of 1789 to pay the gambling debts of the 6th Baronet. Of the unexceptional, plainly furnished rooms on show, the most attractive is the restful drawing-room on the south-west corner of the house, decorated with delicate Adamesque plasterwork of the 1770s, and furnished with sofas round the fire, a suite of 18th-century oval-backed chairs upholstered in pale blue, and a fine, bow-fronted parquetry French commode. Upstairs, modest panelled bedrooms open off an unexpectedly grand landing with pedimented and pilastered doorcases, the status of each room subtly indicated by the choice of Corinthian or Ionic capitals.

County Durham

Raby Castle ☆☆☆

1 m N Staindrop, off A688; tearoom; walled garden and park; *open:* Easter Sat–Wed, May and June, Wed and Sun, July–end Sept, daily, except Sat, and BH wkends, Sat–Tues, 1–5; tel: 0833 60202

Passers-by on the A688 enjoy an uninterrupted view of this great castellated mass set in open parkland in the sweeping Northumbrian countryside. The once formidable curtain wall has been reduced to a parapet, and the moat converted into an ornamental lake, but Raby still looks like a 14th-century fortress, with eight towers ringing a central keep, and the only entrance through a defensible gateway.

The interior is largely Georgian and Victorian. Acquired in 1626 by Sir Henry Vane, whose descendants still live here, Raby was remodelled in the 18th century by James Paine and John Carr, and in the 1840s by William Burn, while most of the furnishings postdate a family row in the early 1700s, when the 1st Lord Barnard was so angered by his son's marriage that he started disposing of the contents, and even attempted to demolish the castle.

The extensive tour starts with the principal rooms on the south front, and then turns inward, towards the older parts of the building. Burn's *tour de force* is an opulent octagonal drawing-room in French style, with yellow silk on the walls, a richly carved ceiling, gilded furniture, and a show of turquoise and midnight blue Sèvres. There is a glimpse of the 17th century in the long library, and of a plaster ceiling by Paine in a delightful small drawing-room, but the main interest is the paintings: sporting pictures by Herring, Sartorius, Marshall and Wootton include Herring's delightful canvas of two shaggy ponies in Raby's stable yard; interiors by Pieter de Hoogh and Teniers the Younger stand out from a clutch of 17th-century Dutch works; and the pink-walled dining-room with its stodgy strapwork ceiling is hung with a mix of portraits and other paintings, among them a dignified middle-aged couple by de Vos, a weak and sentimental Reynolds, a Vernet seascape and an apocalyptic vision of ancient Rome by Luca Giordano.

There is another flood of portraits, some gothic chairs by Pugin and six glorious Venetian candelabra in what was the medieval great hall. This huge room running north to south across the castle had its floor raised 10 ft by Carr and has been thoroughly worked over by Burn, who replaced the original hammerbeam roof with the present unconvincing structure, but the minstrel's gallery and a couple of windows are original. There is a sense of the Middle Ages, too, in some rough stone floors and walls, in the blocked six-light window at the back of the little chapel, and, above all, in the kitchen of 1360, with its lofty ceiling sweeping up to an octagonal ventilation shaft, a passageway circling the room within the thickness of the walls, and splayed window openings set high up, as if the room were dug into the earth.

Rokeby Park ☆

Just SE Barnard Castle, signed off A66 10 m NW Scotch Corner; dramatic riverside walk; *open:* May BH Mon, late May–early Sept, Mon, Tues 2–5; tel: 0833 27268

Perched on the lip of a wooded gorge, where bare cliffs rise sheer from the River Greta, is this trim 18th-century villa, designed for his own use by the colourful amateur architect Sir Thomas Robinson, who contributed to his father-in-law's *Castle Howard*. Devised as a series of receding façades, Rokeby's pedimented central block is attached to lower wings set well back, and they, in the same way, to lowlier, one-storey appendages. Although blurred by later alterations, Rokeby is still much as Sir Thomas conceived it, and there is a nice contrast between the bare stone of the main house and the apricot render on the pavilions. Sir Thomas himself deserted Co. Durham for London, selling the house and much of its contents in 1769 to J. S. Morritt, whose descendants have lived here ever since.

The interior is surprisingly compact, suggesting a bachelor residence rather than a family house. Starting in the low-ceilinged, ground floor hall made out of Robinson's cellar, visitors see some half-dozen rooms before emerging in Rokeby's showpiece: the high-ceilinged saloon, almost a double cube, which was originally devised as the hall. It is furnished as a sitting-room, with comfortable sofas round the green and white marble fireplace, but feels more like a gallery, with a copy of the languid nude by Velazquez known as the

Rokeby Venus (the original is now in the National Gallery) dominating a show of paintings of historical figures and Morritt family portraits, two of them by Benjamin West.

The Velazquez was bought by J. B. S. Morritt, J. S.'s son, and it is the Morritt spirit that predominates here, despite Sir Thomas's architectural cabinets and the views of his London house. A barrel-ceilinged Victorian bedroom with loud lattice wallpaper setting off Pellegrini's *Venus Disarming Cupid* has the four-poster where J.S.'s friend Sir Walter Scott is supposed to have slept, and there are numerous needlework pictures by J. B. S.'s Aunt Anne, whose rather drab and streaky works were all taken from paintings, some of them still in the house. Then, it was J. B. S. Morritt who created the Regency dining-room on the first floor of one of the pavilions, possibly to designs by Carr of York, with a delicate plasterwork ceiling, a domed, apse-like niche on the inner wall, and Gillow chairs round a Regency table. The paintings here include views of Rokeby attributed to Lambert, royal portraits by Jervas and Kent, and the road-building General Wade by Vanderbank, with one of his elegant bridges in the background.

Humberside

Burton Agnes Hall ☆☆☆   In Burton Agnes village, 6 m SW Bridlington, on A166; tearoom; garden; *open:* Apr–end Oct, daily, 11–5; tel: 0262 490324

Within smelling distance of the sea, on the edge of the Yorkshire Wolds, is this gem of a house. Built between 1601 and 1610 by Robert Smythson, architect of *Longleat* and *Hardwick*, Burton Agnes is a glittering late-Elizabethan mansion of red-brick and stone. A charming gatehouse with domed angle turrets leads to the gabled three-storey entrance front, with flamboyant stone carving and cresting on the two central bays and swelling, rounded bows rising the height of the house to either side. This frontispiece melts into the two-storey ranges enclosing the inner courtyard, while just to the west, like an

outbuilding, is the simple manor house built here in 1173, with a vaulted undercroft carried on stumpy Norman columns and a 15th-century timber roof over the great hall.

Sashes rather than stone mullions on the hall point to 18th-century changes, when the house was extensively modernized. Inside is a mix of panelled, primarily Jacobean rooms and elegant Georgian interiors, all of them enriched with family portraits and by the collection of Impressionist and modern art acquired by the late Mr Wickham-Boynton, descendant of the original builder. The tone is set by the light and airy great hall, where a flamboyant screen of wood and plaster is carved with a mix of biblical characters and early-17th-century figures in doublet and hose. An alabaster chimney-piece illustrating the story of the Wise and Foolish virgins is the first of a series of overmantels with moral messages, period furnishings include an oak refectory table and there are languorous full-length portraits by Francis Cotes either side of the fire. A wide staircase with shallow treads leads up to two panelled bedrooms, one with a 17th-century bed hung with original blue Italian damask, the other with a plaster ceiling of 1610 devised as a restless sea of honeysuckle, some fronds hanging free.

The 19th- and 20th-century art is concentrated in the Georgianized rooms and in the re-created, barrel-ceilinged long gallery running across the south front. A show of Impressionists is gathered in the elegant, grey-walled drawing-room looking east and north over the gardens, the inlaid Chippendale-style satinwood commode and tables and other 18th-century pieces here a perfect foil for the small-scale, muted canvases on the walls, among them Gauguin's *Head of a Tahitian Woman*, still lifes by Renoir and Derain, a windswept dune coast by Boudin, and Utrillo's grey study of Montmartre. The gallery, with richly coloured rugs on pale, polished boards, is more of a show-place, the paintings here, hung against peach walls, ranging from Corot's out-of-focus *Woodcutter* of the 1860s, some dark brooding cliffs by Courbet and Pissarro's gentle *Woman Shelling Peas*, to some slabs of scarlet, yellow and green by Bernard Lorjou, and Vlaminck's nightmarish imploding village of 1912. Rooms off are devoted to large, colourful canvases by André Minaux and modern Russian works, and the collection includes several bronzes, among them a couple of Epstein's sloe-eyed beauties.

Despite all these riches, Burton Agnes is still very much a family home, and visitors who arrive at lunchtime may well find the spacious red-walled dining-room, hung with landscapes by Gainsborough and Marlow, a fishing party by Philip Mercier and portraits by Reynolds and Cotes, temporarily closed.

Burton Constable ☆☆

At Burton Constable, 7½ m NE Hull via A165 and B1238; tearoom; garden and park; *open:* Easter Sun–end Sept, Sun–Thurs and Sat in July and Aug, 1–5; tel: 0964 562400

In windswept, pancake-flat country just a couple of miles from the North Sea is this unexpected, dignified great house. Built of warm red brick, with wings coming forward to frame an open courtyard and stone-mullioned windows, Burton Constable looks the Elizabethan mansion it once was, but the splendid interior, where there is much to see, is almost entirely mid-18th-century, with a gloss of extravagant 19th-century embellishments.

Remodelling from the 1750s by the cultivated William Constable has resulted in decorative schemes by Thomas Lightoler, James Wyatt and Thomas Atkinson, and a wealth of contemporary furniture made for the house. Lightoler's elegant staircase, the baluster still carrying the original brass candlesticks, leads off an enfilade of reception rooms on the ground floor. Grandest is Wyatt's beautifully proportioned ballroom running out into a big bay to the garden, with delicate plasterwork by Giuseppe Cortese on the ceiling, gold silk on the walls setting off family portraits, and a set of gilded Chippendale furniture upholstered in the softest pink. An extraordinary umbrella dome in the adjoining drawing-room, a kind of plaster sunshade fringed with midnight blue tassels, is Atkinson's, and so is the dining-room, with its classical bas-reliefs and Hepplewhite-style chairs by the estate carpenter.

Later purchases include the Erard grand piano in a boulle case that was ordered by the ruthlessly extravagant Lady Rosina, second wife of the Victorian Sir Clifford, French Empire pieces, and obscure historical canvases by Andrea Casali. The 19th century also saw the conversion of Atkinson's billiard room into a richly painted chapel, all red, blue and gold, and the creation of a Chinese drawing-room, with little bells hanging from the cornice, a couple of scaly carved dragons gripping the walls, another hovering over the central light, and two more writhing up the frame of a chair.

Amidst all this finery is the enquiring William's museum of curiosities, a mix of mineral specimens, queer and wonderful creatures, unsettling things in bottles, and scientific experiments, with a camera obscura, such as was used by Canaletto, illustrated by the upside down image of a flickering candle. To one side is a show of family documents, among them letters relating to bounty from wrecks along the coast and drawings for the statues in the hall. On the other is a 100 ft long gallery in Jacobean style, lined with books, with a magical plaster frieze full of strange and wonderful creatures, and with a bay window full of Flemish glass at the south end. This pastiche, created by William's father, is hung with portraits, including a Marcus Gheeraerts dated 1599, and furnished with carved Charles II chairs, sadly gilded in the 1830s, and giant oriental vases.

Normanby Hall

4 m N Scunthorpe, on B1430; café; country park; farming museum; *open:* Easter–end Sept, daily, 1–5; tel: 0724 720588

The Sheffield family's chunky Regency house of blackened Ancaster stone was built in 1825–30 by Sir Robert Smirke, with alterations and extensions in the early years of this century. Left empty by the family, it has been refurnished by a local museum as it might have been in c.1830. There is a splendid Edwardian bathroom and an elegant classical hall with branching staircase, but the place as a whole feels forlorn and institutional.

Sledmere ☆☆

24 m E York, between Malton and Great Driffield, junction of B1251 and B1253; tearoom; walled garden; *open:* Easter wkend, mid Apr–late Sept, daily, except Mon and Fri, but open BHs, 1.30–5.30; tel: 0377 86208

The Sykes family's square grey house sits high on a terrace among tree-shaded lawns, looking south over wooded parkland. The austere exterior, with windows grouped beneath great arched recesses, dates from the 1780s, when Sir Christopher Sykes remodelled a mid-18th-century house with advice from John Carr and Samuel Wyatt. The interior is unexpectedly lush. Devastated by fire in 1911, it was restored during the war years by the local architect Walter Brierley, who combined re-creations of the original Adamesque plasterwork by Joseph Rose with an opulent Edwardian treatment, designed for lavish entertaining. Fortunately, the family's portraits and fine furniture, and even doors, banisters and the original plaster moulds, were rescued from the fire.

Striking through the centre of the house is a flamboyant Edwardian hall, with an imperial staircase spilling down behind a screen of brown scagliola columns. Reconstituted plasterwork on walls and ceiling is picked out in mint green and white, a copy of the Apollo Belvedere sits in a niche on the half-landing, and two huge illuminated alabaster vases frame the lower flight. A music room to one side has an organ made for the 1751 house and 18th-century English and Dutch furniture, while on the other are the lush gold and blue drawing-room and red-walled boudoir, the former with late-18th-century giltwood furniture, a highly ornate ceiling and portraits by Lawrence and Francis Grant, the latter with Italian marquetry pieces and a show of Flemish and German works, among them a dreamy landscape by Jan Hackaert, a still-life by Jan Fyt and a portrait by Honthorst. A cool blue and lavender dining-room has the only surviving mid-18th-century ceiling, Chinese Chippendale chairs, a wall hung with blue and white oriental porcelain, and Romney's full-length portrait of Sir Christopher and Lady Sykes, while upstairs, running the length of the south front, is an astonishing library, with a curved vault on a cyclopean scale decorated with plasterwork picked out in gold, blue and wine red.

Horse paintings by Herring, Ferneley, Barraud and others are reminders of the Sledmere stud, which still operates from the classical stable block behind the house, there is a steely, pastel self-portrait of Joseph Rose, who was on intimate terms with Sir Christopher, and the house is enriched by an Italian altar clock, turquoise Sèvres vases and other treasures from the collection of the Duke of Orleans, sold at the Revolution, and by a Turkish room lined with blue and white tiles that was added after the fire. Organ music in the afternoons adds to the general atmosphere of expensive luxury.

Northumberland

Alnwick Castle ☆☆

In Alnwick (E end of Bailiffgate), 30 m N Newcastle; tearoom; museum of antiquities and of Royal Northumberland Fusiliers; *open:* mid Apr–mid Oct, daily, 11–5; tel: 0665 510777

On the edge of the little town of Alnwick, high above the river, is the great fortress of the Percys, with a battlemented curtain wall enclosing a many-towered keep. All around are rolling vistas across the border country, with Scotland only 30 miles to the north.

Originally Norman, Alnwick was largely rebuilt in the 14th century by the 1st and 2nd Lords. Outside, it is all castle, the only entrance a cleft of a passage between the walls of the medieval gatehouse. Inside, all is splendour. Remodelled by Robert Adam in the 18th century, the keep was redesigned again in the 1850s by Anthony Salvin, who fitted a suite of sumptuous state rooms within the shell of the old walls. Approached up a staircase of Carrara marble, each tread a solid 12 ft span, are six interconnected showrooms. Ceilings are coffered and gilded, shutters and door panels carved and inlaid, walls hung with red and yellow damask and painted with deep friezes, and the rooms filled with highly crafted furniture, from Louis XIV *pietra dura* cabinets made at the Gobelins factory to tables by Adam and John Linnell. Salvin was working for the 4th Duke, who wanted Alnwick to be a kind of Italian Renaissance *palazzo*, its rugged exterior contrasted with rooms of palatial magnificence. Distinguished Italians were brought in to advise and assist, and a professor of sculpture in Milan was commissioned to carve marble busts for some of the chimney-pieces.

In this most artificial of settings is one of the great private art collections of England, known particularly for its 16th-century Italian paintings. Here are two Titians, Palma Vecchio's *Lady with a Lute*, set against a mountainous landscape, a curiously unfocused self-portrait by Andrea del Sarto, a Venetian nobleman in an ermine-trimmed gown by Tintoretto, and parts of a fresco from a church in Rome by Sebastiano del Piombo. Here, too, are several Canalettos, one a romantic view of the unrestored castle, another of Westminster bridge under construction, a disconcertingly Claudian Turner and a harbour scene by Claude himself, with a fiery sun sinking into the sea. There is a fine run of family portraits, including works by Ramsay, Hoppner, Reynolds and Batoni, but most have been relegated to a long corridor. In the state rooms are only the Van Dycks and a couple of portraits by William Dobson, one of the bibulous old sculptor Nicholas Stone and his son, the other a triple portrait that includes the artist.

Bamburgh Castle

At Bamburgh, 16 m N Alnwick on B1340, E of A1; tearoom; *open:* Easter–end Sept, daily, Apr 1–4.30; May, June 12–5.30; July, Aug 12–6; Sept 1–5; tel: 066 84 208

On a crag of basalt above the cold North Sea, with views north to Holy Island across wind-swept dunes and breaking surf, is this most ancient of fortresses, 7th-century seat of the powerful Northumbrian kings. Dominated by a massive 12th-century keep of pinkish sandstone, and with a long residential range backing on to the towered and buttressed medieval curtain wall following the contours of the rock, Bamburgh looks every inch a castle still, its bulk shadowing the village sheltering in its lee. But alas, once through the double-towered east gate, romantic illusions rapidly dissolve. Already ruinous and decayed in Elizabethan times, Bamburgh was patched up in the 18th century, and then massively restored between 1894 and 1905, with the help of Charles Ferguson of Carlisle, by the 1st Lord Armstrong, whose *Cragside*, some 25 miles south-west, had been completed only a few years earlier.

Although Lord and Lady Armstrong still live here, much of the building is now divided into flats and the state rooms shown, most of them by Ferguson, are comfortless and dispiriting, with museum-like displays of armour, porcelain and other treasures, or furniture grouped round the edge of a sea of parquet. The high point – if that is the right word – is the 19th-century great hall, complete with lofty hammerbeam roof, minstrel's gallery and portraits against bare stone walls, but with the body of the room filled with a strange mixture of 17th-century armour and cabinets full of precious *objets* and china. A tiny blue-green country scene by Jan Brueghel does something to raise the spirits, and there is a sense of great age in the stone-vaulted undercroft to the keep, with a Saxon well excavated 145 ft through the rock.

Belsay Hall

On A696 14 m NW Newcastle; EH; tearoom; romantic quarry garden; *open:* summer, daily, 10–6, winter, Tues-Sun, 10–4; tel: 066–181 636

Fired by what he had seen on a two-year honeymoon largely spent in Athens, Sir Charles Monck returned to his Belsay estate in 1806 with plans for a new house in an austere classical style. What he built, with some advice from a young local architect, has the look of a temple about it, with the entrance set back behind a recessed portico of tapering, fluted columns, walls of smooth, honey-coloured stone rising to a deep entablature, and a massive projecting cornice that throws deep shadows over the façades. The setting, looking south over terraced gardens, is as beautiful as ever, but the house is now desolate and abandoned, all furnishings gone. The rooms visitors see are empty and characterless, the only memorable feature of the place a strongly architectural, toplit central hall, ringed by double tiers of fluted columns as if this were a courtyard in ancient Greece.

A 15-minute walk away, through the secretive quarry gardens walled by cliffs and pinnacles of naked rock, are the ruins of the 14th-century tower house and adjoining Jacobean manor which preceded the Regency mansion, the whole ensemble now owing much to romantic restoration in the 19th century.

Chillingham Castle

At Chillingham, 12 m NW Alnwick, between A1 and A697; tearoom; Italian garden and lake walk; *open:* Easter wkend, May–end Sept, daily, except Tues, 1.30–5; tel: 06685 359

Rising enticingly from the surrounding woods is a towered and battlemented, romantically decayed courtyard house. The shell is a 14th-century border fortress, but the exuberant frontispiece, all columns and heraldic beasts, is early 17th century, and later alterations culminated in a final remodelling by Sir Jeffry Wyatville, fresh from *Windsor Castle*, in 1828. Sadly, the interior is an anti-climax. Empty for 50 years before being bought by the present owner, whose restoration still has a long way to go, its furnishings long dispersed, Chillingham is a place of rough stone walls and crumbling plaster. There are some crude recreations of medieval times, including a sensationalized torture chamber, a couple of more graciously furnished rooms, one filled with convincing reproduction antiques, and a hugger-mugger collection of bric-à-brac – old baths from Longleat, battered rocking horses, a 1947 railway map – in the museum.

Chipchase Castle

Near Wark-on-Tyne, off B6320, get directions in village; guided tour (c. 30 mins); garden; *open:* 1–28 June, daily, 2–5; tel: 0434 230685

A 14th-century pele tower with massively thick walls marks one corner of this picturesque, rough-walled courtyard house set high above the wide wooded valley of the North Tyne, with panoramic views over the river. The crested, three-storey porch, stone-mullioned windows and rounded bays topped with heraldic beasts on the east front date from 1620, but the long, battlemented south front running up to the tower is Georgian, with rows of sash windows framing a classical doorway. Apart from the stone floor in the hall and some Jacobean court cupboards, there is little of the 17th century inside, which has been much altered. The brief tour takes in Victorian paintings and plasterwork and a Georgian staircase. Most startling are the high-ceilinged billiard room created out of what was a music room, and the huge salmon caught in the Tyne that are mounted over almost every door. The old tower is entered separately, with a worn spiral stair leading to a first floor that is now open to the roof, while across a field to the east, reached only by a grassy path, is a tiny stone chapel with round-headed windows and a diminutive bellcote on one gable end.

Cragside ☆☆

13 m SW Alnwick, 1 m E Rothbury, on B6341; NT; tearoom; garden and country park, with power circuit walk; *open:* Apr–end Oct, daily except Mon, but open BH Mon, 1–5.30; tel: 0669 20333

Cragside plays up to its surroundings. Rising out of a sea of conifers on the slope of a wild and craggy valley, with a huge rock garden tumbling down towards the burn far below, is a romantic display of half-timbered gables, soaring chimneystacks, and stone-mullioned windows, with one gable-topped tower thrusting out of the main mass like a vigorous spring shoot. This huge place, part overgrown cottage, part Tudor mansion, is a period piece, built by Norman Shaw between 1870 and 1874 for Sir William Armstrong, the millionaire industrialist. Armstrong started to buy land in the Debdon valley in 1863, initially contenting himself with building a modest lodge as a weekend retreat from his engineering and armaments business. Over the years he amassed a 1730-acre estate, planted the rough, bare hill-sides with thousands of trees and rhododendrons, laid out miles of carriage drives, and, piece by piece, almost room by room, extended the lodge into the picturesquely varied building seen today, using the inventiveness which fuelled his company to instal hydro-electricity and other technical marvels, such as a hydraulic lift.

Cragside is a huge place and the tour is extensive, exploring most of the ground and first floors, and penetrating to a chilly bath suite in the basement. But because the original lodge was swallowed up by the new building, Shaw's great set-pieces, which make Cragside memorable, are tacked on to either side of a core of surprisingly small and intimate rooms, which do not invite lingering. Shaw's first work, of the 1870s, added the panelled dining-room, with companionable oak settles in a massive inglenook fireplace, and the library looking over the glen, a restless accumulation of red leather sofas, ebonised chairs and potted plants, with stained glass by Burne-Jones and Madox Brown in the windows, turquoise tiles in the fireplace and lamps made out of *cloisonnée* enamel vases. The later additions, which end the tour, are altogether grander, culminating in a top-lit, sculpture-lined gallery leading to a huge barrel-ceilinged drawing-room cut back into the hill. Built for entertaining the foreign dignitaries with whom Armstrong was now doing business, among them the King of Siam, the Shah of Persia, and the Crown Prince of Afghanistan, this is a room to impress, its end wall filled by a carved marble chimney-piece of Jacobean virtuosity designed by W. R. Lethaby, the whole edifice, with its naked cherubs and strapwork, sheltering yet another inglenook.

Sadly, the paintings which once hung here were dispersed only ten years after Armstrong's death by the grand-nephew to whom he bequeathed the estate. There are family portraits still, and several of the sentimental, rustic canvases by the Northumbrian artist H. H. Emmerson which the 1st Lord loved, but elsewhere gaps have been filled by the loan of mannered Pre-Raphaelite compositions by Evelyn de Morgan. Sadly, too, in most rooms visitors are kept away from the windows, with only one opportunity to look down into the glen.

Lindisfarne Castle ☆

On Holy Island, 6 m E A1 across tidal causeway; NT; non-NT car park; *open:* Apr–end Oct, daily except Fri, but open Gd Fri, 1–5.30; check tides before visiting; tel: 0289 89244

A mile or so off the busy A1, a by-road launches out across an expanse of watery mud and sand towards a line of wind-blown, hummocky dunes. This is the first sight of Holy Island: at its furthest point, like a defiant fist raised against the sea, is the romantic outline of Lindisfarne Castle, perched on a steep dolerite crag. Created in 1903 for Edward Hudson, founder of *Country Life*, by the young Edwin Lutyens, this unusual place is an Edwardian summer retreat within the carapace of a little fort, originally built in Tudor times against the Scots. Lutyens worked with what he found, contriving cosy living-rooms out of what had been stone-vaulted ammunition stores, keeping the original approach up a steep, stone ramp, and making a feature out of the constant changes of level.

Tunnel-like passages and rough steps of brick and stone lead to a succession of intimate, curiously shaped, white-washed rooms. Lutyens' touches are everywhere: in inviting seats built in below tiny, deep-set windows, in cottagey plank doors and great arched fireplaces, in floors of brick and slate, and in the primitive, smoothly rounded columns dividing the hall. The castle is fitted out like a 17th-century Dutch interior, with an array of gleaming brass candlesticks, blue and white pottery, mellow oak furniture, some of it by Lutyens himself, and tiny bedrooms half-filled with massive four-posters.

Seaton Delaval Hall ☆

At Seaton Sluice on the A190, between Tynemouth and Blyth, poorly signed; guided tours; garden; *open:* May–end Sept, Wed, Sun and BH Mon 2–6; tel: 091 237 3040

Looking north along a bleak and chilly shore to the smoking stacks of Blyth is this most defiant and restless of houses. Built by Sir John Vanbrugh between 1718 and 1728 for Admiral Sir Ralph Delaval, the hall is a piece of baroque theatre, with long arcaded wings embracing a huge forecourt, and a thrusting central block using every visual trick in Sir John's considerable repertoire: corners are rounded into octagonal turrets, heavy keystones weigh down every window, smooth, trunk-like Doric columns, supporting nothing, rise grandly either side of the entrance, and above, floating free, is a serenely classical top storey.

Gutted by fire in 1822, Seaton Delaval is now an empty, blackened shell, its drama heightened by desolation. Broken statues look down from niches high over the lofty, galleried hall, where two sad caryatids on the chimney-piece still gesture towards the 75 ft saloon across the back of the house. Worn, winding stairs lead up to a fragment of a first floor and down to the vaulted basement, where occasional shafts of sunlight do nothing to dispel an Arctic cold. One wing is now the Delaval family home; the other contains Vanbrugh's stygian stables, spanned by vast arches and with heroic names – Hercules, Julius, Zephyrus – painted over the stalls.

Wallington ☆☆

20 m NW Newcastle, 12 m W Morpeth, on the B6342 off A696; NT; tearoom; wooded lakeside path to walled garden and estate walks; *open:* Apr–end Oct, daily, except Tues, 1–5.30; tel: 067 074 283

The public road running through the park gives the best view of this square, sash-windowed block of warm, honey-coloured stone sitting on a terrace above the valley of the Wansbeck. Originally built in 1688 as an old-fashioned courtyard house, Wallington was remodelled in the mid-18th century by Daniel Garrett, whose symmetrical Georgian façades retain only the outline of the previous building. Garrett was working for Walter Calverley Blackett, whose grandfather had built the 17th-century house, and whose descendants, the Trevelyans, lived here into the 20th century.

The interior, seen in an extensive tour which takes in most of the ground floor and several rooms upstairs, is Georgian and Victorian, although most of the furniture, including the 18th-century pieces, has been assembled since 1880, when everything except the portraits and china was entailed elsewhere. Garrett's finest rooms, with rococo plasterwork by Pietro Francini on walls and ceiling and marble fireplaces attributed to Henry Cheere, form an enfilade down the south front. The library, with its leather-covered chairs, was refitted in 1853, but the coolly blue and white dining-room and saloon are period pieces, the former hung with portraits by Hudson and Johnson, the latter with oval, plaster-framed niches filled with green and blue oriental porcelain, and with portraits by Reynolds and Romney of Sir Walter and his son, both of them russet-coated, portly gentlemen, at either end.

Wallington's cultural heyday was in the mid-19th century, when the talented Lady Pauline and her husband Sir Walter Trevelyan entertained Ruskin, William Bell Scott and others from the pre-Raphaelite circle. Their memorial is the impressive two-storey hall formed out of the central courtyard in 1853–4. Ringed by Romanesque arcades and a baluster copied from Ruskin's *Stones of Venice*, the hall is painted with Bell Scott's romanticized visions of incidents from Northumbrian history, and with naturalistic panels of flowers – poppies and irises, foxgloves and columbines – by a variety of hands, Lady Pauline and Ruskin among them. There is more work by Ruskin and Bell Scott, including portraits of Pauline and her husband, in the little parlour to one side, together with a couple of watercolours by Turner, whom Ruskin much admired, while a study shows off the desk at which Lord Macaulay, whose sister married a Trevelyan, wrote his masterly *History of England*. There are collections of lead soldiers and dolls houses, while upstairs there is a room hung with sparklingly fresh 18th-century needlework and the remnant of a Georgian cabinet of curiosities, all stuffed birds, geological specimens, and spiky porcupine fish.

North Yorkshire

Allerton Park

4½ m E Knaresborough, on A59 just east of A1; guided tours (*c.* 45 mins); vintage cars and mechanical musical instruments; *open:* Easter Sun–end Sept, Sun and BH Mon 1–6; tel: 0423 330927

This sinister, blackened gothic pile rises from the crest of a low rise, with a three-storey porch dominating a jumble of pinnacled gables, gargoyled, octagonal turrets and staring, stone-mullioned windows. Built in 1849–51 by the local architect George Martin to replace an 18th-century house, Allerton has recently been rescued from an institutional limbo and its Victorian interiors restored. In the half-light of drawn curtains and shutters, visitors see a succession of cavernous, sparsely furnished principal rooms. A galleried baronial hall with a vast staircase pouring down one end rises through the centre of the house to a hammerbeam roof; a gloomy library, lined with a boldly coloured and patterned paper, looks like a setting for a Sherlock Holmes mystery; a ballroom is a manic exercise in Strawberry Hill gothick, the fan vaulting and cluster columns menacingly rich, and the dining-room, still with its original table, is a nightmare of heavy traceried panelling beneath a ribbed and pendanted wooden ceiling. A feeling of unreality, and that the whole place might just be some elaborate set, is heightened by glimpses of strip lighting, functional chairs and 'exit' signs.

Beningbrough Hall ☆☆

8 m NW York off A19, just S Newton on Ouse; NT; teas; garden; *open:* Apr–end Oct, daily, except Thurs and Fri, 11–5 (open Gd Fri and Fri in Jul and Aug); tel: 0904 470666

Rising out of flat, low-lying parkland in the flood-plain of the Ouse is this stately, baroque mansion of *c.*1710-16 built by the young John Bourchier, recently returned from an extensive Grand Tour, who is thought to have acted largely as his own architect. Constructed of the reddest of red bricks, with two equal floors below a hipped roof and prominent cornice, Beningbrough's strongly horizontal lines are broken only by strips of stone and the set pieces over the central doorways. Cupola-topped pavilions like parodies of medieval gatehouses stand to either side.

Beningbrough still has its baroque interiors, a sequence of richly carved, pine-panelled rooms, some left stripped, others painted in soft grey, off-white or green. At the corners of the house, off what were the chief bedrooms on the ground floor, are the tiny closets where honoured guests would be received. The original contents have largely gone, but the house has been refurnished with loans and gifts of period pieces and is hung with 17th- and 18th-century paintings from the National Portrait Gallery.

The extensive tour takes in much of the two principal floors and also ventures into the attics, now arranged as a gallery of 18th-century portraiture.

A concern with architectural effect comes through in the enfilade down the south front, in the long arched corridors which run the length of both floors, and in the lofty entrance hall, with its fluted Corinthian pilasters, groin vault, round-headed openings stopped with ornate wrought-iron grilles, and elaborate keystones. Stepped chimney-pieces set across the corners of the closets are stacked with green and blue oriental porcelain in period style, a baroque state bed came here through the 10th Earl of Chesterfield, who bought the house in 1917, and some fine walnut pieces include the Chesterfields' seaweed marquetry pier tables and glasses in the drawing-room.

The portraits, by all the great names of the day, are everywhere. Grey-green panelling in the dining-room is a foil for the wide gilt frames round Kneller's series of members of the Kit-cat Club, there are two Batonis in the sparsely furnished Saloon, Charles Jervas' full length of his friend Alexander Pope hangs in the drawing-room, together with portraits of Handel and Susannah Arne, for whom the composer wrote the contralto arias in *Messiah*, and there is a charming Reynolds sketch of a four-year-old Georgina Spencer and a poignant painting of the bedridden actress Peg Woffington. Best of all, perhaps, is Kneller's disembodied triptych of the hairless, skull-like head of Daniel Finch, 2nd Earl of Nottingham.

Castle Howard ☆☆☆

15 m NE York, 3 m N of A64; costume collection; tearoom; garden; stunning landscape grounds; *open:* late Mar–end Oct, daily, 11–5; tel: 065 384 333

This great baroque palace has the most thrilling approach of any house in England. From the A64, a dead-straight switchback road framed with beeches and limes veers round a huge column and then narrows through two dramatic gateways, one topped by a pyramid, and with turreted walls stretching away on either side. A sharp right turn round an obelisk leads to the house itself, sitting astride a low ridge. Designed for maximum visual effect, this is a restless and exciting composition, with a domed centrepiece, façades bristling with urns and statues, and rhythmically repetitive round-headed windows and fluted pilasters rippling the length of the show south front. To the north, where two wings sweep round to enclose a courtyard, the ground falls steeply to a great lake; to the south are tree-framed vistas to distant temples and a long watery corridor descending in giant steps. Theatrical in the extreme, Castle Howard was designed in 1699 for the 3rd Earl of Carlisle by the young John Vanbrugh, untrained and untried and known only as a witty and irreverent playwright. The grand conception, with a fairly modest number of rooms strung out behind long show frontages, is his, but its realization owes much to his able assistant, Nicholas Hawksmoor. The west wing was still unfinished at Vanbrugh's death in 1726, and was only completed in the 1750s by the gentleman architect Thomas Robinson, the 3rd Earl's son-in-law, whose uninspired, classical treatment does nothing for the earlier work.

Sadly, a devastating fire in 1940 brought down the dome and destroyed all but two of Vanbrugh's state apartments. The dome has been rebuilt and there is still a show of fine paintings and furniture here, but in general the interior is something of an anti-climax. The tour is concentrated on Robinson's west wing, where visitors are initially plunged into a series of small, high-ceilinged bedrooms. Once into Vanbrugh's long, sculpture-lined, stone-vaulted corridor running down the north front, a sense of drama returns, and the hall rising 70 ft into the dome, with shafts of sunlight picking up a bust there, a fragment of a mural there, and tantalizing, shady vistas through round-headed arches, is still magical, despite the pallid recreation of a Pellegrini painting high overhead.

More unconvincing 20th-century murals, by Felix Kelly, decorate the restored garden hall, but then comes a suite of fine rooms filled with late 17th- and 18th-century pieces, including a table by William Kent and a striking Delft tulip vase, and with some lavishly carved and gilded Vanbrugh decoration. The best of the paintings are here, with portraits by Reynolds, a panoramic view of horses exercising on Newmarket Downs by Wootton and a charming, relaxed Gainsborough, of a little girl watching pigs as they feed, augmented by Italian works from the collection of the Duke of Orleans, acquired by the 5th Duke in 1798. These include a roguish self-portrait by Carracci, his hat at a jaunty angle, Fetti's *The Music Master*, thought to be a likeness of Monteverdi, a voluptuous Salome by Rubens, and Bassano's portrait of his aged mother. The tour ends in Robinson's bare, book-lined, peach-walled long gallery running down the west front, the paintings here including a show of exuberant architectural *capriccios* by Panini and Gentileschi's richly coloured *Finding of Moses*. A glittering chapel is a largely 19th-century creation, with stained glass designed by Burne-Jones, and visitors can also wander through the desolate, fire-ruined south-east wing.

Constable Burton ☆

On A684 between Leyburn and Bedale; garden; *open:* guided tours for 1 month in summer, tel: 0677 50428 for information

This Palladian stone cube by John Carr of York is a grand house writ small. Built in the 1760s for Marmaduke Wyville, whose descendants still live here, it stands high above a deeply incised stream, with a picturesque garden tumbling down the slope. The short tour takes in the stone-floored, portrait-hung entrance hall, the top-lit central staircase, pivot of Carr's symmetrical plan, and the high-ceilinged, comfortably furnished principal rooms on the south and east fronts. The cavernous, green-walled dining-room is a Regency interior furnished by Gillows of Lancaster, but the interconnecting library, morning-room and drawing-room have a Georgian flavour, with restrained Adamesque decoration setting off some fine English and Dutch 18th-century furniture, including a serpentine-fronted Chippendale desk veneered in walnut and rosewood. There are portraits by Mercier and Kneller, and a collection of Dutch pictures, among them works by Weenix and Philip Roos, a Hondecoeter bird painting and a Snyders still-life.

Duncombe Park ☆☆

At Helmsley on A170, 14 m E Thirsk; tearoom; dramatic 18th-century landscape garden; *open:* Easter wkend and Apr Suns 11–6; early May–late Oct, Sun–Thurs, 11–6; tel: 0439 70213

Duncombe is a piece of theatre. It starts quietly enough, from a low-key entrance off one of Helmsley's back streets, but the drive soon suggests something of what is to come, with a glimpse of a classical temple and a sweeping view of the ruined 16th-century range of Helmsley Castle, like an eyecatcher on the edge of the park. The house itself is an imposing building of blackened yellowish stone. The west front, set back behind a heavy screen of railings and flanked by low Italianate quadrangles, has a dour clumsiness about it, but round the back Duncombe emerges as a baroque palace, with a broad flight of steps up to an exaggerated portico and a sculptural quality to the receding and advancing bays either side. Huge stone urns like giant chessmen stud the roofline and a broad, grassy ride leads east to a wide turfed terrace high over the Rye, temples by Vanbrugh and William Robinson set half a mile apart at either end and a plunging view to the river glinting far below.

A new house for a *nouveau riche* family on a greenfield site, Duncombe was built between 1711 and 1713 for Thomas Duncombe to designs by the gentleman architect William Wakefield. Thomas' wealth was due to his uncle Charles, a great Restoration banker, who had bought the estate from the executors of the impetuous George Villiers, 2nd Duke of Buckingham. Enlarged in 1846-51 by Sir Charles Barry, who replaced the original wings with the Italianate pavilions, the house was gutted by fire in 1879 and reconstructed in the 1890s, when the spirit of the original was given an opulent Edwardian gloss.

A girls' school for much of this century, when most of the original contents were sold, Duncombe has recently been brought back to life by the 6th Lord Feversham, descendant of the builder. The interior has been comprehensively redecorated and the main rooms furnished with a mix of bought-in 18th-century pieces, new commissions in period style, and surviving Georgian, Victorian and Edwardian family portraits and other paintings. In comparison with the matchless setting, some may find the interior disappointing. Still of the 18th century is the vast stone-floored hall, 40 ft high, its arcaded walls lined with giant fluted Corinthian columns, encrusted with plasterwork, and an array of bearded classical busts inspecting visitors from on high. Off here, filling the centre of the east front, is the 115 ft, sparsely furnished, brown and gold saloon, divided by screens of fluted Ionic columns, peacock-blue curtains at the windows and portraits by Shannon and Beechey on the walls. A heavy, red-walled dining-room fills one end of this front, while on the south side is the most successful of the recreations, a lush and opulent drawing-room hung with gold silk damask, furnished with French pieces in the style of Louis XV, and with two Claudian landscapes framing a sympathetic modern cabinet full of blue and white porcelain. Here, too, is Andrea

Soldi's charming conversation piece of Thomas Duncombe and his family, and portraits attributed to Philip Mercier, Reynolds and George Dance.

Ebberston Hall ☆

Just W Ebberston village, 11 m W Scarborough, on A170; garden; *open:* Easter–end Sept, daily, 2–6; tel: none

A Venetian villa writ small, with the main floor raised over a hidden basement, Ebberston is more dolls' house than mansion, like a scale model for the real thing. Outside, a grand flight of steps sweeps up to a stately pedimented doorway, and there are stone urns on the roofline balustrade; inside, there are carved and gilded friezes, and a delicious, loggia-like dining-room, with a glazed colonnade looking on to a water garden in the valley behind and stone niches crowned with carved dolphins. But each room, although beautifully proportioned, is only a few feet across.

Designed by Colen Campbell, this delight was built in 1718 for the mistress of the local MP, although it seems the lady never visited the place. More fool she. With its back to the moors and a wide prospect south over the Vale of Pickering, Ebberston has a charm all its own, enhanced by the romantically decaying stonework.

Kiplin Hall ☆

6 m SE Richmond, on S side B6271; teas; grounds; *open:* mid May–late Aug, Sun, Wed and BH Mon, 2–5; tel: 0748 818178

This compact, strongly vertical Jacobean house lying low in the Swale valley was built by George Calvert, 1st Lord Baltimore, Principal Secretary to James I and founder of the state of Maryland. Apart from an ecclesiastical library wing added in 1820, and the plate glass in the windows, the exterior is still largely as built: rigorously symmetrical, with an ogee-capped tower projecting from the middle of each gabled, red-brick façade, and a columned Renaissance porch marking the entrance. Inside, though, it is a different story. Much remodelled in c.1730 for the 5th Lord's stepfather, Christopher Crowe, who wanted somewhere to show off the paintings he had acquired while British consul in Livorno, the house was altered again in the 19th century.

Alas, there is only the remnant of the collection here now, and, despite the heroic efforts of the present guardians, Kiplin is a sadly faded place, though with a certain melancholy charm. Visitors see seven rooms on three floors, climbing to the Jacobean gallery running the width of the house. The bedrooms are desolate, the gallery too much of a hotch-potch, but on the ground floor is a gold-walled 18th-century drawing-room with a market scene of 1568 by Bueckelaer inset in the overmantel and family portraits by Angelica Kauffmann, Beechey and Watts. Trevisani's grand painting of Crowe as an antiquary hangs in the entrance hall, together with works attributed to Dahl, Wissing and Zoffany, and there is a Chippendale cabinet that belonged to the consul, inset with *pietra dura* scenes of Venetian villas.

Markenfield Hall

3 m S Ripon, via Hellwath lane off A61 to W, no advance signs; *open:* Apr–Oct, Mon, 10–12.30, 2.15–5; tel: none

A narrow farm lane leads to the picturesque remains of the early 14th-century fortified manor built here by the unsavoury, self-made John de Markenfield before his fall from royal favour in 1312. The buttressed and battlemented three-storey medieval building fills the north-east corner of a moated, grassy courtyard, with low stone outbuildings and what looks for all the world like a row of cottages closing the other sides, and a 16th-century gateway guarding the bridge over the water. Visitors see three bare, rough-walled rooms in the medieval house, where any atmosphere is rather spoilt by an incongruous carpeted stair and other modern intrusions. From the battlements, there is a view of the cottagey gardens edging the moat, of mossy roofs, and stone barns and sheds, and over the Vale of York to the distant moors.

Newburgh Priory ☆☆☆

Just E Coxwold, 7 m SE Thirsk; guided tour (c. 60 mins); teas; extensive grounds; *open:* early Apr–end June, Wed, Sun, and BH Mon, 2.30–4.45; tel: 034 76 435

Set low among sweeping lawns, with the scarp of the Yorkshire Moors, etched with the white horse of Leyburn, rising steeply to the north, is this beautiful and atmospheric house, with three ranges of yellow-grey stone, one now a romantic ruin, framing the entrance courtyard. An Augustinian priory, founded here in 1145, was converted into a grand Tudor mansion, and altered again in the 18th century, when the dignified Georgian stables and offices lining the approach were built. An Elizabethan porch looks on to the courtyard, the windows are a mix of stone mullions and sashes, and at the back, facing on to the gardens, are two Georgianized bows and a delicious three-storey Jacobean tower curiously wedged into an angle of the façade, with huge windows flanked by pairs of classical columns. Descendants of Sir William Bellasis, who first converted the priory, still live here, and the rooms on show, some Jacobean, some Georgian, are filled with a long accumulation of portraits and furniture.

The varied tour, laced with spicy family history, starts in an intimate, panelled Jacobean room furnished with cane-backed Charles II chairs and early family portraits. It finishes in the spacious Georgian drawing-rooms with rococo plasterwork ceilings by Giuseppe Cortese running out into the bows on the south front, one still with its heavy green, arsenic-based 18th-century paper, hung with portraits by Mary Beale, Philip Mercier and Andrea Soldi, and furnished with a suite of formal French chairs, the other a serene room with an Italian sculpture of a boy entwined with a dolphin placed in the deep alcove on the inner wall and a lovely full-length Romney over the fireplace. There is much of interest on the way. On an upper landing, what looks like a coal-bunker is said to hide the remains of Oliver Cromwell, brought here by his third daughter Mary and her husband, Thomas Bellasis, 1st Earl Fauconberg. A patch on the rough timber top shows where Edward VII, on a visit to Newburgh, tried to break in one afternoon, with the help of the estate joiner, when he was supposed to be taking a nap. Just as intriguing is a bare, cheerless room with gaping holes in the ceiling and rough, unplastered walls which has been left unfinished ever since a fire gutted this end of the priory in 1758. The story goes that the then heir chose to save his own neck rather than help a maid to safety, and that the dying girl left a curse on the room and anyone who tried to complete it. There are unusual details too, such as the gleaming silver watch cases used as handles on many of the shutters, and the gravestone of a horse which survived the Crimean War and returned to Newburgh, to die at the ripe old age of 26.

Newby Hall ☆☆☆

4 m SE Ripon on B6265 to Boroughbridge; tearoom; riverside gardens; *open:* Apr–end Sept, daily, except Mon (but open BH Mon), 12–5; tel: 0423 322583

Approaching down the chestnut avenue stretching across the park, visitors see a dignified, brick and stone, William and Mary mansion with two low wings embracing a paved entrance court. The interior, though, is all of the 18th and 19th century. Returning from an Italian tour in 1765 laden with antique sculpture, the cultivated William Weddell, whose father had acquired Newby in 1748, commissioned John Carr and Robert Adam to transform his new house, building on a gallery and remodelling the main rooms. These assured classical interiors contrast with Regency and Victorian additions in the north wing.

The extensive tour starts in Adam's marble-floored entrance hall, decorated with plasterwork by Joseph Rose and with Chippendale wheelback chairs against the walls. Weddell's cousin, the 3rd Lord Grantham, was responsible for the dining-room of 1807, with portraits by Van Loo on egg-yellow walls and inlaid Chippendale sideboards with spindly fluted legs, while upstairs, preceding a run of recently redecorated bedrooms, is a thoroughly 19th-century billiard room, with gilded embossed paper above heavy carved panelling and portraits by Francis Grant and Watts.

Adam's finest rooms, heralded by his staircase hall running across the house, come last. A formal drawing-room in French taste, all muted buff, grey and pink, is hung with Gobelins tapestries featuring romantic scenes by Boucher, decorated with a delicate ceiling incorporating painted panels by Antonio Zucchi and furnished with gilded Chippendale chairs. Forming an enfilade down the south front, with a long vista to the River Ure across the gardens, are Adam's interconnecting library and sculpture gallery. The feminine library, with book-lined apses at each end screened behind fluted Corinthian columns, shows off some of the 3rd Lord's fine French furniture, while the gallery, notable for its central domed rotunda, is as Weddell had it, focused on a huge antique Roman bath at the far end and with his most expensive acquisition, the much-restored Barberini Venus, given pride of place amongst a mixed company of marble busts and statues. The man himself looks on in a bust by Nollekens and in an assured full-length portrait by Batoni on the stairs.

Norton Conyers ☆

3¹/₂ m N Ripon near Wath, 1¹/₂ m from A1; teas BHs only; garden; *open:* BH Sun and Mon, mid May–mid Sept, Sun, and daily in late July, 2–5.30; tel: 0765 640333

Possibly the original for Charlotte Bronte's Thornfield Hall, where the mad Mrs Rochester was locked away in an attic room, Norton Conyers is a smallish house of melancholy charm overlooking serene parkland. Curving Dutch gables on the south and west fronts, bow windows, Georgian sashes and a classical stone porch suggest a 17th- and 18th-century building, but the drab and patchy brown render now covering the walls hides brickwork dating back to 1500, and round the back, looking on to a bowling green where Charles I is said to have played, are some of the original battlements.

Since 1624, apart from one 20-year gap, Norton Conyers has belonged to the Graham family. Like the outside, the interior is a mix of dates and styles, with marble chimney-pieces and stiff plaster ceilings reflecting remodelling in the 1770s, 19th-century panelling, but also some much earlier features, such as the splendid warped and creaking oak staircase of c.1630. Visitors see some half-dozen rooms on two floors, starting off in what was the Jacobean great hall, with a lofty coved ceiling hiding a timber roof and a huge mullioned and transomed window fitted with Georgian sashes. One wall is filled with John Ferneley's vast canvas of the Quorn hunt, said to have been won on the throw of a dice by the spendthrift Sir Bellingham Graham, 7th Baronet, and then master of the hunt, whose extravagance led to the sale of much of the contents and for a time the house itself in the mid-19th century. Sir Bellingham, painted by William Beechey, also dominates the show of mostly rather dim family portraits. To either side are the bow-windowed Georgian parlour and dining-room, the former with a family group by Zoffany's pupil Henry Walton, the latter with a couple of Romneys and a Batoni hung on powder-blue walls, while upstairs, with an original stone-mullioned window, is the dark, panelled room filled with sturdy 17th-century oak pieces and a carved and inlaid four-poster where James II, then Duke of York, and his young wife, Mary of Modena, slept on their way north in 1679. Most intriguing is the deeply incised hoofprint on the stairs, said to have been cut by the horse that carried the wounded Sir Richard Graham home from Marston Moor.

Nunnington Hall ☆

In village of Nunnington, 4¹/₂ m SE Helmsley, 1¹/₂ m N of B1257; NT; teas; garden; Carlisle Collection of Miniature Rooms; open: Apr–end Oct, Tues, Wed, Thurs, Sat, Gd Fri, and Fri in Jul and Aug, 2–6, Sun and BH Mon 12–6; tel: 043 95 283

In the green and wooded Rye valley, just downstream of a 17th-century pack-horse bridge, is this attractive old house of pale yellow stone, its north side right on the river. Massive chimney stacks dominate the east and west façades and Nunnington's only show front looks south, over the semi-wild terraced garden sloping up the side of the valley. Here, gabled end bays and trim sash windows frame a baroque centrepiece, with two pedimented doorways one above the other and a frivolous balcony. This piece of conceit, like the grand gateways that are such a feature of the garden, dates from 1685–8, when an originally Elizabethan house was radically altered by Richard Graham, 1st Viscount Preston, one of those entrusted with the government of England when James II fled.

The interior, with its moulded oak and pine panelling and stepped corner chimney-pieces, is largely the 1st Viscount's. But the contents are a mixed bag, with some pieces left to the Trust by the last owner, others on loan from the V & A and elsewhere, and a display of exquisitely detailed period miniature rooms, embroidery, paintings, silverware, and furniture all to scale, in the attics. Visitors see over most of the south and west sides of the house, a sequence of small rooms furnished with late 17th- and 18th-century pieces and hung with later prints and paintings, including delicate watercolour landscapes by such as Edward Lear and John Varley. There are a couple of baroque closets, the ceiling of one startlingly painted with the arms and crests of Lord Preston and his wife, lavishly red and gold, floating among fluffy clouds, and a little bedroom, the woodwork round the window still showing the damage inflicted by Cromwellian soldiers, has a tiny oratory off, a reminder of the 1st Lord's conversion to Catholicism. The only impressive room is the large, stone-flagged hall on the south front, dignified with a carved stone fireplace and pedimented doorways and with a three-arched screen giving on to the tapestry-hung Stuart staircase.

Ripley Castle ☆

In Ripley, 3½ m N Harrogate; guided tour (c. 60 mins); tearoom; garden; *open:* May–Sept, daily, except Mon and Fri 11.30-4.30 (3.30 Tues–Thurs in May), Apr, Oct, Sat, Sun, 11.30–4.30, Gd Fri and BHs 11–4.30; tel: 0423 770152

At one end of Ripley market place, beyond the rows of picturesque 19th-century cottages, a high wall erupts into the medieval gatehouse that marks the Ingilby family's ancestral home. One corner of the castle is a buttressed stone tower of 1555, but the rest, in a weak gothic style, with sash windows below a castellated roofline, dates from 1783–6.

The tour is divided between rooms of these two periods. Thoroughly Georgian in spirit is the comfortable drawing-room looking over the long lake in the valley behind, with its Hepplewhite chairs, a Dutch marquetry games table and a Louis XV desk, and so too is the long apse-ended hall, with walls painted to simulate stonework, a screen of marbled wooden columns, an elegant, oval staircase and a show of family portraits. The tower rooms, each filling a floor, are of more interest for their links with family history. A show of armour dates from the Civil War, when the royalist Sir William joined the king, and when Cromwell is said to have insisted on a night's shelter after Marston Moor, sitting up in what is now the library; there is the foundation charter of 1296 for Mount Grace Priory, partially funded by Sir John Ingilby, with an exquisite illumination of St Nicholas presenting the donor to the Virgin; and there is a portrait of Francis Ingilby, hung, drawn and quartered for his faith in 1586 and one of the Catholic martyrs beatified in 1987. The large third-floor room reached by a steep corkscrew stair is still lined with rough 16th-century panelling, while the floor below has a Jacobean plaster ceiling put in to honour James I's stay here on his way south in 1603.

Alas, Ripley has sold its soul to commercial interests; visitors are likely to share the castle with conference delegates and to find some of the Georgian rooms closed for functions.

Shandy Hall

Coxwold, SE Thirsk, between A19 and B1363; garden; *open:* June–Sept, Wed, 2–4.30, Sun 2.30–4.30; tel: 034 76 465

This small brick-faced house at the top end of a sleepy Yorkshire village is where Laurence Sterne (1713–68), author of the subversive, teasing *Tristram Shandy*, lived, on and off, for the last eight years of his life. Dating back to the 15th century, it is a place of low-ceilinged, lived-in, cosy rooms, with

exposed, woodwormy beams and some 17th-century panelling. Sterne himself, newly enriched by his novel, was responsible for the neat 18th-century garden frontage, with its round-headed central niche.

Recently brought back from a ruinous state, Shandy Hall has been lovingly restored, but most of the mementoes here, such as the paintings and prints of scenes from his books and porcelain models of his characters, are products of the Sterneana industry rather than direct reflections of the man. More personal are Nollekens' sharp-nosed bust of the author and the tiny, book-lined room looking on to the road, just big enough for a table and a chair, that was Sterne's study. Here are leather-bound copies of his writings and a selection of the works he loved best, among them Montaigne's essays, Cervantes, Rabelais, and Robert Burton's little-known compilation on the causes of melancholy.

Sion Hill Hall

6 m S Northallerton, 4 m NW Thirsk, at Kirby Wiske, $^1/_2$ m W A167; teas; garden; *open:* May–Oct, 1st Sun of month, 2–5; tel: 0845 587206

Built in the Indian summer before World War I, Sion Hill Hall is a rambling, Lutyens-inspired, red-brick house by the Yorkshire architect Walter Brierley in Queen Anne revival style, with tall brick chimneys rising from a hipped roof and louvered green shutters framing the windows on the south side. Bought by the connoisseur H. W. Mawer in 1961, the house is still used to display his collections of furniture, silver, Continental and English porcelain and paintings, only some two-thirds of which can be shown at any one time. Some rooms are furnished as they might be lived-in, with a mix of pieces on show; others are more museum-like, devoted to collections of marquetry, 19th-century lacquer work, or carved oak furniture, again mostly of the 19th century. There are some early works here, such as a 1596 portrait of Elizabeth I, but Mr Mawer's taste seems to have run more to the products of the late Georgian and Regency, and to the ornate and fanciful, such as inlaid and

North Yorkshire

painted commodes and Dresden and Meissen candlesticks bursting with cherubs and rosebuds.

Stockeld Park ☆

2 m N Wetherby, 7 m SE Harrogate on A661; guided tour (*c.* 45 mins); garden; *open:* Apr–early Oct, Thurs, 2–5; tel: 0937 586101

James Paine's modest Palladian house of pinkish stone built between 1758 and 1763 for the Middleton family has been blurred by later alterations. The restless south façade, originally approached by a drive from Wetherby but now looking over parkland, is largely as Paine devised it, with pediments crowning both the wings and the three-storey central block and windows set back within round-headed recesses, but the north front, which visitors see first, is swamped by the huge Victorian portico and wing added by Robert John Foster, the mill-owner who bought the estate in the 19th century and whose descendants still live here. Foster was also responsible for Detmar Blow's Renaissance-style chapel.

Of the six rooms shown, the highlight is Paine's beautiful, apse-ended, blue and white staircase hall running up through the centre of the house to an oval dome. Doorcases are curved to follow the walls and the elegant cantilevered stair has a delicate, wrought-iron baluster. Nothing else is as heart-warming. A mint-green library, with a screen of mock-marble columns at one end, was once the chapel, the Adamesque decor in the drawing-room is an Edwardian scheme by Waring and Gillow, and the decorative ceiling and marble fireplace in Paine's original entrance hall have been hidden beneath a blanket of mushroom paint, perhaps a legacy of the years when Stockeld was a maternity home.

Sutton Park ☆☆

Sutton-on-the-Forest, 8 m N York, on B1363 York-Helmsley road; teas; garden and estate walks; *open:* Easter wkend, early May–end Sept, Wed, Sun and BH Mon, 1.30–5.30; tel: 0347 810249

In the middle of Sutton-on-the-Forest, its gates opening off the main street, is this early Georgian house of rosy red brick. Probably designed by Thomas Atkinson of York, it is a plain, Palladian building with a tall, pedimented central block linked by curving passages to pavilions either side. Despite rococo plaster ceilings by Giuseppe Cortese and fine Adam-style chimney-pieces, this is not a grand place. Now owned by a descendant of the Duke of Buckingham, the man whose London mansion was transformed into a royal palace, Sutton Park combines a lived-in atmosphere with fine furniture and portraits.

The extensive visitor tour takes in ten or so rooms, the best of them looking south on to the enchanting gardens created by the present owners. Here is a chocolate-walled library, lined with bookcases from Normanby Park, the family's Lincolnshire seat, with a self-portrait by Benjamin West among the show of paintings and a row of bluejohn urns along the mantelpiece. The cosy morning room has classical pine panelling by Henry Flitcroft that used to adorn a house outside Leeds, and a softly coloured, green-walled sitting-room, with three long, round-headed windows to the garden, is furnished with some delicate French pieces and hung with views of London by Samuel Scott, with Wren's stone steeples soaring above a red-brick city. Elsewhere, there are displays of Imari, English and Continental porcelain, including a Kaendler teapot made in the shape of a monkey, some fresh 18th-century Chinese wallpaper, rococo mirrors and girandoles, a Canaletto of old Somerset House, a Paul Sandby view of Windsor Castle and van der Meulen's painting of William III's entry into London in 1689.

West Yorkshire

Bolling Hall

S edge of Bradford, signed from ringroad; grounds; *open:* all year, Tues–Sun, 10–6 (5 in winter); tel: 0274 723057

This long smoke-blackened house on a hill above Bradford, its grounds now engulfed by the spreading city, consists of 17th-century ranges attached to a medieval three-storey tower. Intimate panelled rooms with stone-mullioned windows at one end contrast with the Georgian interiors fashioned out of the east wing by Carr of York in 1779–80, one of which has a rococo plaster ceiling. Owned by Bradford corporation since 1912, the house is now used to show off the city's collections of North Country furniture and pictures, with sturdy 17th-century oak cupboards, tables and beds in the Jacobean rooms contrasting with elegant 18th-century and heavier Regency pieces in the Carr wing. Both periods are represented in the lofty, stone-floored great hall, with its Georgian gallery and frieze and a show of richly coloured Tudor glass in the 30-light, stone-mullioned window.

Bramham Park ☆☆☆

5 m S Wetherby, just W A1 at Bramham; guided tours (*c.* 50 mins); spectacular garden; *open:* mid June–end Aug, Sun, Tues, Wed, Thurs, and BH Mon 1.15–5.30; tel: 0937 844265

An Italianate house of golden stone, more villa than palace, floats above a vast, formal garden, with long beech-lined walks leading to temples, urns and obelisks, and a series of hanging ponds forming a great watery staircase. A dignified building in a serene setting, Bramham Park was created by the financier Robert Benson, Chancellor of the Exchequer to Queen Anne, in the first decades of the 18th century, acting, it is thought, as his own architect and garden designer. Giant colonnades, like a piece of the forum, link the main block to pavilions either side, a carriage ramp sweeps up to the first-floor entrance, and a grassy forecort is framed by James Paine's classical stables and by a couple of nonsensical baroque gate piers, topped by anxious heraldic bears.

Surprisingly, given such a build-up, the interior is relatively modest, a reflection of the fact Bramham was designed as a summer retreat. Then, too, most of the house was gutted by fire in 1828 and has only been brought back to life this century, so little is as originally devised. The tour starts in the unaltered, fire-scarred hall, a dignified, blackened stone cube ornamented with giant Corinthian pilasters and round-headed niches and hung with full-length portraits by Reynolds and Kneller. Double doors lead to the long gallery running down the garden front, with a double-sided parquetry desk thought to have been made for Louis XV in the middle of a sparsely furnished expanse, giant Imari urns set on marble-topped tables against the walls, and portraits by Lely, Reynolds, Highmore, Hoppner and Beechey.

These grand spaces, and the green and white drawing-room recently created on the north side of the house, contrast with several more intimate, lived-in rooms, some of them with uncompromisingly strident colour schemes – smoky green and puce, orange and pink – devised by Laura Ashley and the present owners. A mix of furniture includes some Dutch marquetry pieces, comfortable, bun-footed Queen Anne chairs, a lovely Chippendale mirror, and a state bed of the same period as the house hung with 18th-century crewelwork. A massive Georgian sideboard that has always been here, even while Bramham stood empty for 80 years, shows off the mother-of-pearl gambling counters with which the Regency buck George Lane Fox, great-nephew of Benson's daughter, almost destroyed the estate, and the family portraits are accompanied by sporting paintings by Agasse and Ferneley, hunting scenes by John Wootton and Sartorius, a flower piece by Campidoglio, a landscape by Orizonte and a fragment of an *Adoration of the Magi* by Jordaens.

Brontë Parsonage

At Haworth, 4 m SW Keighley, on A6033; parking in public park; *open:* daily, Apr–Sept, 10–5, Oct–Mar, 11–4.30 (closed Christmas and mid-Jan to mid-Feb); tel: 0535 642323

High on the shoulder of the Worth valley, 800 ft up in the Pennines, is the stone-built Yorkshire village which has sold its soul to the Brontë industry, its steep cobbled main street now lined with tea-shops and souvenir emporia. The parsonage where Charlotte, Emily and Anne wrote in the 1840s and where their brilliant brother Branwell slowly disintegrated is a modest, late 18th-century, two-storey building of blackened stone tucked away behind the church. Do not expect too much. Now in the hands of the Brontë Society, its interiors are partly recreated as the Brontës had them, partly given over to museum displays, while later alterations, notably the large wing added on to the back, have blurred the original outlines of the house.

Most convincing are the comfortless dining-room where the sisters gathered to write in the evening, with the sofa on which Emily died against one wall, and Mr Brontë's study across the hall, with a table set for one of his solitary meals, engravings of apocalyptic Biblical paintings on the walls, and a huge magnifying glass which he used as his sight failed by a large-print copy of the psalms. Some of Branwell's portraits hang in a claustrophobic upstairs room, its windows blocked by the new wing, and also on show are such treasures as Charlotte's lacy wedding bonnet and writing desk, samples of the Brontës' writing and drawing, and the cupboard painted with the twelve apostles which Charlotte described in *Jane Eyre*. But those on a literary pilgrimage must battle with the antiseptic, unreal atmosphere and harsh modern lighting. Better to walk up on to the moors behind or to stand in the churchyard below the house, where the gravestones are so tightly packed they look like a great crowd waiting silently on the hillside.

East Riddlesden Hall ☆

1 m E Keighley, on S side A650; NT; tearoom; garden; *open:* Apr–end Oct, Sat–Wed, Gd Fri and Thurs in July and Aug, 12–5.30; tel: 0535 607075

This modest, smoke-blackened stone house on a bluff above the Aire is something of an architectural puzzle, with a great hall wing of indeterminate date wedged between a roomy gabled block finished in 1648 and the ruin of a classical façade. A pinnacled porch projects boldly from the entrance front, and an ancient fishpool and two massive barns help to screen the place from the urban sprawl of Keighley pressing close outside the gates.

Coming to the Trust empty, East Riddlesden has been re-furnished, mostly in 17th-century style, with loaned and donated pieces. The stone-flagged, rough-walled hall is a bare, comfortless space open to the roof, but the panelled rooms in the 1648 wing, some with original plaster ceilings, are much cosier. There are carpet-covered tables in the 17th-century fashion, some Charles II walnut pieces, and displays of pewter and blue and white china, while a bedroom with light green 18th-century panelling is furnished as a Georgian interior.

East Riddlesden is also one of the few Trust properties where ghosts are acknowledged, among them a woman in white, said to have drowned in the fishpond, and a lady of the manor who was starved to death by a sadistic husband after being caught *in flagrante delicto* with her lover.

Harewood House ☆☆☆

At junction of A61 Leeds to Harrogate road and A659, 5 m from A1 at Wetherby; café; bird garden; garden and lakeside walk; *open:* early Apr–end Oct, daily 11-5; tel: 0532 886331

Barbados sugar plantations funded this palatial house set high above a

tree-fringed lake. Built for Edwin Lascelles, 1st Earl of Harewood, from 1759, it was designed by Carr of York, decorated and fitted out in the following decade by Robert Adam, and furnished by Thomas Chippendale. Almost a century later, Carr's chaste Palladian mansion, with pavilions linked to a pedimented and porticoed central block, was blurred by extensions and modifications by Sir Charles Barry. To the north, Harewood is still recognisably Carr's, but to the south, above the steep green slopes of the valley, it looks like an Italianate palazzo in the *Cliveden* mould, with a vast double staircase descending to a fountain-studded terrace.

The tour of the principal floor takes in beautifully presented 18th- and 19th-century rooms, the former embellished with plasterwork by Joseph Rose and William Collins, and by decorative panels by Angelica Kauffmann and Biagio Rebecca. Many of the original furnishings are still here, there is a show of oriental and French porcelain, and a long run of family portraits has been enriched in this century by the 6th Earl's important collection of Italian and Spanish paintings, acquired with the fortune left him by an eccentric great uncle, whom he met only once, quite by chance, just weeks before his death.

The tone is set by Adam's stone-floored entrance hall, with fluted pilasters wine red against grey walls, pedestalled busts in round-headed niches, and Epstein's heavy-buttocked alabaster Adam rooted in the middle, staring up at the ceiling. To the east are mostly intimate, family rooms, one furnished with Chinese Chippendale pieces, another showing portrait sketches by Singer Sargent and Salisbury and Sir Alfred Munnings' painting of the local hunt, with sunshine and shade chasing across the country behind.

The state rooms, some unchanged since Adam's time, are on the west side of the house. Here are crested Chippendale mirrors and an exquisitely inlaid commode, gilded chairs covered in Beauvais tapestry and carpets echoing the plaster swirls on the ceiling. A cinnamon-walled drawing-room with seven portraits by Reynolds and others by Gainsborough, Romney and Hoppner forms an ante-room to the 77 ft long gallery running down the west front, with carved pelmets imitating heavy drapes and marbled columns dividing the Venetian windows at either end. Sparsely furnished in Georgian style, with chairs pushed back against deep red walls, the gallery is hung three deep with the 6th Earl's paintings, among them Titian's portrait of a beak-nosed Francis I, a Madonna and Child by Bellini, with the baby balanced on the frame, a portrait by Veronese, Lorenzo Lotto's intense vision of old age, St Jerome by Sodoma and a bizarre allegory by El Greco.

Nostell Priory ☆☆

On A638, 6 m SE Wakefield; NT; teas; rose garden and lakeside walk; *open:* early Apr-end Oct, Sat 12–5, Sun and BH Mon 11–5, and daily, except Fri, in Jul and Aug, 12–5, Sun 11–5; tel: 0924 863892

A vast and severe Palladian house, its monotonous façades relieved only by pedimented porticoes, Nostell Priory was built for Sir Rowland Winn, 4th Baronet, from 1735. Within this forbidding shell – probably based on plans by the gentleman architect Col. James Moyser – are delicious decorative interiors, the earlier, dating from the 1740s, with sumptuous rococo plasterwork, the later, of the 1760s and '70s, in the chaster Adam style, and all with a range of Chippendale furniture specially made for the house. Sir Rowland had the services of the young James Paine, who also executed and modified Moyser's design, and of the plasterers Thomas Perritt and Joseph Rose the Elder. On the baronet's death in 1765, Robert Adam completed the house for his son, with plasterwork by Joseph Rose the Younger and decorative paintings by Antonio Zucchi.

Visitors do a complete circuit of the principal rooms on the first floor. Except for two interiors badly damaged by fire in 1980, the priory is all of a piece, with a nice contrast between the exuberant work by Paine, seen to particular effect on the two staircases rising through the house, and the Adam rooms, their ornate ceilings coloured in vibrant mint green, wine red and slate blue, or a range of pastel shades. The Chippendale pieces ordered by Sir Rowland are varied to suit each room, from the massive desk in the library and an inlaid commode in the saloon to the green and gold chinoiserie suite and rococo mirrors in the state bedroom, where the walls are hung with a fine Indian paper featuring exotic birds and butterflies on a golden ground.

So rich is the 18th-century decoration that there is little need for pictures, apart from Zucchi's static decorative panels, and the set of classical ruins which he painted for the saloon. Visitors are sometimes offered a glimpse of works by Angelica Kaufmann, Guido Reni and Poussin in the family's private rooms; portraits of Sir Rowland and his brother, by Henry Pickering, hang either end of Paine's magnificent dining-room; and there is a sudden cluster in the restored rooms at the end of the tour, among them Hogarth's illustration of *The Tempest* and Brueghel the Younger's panoramic vision of Christ on his way to Calvary, with a gabled and steepled Flemish town in the distance. A work of art of a different kind is the doll's house attributed to Chippendale which gleams out of a gloomy passage. Miniature furnishings replicate every detail of the period, from drinking glasses to overmantel paintings, and the mouse in the kitchen.

Oakwell Hall

Nutter Lane, Birstall, signed from junction A62 and A652; café; country park; *open:* all year, Mon–Fri 11–5, Sat, Sun 12–5; tel: 0924 474926

The inspiration for Fieldhead in Charlotte Bronte's *Shirley* is a modest, gabled house of smoke-blackened millstone grit sitting in an oasis of green fields just below an elevated section of the M62. Although dating from 1583, the place was substantially refitted and enlarged in the late 17th century, when the hall was given its 30-light mullioned window, and is a good example of the vernacular architecture of the time. Now in the hands of the local council, its modest, panelled rooms, some with remnants of Jacobean plasterwork, others with painted embellishment, are sparsely but appropriately furnished with 16th- and 17th-century pieces, including bulbous-posted Yorkshire beds.

Shibden Hall

1 m E Halifax, off A58; café; gardens and park; *open:* Mar–Nov, Mon–Sat 10-5, Sun 12–5, Feb, Sun, 2–5; tel: 0422 352246

This partly half-timbered, partly stone-faced house set high on the side of a steep and wooded Pennine valley on the outskirts of Halifax is not quite what it seems. Although dating from Tudor and Jacobean times, and with some surviving original features, Shibden Hall as it is now largely reflects the taste of Anne Lister, who inherited the place in 1826. With the help of the architect John Harper, this independent, self-educated woman subjected the old house to a radical restoration that involved demolishing some parts, rebuilding others in a romantic gothic style, and substantially altering the interior plan.

Although now a museum, its outbuildings devoted to displays on Pennine crafts and agriculture, the hall has been well furnished by the local council, who have created realistic 17th- and 18th-century interiors in the intimate panelled rooms.

Temple Newsam

5 m E Leeds, S of A63; tearoom; garden and park; *open:* all year, Tues–Sun, 10.30–5.30 (or dusk, if earlier); tel: 0532 647321

Temple Newsam looks magnificent. Framing three sides of a huge courtyard on a platform above a wooded park, with a long vista east up a grassy ride through the trees, are tall ranges of dark-red brick, with a balustraded roofline and a grid of mullioned and transomed windows wrapped round jutting bays. Later alterations have blurred rather than destroyed the Tudor and Jacobean conception, but inside Temple Newsam is massively changed. The decorative schemes are principally Georgian and later, while the furnishings have almost all been brought in by the Leeds City Art Gallery, who were given the empty house in 1922 and have opened it as a museum of furniture and decorative art. The place comes alive only in the interconnecting Georgian gallery and library in the north wing, with plasterwork by Perritt and Joseph Rose the Elder, Kent-style chimney-pieces, rococo seat furniture made for the house, and a show of paintings that includes several that have always been here.

Scotland

Borders, Central, Dumfries & Galloway, Fife, Grampian, Highland, Lothian, Strathclyde, Tayside

- Dunrobin Castle
- Brodie Castle
- Castle Stuart
- Cawdor Castle
- Dunvegan Castle
- Fyvie Cas
- Leith Hall
- Castle
- Craigievar
- Drum C
- Crathes Castle
- Braemar Castle
- Fas
- Blair Castle
- House of Dun
- Glamis Castle
- Torosay Castle
- Duart Castle
- Scone Palace
- Earlshall Castle
- Hill of Tarvit
- Falkland Palace
- Kellie Castle
- Balcaskie
- Inveraray Castle
- House of the Binns
- Hopetoun House
- Linlithgow Palace
- Lauriston Castle
- Gosford Hou
- Stevenson
- Dalmeny House
- Lennoxlove
- Finlaystone House
- Arniston House
- Ay
- Kelburn Castle
- Mander
- Pax
- Thirlestane Castle
- Mellerstai
- Brodick Castle
- Traquair
- Floors Ca
- Abbotsford
- Bowhill
- Culzean Castle
- Blairquhan Castle
- Drumlanrig Castle
- Maxwelton House
- Rammerscales

Abbotsford ☆

3 m W Melrose, 5 m NE Selkirk, off A72;
tearoom; garden; *open:* late Mar–end Oct,
Mon–Sat 10–5, Sun 2–5; tel: 0896 2043

Anyone who comes to this rambling, vaguely Tudor 19th-century house on the banks of the Tweed knowing nothing of its maker, and with only the arid guide to help them, may well go away feeling bemused. Some houses illuminate those who have lived there; here, you have to know the man to understand his creation. Once a farm, Abbotsford was transformed from 1822 onwards into the gabled, turreted and gargoyled confection seen today by Sir Walter Scott, who, with the help of the architects William Atkinson and Edward Blore, dreamed up an architectural version of his romantic historical novels.

The interior is awash with dark, polished panelling, plaster vaulting, grotesque carved corbels and other gothic details, such as a fireplace copied directly from the cloisters of Melrose Abbey. The effect is gloomy in the extreme, particularly as the rooms shown, many of them with museum display cases, do not feel remotely lived in. Were Scott here there would be roaring fires and the warmth of his personality, both of which are sorely needed.

Visitors do a circuit of the ground floor, taking in the impressive library, still lined with Scott's books and displaying some of the historical relics he collected so avidly, such as a clasp from Napoleon's cloak; the smoking corridor hung with some of his collection of armour; and the dining-room with a wide bay towards the Tweed, where he died on a warm September afternoon in 1832, the murmur of the river in his ears. There is a hint of everyday life in Landseer's painting of Scott's rough-haired terrier Ginger, and in the dog gates dividing the smoking corridor, and the galleried, high-ceilinged study is where, after the financial crash of 1826 left him with mountainous debts, Scott started work at dawn, writing himself into an early grave to repay what he owed.

Ayton Castle

7 m N Berwick-upon-Tweed, on A1; guided
tour (c. 30 mins); *open:* May–Sept, Sun, 2–5;
tel: 089 07 81212

This sprawling red sandstone castle, with pepper-pot turrets corbelled out from the central tower, was built for the Governor of the Bank of Scotland by James Gillespie Graham in 1846. A well-preserved example of the Scottish baronial style, Ayton still has its gilded Italianate plasterwork ceilings, painted decoration and other original features. The Victorian era seems to live on in the cluttered, formal drawing-room with its mass of footstools, little tables covered in *objets* and potted plants, while the gallery-like corridor running down the north side of the house is a rich ensemble of Turkish rugs on mellow parquet, gilded, marble-topped pier tables below huge mirrors, and family portraits. Alas, the perfunctory guided tour imparts almost no information, leaving visitors to glean what they may.

Bowhill ☆☆

3 m W Selkirk, on A708; tearoom; country park; *open:* July, daily, 1–4.30; tel: 0750 20732

Looking south over the green Vale of Ettrick, with wide views to moorland ridges, is this dour barracks of a house, faced in grey whin stone cut to look like brick, the long sash-windowed façades relieved only by an Italianate tower marking the former chapel. Originally a hunting lodge, the present rambling structure was the result of 19th-century remodelling by several hands.

But do not be downcast. Bowhill, like *Boughton* and *Drumlanrig,* is a seat of the Duke of Buccleugh, and the unexceptional interior is filled with a priceless collection of furniture, paintings, porcelain and historical relics. Some parts feel more like a museum or art gallery than a house. A bare billiards room is hung with eight Venetian scenes by Guardi, views of Naples and the south by Joli, and other Italian landscapes; the chilly, high-ceilinged barn that was once the chapel is now devoted to the reckless Duke of Monmouth, Charles II's natural son, from whom the Dukes of Buccleugh are descended, with a portrait by Lely and cases of relics, among them Monmouth's glittering, gold encrusted bridle and saddle, and the surprisingly trim lacy shirt in which he was executed; and there is a study remembering Sir Walter Scott, friend of the 4th Duke, the display of relics here including a leather-bound proof of Scott's life of Napoleon, his dark green and grey plaid, and a copy of *The Lay of the Last Minstrel* dedicated to the 4th Duchess.

The pick of the collection is assembled in the furnished rooms along the south front, looking out over the Ettrick. A long, olive-green Regency dining-room with a display of family silver shows off two portraits by Reynolds, one of a black-eyed, apple-cheeked little girl in cloak and muff that would sit well on any chocolate box, a clutch of Gainsboroughs, and two panoramic views of London, the first, by Jan Griffier, showing barges like scarlet-plumaged birds dotting the Thames, the second, by Canaletto, looking north up old Whitehall, with long shadows and a dawn-tinged sky, and a timeless building site in one corner. A lush, crimson-walled drawing-room with a gilded ceiling is furnished with tapestry-covered French chairs, Boulle cabinets filled with Meissen porcelain, some of it made for Madame du Barry, who went to the guillotine 'vainly whimpering', and a rare longcase clock by Joseph Knibb. Here, too, there are paintings, including a Reynolds portrait accompanied by the artist's original sketch, and some interestingly juxtaposed landscapes, two unreal, gold-tinged scenes by Claude contrasting with a rugged, stormy work by Jacob van Ruisdael and a couple of Vernets, one in the style of the Dutchman, the other showing the influence of Claude.

Elsewhere is the Bowhill collection of miniatures, among them icon-like Hilliards, a bull-necked ageing nobleman by Holbein, and Samuel Cooper's astonishingly detailed, unfinished portrait of Oliver Cromwell, thinning hair above a furrowed brow. Visitors enter the house via a galleried hall, with Mortlake tapestries hung high above portraits by Lely and Mytens and more splendid 18th-century French furniture.

Floors Castle ☆☆

On A6089 just NW Kelso; tearoom; grounds; *open:* Easter-wkend, and late Apr–end Sept, Sun–Thurs (daily in July and Aug), 10.30–5.30, Oct, Sun and Wed, 10.30–4.30; tel: 0573 223333

On a rise above the Tweed, looking over an idyllic pastoral landscape towards the little town of Kelso, is the palace of the Dukes of Roxburghe. Like a sombrely dressed lady with a frivolous hat, Floors combines austere Georgian façades with a fanciful 19th-century roofline. Built in 1718–40 by William Adam as a plain, four-square block with corner towers, the castle was given a fairytale silhouette in 1838 by William Playfair, who added castellations, pepperpot turrets and the toy cannon which poke from the battlements.

Inside, there are still some Adam ceilings and fireplaces, but the grand reception rooms looking out over the Tweed which form the main focus of the tour were largely remodelled early this century by Duchess Mary, the cultivated American heiress who married the 8th Duke. Panelled and tapestry-hung in the style of 18th-century France, they are filled with fine French furniture and oriental porcelain the Duchess brought with her, augmenting the Roxburghe paintings and other treasures.

Both aspects of the collection are on view. In the three intimate rooms which start the tour are portraits by Raeburn, Hudson, Reynolds and Beechey, a Ferneley hunting scene, and Hendrick Danckerts' painting of Charles II walking informally in St James's Park, a pack of little spaniels racing round his feet. Less successful is the confusion of 17th- and 18th-century pieces in the vast ballroom which Playfair added on to the south front, where a mix of capacious Stuart and Georgian chairs, high-backed William and Mary ones, lacquered cabinets and oriental porcelain, with paintings by Gainsborough and Hoppner on the walls, looks rather like a grand antique shop. In between is Duchess Mary's opulent, tapestry-hung drawing-room, with plump-cushioned sofas among a scatter of marquetry cabinets and commodes, a French clock on the purple marble mantelpiece, and candelabra supported on green Meissen parrots. The little tower room off, furnished with formal Louis XVI pieces, is hung with the Duchess's collection of late 19th- and 20th-century art, including still lifes by Matisse and Augustus John, and a river scene by Pierre Bonnard.

The tour of this show-place ends with a formal array of family treasures, from cases of stuffed birds and Meissen and Coalport dinner services to the

Duchess's collection of 18th-century enamelled snuff boxes and parasols with Fabergé handles.

Manderston ☆☆☆

2 m E Duns on A6105; teas; biscuit tin collection; garden; *open:* early May–end Sept, Thurs, Sun and BH Mon, 2–5.30; tel: 0361 83450

Manderston is the peak of Edwardian opulence. Built 1903–5 for the *nouveau riche* Sir James Miller, whose father had made a fortune trading in hemp and herrings, the house was designed, with no expense spared, by the young John Kinross, who incorporated an earlier Georgian building in his plans. The porticoed entrance front is severely classical, but the south façade, looking over Italianate terraces falling to a lake, is softened by two rounded bays and by a white-railed balcony giving on to the garden. The interior is an Adamesque pastiche, with painted and stuccoed ceilings and marble fireplaces closely modelled on *Kedleston,* the childhood home of Miller's wife. Unlike Kedleston, though, this is a house for living in, even the grandest rooms being conceived on a surprisingly intimate scale. And then, Miller was creating an ancestral home from scratch, buying a job lot of portraits to hang on the dining-room walls, mixing genuine antiques with repro pieces, and even acquiring a collection of samplers to give the right touch.

Money was poured into fine materials and craftsmanship. The top-lit hall, with delicate plasterwork on walls and ceiling, is floored in green and grey marble, there is a gleaming silver balustrade to the staircase, and the passage leading to the dining-room is screened by silver-plated grilles set on panels of translucent glowing alabaster. The string of reception rooms along the east and south fronts was designed for balls and house parties. There is a masculine, red-walled billiard-room cum library at one end, a completely circular, feminine morning-room going out into one of the bows at the other, and in the middle the interconnecting ballroom and drawing-room which are Manderston's show-piece, the one all silver and gold, the other white and pale blue, both with pastel plaster ceilings and reproduction Louis XVI furniture pushed back against the walls in the 18th-century fashion. The most elaborate plasterwork, with classical medallions in high relief, is reserved for the dining-room, which is furnished with a set of Chippendale-style, ribbon-back chairs and Lady Miller's collection of bluejohn urns and obelisks, one lit from within to show the rich range of colours in the stone.

Visitors also see a row of north-facing bedrooms and the extensive white-tiled kitchen quarters, fed by a coterie of marble-shelved larders, while across the great expanse of grass at the front of the house, with drifts of bluebells beneath chestnuts and beeches, are the marble and alabaster dairy, vaulted like a chapel, the turret room panelled in Spanish oak where Lady Miller could sip tea and enjoy the view, and the stable block which was Kinross's test commission, with stalls of teak and the horse's names – all beginning with M – engraved on marble slabs. Sadly, Sir James's love of all outdoor pursuits led to his early death, in 1906, from a chill caught while hunting. The house had only been finished a few months and only one ball held.

Mellerstain ☆☆☆

Off A6089, 9 m NE Melrose, 7 m NW Kelso; tearoom; gardens; *open:* Easter wkend, May–end Sept, daily, except Sat, 12.30–5; tel: 057381 225

This chunky castellated house looking south to the Cheviots over a panoramic expanse of Border country was Robert Adam's first important commission in his native Scotland. Built in 1770–8 for the Baillie family, Earls of Haddington, it is flanked by low pavilions of a much rougher stone designed in 1725 by William Adam, Robert's father, while Italianate terraces above the sweep of grass that plunges Gadarene-like to the valley below were Edwardian additions by Sir Reginald Blomfield.

Classically symmetrical and severely plain, Mellerstain has none of the gaiety of *Kenwood* or the drama of the later *Culzean,* but the interior decoration is among Adam's finest. High-ceilinged, interconnecting reception rooms running the length of the south front have delicate plaster friezes and ceilings picked out in their original pastel blues, greens and pinks, marble fireplaces, and Adam side tables and mirrors designed for the house. The comfortable, cluttered library, with busts by Roubiliac set in niches above the doors, Ionic pilasters dividing the bookcases, and a scatter of generous Queen Anne chairs and Dutch marquetry tables among chintzy sofas, contrasts with the more formal, sparsely furnished drawing-rooms and music room to either side. Among a good show of paintings are several portraits by Allan Ramsay, an enchanting Gainsborough of the builder's wife, lit so as to emphasize the fine lace trimming of her dress, works by Maria Varelst and William Aikman, a landscape by J. van Ruisdael, some 16th-century Italian and Flemish pictures, and a child painting by Nicolaes Maes.

The extensive tour takes in Adam's curiously cramped staircase and a clutch of unmemorable bedrooms before climbing, via a narrow back stair, to Mellerstain's most unusual feature: a spacious, barrel-roofed gallery running north to south across the main block. Although unfinished, its decorative plaster ceiling never installed, this is still an extraordinarily impressive room. It is now used to display a collection of 18th- and 19th-century costume and assorted family treasures, among them Bonnie Prince Charlie's bagpipes and the household accounts kept in the 18th century by Lady Grizelda, who wrote detailed instructions to the staff as to how things should be done.

Paxton House ☆☆

5 m W Berwick-upon-Tweed, on B6461; guided tours (*c.* 60 mins); tearoom; garden and river walks; *open:* Gd Fri–end Oct, daily, 12–5; tel: 0289 86291

Crowning a bluff above the Tweed, with views across the water into England, is this trimly symmetrical, Palladian house of dull red stone, with curving screen walls connecting the central pedimented and porticoed block to flanking pavilions. Paxton is a monument to lost hopes. Designed by John and James Adam, it was begun in 1758 for Patrick Home, 13th Laird of Wedderburn, who was expecting to marry the beautiful illegitimate daughter of Frederick the Great. Alas, the bride's father insisted that Patrick move to Germany, and by 1761 it was clear the betrothal would never take place. Building work stopped with only two rooms completed, and the house was finished, decades later, by Patrick's half-brother Ninian. Then, in 1811, the 16th laird engaged Robert Reid to add a library and picture gallery to the east pavilion.

Although Patrick's paintings and *objets d'art* have largely gone, the Chippendale and other furniture made for the house is still here, and the decorative schemes are newly restored. The hall and staircase, with restrained plasterwork by Morrisons of Edinburgh, are as finished for Patrick, but the main rooms along the south front have plasterwork ceilings by Robert Adam, and elsewhere there are small-patterned wallpapers designed by Chippendale the Younger. The elder Chippendale supplied the mahogany dining suite, with its wooden urns, oval mirrors and pier tables, and some of the bedroom furniture, such as a set of painted wheelback chairs, but his son was responsible for the more delicate pieces in the drawing-room.

The full and unhurried tour ends in the Regency additions. The oval-ended library, lined with pine bookcases, shows off rosewood furniture by Trotter of Edinburgh, including three Grecian sofas and a table on lyre supports, while the adjoining apse-ended gallery, the largest such room in a private Scottish house, is hung with a show of paintings on loan from the National Gallery of Scotland, the rather harsh colour scheme here, with a screen of marbled yellow Doric columns against green walls, reflecting Victorian taste.

The sad 13th laird appears in a sequence of portraits in the saloon, the last, after the failure of a second attempt at marriage, showing him as a lonely and dejected old man. Of the beautiful young girl who inspired the house there is no trace, except for a pair of white silk gloves, framed on a wall.

Thirlestane Castle ☆

At Lauder, 28 m SE Edinburgh off A68; tearoom; museum of border country life; woodland walk; *open:* Easter wkend, May, June, Sept, Wed, Thur, Sun; July and Aug, daily, except Sat, 2–5; tel: 0578 722430

A romantic confusion of pepperpot turrets and towers with finialled, pyramidal caps, and the great balustraded staircase up to a raised entrance court, suggest a cross between a French château and Camelot. In fact, the heart of this T-shaped castle of cream and pink stone rising high on a steep slope above the Leader Water is a 16th-century border fortress. Remodelled with a splendid state apartment by William Bruce in the late 17th century for the unpleasant John Maitland, 2nd Earl of Lauderdale, the castle was enlarged

and altered again in the 1840s by David Bryce and William Burn, who gave the place its rose-tinted skyline.

Despite some bold 17th-century plasterwork ceilings in the former state apartment, with bunches of grapes and foliage tendrils hanging free from clusters of fruit and flowers, the interiors are predominantly Victorian and Edwardian. Some are panelled and plastered in a Jacobean style, others lined with floral wallpaper, and there is a profusion of hideous, speckled granite fireplaces. Sadly, too, the Duke and his scheming second wife, the Countess of Dysart, took some 14 carriage-loads of fine 17th-century furniture south to *Ham House*, her London home, and almost everything here now is 19th-century.

The visitor tour is arranged so the best comes last. From a suite of unexciting ground-floor rooms, a spiral stair leads up to the Restoration apartments, where two 17th-century rooms have been turned into a glorious double drawing-room running across the old keep. Huge mirrors reflect the plasterwork ceiling and Edwardian portraits of beautiful women in diaphanous dresses, and the walls are hung with an elegant green and gold paper. Adjoining is the one unaltered 17th-century interior, a splendid baroque anteroom with three great pedimented doorcases and a richly ornate ceiling. One doorway leads to the grand staircase by which the Duke's visitors approached his state rooms, the other to a Victorian dining-room. Here Lely's full-length painting of the Duke dominates family portraits by Reynolds, Lawrence and Romney.

Traquair ☆☆

6 m SE Peebles, 1 m S Innerleithen, at junction of B709 and B7062; tearoom; grounds; open: Easter week, May–end Sept, daily, 1.30–5.30 (10.30–5.30 July and Aug); tel: 0896 830323

Said to be the oldest continuously inhabited house in Scotland, Traquair began in the Middle Ages as a royal hunting lodge on the banks of the Tweed. The present house, with its massive, white-harled walls, steeply pitched roof and tiny sash windows, looks ancient enough. Buried at one end is the 14th-century pele tower built to guard the fertile valley against invasion from the south, but most of the building is of the 16th and mid-17th century, with two long low wings of 1695–9 by James Smith of Edinburgh flanking the entrance court. Later alterations account for a chapel in one of the wings, and a Victorian dining-room and drawing-room, the only interiors with central heating, in the other.

Still lived in by descendants of the James Stewart who came here in 1491, and who fell alongside James IV at Flodden in 1513, Traquair's atmospheric interior is enriched by a rich fund of royal and Jacobite connections. Mary Queen of Scots and her debauched second husband Lord Darnley were entertained here by the 4th Laird, and legend has it that the gates at the end of the main avenue have never been opened since Bonnie Prince Charlie rode out through them in 1745. The house itself is a place of intimate rooms stacked four storeys high; 18th-century gentrification accounts for the panelled first-floor drawing-room with *trompe l'oeil* motifs over the doors, and for the tiny library at the top of the house, with the cove of the ceiling painted with grisaille busts of classical authors, but here and there are fragments of older painted decoration, and there is a wonderfully steep and rough spiral stair in the most ancient part of the building.

The family portraits, many of them hanging in the Victorian dining-room, are unexceptional, but there is a Ruckers harpsichord of 1651, a Flemish cabinet of *c.* 1700 painted with biblical scenes, and a display of Catholic and Stuart treasures, among them vestments and silver used for secret services,

Jacobite glasses, James VI's carved cradle, pristine Jacobean needlework and a tiny 13th-century bible that came from Culross Abbey.

Central

Linlithgow Palace ☆

In Linlithgow, midway between Edinburgh and Stirling; HS; *open:* Mon–Sat, 9.30–6.30, Sun 2–6.30 (4.30 closing in winter); tel: none

On a hillock above the little town, and almost moated by Linlithgow loch, is the ruined palace of Scotland's Stewart kings, birthplace of James V and Mary Queen of Scots. Built over 200 years from 1424, Linlithgow combines the demeanour of a castle – four tall ranges looking inward on to a courtyard – with detailing that proclaims a love of show and beauty: finely carved fireplaces, the strange, ladder-like window designed to light a richly decorated ceiling, and stone bosses fashioned as unicorns. A continuous process of embellishment climaxed in the enchanting 16th-century fountain in the middle of the court and in the breathtaking Renaissance façade with five storeys of pedimented windows added by James I in 1618–24. Destroyed by fire in 1746, the palace is now an atmospheric shell.

Dumfries and Galloway

Arbigland

15 m SW Dumfries, off A710; teas; garden; *open:* 10 days in late May, 2–6, guided tour (*c.* 45 mins) at 3.30 and 4.30; tel: 038788 283

Arbigland is mostly visited for its extensive woodland garden running down to the Solway Firth. The house, set well back from the coast, is a small mid-18th-century building of reddish stone, with a pedimented main block attached to little octagonal pavilions either side. There are wide views from the high-ceilinged, comfortably furnished rooms, and the owner's stream of entertaining anecdotes and gobbets of family history more than makes up for a lack of notable contents.

Drumlanrig Castle ☆☆☆

Off the A76, 18 m N Dumfries; tearoom; falconry displays; garden; woodland walks; *open:* early May–late Aug, daily, except Thurs, 11–5 (Sun 1–5), but advisable to check; tel: 0848 31682

One of the three great houses owned by the Dukes of Buccleugh and Queensberry, Drumlanrig has its share of the family's outstanding collection of paintings and other treasures. The house itself, built between 1679 and 1691 on the site of a medieval stronghold, probably to designs by the royal master mason Robert Mylne or his son-in-law James Smith, is of a grandeur well fitted to what it contains. Set on a low ridge above an Aztec-like sequence of grassy ramps and terraces, Drumlanrig is a quadrangular palace of rose-red sandstone, with virile five-storey towers at each corner and an exuberant baroque entrance front. Here, the hard outlines of the main building are blurred by a sweeping horseshoe stair, by the pedimented windows, fluted pilasters and armorial flourishes, and by the ridiculous pepper-pot turrets on the towers.

This showpiece faces north, down the long lime avenue leading to the house, but the main rooms are all on the other side, looking over the gardens to wooded hills. Three high-ceilinged, panelled rooms display a rich collection of English and Continental 17th-century furniture, many of the pieces reflecting the Buccleugh descent from the Duke of Monmouth, natural son of Charles II. Here are limewood overdoor carvings by Grinling Gibbons, carved chairs by Daniel Marot, gilded Carolean mirrors, two ornate inlaid cabinets supported on lively caryatids made for Versailles in 1675, and examples of fine marquetry and boulle work. Walls are hung with Brussels tapestries and with portraits by Lely, Kneller, Ramsay and Jamesone. Here, too, are some unlikely relics of Bonnie Prince Charlie, who slept at Drumlanrig on his retreat north in December 1745, including a dainty teapot said to have belonged to Flora Macdonald, and the prince's campaign kettle.

Quite different in atmosphere are the feminine, green-walled morning-room dominated by John Merton's pink-stoled marmoreal image of the present duchess, painted in the 1950s, and the equally restful boudoir, with its chintzy easy chairs, and a collection of Dutch cabinet paintings: interiors by Teniers and Van Ostade, a Cuyp landscape and a luminous, immensely detailed Brueghel.

Strangely, Drumlanrig's three greatest treasures – Leonardo's much-debated *Madonna with the Yarnwinder*, Holbein's status-stiff portrait of Sir Nicholas Carew, Henry VIII's Master of the Horse, and Rembrandt's magical painting of an old woman reading, the absorbed, hooded face mysteriously lit from below – are hung at the foot of the 17th-century staircase, where all are difficult to see.

Maxwelton House

13 m N Dumfries on B729; garden and woodland walk; teas; *open:* Easter–end Sept, Wed–Sun 11–5, guided tours (*c.* 40 mins); tel: 084 82 385

Built round three sides of an intimate courtyard, with sweeping views south over the Cairn Water valley, Maxwelton is a tall, three-storey house with white-harled, rubble sandstone walls, sash windows and crow-stepped gables. Although probably dating back to the 17th century or before, the house as it is now owes most to recent restoration, when Victorian accretions were swept away and much of the place rebuilt. An uninformative guided tour takes visitors into some half dozen, lived-in, elegantly furnished rooms, one a little stone-vaulted chamber that may once have been a chapel, another a beautiful long drawing-room in soft green and peach with a big bay looking south over the valley and a scatter of Queen Anne and Georgian pieces. The home of the Laurie family for some 300 years until it was bought by the present owners, Maxwelton is known as the birthplace, in 1682, of the Annie Laurie who inspired the popular ballad.

Rammerscales ☆

5 m W Lockerbie, 2¹/₂ m S Lochmaben, off B7020; garden and woodland walk; *open:* Aug, daily, except Sat, 2–5; tel: 038781 0229

A thickly wooded drive winds slowly up to this red sandstone Georgian box with panoramic views over the Annan valley. Built in the 1760s for Dr James Mounsey, recently returned from Russia, it is intriguingly designed with at least two doors to every room so the fearful doctor, whose meteoric career at the Imperial court came to an abrupt end with the assassination of Tsar Peter, could make a quick get away if need be. It now belongs to the Bell Macdonalds, whose collection of modern art and sculpture, including works by Rodin and Hepworth, a Victor Pasmore nude, and a couple of bleak landscapes by Jean Commerc, dominates the modest, lived-in rooms.

On the first floor is an airy drawing-room furnished with 18th-century pieces, including a Chippendale settee, and with grey silk damask on the walls framing a dark head by Daumier, a clinical reclining nude by Despiau, a Derain, and two sketches by Forain, one of a woman weeping against a chair. Above, with the finest views over the Annan, is a long, oval-ended library, built as a gallery, and some family curiosities include a dining table made of wood from the *Bellerophon,* on which Napoleon surrendered, and a pair of scissors used during the American War of Independence to free soldiers' hair frozen to the ground during the night.

Fife

Balcaskie House ☆

Between St Monance and Pittenweem, off B942; teas; terraced garden; *open:* June–end Aug, Sat–Wed, 2–5; tel: 0333 311202

Looking out over the Firth of Forth, with a grassy vista aligned on the distant hump of the Bass Rock, is this long, rather severe stone house, with a strong vertical thrust from a cluster of turrets and chimneys at each end. Originally an L-shaped tower house, with a crow-stepped gable end, Balcaskie was developed in the 1670s for his own use by the architect William Bruce, who created façades of classical symmetry by simply producing a mirror image of what was already there, and adding towers with pyramidal caps to each corner of the house. Bruce's curving screen walls and low pavilions embracing a gravelled entrance court anticipate 18th-century Palladianism, and the monumental terraces descending in giant leaps towards the sea are similarly innovatory.

Later alterations for the Anstruther family account for a Victorian hall and staircase and the gallery-like landing above, but the three reception rooms looking out toward the sea still have bold 17th-century plasterwork, including massive pendants fashioned as bunches of grapes, and crude, anatomically improbable ceiling paintings by Jacob de Wet. A blue Savonnerie carpet in the elegant drawing-room shows off 18th-century French pieces and a lovely Dutch marquetry bureau, but the portraits are mostly unexceptional and the interior as a whole disappointing, partly because the tour is so brief. A family eccentric comes through in the hooks for slinging a hammock across a corner of the library, and the fetters with which the Chinese confined a 19th-century General Anstruther now form a piece of abstract art.

Earlshall Castle ☆

Leuchars, signed from A919; tearoom; garden and woodland walk; *open:* Easter–end Oct, daily, 1-6; tel: 0334 839205

With only a bank of trees screening it from a noisy RAF airfield is this L-shaped tower house with walls of rough pinkish stone and a roofline of crow-stepped gables, massive chimneys and stone dormers. Built in 1546, it was saved from ruin by the bleach merchant Robert Mackenzie, who bought the place in 1890 and commissioned the young Robert Lorimer to restore it, and to add the romantic, gargoyled gatehouse. Earlshall today is a sympathetic blend of 16th- and 19th-century work, the whole set off by Lorimer's enigmatic topiary garden.

Above stone-vaulted basement rooms is a panelled great hall, furnished with carved 17th-century pieces and arms and armour, and with a bold and colourful display of Wemyss pigs, cats and patterned mugs, some of them painted with the crows and rabbits of the castle. This mix of old and new is seen in almost every room. A little panelled drawing-room with 18th-century furniture shows off some of Leslie Ann Ivory's stylized, icon-like cat paintings, while the 50 ft long gallery on the floor above, with a 16th-century bestiary painted on the high, coved ceiling, is marred by modern chairs along the walls and by the bloodhound and golden retriever – family pets – depicted at either end of the room.

More traditional exhibits include one of Stubbs' paintings of a white stallion held at bay by a lion, and a number of Jacobite relics, among them a silver sermon case that belonged to Bonnie Prince Charlie's brother, Cardinal Duke of York, and a show of drinking glasses. Robert Lorimer was responsible for the lovely wooden screen marking off a dining-room at one end of the hall, for stencilled beams copying the 16th-century decoration, ornamental ironwork and some enchanting stained glass, and for the mischievous stone monkeys perching on a shed in the garden.

Falkland Palace ☆

In Falkland, 11 m N Kirkcaldy on A912; NTS; garden; *open:* Apr–end Sept, Mon–Sat 10–6, Sun 2–6; Oct, Mon–Sat 10–5, Sun 2–5; tel: 0337 57397

Beneath the open Lomond hills, and surrounded by an ancient burgh with wynds of stone-built cottages running back from the main street, are the remains of a great Renaissance palace. Developed as a royal hunting retreat by James II and IV in the mid 15th and early 16th century, Falkland was transformed between 1536 and 1541 by James V, who employed French and Flemish masons to create a building of harmony and elegance surrounding three sides of a spacious court. The north range has now disappeared, the east range is a romantic, broken-walled façade, and only the south range, rescued from 1887 by the 3rd Marquess of Bute, is fully roofed and furnished. From Falkland's main street this looks interesting enough, with a huge twin-towered gatehouse at one end, but on the courtyard side it is sensational, with stone dormers breaking the roofline, lively medallion heads sculpted between the windows, and buttresses disguised as classical columns.

The rooms are late 19th- and 20th-century reconstructions within the shell of the old building. The 3rd Marquess of Bute put in floors, heraldic glass and richly painted ceilings, and furnished the palace with a mix of antiques and meticulous copies of 17th-century pieces, while his grandson, who came to live here, created a comfortable turret bathroom and hid bare walls behind loosely gathered fabrics. What were the family's private quarters in the gatehouse seem warm and opulent, but essentially 20th-century, while a barrel-roofed library, every inch of walls and ceiling painted in a free interpretation of Renaissance decoration, is a kind of 1930s den, with a wind-up gramophone, a well-stocked drinks tray and book-lined walls.

James V's Chapel Royal fills the centre of the range. This great shadowy room still has its original screen of turned oak posts, the canopied royal pew, like a box at the theatre, and the painted ceiling and frieze with *trompe l'oeil* windows created for a visit by Charles I. The shades of the Stewart kings still linger here, but there is no trace of them in the recently reconstructed bedrooms in the east range.

Hill of Tarvit ☆☆

2½ m S Cupar, off A916; NTS; tearoom; garden; *open:* Apr wkends and daily May–end Oct, 2–6; tel: 0334 53127

When Frederick Sharp, son of a wealthy jute merchant, bought the estate in 1904, he was looking for somewhere to display his collection of antique furniture, paintings and porcelain. Sir Robert Lorimer was commissioned to replace an existing 17th-century building with the present house, a pleasant, unshowy affair with a long, grey-harled garden façade looking south over stone-walled terraces. The interior, designed to show off the collection, is a deliberate stylistic mix. The large, oak-panelled hall-cum-sitting-room, with its huge stone chimney-piece, was devised to take Sharp's 16th-century Flemish tapestries, and 17th- and 18th-century oak furniture. Off here, running out into one of the bays on the south front, is a French-style drawing-room, all white and pale green, with tapestry-covered settees and chairs, Louis XV and XVI pieces, and a trellis of plaster ribbons on the ceiling, while the boldly classical dining-room, with its fluted pilasters and prominent plaster shells, shows off a set of Chippendale chairs and other Georgian furnishings. There are some dark kitchen quarters, bedrooms hung with a bold Regency stripe, a splendid parquet-floored Edwardian bathroom, and one genuine old fireplace, a bold, canopied affair of 1627 brought here from the ancient tower house crowning a ridge half a mile to the west.

Almost every room displays pieces of oriental porcelain, from elongated, *blanc-de-chine*, 17th-century figures to large and decorative plates and urns. A sizeable collection of paintings is strong on 17th-century Dutch canvases, with still-lifes by Jan Weenix and Abraham van Beyeren, seascapes by Aelbert Cuyp and Van de Velde the Elder, and a core of winter scenes, one by Brueghel the Younger, which appealed to the golf-loving Sharp because of the little figures engaged in curling and other ice games. Also here are a couple of Herring's horse studies, portraits by Allan Ramsay and Raeburn, Highmore's painting of the actress Peg Woffington dressed as a shepherdess, and a self-satisfied lady in an enormous black hat by Cornelius Johnson.

Kellie Castle ☆☆

On B9171, 3 m NW Pittenweem; NTS; tearoom; luxuriant walled garden; *open:* Apr, Sat, Sun; May–end Oct, daily, 2–6 (5 in Oct); tel: 033 38 271

Set on the easternmost prong of the Fife peninsula, Kellie smells of the sea, with sweeping views south over the Firth of Forth and a wild moorland hill behind. A tall, T-shaped building of rough local sandstone, it is part-fortress, part-mansion, with a range of gracious, high-ceilinged, late 16th-century rooms sandwiched between three earlier towers. Outside, the castle is a picturesque mixture of the austere and the decorative, with trefoil-headed stone dormers breaking the roofline of the main three-storey wing, conically capped turrets corbelled out from the angles of the towers, and a lushly planted walled garden below the massive chimneys and crow-stepped gables of the north front. Inside, rich 17th-century plasterwork and 18th-century fireplaces and pine panelling are set off by furnishings, paintings and sculpture reflecting three generations of the talented Lorimer family. It was Professor James Lorimer who came here in 1876 and rescued the decaying building.

The visitor tour concentrates on the most recent part of the house. A broad stone staircase leads from a vaulted basement to the airy, 60 ft drawing-room, lit by windows on three sides, and with white-panelled walls and a lofty plaster ceiling. This is the heart of the late-16th-century wing, fitted out with a mix of old and modern that is typical of Kellie: comfortable chairs grouped round the two classical fireplaces, copies of Old Masters by John Lorimer on the walls, and some of his architect brother Robert's clean-lined, elegant furniture blending easily with oyster-veneered Dutch cabinets and Jacobean highbacked chairs. Scenes of crumbling fortresses and rushing torrents are painted on the dining-room panelling, and on the floor above, reached by a turnpike stair, is a bedroom with the finest plasterwork in the house: a deep cove decorated with trailing, twisting vine tendrils and more stylized foliage surrounding the painting of cloud-borne deities by de Wet on the ceiling.

Everywhere there are reminders of the Lorimers and their eye for a fine piece of work: a tiny vaulted chapel is enriched with an elongated image of the Virgin and Child by Eric Gill's protégé Anthony Foster and with a bronze by Robert's sculptor son Hew; a gracefully carved pearwood armoire from Normandy stands in the dining-room; and in the smoky-blue bedroom in the south-west tower is one of Robert's beds, with a Virgin and Child carved on the headboard, and his enchanting cradle, an angel kneeling at its foot. Among the family portraits in the professor's study, laid out as it might have been in the 1870s, is John's strongly lit painting of the old man, his beaky nose thrown into high relief.

Grampian

Braemar Castle

½ m NE Braemar, on A93; *open:* May–mid Oct, daily, except Fri, 10–6; tel: 03397 41219

Crowning a grassy knoll in a valley cut deep through forest-clad hills is this picturesquely top-heavy little castle, with battlemented turrets corbelled out

from every angle. Although dating from 1628, Braemar was reduced to a burnt-out shell in 1689 and owes its present romantic skyline to John Adam, elder brother of the more famous Robert, who restored the place, after the 1745 rising, for a garrison of troops, adding the sharply angled, corset-like curtain wall. The castle was massively altered again in the early 19th century to create the family home that visitors see today. It is pleasant enough, with the original spiral stair rising to comfortably furnished rooms stacked one on another, the best of them a virulently pink second-floor drawing-room with three large windows looking south down the valley; but there are few contents of note. The tour ends with collections of national costume, toys and stuffed Scottish wildlife in a warren of top-lit rooms built within Adam's curtain.

Brodie Castle ☆

Off A96, 4^1/$_2$ m W Forres, 24 m E Inverness; NTS; tearoom; woodland walk; *open:* Apr–late Sept, Mon–Sat 11–6, Sun 2–6, wkends in early Oct, Sat 11–5, Sun 2–5; tel: 030 94 371

Surrounded by woodland, as if in a forest clearing, is this substantial L-shaped building, with a 16th-century tower house sandwiched between a small 17th-century addition and an assertive Victorian wing by William Burn in Jacobean style, all large stone-mullioned windows and crow-stepped gables. Burn's remodelling for the 22nd Brodie of Brodie in the 1820s also involved substantial changes to the existing building, which was given decorative stone dormers, and the construction of the low one-storey ranges that straggle northwards to enclose a cobbled service court.

The extensive visitor tour takes in rooms on three floors, most fully furnished, but some primarily picture galleries. The dining-room and a cosy barrel-vaulted sitting-room have early 17th-century plaster ceilings, and there is a scatter of 18th-century French furniture, but the house feels predominantly 19th century. A comfortable low-ceilinged library was created by James Wylson of York in the 1840s and on the first floor is William Burn's light and airy drawing-room, with walls of the palest blue and stencilled decoration picking out the beamed ceiling and door surrounds. Chintzy easy chairs and a brick-red, trellis carpet blend surprisingly well with the 17th-century Dutch paintings acquired by the 22nd laird, among them a fleshy self-portrait by Jacob Cuyp, a work by Ferdinand Bol dated 1669, and Bloemaert's *Boy with a Flute*. More of the 22nd laird's purchases, among them works by Mytens, Gerrit Dou and Ewbank, hang next door, in the soulless, red-walled room that was once the high hall, while on the floor above a blue-walled Victorian bedroom and dressing-room set off softly coloured topographical water colours by Cotman, Sandby, Cox, Copley Fielding and their contemporaries. These 18th- and 19th-century English works were acquired by the 26th laird and his wife, and these two, parents of the present laird, were also responsible for Brodie's collection of modern art. Another gallery-like room shows a changeable display from an eclectic assemblage that includes a gay, child-like Dufy of boats at anchor, landscapes by Paul Nash and David Piper, and an impressionistic Gustave Loiseau.

Castle Fraser ☆

16 m W Aberdeen, 3 m S Kenmay off the B993; NTS; tearoom; walled garden; *open:* May, June, Sept, daily, 2–6, July, Aug, daily 11–6, Apr and Oct, Sat, Sun 2–5; tel: 033 03 463

Rising out of a pastoral landscape is this picturesque variant on the tower house. A tall granite keep bursting into a skyline flowering of crow-stepped gables and pepperpot turrets is married to two low Jacobean service wings framing an intimate courtyard. Started in 1575 by Michael Fraser, who extended a 15th-century building, the castle was finished off by his son Andrew, who added his initials to the dormers on the wings.

The rooms shown are all in the main block of the house, where steep spiral staircases take visitors ever upwards, and even, for the energetic, out on to the roof of one of the towers. Alterations in the 18th and 19th centuries, when some rooms were squared off and large windows and panelling put in, have made for some curious interior contrasts. The east-facing dining-room with Victorian family portraits hung against warm yellow panelling and solid mahogany furniture could be almost anywhere, and a couple of little bedrooms are similarly non-committal, but elsewhere the castle makes its presence felt: in rough stone walls, deep, round-arched window recesses, turret alcoves and strange angles, and in the triple gun loops defending the stone-vaulted ground-floor room that is now the kitchen.

Almost filling the first floor is an airy, barrel-vaulted great hall, once a cluttered Victorian drawing-room but now re-created as a 17th-century interior by the Trust, with plastered walls, sturdy Tudor and Jacobean furniture and period-style rush matting. Three floors above, at the top of the house, is the spacious, barrel-ceilinged library created out of two rooms in the 19th century, the documents and family relics on display here including two bullets – one labelled 'head', the other 'leg' – which wounded Col. Charles Mackenzie Fraser in the Peninsular War of 1812, and the wooden right leg which replaced the one that had to be amputated. Raeburn's portrait of the colonel hangs over the fireplace.

Craigievar ☆☆

On A980, 6 m S Alford, 26 m W Aberdeen; NTS; guided tours except in peak months; refreshments; woodland walk; *open:* May–end Sept, daily, 2–6; tel: 033 98 83635

One of the least altered and most magical of Aberdeenshire's tower houses, Craigievar sits high on a valley side, with sweeping views to open moorland hills. Soaring to the usual fantasy roofline of decorative dormers, crowstepped gables, corbelled angle turrets and even a Georgian-style balustrade, this compact L-shaped building, its solid granite walls covered in a pinkish harl, is still much as it was when first completed in 1626, with steep and narrow spiral staircases linking five storeys of little rooms piled one on another. Built by the master mason John Bell for a wealthy merchant, William Forbes, the castle combines a traditional plan with Renaissance decoration, most of the rooms still boasting their original Italianate plaster ceilings. There is a gallery-like room under the roof, fourth-floor bedrooms have delightful turret closets just big enough for a dressing table or a washstand, and some of the original box beds put in for servants are still here. Forbes family furniture fills the rooms, including a 17th-century gaming table shaped to take the bulging stomachs of the players, and there are portraits by Raeburn and Jamesone.

The highpoint of a tour which explores all five floors is the great hall, its airy spaciousness a contrast to the intimate, mostly low-ceilinged chambers above and below. Arcaded Renaissance panelling lines the walls, tiny musicians' galleries, about big enough for a brace of pipers, perch above the screen at the east end, and some of the most exuberant plasterwork in the house covers the arching stone vault going up into the floor above and describes a huge royal coat of arms above the granite lintel of the fireplace. A collection of studio pottery on one of the deep window recesses includes two bowls by Bernard Leach and a flock of homely ducks by Lady Sempill, daughter of the 19th lord, who gave the castle to the Trust. Only a relentless use of the Forbes tartan for carpets and upholstery mars the overall impact.

Crathes Castle ☆☆

On A93, 3 m E Banchory, 15 m W Aberdeen; NTS; restaurant; walled garden; woodland walks; *open:* Apr–end Oct, daily 11–6; tel: 033 044 525

With its outstanding garden and 15 miles of waymarked trails through varied scenery, Crathes is the kind of property where visitors come for the day. At the centre of the estate, sitting high on the shoulder of the Dee valley and set off by a sweep of tree-shaded lawns, is the 16th-century tower house of the Burnetts, built by the Bell family of master masons. Harled granite walls rise four floors to the usual skyline profusion of dormers, turrets and steeply pitched gables, but here the clean outlines of the original L-shaped tower house are softened by the low Queen Anne wing joined on to the north-east corner, and by the luxuriant planting in the walled garden on the slopes below, divided by architectural bastions of yew planted in 1702.

Despite a disastrous fire in 1966, when the Queen Anne wing was gutted, and Victorian alterations, when a Venetian window was put into the lofty great hall and other openings blocked, Crathes is still rich in original features and furnishings: bold, charmingly naive painted ceilings mix figures in 16th-century dress with wise sayings and biblical texts in a scramble of old Scots and English; carved chairs and beds and a superb oak-panelled ceiling illustrate the contemporary Aberdeenshire school of woodworkers; and tight spiral staircases lead to a stack of small low-ceilinged rooms, many of them still lit by tiny shuttered casements, the openings only partly glazed. Always there is a feeling of light and air, with even the smallest window giving a panoramic view to high moorland hills rising above wooded ridges.

Visitors see some dozen rooms on five floors, from the stone-vaulted basement kitchen to the gallery running east to west under the roof, the rough oak table at one end perhaps once used for the laird's court. The lofty hall with its comfortable sofas, original refectory table and lovely Flemish brass chandeliers is the heart of the house, but most of the painted decoration has sadly disappeared, and the 16th-century Italian stone fireplace was only installed in the 1870s. Above it hangs Crathes' greatest treasure, the carved ivory horn inset with red carbuncles traditionally given to the family by Robert the Bruce, giving authority over the royal hunting forest in the Dee valley.

Drum Castle ☆

Off A93, 3 m W Peterculter, 10 m W Aberdeen; NTS; tearoom; garden and woodland walks; *open:* May–end Sept, daily 2–6, Apr and Oct, Sat, Sun 2–5; tel: 033 08 204

Home of the Irvine family for some 650 years, Drum still looks out on a remnant of the medieval hunting forest entrusted to the family by Robert the Bruce. The main house is a substantial, much-altered, three-storey Jacobean mansion, its dignified show front ornamented with Renaissance dormers, stone steps up to a Georgian doorway, and a delicious pepperpot tower in an angle of the façade. Behind, partly enclosed by period-style Victorian additions, is an intimate courtyard, its east side filled by the muscular bulk of a 13th-century keep, one of the three oldest tower houses in Scotland, its walls of pinkish grey granite rising 70 ft to a battlemented skyline.

From the courtyard entrance, a Jacobean stone stair rises to the elegant drawing-room and interconnecting dining-room on the first floor of the mansion house. These interiors, like most of those on view, are 18th- and 19th-century in spirit, with Victorian oak ceilings and fireplaces, Georgian sash windows, and a mix of Georgian and later furnishings. Irvine family portraits include works by Raeburn and Reynolds, a moody likeness of the red-haired painter Hugh Irvine, friend of Byron, and a picture of the author Washington Irving, creator of Rip van Winkle, of the American branch of the family. Hugh's embarrassing painting of himself as a naked Archangel Gabriel dominates the plaster-vaulted Victorian library created out of the first floor of the medieval keep. Above and below are dark, rough-walled chambers reached only by an outside stair on the south side of the tower, while on the second floor of the main house visitors see a couple of Victorian bedrooms furnished with loaned and gifted pieces. The charm of Drum lies in detail: in the date 1619 inserted upside down by masons who could not read, in a 17th-century window now looking on to a passage, and in a padouk wood bureau made in China, its Corinthian pilasters topped with palm leaf capitals.

Fasque ☆

On B974, 1 m N Fettercairn, 12 m N Montrose; *open:* May–end Sept, daily, except Fri, 1.30–5.30; tel: 0561 340202

From the drive, there is a glimpse of an imposing, castellated red sandstone façade with turrets and a central tower, but this is the only opportunity to size up this grandiose early-19th-century mansion. Visitors are kept well away from the main front and ushered in through a gloomy service court and the dankly dark kitchen quarters. Beyond, there is not much to lift the spirits, but something of Fasque's Edwardian heyday comes through in the vast hall running across the house to a graceful double staircase, and in the interconnecting library and drawing-room looking out over the park, the former a quiet sanctuary of leather-covered chairs, the latter a long, uncluttered interior with inlaid tables, commodes and cabinets among the chairs and sofas, giant oriental urns ringing the window bay, and walls hung with land- and seascapes attributed to Van de Velde, Richard Wilson and Wouwerman and a typically rustic George Morland. Bought by John Gladstone, father of the future Prime Minister, in 1829, Fasque has various mementoes of the great W.E., notably a heap of capacious Gladstone bags at the foot of the stairs, and there are portraits by Raeburn in the dining-room.

Fyvie Castle ☆☆☆

Off A947, 8 m SE Turriff, 25 m NW Aberdeen; NTS; tearoom; grounds; *open:* May–end Sept, daily, 2–6 (11–6 Jun–Aug), Apr and Oct, Sat and Sun, 2–5; tel: 0651 891 266

For centuries a royal stronghold on a bare bluff above the River Ythan, Fyvie's two ranges, now surrounded by Victorian shrubberies, are the remnants of a 16th-century courtyard house formed out of the earlier castle. Brash and assertive, Fyvie stands four and five storeys tall in the shape of a massive L, drawing all eyes upwards to a skyline display of turrets, carved dormers, steeply pitched roofs and crow-stepped gables, with the boldly sculpted figures of pipers, hunters and bears crowning every cap and pinnacle.

The interior is Edwardian. In 1889, a self-made local boy, the millionaire industrialist Alexander Leith, founder of the Illinois Steel Company, returned from America to buy the house he had always wanted. The contents were included in the sale, but Lord Leith added greatly to the collection, buying portraits, arms and armour, tapestries and porcelain, and carrying out much redecoration in an antiquarian style, with rich panelling and stiff plasterwork. None of the rooms feels very old, but the house is pinned by a late 17th-century wheel stair of worn red sandstone, each tread 10 ft across, and there are still a couple of Jacobean plaster ceilings, with panels of fluid vine and oak foliage.

The extensive visitor tour takes in most of the first and second floors, climaxing in the tapestry-hung, barrel-roofed gallery that was entirely Lord Leith's creation. Filling a floor of the tower he built on at the turn of the century, this rich and sumptuous room with its boldly ribbed plasterwork is a romanticized vision of the past. An exquisite stone fireplace was brought here from a French château, the organ gallery is composed of carved 17th-century woodwork from a Dutch church, old furniture has been embellished by additional carving, the tapestries have been chopped about to fit, and a multi-coloured Tiffany lamp glitters in a corner.

On the way, visitors can feast on an exceptional collection of Raeburns, including his sharp-faced image of Dr Reid, Professor of Moral Philosophy at Glasgow, and on portraits by Batoni, Cotes, Hudson, Reynolds, Gainsborough, Romney and Hoppner. There are seascapes by Van de Velde and Van Minderhout, a wintery river by Sir John Millais, a show of blue and white Delftware and oriental porcelain, and fine 17th- and 18th-century tapestries. Apart from a set of Louis XV armchairs, though, much of the furniture is Victorian and Edwardian, with a fair show of chintz and the obligatory billiard room. Most entertaining, perhaps, are the plaster heads surmounting the bookcases in the library, made at a time when skull shape was supposed to indicate character.

Haddo House ☆☆

Off B999, 4 m N Pitmedden, 19 m N Aberdeen; NTS; restaurant; garden and country park; *open:* May–end Sept, daily, 2–6 (June–Aug 11–6), Apr and Oct, Sat, Sun 2–5; tel: 0651 851440

Aberdeenshire's first classical house was built by William Adam in 1731–5 for the rapacious, acquisitive William Gordon, 2nd Earl of Aberdeen, in what was then a bleak and treeless landscape. Built of pinkish-grey local granite and field stone and now surrounded by a mature wooded park, Haddo is a mansion of a place, suited to the 2nd Earl's social pretensions, with a pedimented central block linked by curving corridors to pavilions either side. But Adam's original design, with a graceful double stair up to the first-floor entrance, has been blurred by 19th-century alterations, when the single-storey links were doubled in height, a chapel designed by G. E. Street added to the north pavilion, and the entrance moved down to the ground floor, with a long balcony inserted above.

Inside, not much of Adam's work survives. Haddo today is largely as remodelled in 1880 by the Edinburgh architects Wardrop and Reid and the fashionable London interior designers Wright and Mansfield for the 7th Earl and Countess Ishbel, with neo-classical decorative schemes married to a mix of Adam-style furniture and comfortably upholstered pieces specially made for the house, heavy Victorian curtains and re-creations of boldly patterned 19th-century carpets.

A portrait-hung staircase dominated by Batoni's painting of Lord Haddo, heir to the 3rd Earl, leads to the first-floor rooms which are the focus of the tour: a bow-windowed morning room hung with watercolours by Countess Ishbel and her tutor and furnished with chintzy easy chairs and some of Wright and Mansfield's repro 18th-century pieces; a formal drawing-room with some of the best of the paintings, among them a grizzled St Peter by Van Dyck, and Domenichino's *David with the Head of Goliath;* and a dining-room with classical plasterwork made of papier-mâché, and a show of family silver that includes models of the family pets and salt cellars in the shape of deer. A spacious Victorian library lined with bookshelves of cedar inlaid with ebony has its original gas chandeliers, full-length portraits of the 7th Earl and Ishbel over the fireplaces, leather-seated chairs and an ink stand and blotter of polished Peterhead granite on the large partner's desk in the middle of the room.

There is a collection of family memorabilia, a display of the watercolours of Scottish castles by James Giles commissioned by the 4th Earl, who was briefly Prime Minister in the 1850s, and a corner of 20th-century paintings, among them Maggi Hambling's unrelenting portrait of the 5th Marquess.

Leith Hall ☆

On B9002, 1 m W Kennethmont, 34 m NW Aberdeen; NTS; tearoom; walled garden and countryside walks; *open:* May–end Sept, daily, 2–6, Oct, Sat, Sun, 2–5; tel: 046 43 216

The lime avenue leading to the Leith family's courtyard house frames the white-harled west front, with four stone dormers breaking the roofline, long sash windows lighting the first floor, and an ornamental arch giving access to the yard. Almost the last addition to a house which grew slowly over two centuries, range by range, this 1868 façade blends comfortably with a more elegant 18th-century south range, with countrified Venetian windows, and the old tower house dating from 1650 on the north side, with turrets corbelled out at the corners.

Visitors do a circuit of the first floor, entering the house through a self-important hall added on early this century. Modest rooms enriched with simple provincial plasterwork and furnished with Georgian and 19th-century pieces suggest a quiet country life, the one whiff of frivolity being a pink-walled oval boudoir on the south front, with round-headed niches full of porcelain, tiny rococo mirrors either side of the fireplace, and lacy plasterwork on the ceiling. Leith family portraits, among them an unconvincing Opie, and works by Ramsay, Westmacott and Northcote, rub shoulders with some Italian and Spanish religious pictures, such as Ribera's *Flight into Egypt;* several examples of 18th- and 19th-century needlework include tapestry bell pulls, pictures of silk and horsehair, and a bedspread of knitted cotton; and a couple of rooms are devoted to the family's military exploits, the mementoes here including ivory writing tablets said to have belonged to Bonnie Prince Charlie, and relics of the Crimean War and Indian Mutiny.

Castle Stuart

5 m E Inverness, on B9039; guided tours (*c.* 30 mins); *open:* all year, daily, 10–5; tel: 0463 790745

This tall, keep-like house of rough, lichen-stained rubble, with decorative stone dormers between a brace of taller towers, was completed in 1625 by the 3rd Earl of Moray, descendant of Mary Queen of Scots' half brother. Only lived in for some thirty years before being abandoned for three centuries, the castle has been rescued by the present owners, whose extensive restoration has involved new oak panelling, new floors of Douglas fir, reproduction 17th-century furniture, and carpets of red Stuart tartan, not to mention a set of breathtakingly brash murals which are used to regale visitors with the story of Bonnie Prince Charlie. Visitors are taken up one tower and down the other, emerging into the large rooms which fill each floor of the central block and out on to the roof, with views over the Moray Firth and the battlefield of Culloden, 3 miles away, the graveyard of Prince Charlie's hopes.

Cawdor Castle ☆☆☆

Near village of Cawdor, on B9090, 6 m SW Nairn; teas; garden and woodland walks; *open:* May–early Oct, daily, 10–5.30; tel: 06677 615

Seat of the Campbells, thanes of Cawdor, from the 13th century, the castle is a photogenic mix of crow-stepped gables, pepperpot turrets, steeply pitched roofs and pedimented dormers, with a four-storey medieval keep rising out of a fringe of domestic ranges built round tiny courtyards. Some of these additions are 17th-century, others Victorian embellishments, but all are in traditional style. Grey stone is softened by smooth green lawns and a charming flower garden, all long borders and pergolas, but at the back the castle is much grimmer, standing high above a deep wooded valley.

Visitors take in the great hall wing, part of the central keep, and a trio of bedrooms in the range looking west over the burn. There is a basement kitchen with tiny, deep-set windows, and a stone-vaulted guard room, but much remodelling has resulted in rooms that are comfortable and welcoming rather than period pieces, with some recent pine panelling and soft furnishings as well as old stone fireplaces and antiques, and a glimpse of a modern Scandinavian-style kitchen. There is a strong sense, too, that the collections are still growing.

What was the great hall is now a long, peach-coloured drawing-room, with a scatter of porcelain on delicate side tables, 18th-century mirrors between the windows, easy chairs round the fire, and a fine display of late 18th-century portraits, including works by Cotes and Lawrence, and full-lengths by Reynolds and Beechey of the 1st Lord Campbell, collector and connoisseur, and his beautiful wife. One bedroom is hung with biblical 17th-century Flemish tapestries, including a *Flight into Egypt* in which the Virgin, trim in a broad-brimmed hat, looks for all the world as if she is out for a picnic; others are furnished with Georgian pieces, such as a domed Sheraton four-poster and a set of painted chairs.

A rich accumulation in a sitting-room with a bold Restoration cornice includes a marquetry longcase clock by Jeremiah Johnson and a Chinese stoneware jar of the 1st century decorated with a splendid leaping dragon, while a similarly cluttered drawing-room in the tower, with a deep bay looking over the gardens, shows off a dark blue Venetian gondola chair, a Georgian roll-top desk, Sheraton card tables and a white marble lotus bowl on a long refectory table. A seascape by Vernet is one of the paintings which escaped a sale of the 1st Lord's London collection, and there is also an intriguing clutch of more modern works: pencil sketches of Greece and Albania by Edward Lear, a desolate Cornish beach by Stanley Spencer, indeterminate watercolours by John Piper, a Charles Adams cartoon of Edgar Allen Poe, surrounded by croking ravens, and Dali's vision of Shakespeare's Macbeth, loosely based on an 11th-century Scottish king but created Thane of Cawdor by the bard.

Dunrobin Castle

¹/₂ m NE Golspie, on A9; tearoom; formal gardens; *open:* May, Mon–Thurs, 10.30–12.30, June–mid Oct, Mon-Sat, 10.30–5.30, Sun 1–5.30 (4.30 in Oct); tel: 0408 633177

Standing high over Italianate terraces descending in great leaps to a lonely, tree-fringed coast is the most northerly great house in Britain, its slender, conically capped turrets, roofline dormers and elaborate stone balconies like a Loire château transported to Scotland. Designed by Charles Barry for the 2nd Duke of Sutherland after 1833, Dunrobin's show fronts were added on to a rough sandstone medieval keep and the white-harled 18th-century ranges that still make up the southern end of the house.

Most of the interior was gutted by fire in 1915 and the rooms visitors see, concentrated in the 19th-century part of the house, are largely as restored by Sir Robert Lorimer, with panelling in sycamore and larch and decorative plaster ceilings. A massive stone staircase, with tiger skins slung casually over the landing balustrade, leads up to Lorimer's elegant drawing-room facing over the sea, hung with chocolate brown 18th-century Mortlake tapestries and a couple of busy Venetian views by Canaletto and furnished with high-backed, capacious, Louis XV chairs. Elsewhere, apart from a grandfather clock by Joseph Knibb, a show of Wemyss pottery, and the bed, its posts topped with fluttering doves, on which Queen Victoria slept on a visit in 1872, it is the family portraits which command attention. The panelled dining-room, curiously embellished with a classical frieze, shows off Winterhalter's full-length of the 2nd Duchess, dressed as a gipsy, with a black mantilla over her head, and works by Romney, Lawrence and Ramsay, the library has a de Laszlo of another duchess, a blue wrap pulled loosely round her diaphanous yellow dress, and there are more Ramsays, a Jameson and another Lawrence in the apse-ended breakfast room, with heavy wooden porringers among the dainty wooden porcelain on the table. The 5th Duke's study has a tiny balcony where he could listen to a piper on the terrace below, and out in the garden, in a former summer house, is the family museum, where antlered and tusked heads are mixed with relics of the Crimea and Waterloo, Pictish stones and curiosities brought back from all round the world.

Dunvegan Castle ☆

Outside Dunvegan village, 23 m W Portree on Isle of Skye; café; picturesque gardens; boat trips; open: late Mar–end Oct, Mon–Sat 10–5.30, Sun, 1–5.30; tel: 047 022 206

Set above a long, island-studded loch on the west coast of Skye is the only stately home on the island, seat of the Chiefs of the Clan MacLeod and a magnet for summer visitors. Although dating back to the 13th century, with a medieval keep marking one end of the long range that perches on a rock above the sea, any sense of age has been blurred by extensive remodelling in the late 18th and 19th centuries. Dunvegan is now drenched in a drab harl, its skyline a romantic Victorian vision of battlements and pepperpot turrets, the entrance a baronial hall.

The interior is relatively modest. Largely 19th-century furnishings are mixed with a good run of family portraits, including works by Beechey, Devis, Raeburn and Hoppner and Ramsay's extraordinary portrait of the dandified 22nd Chief, dressed from head to foot, stockings and all, in a checked red plaid. Civilization here, though, is only skin deep. In the pink-walled 18th-century drawing-room, lit by large windows on both sides, marquetry spoonback chairs are grouped round a Georgian games table, and there are portraits by Zoffany on the walls, but just outside, a stone-walled passage leads to a dungeon cut into the rock, and a narrow stone stair runs down through the curtain wall to the heavily defended sea gate. A show of Jacobite and MacLeod relics includes Flora Macdonald's stays, an ancient drinking cup and a tattered silk banner, and there are letters from Dr Johnson, who came here with Boswell in 1773, and from Sir Walter Scott.

Lothian

Arniston House ☆☆

Gorebridge, off B6372 S of A7; guided tours (c. 90 mins); teas; *open:* July–mid Sept, Tues, Thurs, Sun, 2–5; tel: 087530 238

A broad lime avenue leads to this impressive house of pink local stone looking north towards Edinburgh. Designed by William Adam for Robert Dundas, a successful lawyer, Arniston is a symmetrical Palladian composition, with curving colonnades connecting the three-storey central block to low pavilions, sash windows, and a heraldic pediment supported on four Tuscan columns. Built over 30 years from 1726, the later stages were under the direction of William's son John, who created a suite of high-ceilinged ground-floor reception rooms, now empty and desolate. Victorian alterations are responsible for the ugly porch and a square garden bay spoiling the original lines.

Visitors walk straight into Adam's breathtaking two-storey hall, ringed by round-headed arches and smothered with bold and vigorous plasterwork by Joseph Enzer. Two fireplaces are incongruously placed beneath arches, and there is a set of wide-seated, tapestry-covered Louis XIV chairs. A south-facing panelled room hung with early portraits is a remnant of an earlier house, and on the second floor is Adam's serene library, where Boswell once sat reading, its shelves now used to display porcelain.

An astonishing collection of Raeburns and Romneys is crowded in an otherwise unexceptional room, and the staircase shows off an unusual Raeburn double portrait and Brueghel's view of the Scheldt, with rickety windmills and overloaded boats against a vast blue distance.

Dalmeny House ☆☆

3 m E South Queensferry, 7 m W Edinburgh, on B924; partly guided tour; teas; valley garden and spectacular shore walk; *open:* May–end Sept, Sun 1–5.30, Mon, Tues 12–5.30

Set on a terrace above a grassy sweep running down to the sea is a

picturesque Regency interpretation of the gothic style, with huge stone-mullioned windows, slender octagonal turrets and banks of ornate chimneys fitted into an essentially ordered composition. Designed by William Wilkins in 1814, Dalmeny was built for the 4th Earl of Rosebery, whose forbears had inhabited an uncomfortable castle just down the coast. Inside, there is a hammerbeam roof over the staircase hall and a fan-vaulted corridor with 16th-century Flemish glass in the windows, but the decoration of the main rooms is unassertive.

Visitors see some half-dozen rooms on the ground floor, some of them lived in, others clearly set pieces. Most striking is the collection of French furniture and porcelain from *Mentmore*, which came to Dalmeny as a result of the marriage of Mayer Amschel Rothschild's only child to the 5th Earl. A darkened, artificially lit drawing-room looking over the sea is hung with Beauvais tapestries, and furnished with exquisite marquetry and ormolu-mounted pieces from the reigns of Louis XIV, XV and XVI. The pink and beige Savonnerie carpet was ordered by the Sun King himself, a rococo writing table was made for the Dauphin in 1756, and a massive desk is the one at which Louis XVI's Swiss banker struggled to avert disaster before the Revolution. A show of Vincennes and Sèvres porcelain includes a model of a bulging-eyed spaniel said to have belonged to Marie Antoinette, and some of the artificial flowers loved by Madame de Pompadour.

The politician 5th Earl, who briefly succeeded Gladstone as Prime Minister, was also responsible for a shrine-like collection of Napoleonic relics, among them the desk, chair and screen which the exiled Emperor used in his study on St Helena, a vastly unflattering portrait by Eastlake and the great man's shaving stand from Malmaison, studded with imperial bees. The finest paintings are in the green-walled dining-room, where works by Gainsborough, Reynolds, Hoppner, Raeburn and Lawrence, and busts by Joseph Nollekens, portray leading figures in 18th-century society, while a cosy sitting-room is kept as it was in the 6th Earl's lifetime, with a little chair for his grandchildren by his own large one and paintings of some of his racehorses on the walls.

Gosford House ☆

On A198 between Aberlady and Longniddry; grounds; *open:* 2 months in early summer, Wed, Sat, Sun, 2–5; tel: 08757 201

Set back from a low shore, with wind-sculpted trees sheltering it from winter gales, is this melancholy great house, one of Robert Adam's last commissions. Built for the 7th Earl of Wemyss by 1800, Gosford then stood empty for almost a century, but was rescued in the 1880s by the 10th Earl, who needed somewhere to hang his collection of Italian Renaissance paintings. The serene, clean-lined central block, domed and pedimented, with three great round-headed windows looking towards the sea, is still as originally designed. But the wings are restless, fussy additions of the 1880s by William Young, built to replace the Adam pavilions demolished by the 8th Earl.

Gosford is an impressive house, but as you approach from the coast road it becomes clear that all is not quite what it seems. The northern end is open to the sky, its windows all false, while the Adam centrepiece, gutted by fire in 1940, is roofed but unrestored, its stonework romantically decayed, with tendrils of wisteria across the steps leading up to the first-floor terrace. Only Young's south wing is habitable, and this is astonishing enough. Most of the space is taken up by a domed and galleried marble hall rising through the house, with an alabaster handrail to the grand, double-armed staircase and a pink alabaster arcade ringing the upper floor. Every inch of the gallery is crammed with paintings. Early Italian works are dominated by a Virgin and Child by Botticelli and the identical subject, but in a very different style, by Mantegna, and there are landscapes attributed to Jacob van Ruisdael and Richard Wilson, portraits attributed to Lely, Mercier, Reynolds, Dahl, Ramsay, Raeburn and Singer Sargent, and a fleshy classical Rubens. Even if some are clearly copies, the general effect is superb, and this display is enriched by a set of William and Mary chairs and settees with contemporary needlework seats, and by inlaid commodes carrying porcelain urns. The discerning will also want to see Adam's stable block to the east of the house, which is richly ornamented with Coade stone plaques.

Hopetoun House ☆☆☆

12 m W Edinburgh, off A904 near South Queensferry; tearoom; grounds with coast walk; *open:* mid Apr–early Oct, daily, 10–5.30; tel: 031 331 2451

Only yards from the Firth of Forth, set sideways on to the sea, is the largest country house in Scotland, a grey stone palace on an almost superhuman scale. To the east, looking down a broad grassy ride towards the main gates, is a wide baroque frontage of swelling curves, with colonnaded screen walls linking the central block to cupola-topped pavilions either side. This piece of ostentation was designed in the 1720s for Charles Hope, 1st Earl of Hopetoun, by William Adam, who was called in to remodel the house built by Sir

William Bruce only 20 years before. The earlier work, in an imposing Palladian idiom, still survives on the garden side, where the central bay is marked by a decorous pediment.

Inside, a chaste entrance hall divides the Bruce rooms from the Georgian state apartment on the north side of the house, completed by John and Robert Adam after their father's death. The contrast is so great that touring Hopetoun is like visiting two houses under the same roof. The Bruce interiors are intimate, oak and pine-panelled rooms, some with chimney-pieces set across the corner in Restoration style, and several with shadowy overdoor paintings by the Dutch artist Philip Tideman. There are some 17th-century tapestries and a suite of ornate contemporary Dutch furniture, but the highlights of this part of the house are the tiny stone-vaulted, fire-proof chamber that is still stuffed with 18th-century deedboxes and account books, and Bruce's flamboyant, pine-panelled stairwell, encrusted with three-dimensional carvings of fruit and flowers. Tideman's original painted panels have been replaced by witty *trompe l'oeil* fantasies by William McLaren, but these blend beautifully with a recently discovered baroque painting on the cupola overhead.

The three state-rooms, hung with the pick of the family paintings, form the climax of the tour. The yellow drawing-room is lined with 1850s silk damask, and the dining-room is a Regency creation, but the great empty space known as the red drawing-room is still as it was in the mid-18th century, with a froth of rococo plasterwork on the high coved ceiling, red damask purchased in 1766 on the walls, and gilded pier glasses and console tables and substantial mahogany chairs and sofas made for the room by James Cullen of London.

A fine collection of family portraits includes three commissioned from Nathaniel Dance in Rome in 1753, a soft-faced Gainsborough, David Allan's painting of the 1st Earl, and works by Allan Ramsay, Raeburn and Procaccini. Also here is a show of mostly 16th- and 17th-century Venetian, Flemish and Dutch paintings, most of them bought in the 19th century on the advice of an Edinburgh art dealer. There are sombre portraits by Koninck, Cornelius Johnson and Annibale Carracci, David Teniers the Younger's *Temptation of St Anthony*, an atmospheric, crowded courtyard scene by Philips Wouwerman, one of Canaletto's Venetian panoramas, and Jacopo Palma the Younger's portrait of the Doge himself, eyes full of intelligence and guile.

House of the Binns ☆

15 m W Edinburgh, off A904; NTS; viewpoint walk; guided tour (*c.* 60 mins); *open:* Easter wkend, May–end Sept, daily, except Fri, 2–5; tel: 050 683 4255

A battlemented and turreted Regency entrance front looking north over the Forth is just a veneer by William Burn on a largely 17th-century building. Begun in 1612–30 by Thomas Dalyell, an Edinburgh butter merchant, the house was extended by his ardently royalist son, General Tam, who added wings framing a courtyard to the south. It was enlarged again in the 1740s.

A modest place with a mixed bag of Dalyell family furnishings, and with a strong contrast between the cosy 17th-century rooms and the high-ceilinged Georgian morning- and dining-room, the Binns is of interest for its connections as much as for its architecture or what it contains. Sadly, visitors cannot wander into the courtyard to see the picturesque, stone-dormered south front, but the flagged hall still has its original fireplace, carved with the date 1622, and two first-floor rooms have ornate Jacobean plaster ceilings, one of them with a massive central pendant, the other decorated with Stuart motifs in honour of a projected visit by Charles I. The presiding spirit is that of General Tam, who vowed never to cut his hair until the Stuarts were returned to the throne. There is a portrait of him looking like Father Time, and a show of some of his belongings, among them a huge comb, his camp spoon and his Bible printed in lowland Scots.

Lauriston Castle ☆

Cramond Road South on NW outskirts of Edinburgh, off A90 Queensferry road, no advance signs; guided tours (40–50 mins); garden; *open:* Apr–Oct, daily, except Fri, 11–1, 2–5; Nov–Mar, Sat, Sun 2–4; tel: 031 336 2060

Set in spacious grounds on the edge of the Forth is a small 16th-century tower house joined to modest 19th-century additions in a loose Jacobean style. The interior, with both living-rooms and bedrooms all comfortably arranged on one foor, is still as planned by Mr and Mrs Reid, the unconventional, slightly Bohemian couple who took Lauriston over in 1902. Mr Reid, a cabinet-maker, had made a fortune from fitting out luxury trains, an occupation which took him all over Europe, and it is his spirit which infuses the place. Railway carpeting, in a small blue pattern, is used extensively, railway chairs surround the table in the dining-room, and the long library ceiled in pine is rather like an opulent carriage. Inlaid furniture, much of it carefully restored, a rich assemblage of Turkish rugs and hangings, and a large collection of bluejohn urns, bowls and other *objets* were treasured for the skill that went into making them rather than for their beauty. So too were the garishly coloured wool mosaics reproducing well-known paintings, such as Landseer's *Monarch of the Glen* and *Dignity and Impudence*, that were the Victorian equivalent of mass-produced prints. In winter, the Reids sat round the fire in the cosy, blue-walled study on the ground floor of the old tower, and they entertained their friends to tea in the sitting-room with a wide bay to the Forth, where his binoculars, for watching passing boats, are still out on the table.

Lennoxlove ☆☆

1¹/₂ m S Haddington on B6369; guided tours (*c.* 60 mins); teas; garden; *open:* Easter wkend, May–Sept, Wed, Sat, Sun 2–5; tel: 062 082 3720

This intriguing old building of rough brownish stone, with later wings attached to a medieval tower house at one corner, is romantically linked to Frances Teresa Stewart, described by Pepys as 'the beautifullest creature that I ever saw'. 'La Belle Stewart' enjoyed a tragically short marriage to her cousin, the last Duke of Lennox, with whom she was deeply in love, and at her death arranged for a property to be purchased and renamed Lennoxlove after him.

Acquired by the Duke of Hamilton in 1946, Lennoxlove is full of treasures brought here from the now-demolished Hamilton Palace. The house itself is an architecturally undistinguished, rambling place with alterations of various periods, the most recent by Sir Robert Lorimer in the early years of this century. The informative, relaxed guided tour starts in a series of largely 18th-century rooms. A lemon and egg-yellow hall and staircase hung with portraits by Raeburn, Mytens and Gavin Hamilton lead to a sunny, blue and white drawing-room decorated with touches of rococo plasterwork and with a grand piano that may have been played by Chopin among a display of elegant 18th-century French furniture. The finest paintings – portraits by Van Dyck, Lely and Cornelius Johnson – are gathered in the dining-room, and there are relics of La Belle Stewart, in particular a monstrous cabinet studded with tortoiseshell hearts which was a present from Charles II, who tried without success to add her to his string of conquests.

A doorway pushed through a massive wall leads into the lofty, rough-walled, stone-vaulted great hall in the old tower, now with generous windows and a baronial fireplace put in by Sir Robert Lorimer, but still with the original smoke vents in the roof. An undercroft has been turned into a crypt-like chapel, with the medieval castle well, water glinting in its depths, in one corner, and the old kitchen now displays relics of Mary, Queen of Scots, whose kinsman, the 1st Marquess of Hamilton, was once a candidate for her hand. Here is her death mask, smooth and untroubled, the silver casket given to her by her first husband, Francis II, in which she is said to have kept incriminating letters relating to the murder of Lord Darnley, and the blue sapphire ring which she gave to the 1st Marquess. The 14th Duke was the target of Rudolf Hess's abortive peace mission in 1941, when the Deputy Führer made his solo flight to Scotland, and Hess's compass and map, annotated in precise German, head the displays in the museum.

Stevenson House ☆

20 m E Edinburgh, outside Haddington, signed from A1; guided tour only (c. 1¼ hrs), at 3; refreshments; garden; *open:* July-mid Aug, Thurs, Sat, Sun, 2-5; tel: 062 082 3376

Standing tall and four-square round a courtyard, with turnpike stairs in each corner and façades of rough rubble stone, Stevenson is one of very few examples of the old Scottish grange, or farm, a step down from the grander laird's house. The main fabric dates from the latter half of the 16th century, but a show of sash windows and two large late Georgian bows on the south front were the result of improvements in the late 17th and early 19th century, when the courtyard was for the first time ringed by corridors.

The present owner, who rescued Stevenson from wartime devastation, gives an informal and enthusiastic tour taking in all three floors. A stately Restoration staircase leads up to the spacious high-ceilinged drawing-room lined with classical panelling that runs out into one of the bows, but other parts of the house, where the rooms are still a 16th-century size, can only be reached by the spiral stairs. There are a number of bedrooms to be seen, an unrestored room shows the extent of wartime damage, and an eyrie of a library at the top of the house is lined with sweet-smelling cedar panelling taken from a broken-up cruise liner. Mostly English furniture includes a table that is said to have belonged to Dr Johnson, a lovely Queen Anne bureau and a rare collapsible coach table, and there are portraits by Marcus Gheeraerts the Younger and the early-19th-century American artist C. B. King, a moonlit seascape by Ewbank and works by modern Scottish artists.

Strathclyde

Blairquhan Castle ☆

14 m S Ayr, off B7045 $\frac{1}{2}$ m S Kirkmichael, signed from A77; teas; walled garden and grounds; *open:* mid July–mid Aug, daily, except Mon, 1.30–4.30; tel: 065 57 239

A scenic, 3-mile approach along an unmetalled drive gives glimpses of the dark, romantic shape of Cloncaird Castle, of the tempestuous River Girvan far below and finally of Blairquhan itself, a stolid, castellated effort set on a bluff above the valley, with a central tower rising out of the main block. Built for Sir David Hunter Blair in 1820–4, the castle was designed by William Burn. What remained of the ruinous old house was used to make up the charming, cobbled kitchen court, with its stone dormers and carved decoration.

Visitors see a series of high-ceilinged, airy, very 19th-century interiors, including a double drawing-room with a big bay to the valley and a clutch of bedrooms, each with a bathroom en suite, and still furnished with the plush mahogany pieces that were specially made for the house. Most astonishing is the galleried gothic saloon rising into the tower, with plaster vaulting white on blue, traceried clerestory windows and carved and hooded doors. A show of paintings includes portraits by Mercier and Raeburn, landscapes by Alexander and Patrick Nasmyth and Locatelli, a shadowy Moucheron and exotic eastern figures by David Wilkie, while stone-vaulted rooms in the basement are given over to works by the early 20th-century group known as the Scottish colourists – F. C. B. Cadell, J. D. Fergusson, S. J. Peploe and Leslie Hunter – whose bold, free compositions owed much to Matisse and the Fauves.

Brodick Castle ☆

Isle of Arran, 40-minute walk or by connecting bus from Brodick pier head; NTS; tearoom; extensive woodland and rhododendron garden and country park; *open:* Apr and early Oct, Mon, Wed, Sat, 1–5; May–end Sept, daily, 1–5; tel: 0770 2202

Brodick Castle is best approached on foot, along the path running round the curve of the bay between the golf course and the sea. Only visitors who take this route have the thrill of seeing the castle as it should be seen, a towering block of red sandstone rising out of a wooded promontory, with the 2,866 ft pyramid of Goatfell at its back. Close to, the surroundings dissolve into the terraced lawns and rhododendron gardens which drop steeply away below the house, and the castle itself is revealed as a mainly 19th-century creation in Scots baronial style by James Gillespie Graham, with large sash windows below a battlemented roofline and a fanciful tower at the south-west corner, all crow-step gables and angle turrets. Rougher masonry and smaller windows at the east end identify the former fortress dating back to the early 14th century. Although a seat of the Earls of Arran, later Dukes of Hamilton, since the 15th century, Brodick was too inaccessible to be a viable family home until Victorian times.

The six or so rooms on show, most of them with stiff Jacobethan plaster ceilings, are strung out along the first floor of the south front. The most thrilling is the sunny, white-panelled drawing-room, furnished with ornate Italian mirrors, gilded French chairs and settees, and two enchanting oriental goose tureens, their porcelain feathers coloured plum purple, rose pink, jade green and smoky blue, and hung with cabinet paintings, among them works by Watteau, a portrait by Clouet in a heavy gold frame that was once in the collection of Charles I, church interiors by Pieter Neeffs, landscapes by Moucheron and a dramatic view of Edinburgh castle by Alexander Nasmyth. Most of these pictures once belonged to the eccentric, 19th-century connoisseur William Beckford, builder of legendary Fonthill Abbey, whose daughter married the 10th Duke, and more Beckford treasures are on show on a dark landing, among them a cabinet full of Fabergé-style trinkets, such as an agate spoon mounted in gold, and Turner's watercolour of a distant view of the abbey. More assertive are the sporting trophies and paintings acquired by the 10th, 11th and 12th Dukes. The walls of the main staircase are covered with almost a hundred antlered heads and there are paintings of boxing, dog fights, hunting and horse-racing by Herring, Reinagle, Sartorius, Rowlandson and others.

Culzean Castle ☆☆

12 m S Ayr, off A719; NTS; tearoom; garden and country park with cliff walks; *open:* Apr–late Oct, daily, 10.30–5.30; tel: 065 56 274

On a clifftop 150 ft above the sea, looking north-west to Arran and Holy Island, is a towered and castellated mass of creamy yellow stone. Robert Adam's most romantic house, with one huge round tower breaking forward to stand on the brink of the precipice, Culzean competes with its setting. Inside, delicate plaster ceilings and elegant Georgian furnishings contrast with the wild without.

Adam was at Culzean for over a decade. Called in by David, 10th Earl of Cassilis in 1777 to transform a 16th-century fortified building, he started on his final addition some ten years later. Subsequent changes, particularly in the 1870s, have blurred the Georgian plan and much of the original furniture is no longer here, but enough remains to appreciate Adam's grand designs. Since taking the house over, too, the Trust has meticulously recreated the 18th-century decorative schemes, commissioning copies of key items where necessary and adding appropriate furnishings.

The principal rooms are arranged around Adam's theatrical oval staircase, plugging what was a courtyard in the centre of the house, with a screen of classical columns ringing each floor. Equally dramatic is the circular saloon filling the first floor of the great round tower which leads off to the north. Furnished only with some gilded chairs pushed back against the walls and with a carpet echoing the pattern of Adam's geometric ceiling, this formal space seems suspended on the edge of a void, its great windows filled with an unrelenting expanse of sea.

To the south, looking over a sunken terraced garden, are the main living-rooms. The dining-room with its paintings by Ben Marshall and Ferneley is a largely 19th-century creation, a drawing-room is an almost total reconstruction, but elsewhere are original plaster ceilings with inset panels by Antonio Zucchi and pier glasses and tables, girandoles and fireplaces designed by Adam. An apse-ended eating room is hung with Luny's seascape of the Kent coast, and the lofty picture room in what was the high hall of the old house shows off Batoni's striking portrait of the 10th Earl between two romantic views of the castle by Alexander Nasmyth.

The 14th Earl, who designed and built many of his own yachts at Culzean, was responsible for a bizarre boat-shaped cradle in a dressing-room, and visitors can also see an exhibition devoted to General Eisenhower, who was given part of the castle for his lifetime after World War II. Gun batteries and grassy earthworks west of the house were constructed to defend the coast against Napoleon, and the weapons which the 12th Earl issued at the time now form geometric patterns in the armoury beyond the entrance hall.

Duart Castle

Off A849 on E point of Mull, about 50 mins on foot, via *Torosay Castle*, from Craignure pier head; teas; *open:* May–Sept, daily, 10.30-6; tel: 068 02 309

Nowhere looks more romantic than this little grey-walled castle perched on a wild and craggy headland reaching out into the Sound of Mull. Massively thick, almost windowless walls enclose a sheltered courtyard; one side, towards the sea, is filled by a four-storey, 14th-century keep, but two others are lined by charming, originally 16th-century ranges, with gabled roofs, stone dormers and cottagey casements. Ancient stronghold of the Macleans, Duart was left a ruin in the 18th century, and was bought back and restored, from 1912, by Sir Fitzroy Maclean, great-grandfather of the present owner.

Alas, the rooms on view, all in the keep, have none of the character of the exterior, and are largely given over to diverse displays, from a cannon from an Armada galleon that went down in Tobermory Bay to stiffly mounted uniforms and cases of medals, dirks, and ornate 20th-century silver. Most atmospheric is an unaltered World War II bathroom, with original cork linoleum, and visitors can enjoy the stupendous views from the wall walk ringing the keep.

Finlaystone House

On A8 between Port Glasgow and Langbank; tearoom; garden and woodland walks; *open:* Apr-Aug, Sun 2.30-4.30; tel: 047 554 285

There is little to enthral those who visit this large, grey-harled house sitting end on to the Clyde, with views across the water to the housing estates of Dumbarton. Classical 18th-century façades have been blurred by Sir John James Burnett's lumpish alterations of *c*.1900, and the few rooms on show are lacklustre and dreary, one of them used for a display of dolls and puppets from all over the world, another with cases of Victoriana. Neither the signature of Robert Burns scratched on a pane of glass, nor the knowledge that John Knox gave his first Protestant communion at Finlaystone, can lift the spirits.

Inveraray Castle ☆

At Inveraray on Loch Fyne, 58 m NW Glasgow; tearoom; estate walks; *open:* early Apr–mid Oct, Mon–Sat 10–6, Sun 1–6 (closed Fri and 1–2 on weekdays except in July and Aug); tel: 0499 2203

In a dramatic loch and mountain landscape, with forested slopes rising steeply from cleft-like valleys, is this uncompromisingly four-square towered and turreted gothic pile. Built of dour grey stone, Inveraray was deliberately designed with rigid symmetry by the London architect Roger Morris to contrast with the untamed Scottish hills. Now a staging post on any tour of the highlands, the little planned town on the loch always awash with summer visitors, the castle feels anything but remote, but when begun, in 1744, for the 3rd Duke of Argyll, it was 40 miles to the nearest carriage road. Following a fire in 1877, the 18th-century lines were blurred by alterations by Anthony Salvin, who replaced Morris' battlements with a dormered top storey and added conical caps to the corner turrets.

Morris' gothic hall still rises into the tower, lit by traceried windows high above and with wheels and fans of muskets, axes and broadswords covering the walls, but the high-ceilinged drawing-room and dining-room on the north front are the work of Robert Mylne, who recast the interior for the 5th Duke

Strathclyde

some thirty years later. Decorated in the French style that was the acme of sophistication in the 1780s, the dining-room is painted with delicate arabesques and richly coloured garlands, the drawing-room is hung with faded tapestries full of Dresden shepherdesses and other idealized rustics, and both are filled with gilded chairs and settees covered with Beauvais and Aubusson tapestry, some from the workshops of John Linnell, others made by estate craftsmen. These set-pieces are the best part of a brief tour which also takes in a lacklustre saloon and a couple of unexciting upstairs rooms, one full of mementoes of the 6th Duke's marriage to one of Queen Victoria's daughters.

A fine display of portraits includes works by Gainsborough, Francis Cotes, Reynolds, Batoni, Hoppner and Ramsay, and some charming paintings of the 5th Duke's children by John Opie, and there are cases of family relics, among them a Bible that belonged to the executed 9th Earl, with some of the more desperate verses from St Matthew marked with his blood. Overall, this is a soulless place, with intrusive rope barriers and little sense it is ever lived in. Most incongruous is the geranium-hung glass and iron canopy over the entrance by Matthew Digby Wyatt, who clearly thought he was still at work on Paddington Station.

Kelburn Castle ☆

On the A78, between Largs and Fairlie; guided tours (c. 30 mins, booking advisable); café; country park; *open:* two months in summer; tel: 0475 568685

Perched above the steep, wooded glen of the Kel Burn, and with stunning views west over the sea, is this unpretentious old place, seat of the Earls of Glasgow. A gentle William and Mary wing, gabled and sash-windowed, is grafted on to a four-storey tower house dating back to c.1200, and one side of the entrance court is framed by an agreeable, *sotto voce* Victorian extension. Visitors assemble at the information office in the country park and are taken up to the house via a path across the glen. Once within the precincts, the crowds thronging the popular attractions down the hill are left behind, and the castle is seen for what it is, a quiet, lived-in family house. Most of the original contents were sold in the 19th century to meet the debts of the improvident 6th Earl, but Kelburn survives remarkably unchanged.

The short, informal tour takes in something of every period. A grandiose staircase smothered in colonial and sporting trophies that include a Kiwi rug and a stuffed gavial leads to a glorious high-ceilinged drawing-room running right across the house. Almost 40 ft long, and now without the paintings it was designed to display, this baroque interior, with fluted Corinthian pilasters framing doorcases and fireplaces, is enhanced by a Victorian colour scheme in blue, stone and gold, with twinkling stars covering the panels intended for portraits. The plaster cornice, featuring both the English rose and the Scottish thistle, anticipated the Act of Union of 1707, in which the 1st Earl was involved, and the comfortable furnishings include a Chippendale sofa and some generous, oval-backed Louis XVI chairs with silk upholstery. A corridor curved round the outer wall of the old tower leads to the portrait-hung Victorian dining-room with a big bay looking west to the sea, original William Morris wallpaper, in a swirling acanthus leaf pattern, and sinuous Morris door furniture. A couple of little bedrooms in the tower were panelled in c.1700, when the new wing was built.

Torosay Castle ☆

Isle of Mull, 1½ m from pier head at Craignure by forest walk or narrow-gauge railway; teas; terraced gardens; *open:* late Apr–mid Oct, daily, 10.30–5.30, plus some days earlier in season according to boats; tel: 068 02 421

This compact grey stone house rising out of forested slopes above the great curve of Duart Bay looks east over Italianate terraces to the romantic silhouette of *Duart Castle* and the distant Ben Nevis range. Completed in 1858 to designs by David Bryce, Torosay is capacious rather than grand, with comfortable family rooms beneath a profusion of pepper-pot turrets, crow-stepped gables, and steeply pitched dormers.

Bought by the 1st Laird, the present owner's great-great-grandfather, in 1865, Torosay is a lived-in, friendly house, with chatty, handwritten information and invitations to sink into easy chairs. There are paintings by Sir John Leslie, another great-great-grandfather, and de Laszlo, and Singer Sargent's charcoal sketch of the mortally ill 2nd Laird, dying of diabetes, but Torosay's sunny main rooms are chiefly memorable for their panoramic views, with a telescope thoughtfully provided for visitors' use. There is an interesting family archive, with mementoes of the 4th Laird's days on one of the last commercial sailing ships and the uniform and papers with which he escaped from a German PoW camp disguised as a Bulgarian naval officer, and there are nostalgic paintings by Ian Orchardson of the little paddle steamers that used to serve the islands and which helped in the evacuation from Dunkirk.

Tayside

Blair Castle ☆

8 m NW Pitlochry, off A9 Inverness road; tearoom; woodland walks; *open:* Apr–late Oct, daily 10–6; tel: 0796 481207

Passers-by on the A9 get the best view of the impressive seat of the Murrays, Dukes of Atholl. Set low in a broad valley just north of the deep wooded cleft of Killiecrankie, with forested and heather-clad hills closing every horizon, Blair developed from a 13th-century tower guarding one of the few feasible routes through the Highlands. For long more fortress than house, massive remodelling by the architect James Winter in the 18th century gave the castle its elegant Georgian interiors, while the romantic assemblage of crow-stepped gables, battlements and angle turrets which now crowns the white-harled façades is a Victorian vision of baronial splendour by David Bryce.

The tour, taking in 32 rooms on three floors, is one of the longest on offer, and requires time and stamina. The interiors are mostly 18th- or 19th-century, with a fine suite of Georgian rooms on the south front fitted out with marble chimney-pieces, carved overmantels and lavish plasterwork by Thomas Clayton, who had worked for William Adam. Most of the furniture, too, was bought in London in the mid-18th century by the 2nd Duke, but there are earlier pieces of oak and elm in a vaulted ground-floor room, some extraordinary creations veneered in broom for the 3rd Duke, including a coin cabinet designed as a miniature Roman temple, and some heavy Victorian pieces made for a visit by Victoria and Albert in 1844.

High points in what can easily become a half-remembered blur are the Georgian white and mint-green dining-room created out of what was the great hall and the drawing-room immediately above, the former with a dazzle of plasterwork on both walls and ceiling, a set of dramatic views of the estate by the little-known Charles Stewart, and 18th-century chairs round a Regency table, the latter with rococo pier glasses against crimson walls, gilded settees and chairs, and a show of portraits headed up by Zoffany's charming painting of the 3rd Duke and his family. Elsewhere are flamboyant four-posters sporting tufts of ostrich feathers or rococo cresting, Sèvres porcelain in Chippendale cabinets, portraits by Honthorst, Lely, Landseer and Lawrence, and a range of family treasures, from Jacobite relics and the breastplate of Bonnie Dundee, mortally wounded at the Battle of Killiecrankie in 1689, to coinage from the Isle of Man, over which the Murrays had sovereignty in the 18th century, and the fiddle, whisky glass and portrait, by Raeburn, of Neil Gow, musician to the 2nd, 3rd and 4th Dukes. This last hangs in the cavernous ballroom of 1876–7, where the walls are smothered with antlered heads and Sudanese weapons brought back by the 8th Duke.

How sad that so rich a place should feel tawdry and tired, the mechanically numbered rooms and frequent display cases speaking of a house that now exists mainly for its streams of visitors.

Glamis Castle ☆☆

1 m N Glamis, off A928; guided tour (c. 50 mins); tearoom; garden and nature trail; *open:* mid Apr–early Oct, daily, 10.30–5.30; tel: 0307 84242

Seat of the Bowes Lyons, Earls of Strathmore and Kinghorne, Glamis is the most haunted castle in Scotland, the place where Macbeth traditionally slew Duncan, and childhood home of the Queen Mother. Set low in a pastoral landscape, and approached by a wide oak avenue, the central block of the castle, developed from a 14th-century tower house, shoots skywards to a fairytale roofline of turrets, cupolas and dormers. Low castellated wings splay out on either side to form a trunkless Y, and a long Victorian range stretches away to the east.

Inside, the guided tour leaps back and forwards between rooms of different periods, moving from a cavernous Victorian dining-room to a stone-vaulted, armour-hung medieval hall furnished with sturdy oak pieces, and on to fine Stuart interiors and the modern apartment made for the Queen Mother, before plunging back into the Middle Ages. The second floor of the tower, once the Jacobean great hall, is now an airy, 60 ft drawing-room, with plasterwork of 1621 on the high barrel ceiling, and an overmantel with an intertwined thistle and rose celebrating the union of Scotland and England. There are comfortable sofas round the fire and a mass of 17th-century lacquered cabinets and the walls are closely hung with portraits, among them works by Lely, Kneller, Verelst, Aikman and Dance. The chapel off, where the Old Pretender touched for scrofula, is from the 1680s, when the Dutch artist Jacob de Wet covered every inch of walls and ceiling with richly coloured, charmingly naive panels illustrating biblical themes, among them the listening ear of god, and Jesus as a gardener, with broad-brimmed hat and spade. After all this and a couple of other interiors, one with 17th-century needlework hangings, the other with a huge painting of a fruit market by Snyders and Rubens, the 1920s royal apartment, where Princess Margaret was born, is something of an anti-climax, although the sitting-room, with its fireplace lined with Delft tiles and a display of blue and white porcelain, is cosy enough.

The tour ends in the stone-walled guard room where Duncan is supposed to have met his end, and there are ghost stories and mysteries a-plenty,

among them the tale of a secret room where a lord of the castle played cards with the devil. But avoid Glamis at high season, when the tour groups become too large for comfort.

House of Dun ☆☆

On A935, 3 m W Montrose, signed from A94; NTS; tearoom; garden and woodland walk; *open:* Easter wknd and May–mid Oct, daily, 11–5.30; tel: 067 481 264

Set on gently rising ground looking south over a vast tidal lagoon, this dignified Palladian house of pinkish grey stone, more villa than mansion, is an important example of the work of William Adam. On the striking north front, the entrance is set back in a round-headed recess flanked by pairs of fluted pilasters rising the height of the façade, as if the house incorporated a triumphal arch. The south front is simpler and less dramatic, its lines softened by a horseshoe stair to the first floor, with flowering pots hung from the balustrade.

Dun was built between 1730 and 1742 for David Erskine, 13th laird, whose family had owned the estate since 1375. Recently used as a hotel, it has been restored by the Trust, who have mixed original furnishings with re-creations of light fittings and other fixtures and some loaned pieces to conjure up the house as it was in the first decades of the 19th century, when Lady Augusta, daughter of the future King William IV and the actress Dorothy Jordan, married into the family. Adam's original room plan has been much modified, but his lofty saloon in the centre of the south front survives unaltered, the walls and ceiling covered with exuberant plasterwork by Joseph Enzer, each motif – Neptune with his triton, urns brimming with seashells, musical instruments, arms and armour and a stag hunt – conjuring up an appropriate allusion. To either side are the 19th-century dining-room created out of the former state apartment, and the tobacco-tinged Victorian library, all leather armchairs and historical prints and with red concertina folds hiding the bookshelves. Adam's first-floor library above the saloon, reached by a miniature horseshoe stair, has been re-created as a comfortable sitting-room.

Dun's royal connection comes through in silk embroidery by Lady Augusta, in William IV's shaving chair, seen in one of the many Victorian bedrooms, and in numerous paintings and drawings, among them Hayter's group portrait of the Fitzclarence children, with a marble bust to represent the future king and a copy of a Romney, tactfully reversed, to indicate their thespian mother. A sweep of family portraits includes some wonderfully naive 17th-century likenesses and a couple of clear-eyed little girls by Allan Ramsay, and there is a mistily romantic Alexander Nasmyth of *Culzean*, with the sun going down over the sea.

The extensive tour also takes in a tiny business room, with bundles of bills on a desk built in under the window and a pile of brass-bound deed boxes, and the basement service quarters. Visitors leave through the stable court, where a game larder is hidden among the lime trees in the middle.

Scone Palace ☆☆

2 m NE Perth on A93; tearoom; grounds;
open: Easter–mid Oct, Mon–Sat 9.30–5, Sun
1.30–5 (10–5 July and Aug); tel: 0738 52300

This towered and castellated sandstone palace above the Tay is a piece of
light-hearted, late-Georgian gothic built from 1803 by the young William
Atkinson, whose first major commission this was. The interior is positively
ecclesiastical, with plaster vaulting, canopied niches, cloister-like galleries,
traceried windows, and grand spaces divided by chapel-like anterooms. Seat
of the Murray family, Viscounts Stormont and Earls of Mansfield, who have
been here since 1604, Scone is hung with a fine collection of 18th-century
portraits and 17th-century Dutch paintings and stuffed with accumulated
treasures, some of them acquired through the 7th Viscount's diplomatic postings to Vienna, Dresden, Warsaw and Paris in the 1750s, '60s and '70s, others
brought here from *Kenwood,* the 1st Earl's London home.

Each of the main rooms highlights a different aspect of the collection. The
vast dining-room, presided over by Hudson's portrait of the 1st Earl, is used
to display the 4th Earl's Continental ivories, with some carved 17th-century
German tankards among a profusion of mannered statuettes, while the gothic
bookshelves in the former library are now laden with English, German and
French porcelain, including some green and white Sèvres that Louis XVI presented to the 7th Viscount, and the 1st Earl's lovely rust and blue Derby service. The ambassador's bed with its original crimson hangings is set off by
inlaid French pieces, such as a writing table with a marquetry portrait of
Francis I, and by paintings by Batoni, Hoppner, Gainsborough and Zoffany,
and a set of wide-bodied French armchairs covered in the finest needlework
is stiffly arranged in the elegant drawing-room hung with blue and gold silk
on the south-west corner of the house.

The Murray's old house, partly incorporated in the new palace, comes
through in the gallery running the length of the east front, with its 16th-
century parquetry floor inlaid with bog oak, and this is also the setting for an
astonishing collection of gold-mounted urns, flagons and vases that look as if
they have been dipped in amber: made for Louis XV by the Martin brothers,
they are in fact of varnished papier mâché and are thought to be unique.
Alas, Scone's greatest treasure, the venerated stone on which Kings of
Scotland were anointed for centuries, was taken south by Edward I in 1296
and is now in Westminster Abbey. To the east of the house, crowned by a
tiny chapel, is the mound where the monarchs were enthroned, and a ruined
gateway is all that remains of the ancient abbey dating from the 6th century
that was sacked by a mob in 1559.

Glossary

apse A semicircular or polygonal feature, often vaulted, such as is often found at the east end of a church

arch-braced Where the subsidiary timbers strengthening the main frame of a roof are curved like an arch

armorial Displaying coats of arms or other heraldic emblems

art deco Referring to the decorative arts of the 1920s and 1930s, characterized by streamlined, emphatic lines and shapes, the use of man-made materials, and strong colours

art nouveau A decorative style of the 1890s and early 1900s, characterised by sinuous, undulating designs based on natural forms

Arts and Crafts An aesthetic movement primarily inspired by the artist-designer William Morris (1834-96), who responded to the 'evils' of industrialization by reviving traditional crafts, and who founded a firm to make handmade furnishings. Morris's designs for wallpapers and fabrics show a preference for restful colours, particularly blue and green, and for patterns based on flowers and foliage

barge-board A board, often decoratively carved, used to finish the edge of a gable or other sloping roof

baroque The theatrical and exuberant architectural and artistic style of the 17th and early 18th centuries, characterized, in buildings, by elaborate spatial effects, a sense of mass, and ornate decoration, and associated with Popery

barrel-vault A roof of semi-circular section like a continuous round-headed arch

blanc-de-chine Pure white Chinese porcelain, mostly of the 17th and 18th centuries

blue-john A decorative fluorspar marked in deep blue, purple and brown and much used for ornamental urns, vases etc

boss A knob-like projection, often carved, found where the ribs of a vault intersect

boulle 18th- and 19th-century furniture intricately inlaid with tortoiseshell, pewter, brass and mother-of-pearl, and called after the French cabinet-maker André-Charles Boulle (1642-1732), who specialized in this type of work

buttress A masonry projection strengthening a wall

campanile An italianate bell-tower, usually tall and slender

cantilever A beam, canopy or other horizontal projection supported at one end only

Carolean Of the time of Charles II

caryatid A supportive column sculpted as a human figure; often found either side of a fireplace

castellated With battlements

chancel The east end of a church, containing the altar and choir

chinoiserie The 17th- and 18th-century fashion for all things Chinese, with often fanciful interpretations of oriental buildings, furniture and decorative schemes

Cistercian An order of Roman Catholic monks

clerestory A row of windows set high up in a wall, so light streams down from above; commonly found in churches, where the clerestory windows light the nave above the level of the aisle roofs

cluster-column A column carved to suggest it is composed of a cluster of slender shafts

coffered Refers to a geometric pattern on a ceiling or vault created by square or polygonal recessed panels

colonette A little column

colonnade A row of columns, often forming an arcaded walk

corbel A wall projection, usually of stone and often carved, supporting a beam

Corinthian One of the five main types of column found in classical architecture, characterized by a fluted shaft and ornate capitals carved with acanthus foliage

cornice A projecting ornamental moulding along the top of a wall

Coromandel Refers to the Coromandel coast, i.e. SE India; large 17th-century Chinese screens shipped from here were known as Coromandel screens

cove A concave moulding, usually found at the junction of wall and ceiling

crenellated Battlemented

crewel work Embroidery in coloured wools, generally on a neutral ground; much used for

bed hangings of the late 17th and early 18th centuries, when designs featuring bold
curling leaves and brilliant blooms were popular

crocket A decorative feature, usually carved with curled leaves, projecting at regular
intervals from a canopy, gable, or pinnacle

crown post A prominent vertical beam supporting the main longitudinal timber of a roof,
and itself resting on a cross beam

cruck construction A simple form of timber-framing, in which pairs of massive timbers
(the crucks) forming an inverted V support both walls and roof

crypt A vault or chamber beneath the main floor; often underground

cupola A little dome, usually perching on a roof or crowning a turret

cusp A curved and pointed projection found on the tracery of a gothic arch or window

Delftware Ceramic ware called after the Dutch town of Delft, which became a centre of the
pottery industry in the mid 17th century; a range of colours was largely abandoned for
blue and white as a result of the impact of Chinese porcelain

diapering A form of decorative brickwork, where bricks of a contrasting colour to the main
body of a wall are used to make repeated patterns

dole gate An abbey or monastery gate where food was given to the poor

dormer window A window projecting from a sloping roof

ebonized Veneered in ebony

Elizabethan From the reign of Elizabeth I, i.e. 1558-1603

empire style An early 19th-century style of furniture and interior decoration named after
First Empire France, where it originated; it is basically neo-classical, but makes much use
of Egyptian and other exotic motifs

enfilade When doors from one room to another are aligned, thus creating a vista through a
series of rooms when they are all open

fan-vaulting A form of vault in which the ribs radiate out from a common point, thus
forming fan shapes

finial A carved ornament topping off a gable or pinnacle

fleur-de-lis An emblem in the form of a stylized lily flower, widely used in heraldry and
associated with the French royal arms.

fluting Refers to closely spaced vertical channels decorating the shafts of columns and pilasters

fresco A form of wall decoration, in which colours are applied directly onto a wet,
lime-plastered surface

frieze A decorative band along the upper part of a wall

gable The end of a pitched roof, forming an inverted V

gargoyle A decorative waterspout, often carved as a grotesque head or creature, projecting
from a wall or roof, and designed to throw rainwater clear of the walls

garth The open space ringed by a cloister

gazebo A lookout tower or summerhouse

Georgian Literally, from the reigns of the first four Georges, i.e. 1714-1830; in architecture,
the term Georgian used alone generally means classical, although the Georgians employed
a wide diversity of styles

gesso A composition of chalk and glue that was applied to furniture in the early 18th
century, and then carved and gilded or silvered

girandole A standing candelabra

gothic/gothick This is the architecture of the pointed arch, the traceried window, the rib
vault and the gargoyle; originally medieval, the gothic style was consciously revived in
the 19th century, while the term gothick is applied to the light-hearted and fanciful
interpretations of the later 18th century, sparked off by the design of Strawberry Hill,
Horace Walpole's house at Twickenham (hence **Strawberry Hill gothick**)

grisaille Monochrome painting in tones of grey

ha-ha A sunken ditch separating a park from the gardens around a house, so the view is
unbroken

half-timbered Refers to a timber-framed building, in which the structure is composed of
interlocking vertical and horizontal timbers, which are often exposed

hammer-beam roof A timber roof in which the main timbers spring from short, often
richly carved beams projecting from the wall

Hepplewhite Name given to the light and elegant furniture of the late 18th century, many designs for which were illustrated in the cabinet-maker George Hepplewhite's *The Cabinet-Maker and Upholsterer's Guide*, hence 'Hepplewhite'

hipped roof A roof which slopes on all sides, rather than forming gable ends

inglenook A recess for a seat built in by a fireplace

Ionic One of the five main types of column found in classical architecture, characterized by a fluted shaft and capitals carved with tightly-wound scrolls

Jacobean Of the reign of James I, i.e. 1603-25; **Jacobethan** refers to a meld of Elizabethan and Jacobean, as frequently used in the 19th century

jib door A concealed door flush with the wall surface

keystone The central stone of an arch or window opening

lancet A narrow, pointed window

linenfold A stylized design representing folded linen found carved on panelling, chests, doors etc

loggia An often garden room open on one or more sides, which are usually arcaded

lozenge A diamond shape

lunette A half-moon window

majolica Boldly-decorated, lustrous pottery originally developed by Moorish potters in Spain and which came to Renaissance Italy by way of Majorca, hence majolica

mansard roof A double-angled roof, with a gently sloping upper part and a much steeper – often almost vertical – lower section

marquetry A decorative veneer of contrasting woods or other materials, used to create floral and pictorial designs

William Morris See Arts and Crafts

mullions The vertical bars, of wood or stone, dividing a window

nave The main body of a church, often flanked by aisles

neo-classical Refers to the mid-18th-century and later revival of classical architecture, as based on a study of the buildings of Italy and Greece, rather than as filtered through Palladio (see Palladian)

obelisk A tall, tapering shaft of stone, with a pyramidal top

ogee arch A form of gothic arch with a head formed of serpentine curves

oratory A small chapel

oriel A bay window projecting from an upper floor

ormolu Gilt bronze decorative metalwork used on furniture of the late 18th and 19th centuries

overmantel Literally 'above the mantelpiece', but used to refer to the carved panels placed above fireplaces by the Elizabethans and Jacobeans

pagoda An oriental tower, with elaborate roofs projecting from each storey

Palladian Classical architecture of the earlier 18th century, which was modelled on the writings and buildings of the Italian architect Andrea Palladio (1508-80), rather than on direct study of Greek and Roman remains

parquetry A decorative veneer or inlay using contrasted woods and other materials to produce a geometric design

pediment A low-pitched gable above a portico, door, window etc; the sides may be straight or curved, and a broken pediment has a central gap

pele tower A defensive, tower-like house found in northern England and Scotland

pendant An elongated, hanging feature characteristic of 16th- and 17th-century plasterwork ceilings and of gothic vaults

pietra dura work A mosaic of coloured, often semi-precious stones, used to decorate table tops and cabinets

pilaster A shallow rectangular column projecting from a wall

pinnacle A spiky ornament

piscina In churches and chapels, a shallow basin for washing Communion vessels, usually set within a niche in the chancel

porte-cochère A drive-through porch, so those in carriages could step out under cover

portico The columned and usually pedimented entrance to a classical building

Pre-Raphaelites A group of British painters, including Rossetti, Millais, and Holman Hunt, who banded together in 1848 in reaction to what they saw as the banality of contemporary art. Their paintings are characterised by luminous, intense colours and meticulous detail, and are often romantic interpretations of history and legend

quatrefoil A four-lobed feature

Queen Anne Architecture of the early-18th century, characterized by a sensible and pleasing plainness; the 'Queen Anne Revival' of the later 19th century is misleadingly named, as it derived primarily from the modest, Dutch-influenced gabled brick houses of the 17th century

Regency Referring to the early 19th century, when the future George IV was Prince Regent; architecture and decorative styles were still essentially classical, but with injections of Egyptian and oriental motifs, and, in furniture, a tendency towards heaviness

Renaissance The revival of classicism which began in Italy in the early 15th century, and reached England about a hundred years later

reredos A decorative screen behind an altar

Restoration Referring to the time of Charles II, when the monarchy was restored after the Civil War

rib A projecting band, usually on a ceiling or vault

rococo A light and elegant form of decoration popular in the mid-18th century and characterized by asymmetry and sinuous, naturalistic forms

romanesque Synonymous in Britain with Norman, this is pre-gothic architecture of the round-headed arch

rotunda A circular, usually domed building

scagliola An imitation marble, used particularly for columns

solar The first-floor parlour of a medieval and Tudor manor

strapwork Interlaced bands imitating leather straps that were a popular decorative motif in Elizabethan and Jacobean times

Stuart 17th-century, i.e. relating to the reigns of the Stuart kings

stucco Plaster, used to create decorative ceilings and to face buildings

stumpwork Raised embroidery, in which the principal motifs are worked over padding or shaped blocks of wood

swag An ornamental garland of fruit or flowers hanging in a gentle curve

topiary Shrubs and trees clipped into balls, pyramids, birds and other shapes

torchère A decorative stand for a candelabra

tracery The ornamental division of a window, blind arch or vault

transepts The transverse arms of a cross-shaped church

transom The horizontal bar, of wood or stone, dividing a window

trefoil Three-lobed

triptych A picture on three panels

trompe l'oeil Painting which, through use of shadows etc, deceives the eye into seeing three dimensions; often used to suggest arcades and other architectural features, or views through non-existent windows

Tudor Of the time of the Tudor dynasty; literally, this means from 1485 to 1603, but in architecture Tudor is usually only used up to 1558, when Elizabeth I ascended the throne

undercroft A vaulted basement room, below a church, chapel or hall

vargueño A richly decorated 16th-century Spanish chest or cabinet

Victorian Of the reign of Queen Victoria, i.e. 1837–1901

William and Mary Of the reign of William III and Mary, i.e. 1689–1702; the monarchs are associated with Wren and, in domestic architecture, with quietly-pleasing, Dutch-influenced brick houses

wyvern A winged and two-legged dragon with a barbed, snaky tail

Index

A la Ronde 24
Abbotsford 335
Acland family 33
Acton Round Hall 273
Adam, James 340
Adam, John 340, 350, 361, 364
Adam, Robert 36, 39, 86, 103, 105, 116, 130,
    144, 146, 147, 181, 220, 272, 308, 321,
    330, 331, 339, 340, 363–4, 369–70
Adam, William 337, 339, 356, 361, 363–4,
    376
Addison, Edward 285
Adlington Hall 164
Aelst, Pieter van 287
Agasse, Jacques Laurent 190, 328
Aikman, William 140, 339, 375
Albert, Prince 68–9
Albury Park 84
Alfriston Clergy House 89
Allan, David 364
Allerton Park 314–15
Allom, Thomas 61
Allori, Alessandro 144
Alma-Tadema, Sir Lawrence 218, 245
Alnwick Castle 308
Althorp 186–7
Amigoni, Jacopo 138
Angeli, Heinrich von 235
Anglesey Abbey 215
Anne of Cleves 75
Anne Hathaway's Cottage 202
Anne, Queen 149–50
Antony House 14
Appuldurcombe House 67
Arbigland 343
Arbury Hall 202
Archer, Thomas 41, 73, 119, 176, 187
Ardington House 148
Argyll, Dukes of 371
Arley Hall 164–5
Arlington Court 24–5
arms and armour, collections of 15, 38, 108,
    153, 267, 273
Armstrong, William, 1st Lord 309, 311
Arniston House 361
Arnold, William 53
Arp, Jean 276
art collections: 34, 36, 44, 83, 86, 88, 92,
    101, 104–6, 117, 118, 123, 124, 132, 144,
    145, 152, 159, 176–8, 184, 188–9, 202,
    209, 215, 217–18, 225, 231, 232, 236, 245,
    253, 287, 305, 308, 331, 336, 339, 344,
    348, 363, 364, 374, 377; bird, flower and
    nature 89, 152, 225, 276; Bloomsbury
    90–1; Dutch 13, 61, 65, 88, 117, 124, 132,
    141, 145, 176–8, 188–9, 209, 303, 348,

377; French 132, 145, 305, 337; landscape
101, 215, 218, 232, 336; miniatures 48,
141, 185, 336; modern art 44, 152, 248,
276, 305, 345, 351; portraits 19, 23, 36,
44, 48, 53, 55, 61, 96, 99–100, 101, 118,
132, 143–4, 145, 148, 150, 152, 156, 158,
209, 232, 236, 293, 308, 316, 328, 331,
336, 337, 356, 361, 364, 372, 377; pre-
Raphaelite 152, 154–5, 213, 230, 312,
314; Scottish colourists 368; sea and
naval 231, 240, 265; sporting 14, 119,
176, 190, 209, 223, 303, 307, 328, 369;
Victorian 103, 204, 245, 282; water-
colours 103, 276, 287, 351, 357
Artari, Giuseppe 85, 233
Arundel Castle 96
Arundell family 22
Ascott 123–4
Ash, Graham Baron 208
Ashdown House 148
Ashfield, Edmund 257
Ashton, Henry 217
Aspinall, John 81
Asprucci, Mario 238
Astley Hall 292–3
Aston Hall 211
Astor, Lady Nancy 127
Astor, William Waldorf 74–5, 127
Athelhampton 40
Atholl, Dukes of 373
Atkinson, Thomas 306, 326
Atkinson, William 72, 335, 377
Attingham Park 273–4
Aubourn Hall 224
Audley End 219–20
Austen, Jane 63, 190
Avington Park 58
Aynhoe Park 187
Ayton Castle 335–6

Babbage, Charles 276
Baccelli, Giannetta 77
Bacon, Sir Francis 135
Baddesley Clinton 203–4
Bagutti, Giovanni 85, 233
Baillie, Lady Olive 79
Baker, Sir Herbert 80, 81
Bakewell, Robert, of Derby 182
Balcaskie House 345–6
Bamburgh Castle 309
Bankes, William 44
Barraud, Henry 190
Barraud, William 83, 190
Barry, Sir Charles 44, 61, 127, 294, 318, 330,
360
Bartolommeo, Fra 92
Basildon Park 120–1
Baskett, William 78

Wolff, Emil 69
Wolsey, Cardinal 141
Woodchester Park Mansion 264
Woodforde, Samuel 112
Woolf, Virginia 90, 95
Woolsthorpe Manor 228–9
Wootton, John 14, 16, 83, 90, 98, 109, 112, 187, 190, 209, 212, 215, 219, 233, 248, 303, 317, 328
Wordsworth, William 283, 287, 289–90
Wotton House 134
Wouwerman, Philips 124, 354, 364
Wren, Sir Christopher 133, 142–3, 202
Wrest Park 119
Wright and Mansfield 356
Wright, John Michael 160, 184, 192
Wright, Joseph, 'of Derby' 61, 190
Wright, Stephen 156
Wright, Thomas, of Durham 200
Wyatt, Benjamin Dean 65

Wyatt, James 33, 35, 45, 72, 114, 116, 121, 123, 153, 184, 208, 225, 247, 254, 272, 306
Wyatt, Lewis 170, 172, 173
Wyatt, Matthew Cotes 184
Wyatt, Matthew Digby 372
Wyatt, Samuel 69, 173, 200, 307
Wyatville, Sir Jeffry (formerly Jeffrey Wyatt) 109, 122, 176, 225, 293, 298, 310
Wyck, Jan 140, 141
Wylson, James, of York 351
Wyndham family 55

Yorke family 247
Young, William 363

Zoffany, Johann 20, 85, 92, 164, 190, 194, 233, 283, 298, 361, 374, 377
Zuccarelli, Francesco 112, 201
Zuccaro, Taddeo 188
Zucchi, Antonio 144, 146, 322, 331, 370
Zurbarán, Francisco 55

Reader's report form

Please send to: *The Good Country House Guide*, Pavilion Books Ltd, 26 Upper Ground, London SE1 9PD

I visited _____ house on _____ 19___

Please delete or amend as applicable

The directions given would be clearer if they also mentioned that:

_____

A guided tour was/was not available and took approx. _____ minutes

Refreshments were/were not available

The opening hours have been changed to _____

The telephone number has been changed to _____

The house description needs amending because the property has had a major fire/been sold/re-organized the visitor route (please explain):

_____

_____

_____

The following country house has recently opened (please give details)

_____

_____

_____

Name and address (BLOCK CAPITALS)

_____

_____

_____

Signed